RANKING AMERICA'S FIFTY STATES

A COMPARISON IN GRAPHIC DETAIL

MICHAEL D. DULBERGER

Published in the United States of America
by Bernan Press, a wholly owned subsidiary of
The Rowman & Littlefield Publishing Group, Inc.
4501 Forbes Boulevard, Suite 200
Lanham, Maryland 20706

Bernan Press
800-865-3457
www.bernan.com

ISBN-13: 978-1-59888-669-6

∞™ The paper used in this publication meets the minimum requirements of
American National Standard for Information Sciences—Permanence of
Paper for Printed Library Materials, ANSI/NISO Z39.48-1992.
Manufactured in the United States of America.

~ Contents ~

Chapter 3: Lifestyle

Chapter 4: Education

Chapter 5: Crime

Chapter 6: Environment

Chapter 7: Resources

Chapter 8: Personal Finances

Chapter 9: State Economy

Chapter 10: Federal Influence

Appendices

Index

Chapter 9: State Economy

Chapter 10: Federal Influence

Appendices

Index

~ <u>Introduction</u> ~

This book provides a compendium of stimulating facts about the states, presented graphically, and covering a wide array of topics including demographic, economic, environmental, health, and crime variables. Hundreds of attributes are compared side-by-side, from life expectancy to murder rates; from fourth-grade math proficiency scores to the number of food stamp recipients, and from illicit drug use to the rate of firearm background checks per state.

It is the author's intent to deliver maximum knowledge with minimum effort on the part of the reader. Through meticulous organization and use of graphic formats, retrieval of specific information the reader may seek has been greatly facilitated. In addition to the graphs comparing the fifty states for each individual metric, a summary table is provided at the beginning of each chapter. This uniquely formatted summary table provides a simultaneous view for all metrics within the chapter and across all fifty states. Each table provides a visual snapshot identifying the five states with highest values for each metric and is shaded green while the five states with lowest values are shaded red. These tables enable the reader to see, at a glance, which states have the highest and lowest concentration of values for that chapter's subject matter.

All charts include their attributed sources to enable verification or augmentation of the data. The data used to create this book have been rigorously vetted and distilled from official, public databases—primarily United States government agencies, presented in an unbiased, objective manner, however even these "facts" should be viewed with healthy skepticism. The author has refrained from interpreting the merits of any metric even when doing so would appear to be self-evident and beyond dispute—such as declaring high life expectancies as desirable—since other metrics that also seem obvious to judge may actually be considered subjective by other people. For example, Chapter 8 includes a chart of owner-occupied home values. Are home values better to be high or low? Although a low value may be considered a desirable attribute for someone with limited financial resources looking to purchase a home, high home values may be attractive to a wealthy person looking for an exclusive place to live.

An obvious benefit in contrasting states is the opportunity to highlight those states that excel relative to others, in areas such as education, health, and crime prevention. The achievements of the most successful states can become benchmarks for the others. The underachieving states can examine specific differences in state laws and public policies which may be contributing to their weaker performance. Why do one percent of infants in Mississippi die before their first birthday—more than double the rate in Iowa? Why do eighth grade students in Hawaii score at just one-third the science proficiency level as eighth grade students in North Dakota? While the causations for these profound differences are undoubtedly highly complex, the most important first step is to become disturbed by these results.

Of course, not all the metrics compared in this book are within the powers of government to control or improve, such as environmental disasters. However, even these natural events raise questions as to how their financial consequences should be allocated between individual property owners, state, local, and federal governments.

For many metrics, the wide range of values between the lowest and highest states is a stark reminder of the multi-cultural ancestry and wide spectra of preferred lifestyles for America's residents. While we are one, indivisible nation, at the same time Americans are as diverse from state-to-state as many nations are when compared with other nations. For example: in 2010, 95 percent of Vermont residents were white compared with only 24 percent of residents in Hawaii and 1-in-12 New York residents were Jewish compared with less than 1-in-1,000 Arkansas residents. In Texas, 464 prisoners have been executed over the past 35 years while 16 states have not executed any.

Appendix two titled "Top and Bottom Ranked States", on page 195, was created to summarize those states ranking highest or lowest for each metric, organized according to state. At a glance, this listing demonstrates how some states stand out dramatically since they rank number one (or 50) in a large number of metrics. Alaska ranked highest or lowest in 31 metrics—more than any other state—followed by Mississippi at 25 and Texas at 20. In contrast, seven states—Alabama, Illinois, Kansas, Missouri, Nebraska, Oklahoma, and Wisconsin—did not rank highest or lowest in any metric.

- Alaska is the only state that does not have a state income tax or a state sales tax. It had the highest revenues per capita from taxes levied on businesses for the extraction of oil and gas and receives the highest federal aid per capita. Alaska had the lowest percent of households with annual income below $15,000.

- Mississippi had the lowest personal income per capita, median household income, gross domestic product per capita, and lowest male life expectancy rate. Additionally, it had the highest food stamp recipient rate, rate of persons below the poverty level, and infant mortality rate.

- Texas had the most extreme environmental metrics including the highest major disaster, storm, and wildfire emergency declarations. Texas also had the highest summer air temperature and carbon dioxide emissions level. In addition to extreme environmental metrics, Texas also had the highest property crime rate and high school dropout rate. Harlingen, Texas had the lowest costs of living in the nation.

One freedom enjoyed in America—and often taken for granted—is the ability to travel and relocate across state lines seamlessly. An indicator of this mobility is the 27 percent of the population who choose to reside in a state other than their birth state. Over the past decade, New York and California have seen a combined net loss of three million residents relocating to other states while Florida and Texas added a combined two million from other states. Mobility is also evidenced by the migration of college freshmen, when each year a new crop of 400,000 college freshmen leave their home state to attend college in a different state—one of six going to either Pennsylvania or New York.

The tenth amendment to the United States Constitution grants state governments and the people, all powers not specifically reserved for the federal government. In 1932, Supreme Court Justice Louis Brandeis may have been the first to use the expression "Laboratories of Democracy" to describe the collection of individual states when he wrote an opinion which said: "It is one of the happy incidents of the federal system that a single courageous state may, if its citizens choose, serve as a laboratory; and try novel social and economic experiments without risk to the rest of the country." These laboratories of democracy have created a diverse patchwork of governmental practices that have evolved since the birth of the fledgling American experiment in self-governance. Since the time the tenth amendment ink dried, America's states have embarked on developing a wide diversity of laws and forms of government to suit their individual needs, which now include 3,000 counties and 36,000 municipalities plus townships. In view of the heterogeneous composition of America's population and generous disbursement of natural resources, it is not surprising that the states have developed into highly individualized, eclectic entities.

The author is confident you will readily learn facts that will stimulate your thinking and when you finish this book you'll return to it, again and again, as a refresher of the facts.

~

Chapter 1: Demographics Overview

One-third of the population of the United States lives in four states: California, Texas, New York and Florida. The majority of their students, grades K-12, are of non-white race or of Hispanic origin.

With 38 million residents, California has a population size equivalent to the least-populated 21 states. In 2009, 28 percent of all of California residents were born outside the United States and two of five babies born in California were born to women who were born outside the United States.

In 2009, approximately half of New Mexico's residents were of Hispanic or Latino origin, primarily of Mexican origin; Connecticut had the largest proportion of residents of Puerto Rican origin at 7.1 percent; Florida had the largest proportion of residents of Cuban origin at 6.5 percent; and Mississippi, the largest proportion of black residents at 37 percent.

Vermont had the largest proportion of white population at 95.3 percent while Hawaii the smallest portion at 24.7 percent.

Over the past decade Michigan was the only state to experience a reduction in population. Meanwhile, Nevada had the largest growth rate at 35 percent. Florida had the greatest influx of people at approximately two million while New York experienced the greatest decrease with approximately 800,000 leaving the state.

More than one-half of the residents of Nevada, Wyoming, New Hampshire, and Alaska were born in other states.

Utah was the youngest state in the nation in 2010. One-half of its population was under 29 years. The median age in the U.S. was 37 years.

New Jersey is the most densely populated state in the nation while Alaska is the least densely populated. The population density in New Jersey is one thousand times greater than in Alaska and 200 times greater than in Wyoming.

~

Demographics Summary Table

States Legend: ☐ Highest 10% ☐ Middle 80% ☐ Lowest 10%

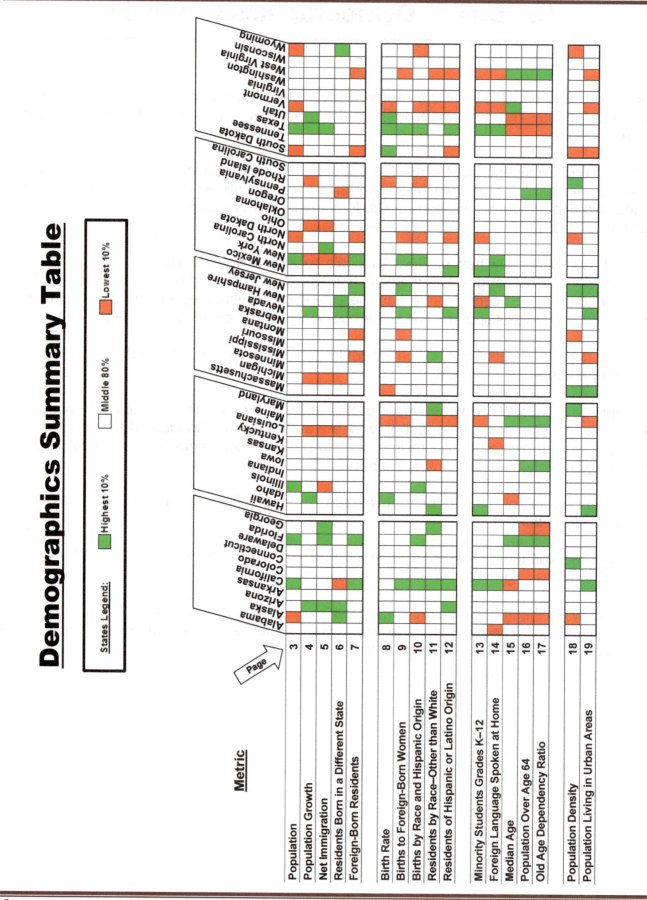

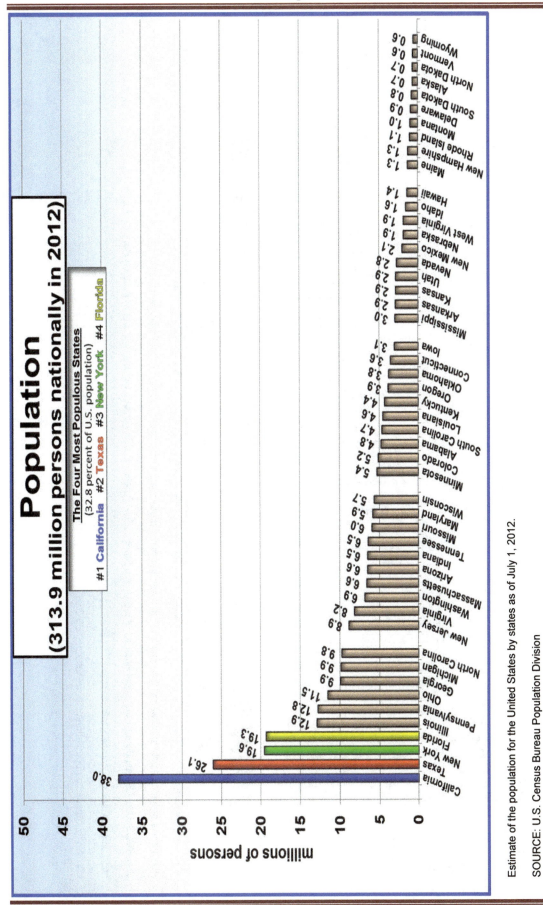

Population
(313.9 million persons nationally in 2012)

The Four Most Populous States
(32.8 percent of U.S. population)
#1 California #2 Texas #3 New York #4 Florida

State	Millions
California	38.0
Texas	26.1
New York	19.6
Florida	19.3
Illinois	12.9
Pennsylvania	12.8
Ohio	11.5
Georgia	9.9
Michigan	9.9
North Carolina	9.8
New Jersey	8.9
Virginia	8.2
Washington	6.9
Massachusetts	6.6
Arizona	6.6
Indiana	6.5
Tennessee	6.5
Missouri	6.0
Maryland	5.9
Wisconsin	5.7
Minnesota	5.4
Colorado	5.2
Alabama	4.8
South Carolina	4.7
Louisiana	4.6
Kentucky	4.4
Oregon	3.9
Oklahoma	3.8
Connecticut	3.6
Iowa	3.1
Mississippi	3.0
Arkansas	2.9
Kansas	2.9
Utah	2.8
Nevada	2.8
New Mexico	2.1
Nebraska	1.9
West Virginia	1.9
Idaho	1.6
Hawaii	1.4
Maine	1.3
New Hampshire	1.3
Rhode Island	1.1
Montana	1.0
Delaware	0.9
South Dakota	0.8
Alaska	0.7
North Dakota	0.7
Vermont	0.6
Wyoming	0.6

millions of persons

Estimate of the population for the United States by states as of July 1, 2012.

SOURCE: U.S. Census Bureau Population Division

http://www.census.gov/popest/data/state/totals/2012/index.html

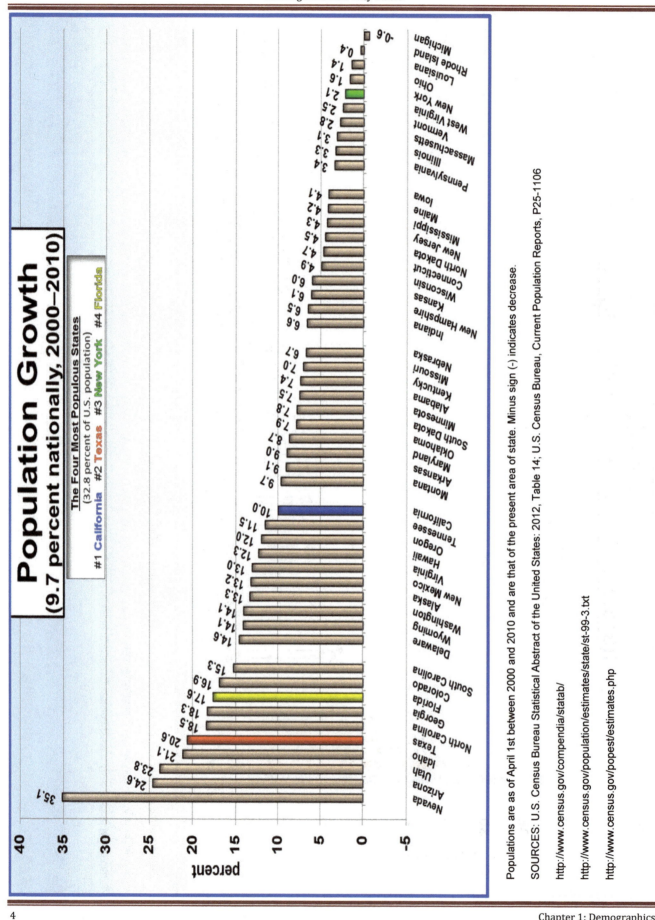

Population Growth
(9.7 percent nationally, 2000–2010)

The Four Most Populous States
(32.8 percent of U.S. population)

#1 California   #2 Texas   #3 New York   #4 Florida

State	Percent
Nevada	35.1
Arizona	24.6
Utah	23.8
Idaho	21.1
Texas	20.6
North Carolina	18.5
Georgia	18.3
Florida	17.6
Colorado	16.9
South Carolina	15.3
Delaware	14.6
Wyoming	14.1
Washington	14.1
Alaska	13.3
New Mexico	13.2
Virginia	13.0
Hawaii	12.3
Oregon	12.0
Tennessee	11.5
California	10.0
Montana	9.7
Arkansas	9.1
Maryland	9.0
Oklahoma	8.7
South Dakota	7.9
Minnesota	7.8
Alabama	7.5
Kentucky	7.4
Missouri	7.0
Nebraska	6.7
Indiana	6.6
New Hampshire	6.5
Kansas	6.1
Wisconsin	6.0
Connecticut	4.9
North Dakota	4.7
New Jersey	4.5
Mississippi	4.3
Maine	4.2
Iowa	4.1
Pennsylvania	3.4
Illinois	3.3
Massachusetts	3.1
Vermont	2.8
West Virginia	2.5
New York	2.1
Ohio	1.6
Louisiana	1.4
Rhode Island	0.4
Michigan	-0.6

Populations are as of April 1st between 2000 and 2010 and are that of the present area of state. Minus sign (-) indicates decrease.

SOURCES: U.S. Census Bureau Statistical Abstract of the United States: 2012, Table 14; U.S. Census Bureau, Current Population Reports, P25-1106

http://www.census.gov/compendia/statab/

http://www.census.gov/population/estimates/state/st-99-3.txt

http://www.census.gov/popest/estimates.php

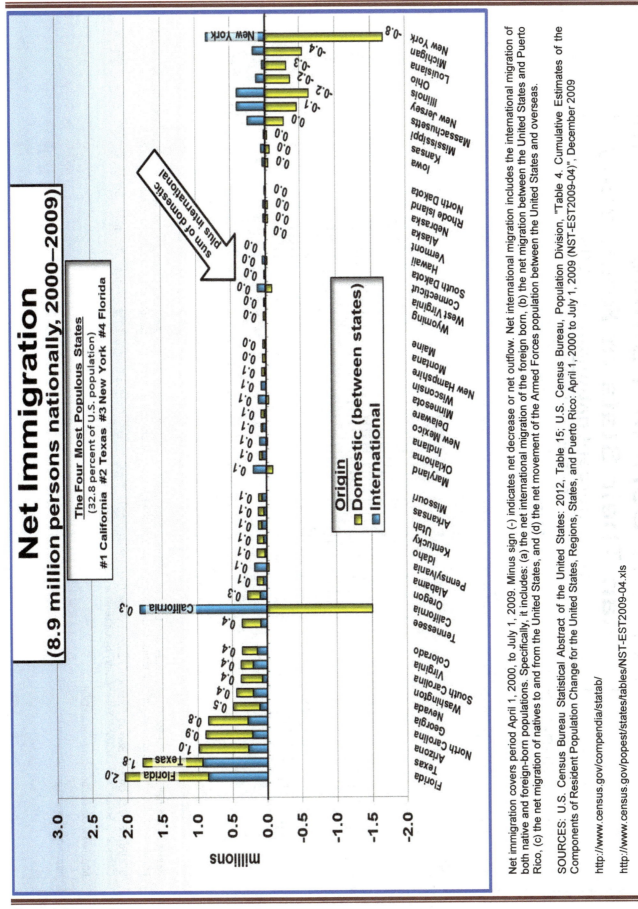

Net Immigration
(8.9 million persons nationally, 2000–2009)

The Four Most Populous States
(32.8 percent of U.S. population)
#1 California #2 Texas #3 New York #4 Florida

Origin
- Domestic (between states)
- International

sum of domestic plus international

Florida 2.0
Texas 1.8
Arizona 1.0
North Carolina 0.9
Georgia 0.8
Nevada 0.5
Washington 0.4
South Carolina 0.4
Virginia 0.4
Colorado 0.4
Tennessee 0.4
California 0.3
Oregon 0.3
Alabama 0.1
Pennsylvania 0.1
Idaho 0.1
Kentucky 0.1
Utah 0.1
Arkansas 0.1
Missouri 0.1
Maryland 0.1
Oklahoma 0.1
Indiana 0.1
New Mexico 0.1
Delaware 0.1
Minnesota 0.1
Wisconsin 0.1
New Hampshire 0.0
Montana 0.0
Maine 0.0
Wyoming 0.0
West Virginia 0.0
Connecticut 0.0
South Dakota 0.0
Hawaii 0.0
Vermont 0.0
Alaska 0.0
Nebraska 0.0
Rhode Island 0.0
North Dakota 0.0
Iowa 0.0
Kansas 0.0
Mississippi 0.0
Massachusetts 0.0
New Jersey -0.1
Illinois -0.2
Ohio -0.3
Louisiana -0.4
Michigan -0.4
New York -0.8

millions

3.0 2.5 2.0 1.5 1.0 0.5 0.0 -0.5 -1.0 -1.5 -2.0

Net immigration covers period April 1, 2000, to July 1, 2009. Minus sign (–) indicates net decrease or net outflow. Net international migration includes the international migration of both native and foreign-born populations. Specifically, it includes: (a) the net international migration of the foreign born, (b) the net migration between the United States and Puerto Rico, (c) the net migration of natives to and from the United States, and (d) the net movement of the Armed Forces population between the United States and overseas.

SOURCES: U.S. Census Bureau Statistical Abstract of the United States: 2012, Table 15; U.S. Census Bureau, Population Division, "Table 4. Cumulative Estimates of the Components of Resident Population Change for the United States, Regions, States, and Puerto Rico: April 1, 2000 to July 1, 2009 (NST-EST2009-04)", December 2009

http://www.census.gov/compendia/statab/

http://www.census.gov/popest/states/tables/NST-EST2009-04.xls

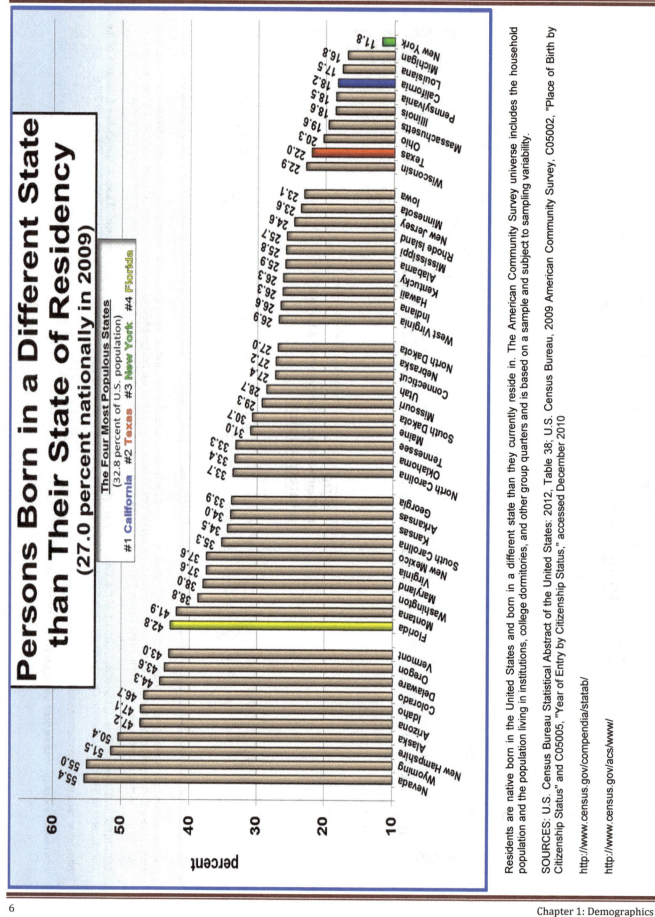

Persons Born in a Different State than Their State of Residency
(27.0 percent nationally in 2009)

The Four Most Populous States
(32.8 percent of U.S. population)
#1 California #2 Texas #3 New York #4 Florida

State	Percent
Nevada	55.4
Wyoming	55.0
New Hampshire	51.5
Alaska	50.4
Arizona	47.2
Idaho	47.1
Colorado	46.7
Delaware	44.3
Oregon	43.6
Vermont	43.0
Florida	42.8
Montana	41.9
Washington	38.8
Maryland	38.0
Virginia	37.6
New Mexico	37.6
South Carolina	35.3
Kansas	34.5
Arkansas	34.0
Georgia	33.9
North Carolina	33.7
Oklahoma	33.4
Tennessee	33.3
Maine	31.0
South Dakota	30.7
Missouri	29.3
Utah	28.7
Connecticut	27.4
Nebraska	27.2
North Dakota	27.0
West Virginia	26.9
Indiana	26.6
Hawaii	26.3
Kentucky	26.3
Alabama	25.9
Mississippi	25.8
Rhode Island	25.7
New Jersey	24.6
Minnesota	23.6
Iowa	23.1
Wisconsin	22.9
Texas	22.0
Ohio	20.3
Massachusetts	19.6
Illinois	18.6
Pennsylvania	18.5
California	18.2
Louisiana	17.5
Michigan	16.8
New York	11.8

percent

Residents are native born in the United States and born in a different state than they currently reside in. The American Community Survey universe includes the household population and the population living in institutions, college dormitories, and other group quarters and is based on a sample and subject to sampling variability.

SOURCES: U.S. Census Bureau Statistical Abstract of the United States: 2012, Table 38; U.S. Census Bureau, 2009 American Community Survey, C05002, "Place of Birth by Citizenship Status" and C05005, "Year of Entry by Citizenship Status," accessed December 2010

http://www.census.gov/compendia/statab/

http://www.census.gov/acs/www/

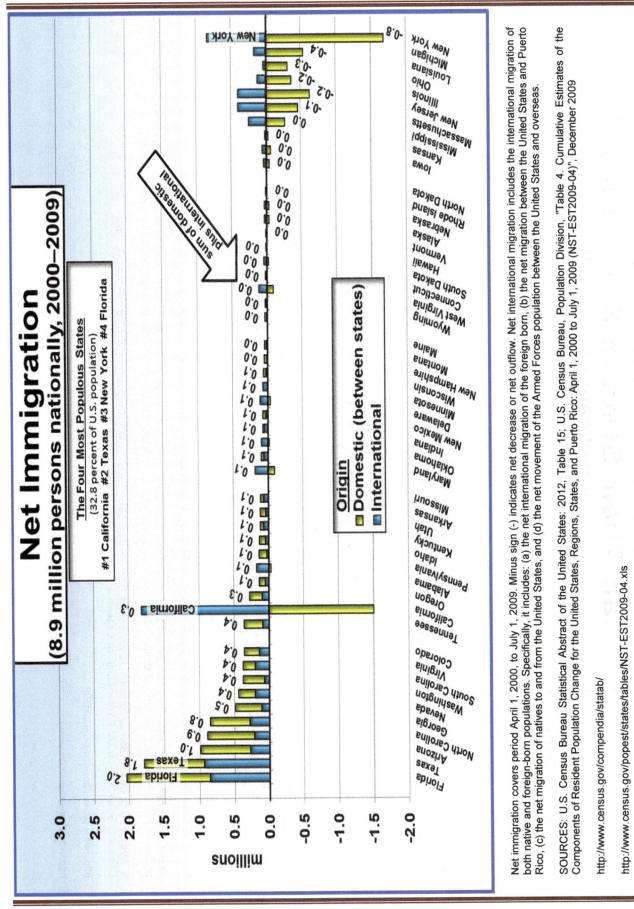

Net Immigration
(8.9 million persons nationally, 2000–2009)

The Four Most Populous States
(32.8 percent of U.S. population)
#1 California #2 Texas #3 New York #4 Florida

Origin
- Domestic (between states)
- International

sum of domestic plus international

Net immigration covers period April 1, 2000, to July 1, 2009. Minus sign (-) indicates net decrease or net outflow. Net international migration includes the international migration of both native and foreign-born populations. Specifically, it includes: (a) the net international migration of the foreign born, (b) the net migration between the United States and Puerto Rico, (c) the net migration of natives to and from the United States, and (d) the net movement of the Armed Forces population between the United States and overseas.

SOURCES: U.S. Census Bureau Statistical Abstract of the United States: 2012, Table 15; U.S. Census Bureau, Population Division, "Table 4. Cumulative Estimates of the Components of Resident Population Change for the United States, Regions, States, and Puerto Rico: April 1, 2000 to July 1, 2009 (NST-EST2009-04)", December 2009

http://www.census.gov/compendia/statab/

http://www.census.gov/popest/states/tables/NST-EST2009-04.xls

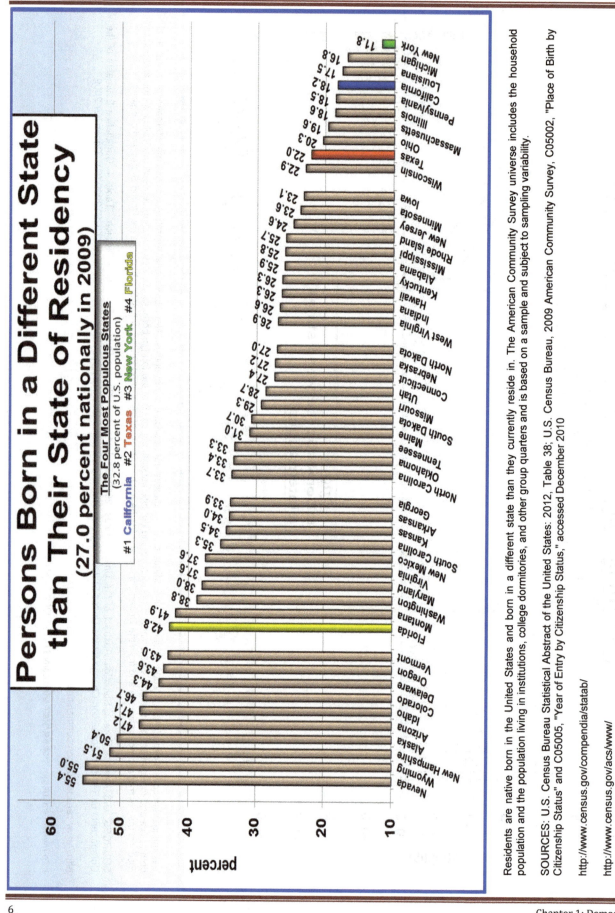

Persons Born in a Different State than Their State of Residency
(27.0 percent nationally in 2009)

The Four Most Populous States
(32.8 percent of U.S. population)
#1 California   #2 Texas   #3 New York   #4 Florida

State	percent
Nevada	55.4
Wyoming	55.0
New Hampshire	51.5
Alaska	50.4
Arizona	47.2
Idaho	47.1
Colorado	46.7
Delaware	44.3
Oregon	43.6
Vermont	43.0
Florida	42.8
Montana	41.9
Washington	38.8
Maryland	38.0
Virginia	37.6
New Mexico	37.6
South Carolina	35.3
Kansas	34.5
Arkansas	34.0
Georgia	33.9
North Carolina	33.7
Oklahoma	33.4
Tennessee	33.3
Maine	31.0
South Dakota	30.7
Missouri	29.3
Utah	28.7
Connecticut	27.4
Nebraska	27.2
North Dakota	27.0
West Virginia	26.9
Indiana	26.6
Hawaii	26.3
Kentucky	26.3
Alabama	25.9
Mississippi	25.8
Rhode Island	25.7
New Jersey	24.6
Minnesota	23.6
Iowa	23.1
Wisconsin	22.9
Texas	22.0
Ohio	20.3
Massachusetts	19.6
Illinois	18.6
Pennsylvania	18.5
California	18.2
Louisiana	17.5
Michigan	16.8
New York	11.8

Residents are native born in the United States and born in a different state than they currently reside in. The American Community Survey universe includes the household population and the population living in institutions, college dormitories, and other group quarters and is based on a sample and subject to sampling variability.

SOURCES: U.S. Census Bureau Statistical Abstract of the United States: 2012, Table 38; U.S. Census Bureau, 2009 American Community Survey, C05002, "Place of Birth by Citizenship Status" and C05005, "Year of Entry by Citizenship Status," accessed December 2010

http://www.census.gov/compendia/statab/

http://www.census.gov/acs/www/

Foreign-Born Residents
(13.9 percent nationally in 2009)

The Four Most Populous States
(32.8 percent of U.S. population)
#1 California #2 Texas #3 New York #4 Florida

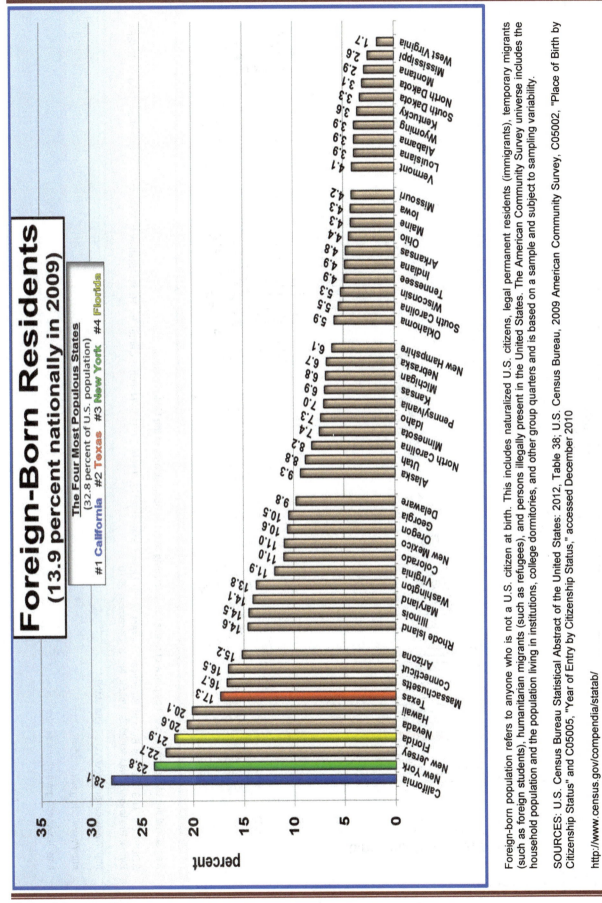

State	Percent
California	28.1
New York	23.8
New Jersey	22.1
Florida	21.9
Nevada	20.6
Hawaii	20.1
Texas	17.3
Massachusetts	16.7
Connecticut	16.5
Arizona	15.2
Rhode Island	14.6
Illinois	14.5
Maryland	14.1
Washington	13.8
Virginia	11.9
Colorado	11.0
New Mexico	11.0
Oregon	10.6
Georgia	10.5
Delaware	9.8
Alaska	9.3
Utah	8.8
North Carolina	8.2
Minnesota	7.4
Idaho	7.3
Pennsylvania	7.0
Kansas	6.9
Michigan	6.8
Nebraska	6.7
New Hampshire	6.1
Oklahoma	5.9
South Carolina	5.5
Wisconsin	5.3
Tennessee	4.9
Indiana	4.9
Arkansas	4.8
Ohio	4.4
Maine	4.3
Iowa	4.3
Missouri	4.2
Vermont	4.1
Louisiana	3.9
Alabama	3.9
Wyoming	3.6
Kentucky	3.3
South Dakota	3.1
North Dakota	2.9
Montana	2.6
Mississippi	1.7
West Virginia	1.7

Foreign-born population refers to anyone who is not a U.S. citizen at birth. This includes naturalized U.S. citizens, legal permanent residents (immigrants), temporary migrants (such as foreign students), humanitarian migrants (such as refugees), and persons illegally present in the United States. The American Community Survey universe includes the household population and the population living in institutions, college dormitories, and other group quarters and is based on a sample and subject to sampling variability.

SOURCES: U.S. Census Bureau Statistical Abstract of the United States: 2012, Table 38; U.S. Census Bureau, 2009 American Community Survey, C05002, "Place of Birth by Citizenship Status" and C05005, "Year of Entry by Citizenship Status," accessed December 2010

http://www.census.gov/compendia/statab/

Birth Rate

(66.7 births per 1,000 women nationally in 2009)

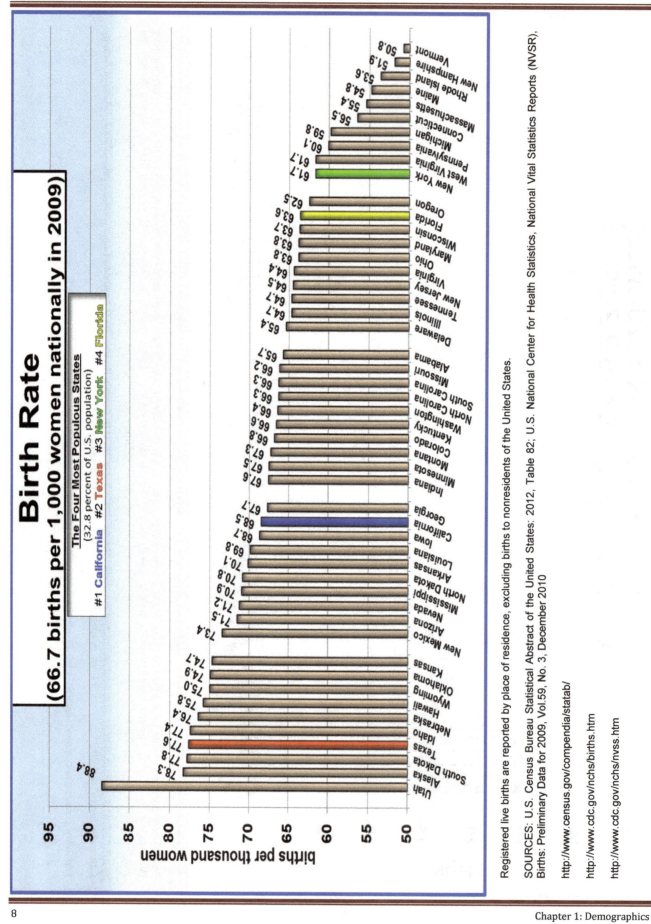

The Four Most Populous States
(32.8 percent of U.S. population)

#1 California   #2 Texas   #3 New York   #4 Florida

births per thousand women

Utah	88.4
Alaska	78.3
South Dakota	77.8
Texas	77.6
Idaho	77.4
Nebraska	76.4
Hawaii	75.8
Wyoming	75.0
Oklahoma	74.9
Kansas	74.7
New Mexico	73.4
Arizona	71.5
Nevada	71.2
Mississippi	70.9
North Dakota	70.8
Arkansas	70.1
Louisiana	69.8
Iowa	68.7
California	68.5
Georgia	67.7
Indiana	67.6
Minnesota	67.5
Montana	67.3
Colorado	66.8
Kentucky	66.6
Washington	66.4
North Carolina	66.3
South Carolina	66.3
Missouri	66.2
Alabama	65.7
Delaware	65.4
Illinois	64.7
Tennessee	64.7
New Jersey	64.5
Virginia	64.4
Ohio	63.8
Maryland	63.8
Wisconsin	63.7
Florida	63.6
Oregon	62.5
New York	61.7
West Virginia	61.7
Pennsylvania	60.1
Michigan	59.8
Connecticut	56.5
Massachusetts	55.4
Maine	54.8
Rhode Island	53.6
New Hampshire	51.9
Vermont	50.8

Registered live births are reported by place of residence, excluding births to nonresidents of the United States.

SOURCES: U.S. Census Bureau Statistical Abstract of the United States: 2012, Table 82; U.S. National Center for Health Statistics, National Vital Statistics Reports (NVSR), Births: Preliminary Data for 2009, Vol.59, No. 3, December 2010

http://www.census.gov/compendia/statab/

http://www.cdc.gov/nchs/births.htm

http://www.cdc.gov/nchs/nvss.htm

Births to Foreign-Born Women
(20.3 percent nationally in 2009)

The Four Most Populous States
(32.8 percent of U.S. population)
#1 California #2 Texas #3 New York #4 Florida

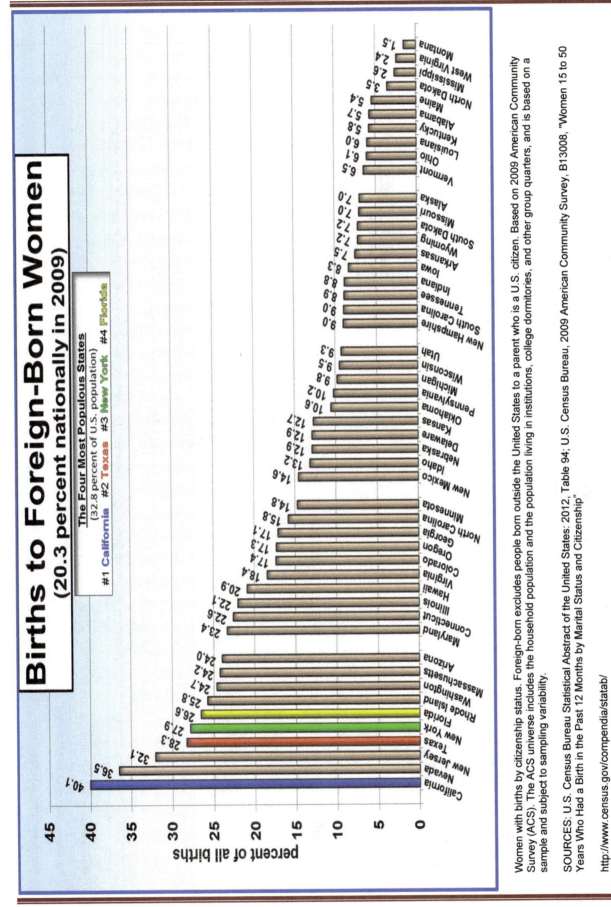

State	percent of all births
California	40.1
Nevada	36.5
New Jersey	32.1
Texas	28.3
New York	27.9
Florida	26.6
Rhode Island	25.8
Washington	24.7
Massachusetts	24.2
Arizona	24.0
Maryland	23.4
Connecticut	22.6
Illinois	22.1
Hawaii	20.9
Virginia	18.4
Colorado	17.4
Oregon	17.3
Georgia	17.1
North Carolina	15.8
Minnesota	14.8
New Mexico	14.6
Idaho	13.2
Nebraska	12.9
Delaware	12.9
Kansas	12.7
Oklahoma	10.6
Pennsylvania	10.2
Michigan	9.8
Wisconsin	9.5
Utah	9.3
New Hampshire	9.0
South Carolina	9.0
Tennessee	8.9
Indiana	8.8
Iowa	8.3
Arkansas	7.5
Wyoming	7.2
South Dakota	7.0
Missouri	7.0
Alaska	7.0
Vermont	6.5
Ohio	6.1
Louisiana	6.0
Kentucky	5.8
Alabama	5.7
Maine	5.4
North Dakota	3.5
Mississippi	2.6
West Virginia	2.4
Montana	1.5

Women with births by citizenship status. Foreign-born excludes people born outside the United States to a parent who is a U.S. citizen. Based on 2009 American Community Survey (ACS). The ACS universe includes the household population and the population living in institutions, college dormitories, and other group quarters, and is based on a sample and subject to sampling variability.

SOURCES: U.S. Census Bureau Statistical Abstract of the United States: 2012, Table 94; U.S. Census Bureau, 2009 American Community Survey, B13008, "Women 15 to 50 Years Who Had a Birth in the Past 12 Months by Marital Status and Citizenship"

http://www.census.gov/compendia/statab/

http://factfinder.census.gov/servlet/DatasetMainPageServlet?_program=ACS&_submenuId=&_lang=en&_ts=

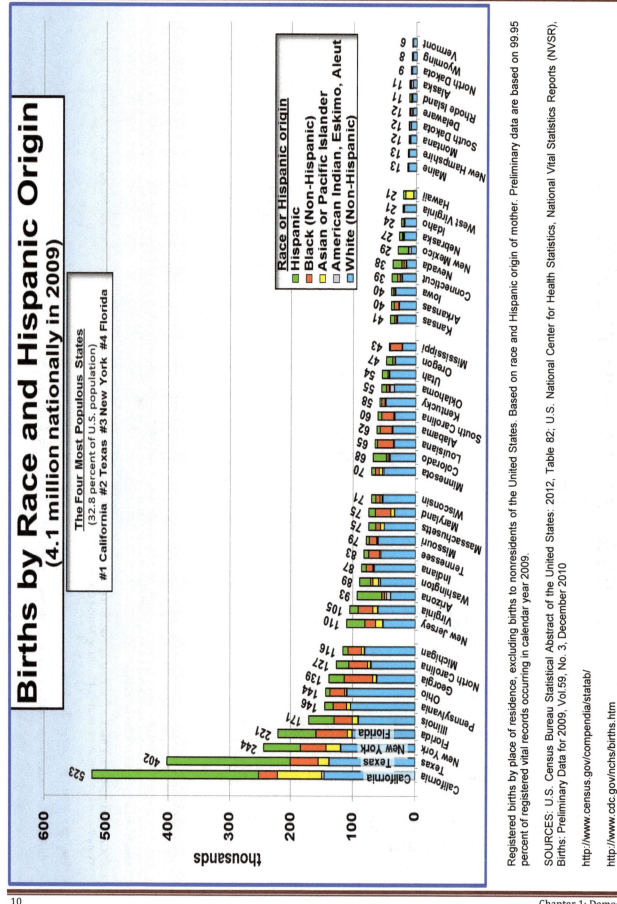

Births by Race and Hispanic Origin
(4.1 million nationally in 2009)

The Four Most Populous States
(32.8 percent of U.S. population)
#1 California #2 Texas #3 New York #4 Florida

Race or Hispanic origin
- Hispanic
- Black (Non-Hispanic)
- Asian or Pacific Islander
- American Indian, Eskimo, Aleut
- White (Non-Hispanic)

thousands

California	523
Texas	402
New York	244
Florida	221
Illinois	171
Pennsylvania	146
Ohio	144
Georgia	139
North Carolina	127
Michigan	116
New Jersey	110
Virginia	105
Arizona	93
Washington	89
Indiana	87
Tennessee	83
Missouri	79
Massachusetts	75
Maryland	75
Wisconsin	71
Minnesota	70
Colorado	68
Louisiana	65
Alabama	62
South Carolina	60
Kentucky	58
Oklahoma	55
Utah	54
Oregon	47
Mississippi	43
Kansas	41
Arkansas	40
Iowa	40
Connecticut	39
Nevada	38
New Mexico	29
Nebraska	27
Idaho	24
West Virginia	21
Hawaii	21
Maine	13
New Hampshire	13
Montana	12
South Dakota	12
Delaware	12
Rhode Island	11
Alaska	11
North Dakota	9
Wyoming	8
Vermont	6

Registered births by place of residence, excluding births to nonresidents of the United States. Based on race and Hispanic origin of mother. Preliminary data are based on 99.95 percent of registered vital records occurring in calendar year 2009.

SOURCES: U.S. Census Bureau Statistical Abstract of the United States: 2012, Table 82; U.S. National Center for Health Statistics, National Vital Statistics Reports (NVSR), Births: Preliminary Data for 2009, Vol.59, No. 3, December 2010

http://www.census.gov/compendia/statab/

http://www.cdc.gov/nchs/births.htm

http://www.census.gov/acs/www/

Residents by Race—Other than White
(27.6 percent nationally in 2010)

The Four Most Populous States
(32.8 percent of U.S. population)
#1 California #2 Texas #3 New York #4 Florida

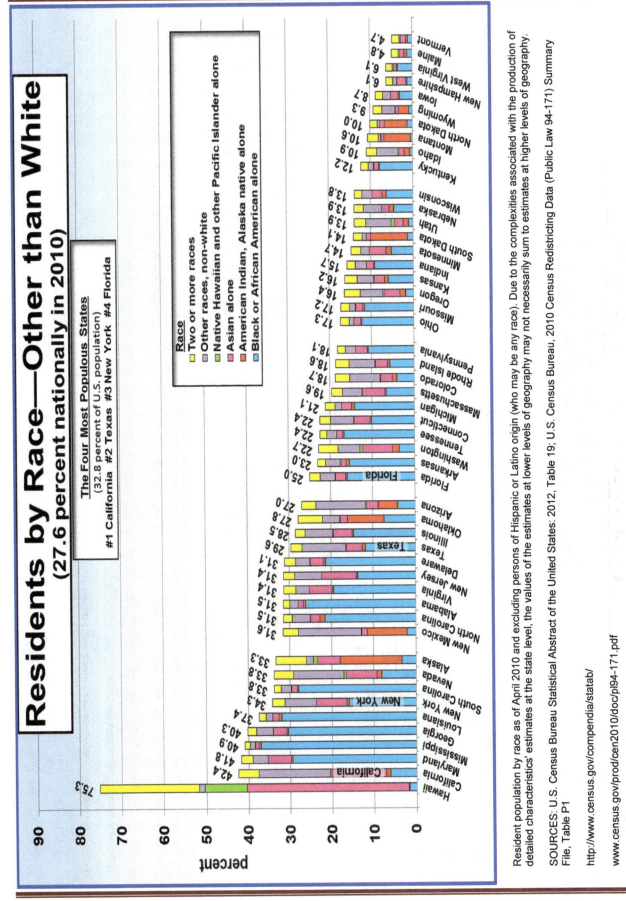

Race
- Two or more races
- Other races, non-white
- Native Hawaiian and other Pacific Islander alone
- Asian alone
- American Indian, Alaska native alone
- Black or African American alone

State	Percent
Hawaii	75.3
California	42.4
Maryland	41.8
Mississippi	40.9
Georgia	40.3
Louisiana	37.4
New York	34.3
South Carolina	33.8
Nevada	33.8
Alaska	33.3
New Mexico	31.6
North Carolina	31.5
Alabama	31.5
Virginia	31.4
New Jersey	31.1
Delaware	29.6
Texas	28.5
Illinois	27.8
Oklahoma	27.0
Arizona	25.0
Florida	23.0
Arkansas	22.7
Washington	22.4
Tennessee	22.4
Connecticut	21.1
Michigan	19.6
Massachusetts	18.7
Colorado	18.6
Rhode Island	18.1
Pennsylvania	17.3
Ohio	17.2
Missouri	16.4
Oregon	16.2
Kansas	15.7
Indiana	14.7
Minnesota	14.1
South Dakota	13.9
Utah	13.9
Nebraska	13.8
Wisconsin	12.2
Kentucky	10.9
Idaho	10.6
Montana	10.0
North Dakota	9.3
Wyoming	8.7
Iowa	6.7
New Hampshire	6.4
West Virginia	4.8
Maine	4.7
Vermont	

Resident population by race as of April 2010 and excluding persons of Hispanic or Latino origin (who may be any race). Due to the complexities associated with the production of detailed characteristics' estimates at the state level, the values of the estimates at lower levels of geography may not necessarily sum to estimates at higher levels of geography.

SOURCES: U.S. Census Bureau Statistical Abstract of the United States: 2012, Table 19; U.S. Census Bureau, 2010 Census Redistricting Data (Public Law 94-171) Summary File, Table P1

http://www.census.gov/compendia/statab/

www.census.gov/prod/cen2010/doc/pl94-171.pdf

http://www.census.gov/popest/estimates.php

Residents of Hispanic or Latino Origin
(16.3 percent nationally in 2010)

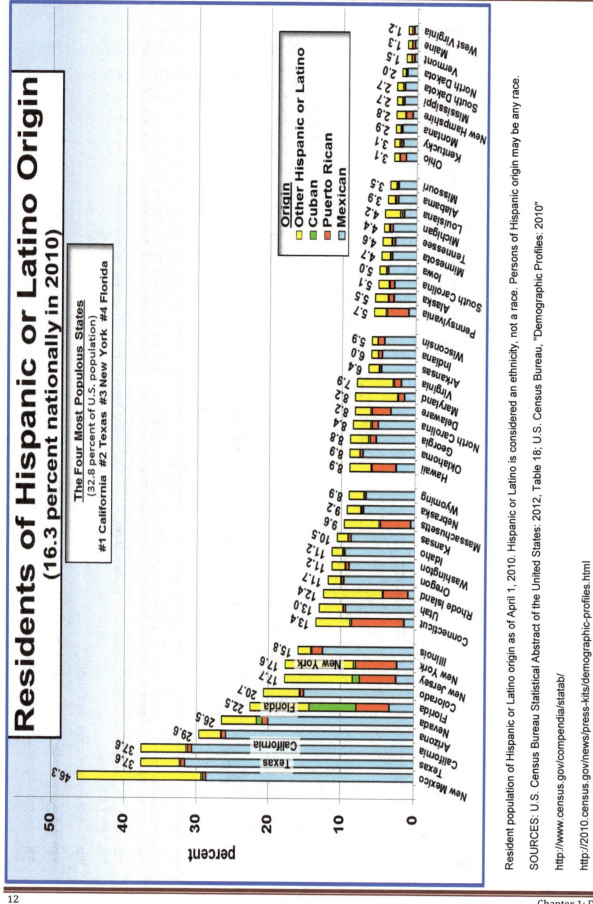

The Four Most Populous States
(32.8 percent of U.S. population)
#1 California #2 Texas #3 New York #4 Florida

Origin
- Other Hispanic or Latino
- Cuban
- Puerto Rican
- Mexican

New Mexico	46.3
Texas	37.6
California	37.6
Arizona	29.6
Nevada	26.5
Florida	22.5
Colorado	20.7
New Jersey	17.7
New York	17.6
Illinois	15.8
Connecticut	13.4
Utah	13.0
Rhode Island	12.4
Oregon	11.7
Washington	11.2
Idaho	11.2
Kansas	10.5
Massachusetts	9.6
Nebraska	9.2
Wyoming	8.9
Hawaii	8.9
Oklahoma	8.9
Georgia	8.8
North Carolina	8.4
Delaware	8.2
Maryland	8.2
Virginia	7.9
Arkansas	6.4
Indiana	6.0
Wisconsin	5.9
Pennsylvania	5.7
Alaska	5.5
South Carolina	5.1
Iowa	5.0
Minnesota	4.7
Tennessee	4.6
Michigan	4.4
Louisiana	4.2
Alabama	3.9
Missouri	3.5
Ohio	3.1
Kentucky	3.1
Montana	2.9
New Hampshire	2.8
Mississippi	2.7
South Dakota	2.7
North Dakota	2.0
Vermont	1.5
Maine	1.3
West Virginia	1.2

percent

Resident population of Hispanic or Latino origin as of April 1, 2010. Hispanic or Latino is considered an ethnicity, not a race. Persons of Hispanic origin may be any race.

SOURCES: U.S. Census Bureau Statistical Abstract of the United States: 2012, Table 18; U.S. Census Bureau, "Demographic Profiles: 2010"

http://www.census.gov/compendia/statab/

http://2010.census.gov/news/press-kits/demographic-profiles.html

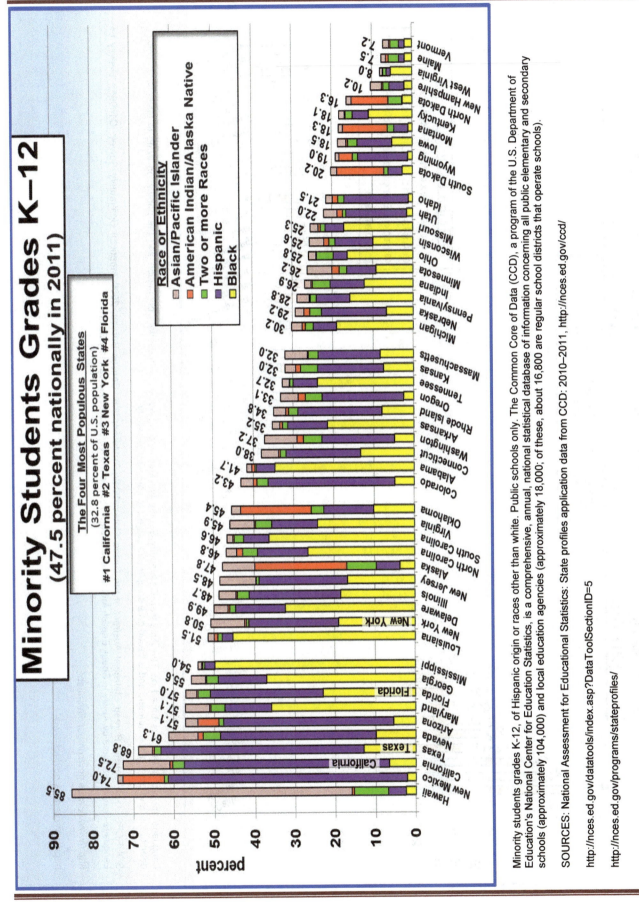

Minority Students Grades K–12
(47.5 percent nationally in 2011)

The Four Most Populous States
(32.8 percent of U.S. population)
#1 California #2 Texas #3 New York #4 Florida

Race or Ethnicity
- Asian/Pacific Islander
- American Indian/Alaska Native
- Two or more Races
- Hispanic
- Black

State	Percent
Hawaii	85.5
New Mexico	74.0
California	72.5
Texas	68.8
Nevada	61.3
Arizona	57.1
Maryland	57.1
Florida	57.0
Georgia	55.6
Mississippi	54.0
Louisiana	51.5
New York	50.8
Delaware	49.9
Illinois	48.7
New Jersey	48.5
Alaska	47.8
North Carolina	46.8
South Carolina	46.6
Virginia	45.9
Oklahoma	45.4
Colorado	43.2
Alabama	41.7
Connecticut	38.0
Washington	37.2
Arkansas	35.2
Rhode Island	34.8
Oregon	33.1
Tennessee	32.7
Kansas	32.0
Massachusetts	32.0
Michigan	30.2
Nebraska	29.2
Pennsylvania	28.8
Indiana	26.9
Minnesota	26.2
Ohio	25.8
Wisconsin	25.6
Missouri	25.3
Utah	22.0
Idaho	21.5
South Dakota	20.2
Wyoming	19.0
Iowa	18.5
Montana	18.3
Kentucky	18.1
North Dakota	16.3
New Hampshire	10.2
West Virginia	8.0
Maine	7.5
Vermont	7.2

Minority students grades K–12, of Hispanic origin or races other than white. Public schools only. The Common Core of Data (CCD), a program of the U.S. Department of Education's National Center for Education Statistics, is a comprehensive, annual, national statistical database of information concerning all public elementary and secondary schools (approximately 104,000) and local education agencies (approximately 18,000; of these, about 16,800 are regular school districts that operate schools).

SOURCES: National Assessment for Educational Statistics: State profiles application data from CCD: 2010–2011, http://nces.ed.gov/ccd/

http://nces.ed.gov/datatools/index.asp?DataToolSectionID=5

http://nces.ed.gov/programs/stateprofiles/

Foreign Language Spoken at Home

(20.0 percent of households nationally in 2009)

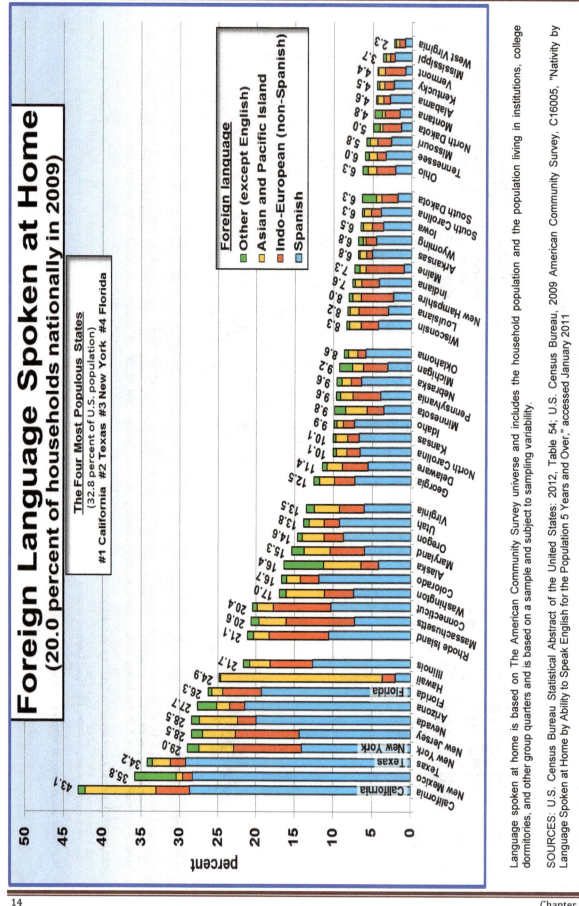

The Four Most Populous States
(32.8 percent of U.S. population)
#1 California #2 Texas #3 New York #4 Florida

Foreign language
- Other (except English)
- Asian and Pacific Island
- Indo-European (non-Spanish)
- Spanish

State	Percent
California	43.1
New Mexico	35.8
Texas	34.2
New York	29.0
New Jersey	28.5
Nevada	28.5
Arizona	27.7
Florida	26.3
Hawaii	24.9
Illinois	21.7
Rhode Island	21.1
Massachusetts	20.6
Connecticut	20.4
Washington	17.0
Colorado	16.7
Alaska	16.4
Maryland	15.3
Oregon	14.6
Utah	13.8
Virginia	13.5
Georgia	12.5
Delaware	11.4
North Carolina	10.1
Kansas	10.1
Idaho	9.9
Minnesota	9.8
Pennsylvania	9.6
Nebraska	9.6
Michigan	9.2
Oklahoma	8.6
Wisconsin	8.3
Louisiana	8.2
New Hampshire	8.0
Indiana	7.6
Maine	7.3
Arkansas	6.8
Wyoming	6.8
Iowa	6.5
South Carolina	6.3
South Dakota	6.3
Ohio	6.3
Tennessee	6.0
Missouri	5.8
North Dakota	5.0
Montana	4.8
Alabama	4.6
Kentucky	4.5
Vermont	4.4
Mississippi	3.7
West Virginia	2.3

Language spoken at home is based on The American Community Survey universe and includes the household population and the population living in institutions, college dormitories, and other group quarters and is based on a sample and subject to sampling variability.

SOURCES: U.S. Census Bureau Statistical Abstract of the United States: 2012, Table 54; U.S. Census Bureau, 2009 American Community Survey, C16005, "Nativity by Language Spoken at Home by Ability to Speak English for the Population 5 Years and Over," accessed January 2011

http://www.census.gov/compendia/statab/

http://www.census.gov/acs/www/

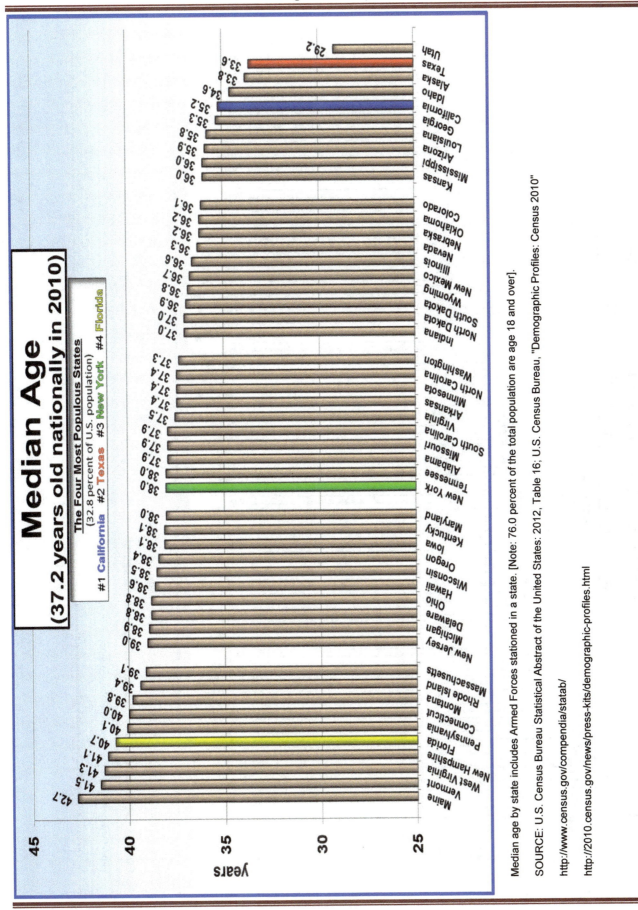

Median Age
(37.2 years old nationally in 2010)

The Four Most Populous States
(32.8 percent of U.S. population)
#1 California #2 Texas #3 New York #4 Florida

State	years
Utah	29.2
Texas	33.6
Alaska	33.8
Idaho	34.6
California	35.2
Georgia	35.3
Louisiana	35.8
Arizona	35.9
Mississippi	36.0
Kansas	36.0
Colorado	36.1
Oklahoma	36.2
Nebraska	36.2
Nevada	36.3
Illinois	36.6
New Mexico	36.7
Wyoming	36.8
South Dakota	36.9
North Dakota	37.0
Indiana	37.0
Washington	37.3
North Carolina	37.4
Minnesota	37.4
Arkansas	37.4
Virginia	37.5
South Carolina	37.9
Missouri	37.9
Alabama	37.9
Tennessee	38.0
New York	38.0
Maryland	38.0
Kentucky	38.1
Iowa	38.1
Oregon	38.4
Wisconsin	38.5
Hawaii	38.6
Ohio	38.8
Delaware	38.8
Michigan	38.9
New Jersey	39.0
Massachusetts	39.1
Rhode Island	39.4
Montana	39.8
Connecticut	40.0
Pennsylvania	40.1
Florida	40.7
New Hampshire	41.1
West Virginia	41.3
Vermont	41.5
Maine	42.7

Median age by state includes Armed Forces stationed in a state. [Note: 76.0 percent of the total population are age 18 and over].

SOURCE: U.S. Census Bureau Statistical Abstract of the United States: 2012, Table 16; U.S. Census Bureau, "Demographic Profiles: Census 2010"

http://www.census.gov/compendia/statab/

http://2010.census.gov/news/press-kits/demographic-profiles.html

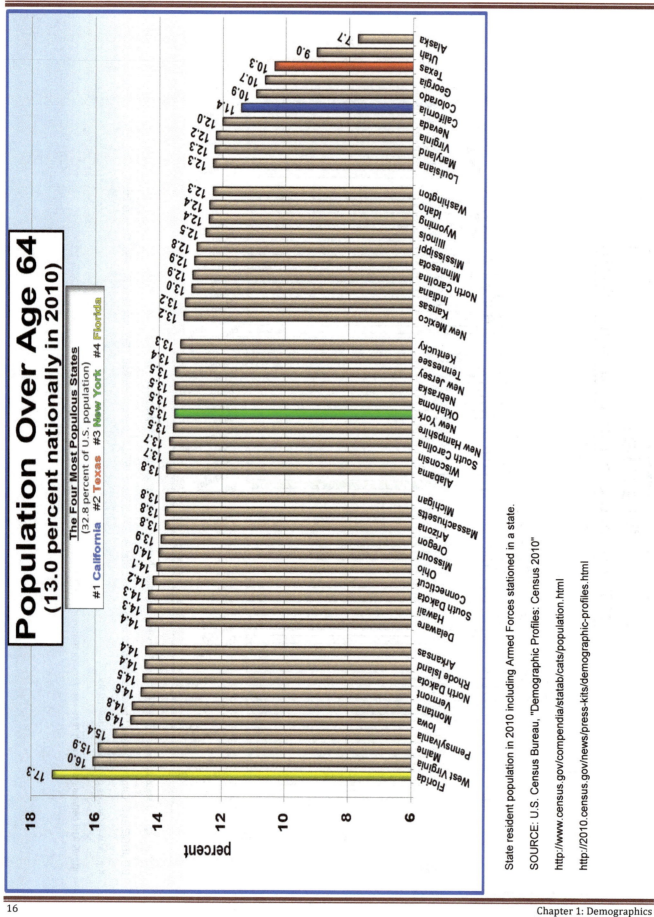

Population Over Age 64
(13.0 percent nationally in 2010)

The Four Most Populous States
(32.8 percent of U.S. population)

#1 California #2 Texas #3 New York #4 Florida

State	Percent
Florida	17.3
West Virginia	16.0
Maine	15.9
Pennsylvania	15.4
Iowa	14.9
Montana	14.8
Vermont	14.6
North Dakota	14.5
Rhode Island	14.4
Arkansas	14.4
Delaware	14.3
Hawaii	14.3
South Dakota	14.2
Connecticut	14.1
Ohio	14.0
Missouri	13.9
Oregon	13.8
Arizona	13.8
Massachusetts	13.8
Michigan	13.8
Alabama	13.7
Wisconsin	13.7
South Carolina	13.5
New Hampshire	13.5
New York	13.5
Oklahoma	13.5
Nebraska	13.5
New Jersey	13.4
Tennessee	13.3
Kentucky	13.3
New Mexico	13.2
Kansas	13.0
Indiana	12.9
North Carolina	12.9
Minnesota	12.8
Mississippi	12.5
Illinois	12.4
Wyoming	12.4
Idaho	12.3
Washington	12.3
Louisiana	12.3
Maryland	12.2
Virginia	12.0
Nevada	11.4
California	10.9
Colorado	10.7
Georgia	10.3
Texas	9.0
Utah	7.7
Alaska	

percent: 18, 16, 14, 12, 10, 8, 6

State resident population in 2010 including Armed Forces stationed in a state.

SOURCE: U.S. Census Bureau, "Demographic Profiles: Census 2010"

http://www.census.gov/compendia/statab/cats/population.html

http://2010.census.gov/news/press-kits/demographic-profiles.html

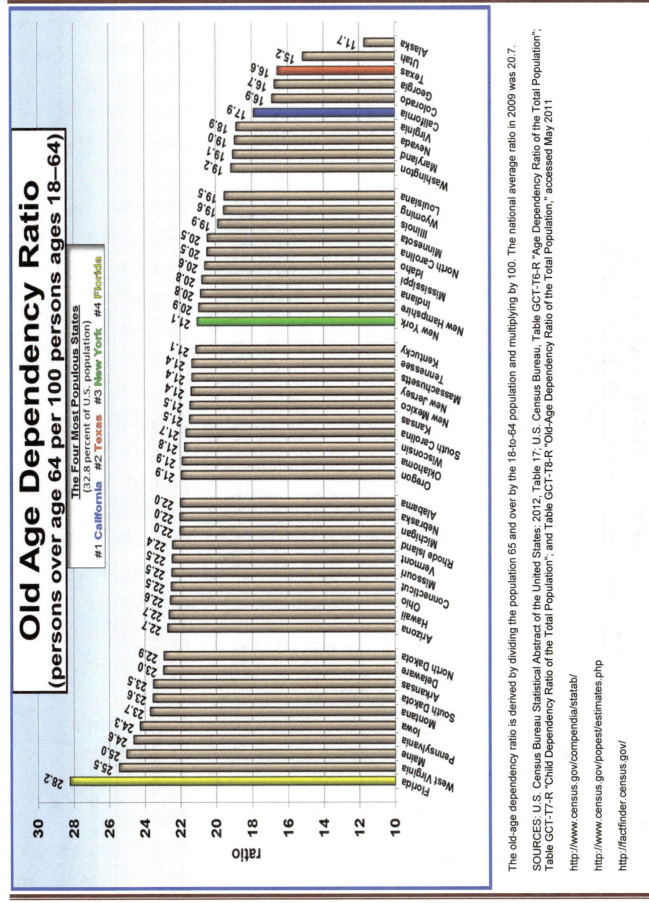

Old Age Dependency Ratio
(persons over age 64 per 100 persons ages 18–64)

The Four Most Populous States
(32.8 percent of U.S. population)
#1 California   #2 Texas   #3 New York   #4 Florida

State	Ratio
Alaska	11.7
Utah	15.2
Texas	16.6
Georgia	16.7
Colorado	16.9
California	17.9
Virginia	18.9
Nevada	19.0
Maryland	19.1
Washington	19.2
Louisiana	19.5
Wyoming	19.6
Illinois	19.9
Minnesota	20.5
North Carolina	20.5
Idaho	20.6
Mississippi	20.8
Indiana	20.8
New Hampshire	20.9
New York	21.1
Kentucky	21.1
Tennessee	21.4
Massachusetts	21.4
New Jersey	21.4
New Mexico	21.5
Kansas	21.5
South Carolina	21.7
Wisconsin	21.8
Oklahoma	21.9
Oregon	21.9
Alabama	22.0
Nebraska	22.0
Michigan	22.0
Rhode Island	22.4
Vermont	22.5
Missouri	22.5
Connecticut	22.6
Ohio	22.7
Hawaii	22.7
Arizona	22.7
North Dakota	22.9
Delaware	23.0
Arkansas	23.5
South Dakota	23.6
Montana	23.7
Iowa	24.3
Pennsylvania	24.6
Maine	25.0
West Virginia	25.5
Florida	28.2

ratio

The old-age dependency ratio is derived by dividing the population 65 and over by the 18-to-64 population and multiplying by 100. The national average ratio in 2009 was 20.7.

SOURCES: U.S. Census Bureau Statistical Abstract of the United States: 2012, Table 17; U.S. Census Bureau, Table GCT-T6-R "Age Dependency Ratio of the Total Population"; Table GCT-T7-R "Child Dependency Ratio of the Total Population"; and Table GCT-T8-R "Old-Age Dependency Ratio of the Total Population," accessed May 2011

http://www.census.gov/compendia/statab/

http://www.census.gov/popest/estimates.php

http://factfinder.census.gov/

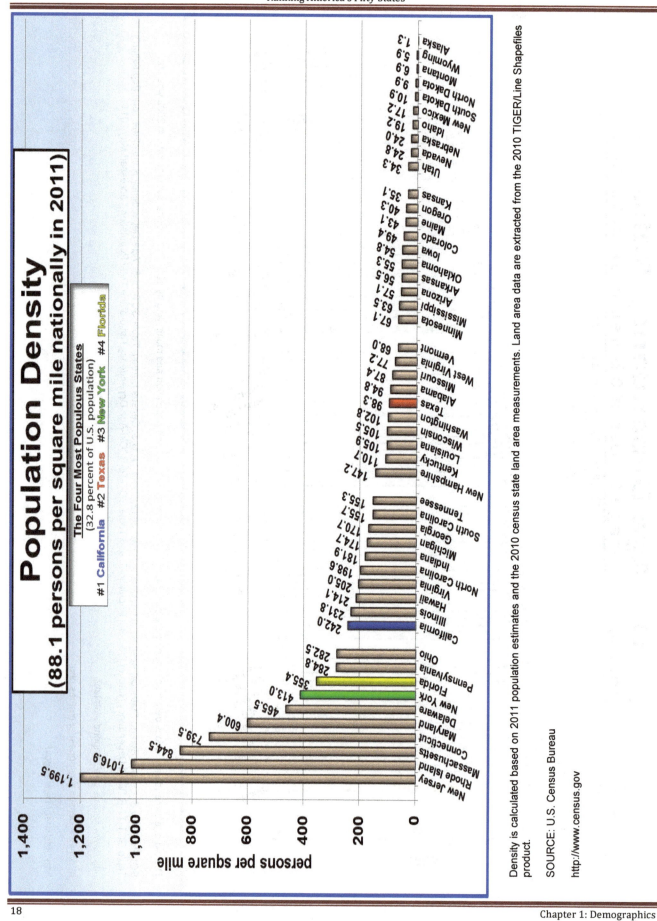

Population Density
(88.1 persons per square mile nationally in 2011)

The Four Most Populous States
(32.8 percent of U.S. population)
#1 California   #2 Texas   #3 New York   #4 Florida

State	persons per square mile
New Jersey	1,199.5
Rhode Island	1,016.9
Massachusetts	844.5
Connecticut	739.5
Maryland	600.4
Delaware	465.5
New York	413.0
Florida	355.4
Pennsylvania	284.8
Ohio	282.5
California	242.0
Illinois	231.8
Hawaii	214.1
Virginia	205.0
North Carolina	198.6
Indiana	181.9
Michigan	174.7
Georgia	170.7
South Carolina	155.7
Tennessee	155.3
New Hampshire	147.2
Kentucky	110.7
Louisiana	105.9
Wisconsin	105.5
Washington	102.8
Texas	98.3
Alabama	94.8
Missouri	87.4
West Virginia	77.2
Vermont	68.0
Minnesota	67.1
Mississippi	63.5
Arizona	57.1
Arkansas	56.5
Oklahoma	55.3
Iowa	54.8
Colorado	49.4
Maine	43.1
Oregon	40.3
Kansas	35.1
Utah	34.3
Nevada	24.8
Nebraska	24.0
Idaho	19.2
New Mexico	17.2
South Dakota	10.9
North Dakota	9.9
Montana	6.9
Wyoming	5.9
Alaska	1.3

Density is calculated based on 2011 population estimates and the 2010 census state land area measurements. Land area data are extracted from the 2010 TIGER/Line Shapefiles product.

SOURCE: U.S. Census Bureau

http://www.census.gov

Chapter 1: Demographics

Population Living in Urban Areas
(79.0 percent nationally in 2000)

The Four Most Populous States
(32.8 percent of U.S. population)
#1 California #2 Texas #3 New York #4 Florida

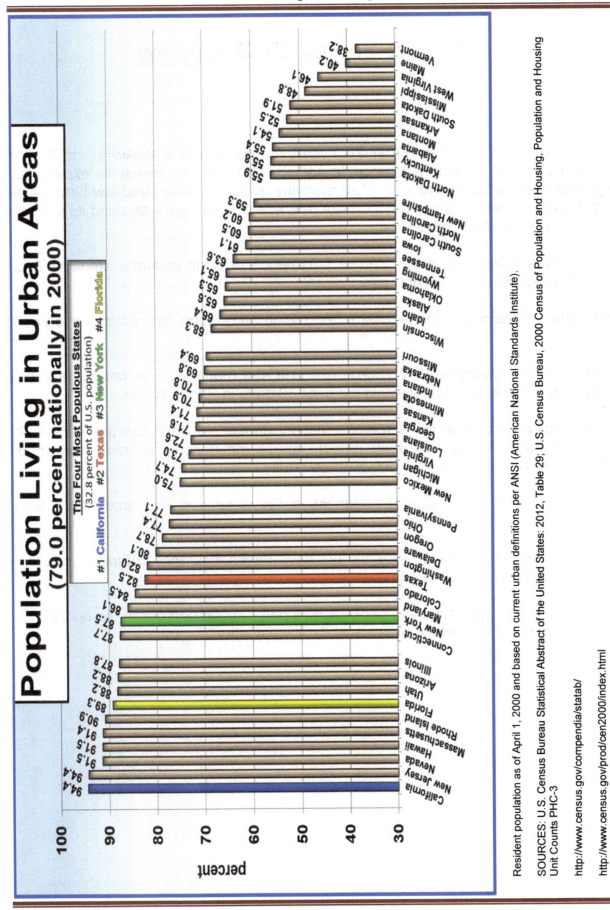

State	Percent
California	94.4
New Jersey	94.4
Nevada	91.5
Hawaii	91.5
Massachusetts	91.4
Rhode Island	90.9
Florida	89.3
Utah	88.2
Arizona	88.2
Illinois	87.8
Connecticut	87.7
New York	87.5
Maryland	86.1
Colorado	84.5
Texas	82.5
Washington	82.0
Delaware	80.1
Oregon	78.7
Ohio	77.4
Pennsylvania	77.1
New Mexico	75.0
Michigan	74.7
Virginia	73.0
Louisiana	72.6
Georgia	71.6
Kansas	71.4
Minnesota	70.9
Indiana	70.8
Nebraska	69.8
Missouri	69.4
Wisconsin	68.3
Idaho	66.4
Alaska	65.6
Oklahoma	65.3
Wyoming	65.1
Tennessee	63.6
Iowa	61.1
South Carolina	60.5
North Carolina	60.2
New Hampshire	59.3
North Dakota	55.9
Kentucky	55.8
Alabama	55.4
Montana	54.1
Arkansas	52.5
South Dakota	51.9
Mississippi	48.8
West Virginia	46.1
Maine	40.2
Vermont	38.2

Resident population as of April 1, 2000 and based on current urban definitions per ANSI (American National Standards Institute).

SOURCES: U.S. Census Bureau Statistical Abstract of the United States: 2012, Table 29; U.S. Census Bureau, 2000 Census of Population and Housing, Population and Housing Unit Counts PHC-3

http://www.census.gov/compendia/statab/

http://www.census.gov/prod/cen2000/index.html

Chapter 2: Health Overview

Life expectancy for newborns ranged from 70.3 years for males born in Mississippi to 77.2 for males born in Hawaii—a 6.9 year difference. In addition to having the lowest life expectancy, Mississippi also had the highest rate of infant mortality, pre-term births, and low-birth weight babies in the nation. Mississippi's infant mortality rate was double Iowa's rate and its pre-term birth rate was double Vermont's rate.

Kentucky and West Virginia had the highest prevalence of adult cigarette smoking at 25 percent, and the highest cancer death rates in 2009.

The suicide rate in Alaska was the highest in the nation and double the national average in 2007.

Rhode Island led the country in all illicit drug use rate and marijuana use rate. One-in-nine persons over age 12 used marijuana within the prior 30 days in Rhode Island.

Nearly one-in-four American adults is a binge alcohol drinker. In North Dakota—where the alcohol-impaired traffic fatality rate is 42 percent above the national average and double Utah's rate—this number increases to one-in-three adults.

The overall traffic fatality rate was the highest in Wyoming and five times the rate in Massachusetts.

In 2009, 26.1 percent of people in Texas did not have health insurance compared with only 4.4 percent of people in Massachusetts.

Massachusetts had the highest number of physicians per 100,000 persons in the country and nearly three times higher than Idaho, which had the lowest level.

~

Health Summary Table

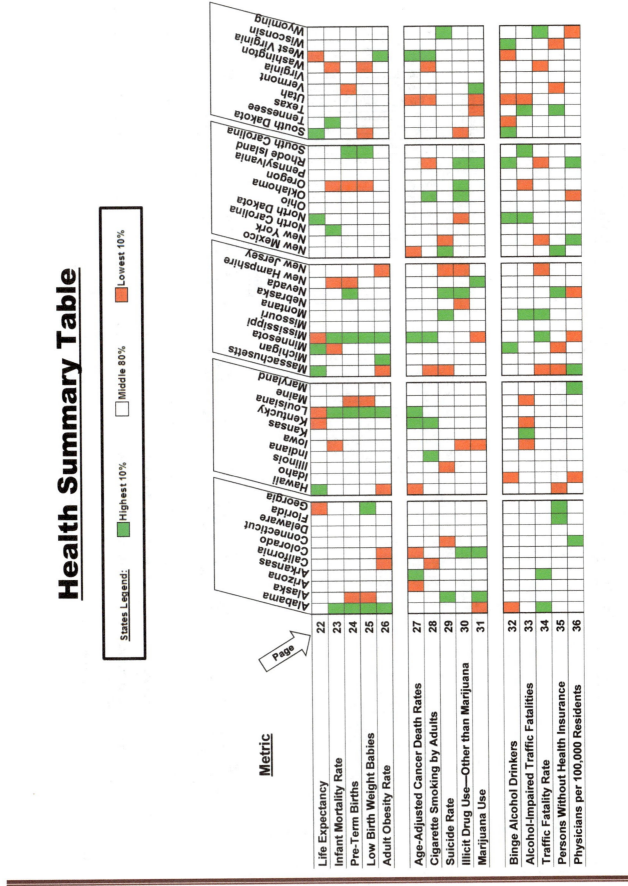

States Legend: ■ Highest 10%   □ Middle 80%   ■ Lowest 10%

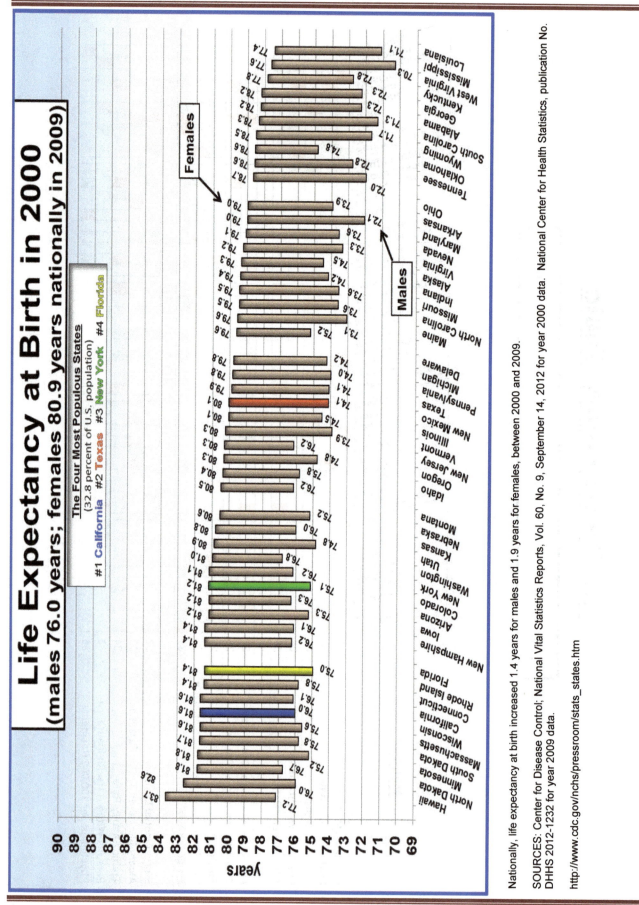

Life Expectancy at Birth in 2000
(males 76.0 years; females 80.9 years nationally in 2009)

The Four Most Populous States
(32.8 percent of U.S. population)
#1 California #2 Texas #3 New York #4 Florida

Females

Males

years

Nationally, life expectancy at birth increased 1.4 years for males and 1.9 years for females, between 2000 and 2009.

SOURCES: Center for Disease Control; National Vital Statistics Reports, Vol. 60, No. 9, September 14, 2012 for year 2000 data. National Center for Health Statistics, publication No. DHHS 2012-1232 for year 2009 data.

http://www.cdc.gov/nchs/pressroom/stats_states.htm

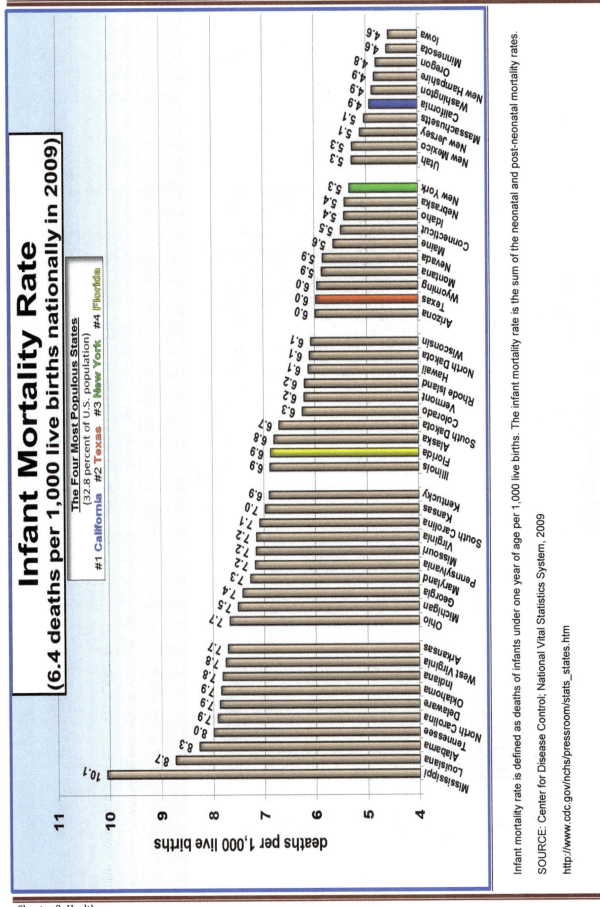

Infant Mortality Rate
(6.4 deaths per 1,000 live births nationally in 2009)

The Four Most Populous States
(32.8 percent of U.S. population)
#1 California #2 Texas #3 New York #4 Florida

State	Rate
Mississippi	10.1
Louisiana	8.7
Alabama	8.3
Tennessee	8.0
North Carolina	7.9
Delaware	7.9
Oklahoma	7.9
Indiana	7.8
West Virginia	7.8
Arkansas	7.7
Ohio	7.7
Michigan	7.5
Georgia	7.4
Maryland	7.3
Pennsylvania	7.2
Missouri	7.2
Virginia	7.2
South Carolina	7.1
Kansas	7.0
Kentucky	6.9
Illinois	6.9
Florida	6.9
Alaska	6.8
South Dakota	6.7
Colorado	6.3
Vermont	6.2
Rhode Island	6.2
Hawaii	6.1
North Dakota	6.1
Wisconsin	6.1
Arizona	6.0
Texas	6.0
Wyoming	6.0
Montana	5.9
Nevada	5.9
Maine	5.6
Connecticut	5.5
Idaho	5.4
Nebraska	5.4
New York	5.3
Utah	5.3
New Mexico	5.3
New Jersey	5.1
Massachusetts	5.1
California	4.9
Washington	4.9
New Hampshire	4.9
Oregon	4.8
Minnesota	4.6
Iowa	4.6

deaths per 1,000 live births

Infant mortality rate is defined as deaths of infants under one year of age per 1,000 live births. The infant mortality rate is the sum of the neonatal and post-neonatal mortality rates.

SOURCE: Center for Disease Control; National Vital Statistics System, 2009

http://www.cdc.gov/nchs/pressroom/stats_states.htm

Pre-Term Births
(12.0 percent nationally in 2010)

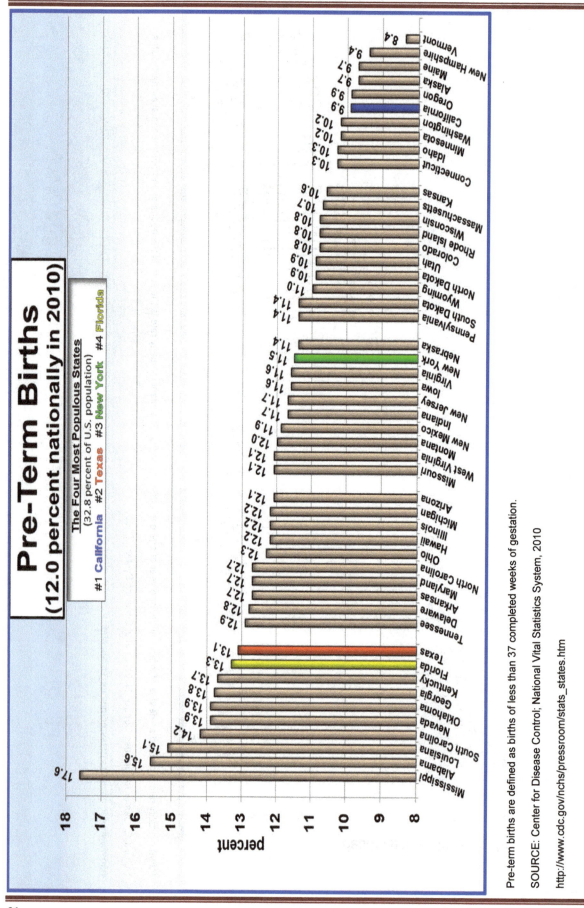

The Four Most Populous States
(32.8 percent of U.S. population)
#1 California #2 Texas #3 New York #4 Florida

State	Percent
Mississippi	17.6
Alabama	15.6
Louisiana	15.1
South Carolina	14.2
Nevada	13.9
Oklahoma	13.9
Georgia	13.8
Kentucky	13.7
Florida	13.3
Texas	13.1
Tennessee	12.9
Delaware	12.8
Arkansas	12.7
Maryland	12.7
North Carolina	12.7
Ohio	12.3
Hawaii	12.2
Illinois	12.2
Michigan	12.2
Arizona	12.1
Missouri	12.1
West Virginia	12.1
Montana	12.0
New Mexico	11.9
Indiana	11.7
New Jersey	11.7
Iowa	11.6
Virginia	11.6
New York	11.5
Nebraska	11.4
Pennsylvania	11.4
South Dakota	11.4
Wyoming	11.0
North Dakota	10.9
Utah	10.9
Colorado	10.8
Rhode Island	10.8
Wisconsin	10.7
Massachusetts	10.6
Kansas	10.6
Connecticut	10.3
Idaho	10.3
Minnesota	10.2
Washington	10.2
California	9.9
Oregon	9.9
Alaska	9.7
Maine	9.7
New Hampshire	9.4
Vermont	8.4

percent

Pre-term births are defined as births of less than 37 completed weeks of gestation.

SOURCE: Center for Disease Control; National Vital Statistics System, 2010

http://www.cdc.gov/nchs/pressroom/stats_states.htm

Low Birth Weight Babies
(8.2 percent nationally in 2009)

The Four Most Populous States
(32.8 percent of U.S. population)
#1 California #2 Texas #3 New York #4 Florida

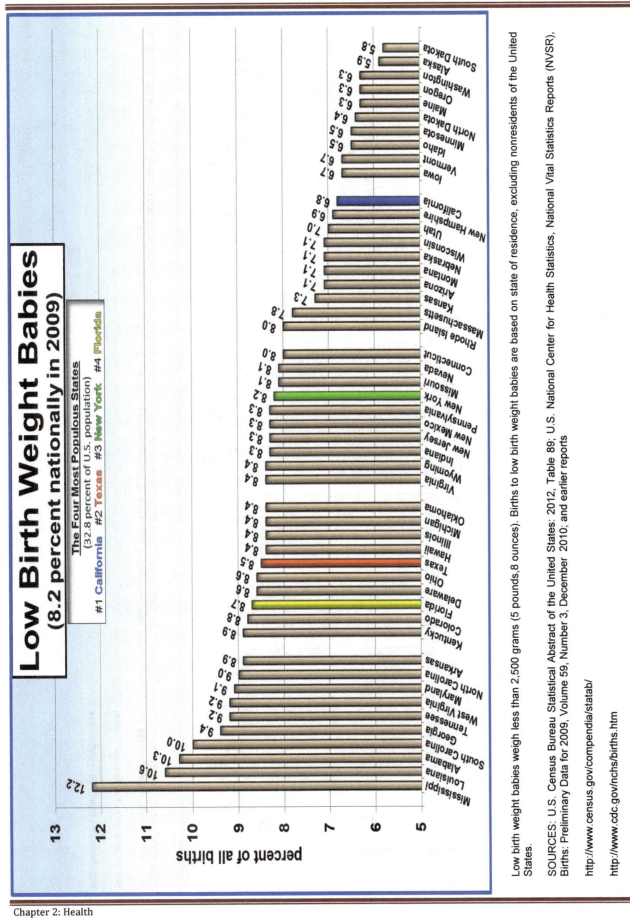

State	Percent
Mississippi	12.2
Louisiana	10.6
Alabama	10.3
South Carolina	10.0
Georgia	9.4
Tennessee	9.2
West Virginia	9.2
Maryland	9.1
North Carolina	9.0
Arkansas	8.9
Kentucky	8.9
Colorado	8.8
Florida	8.7
Delaware	8.6
Ohio	8.6
Texas	8.5
Hawaii	8.4
Illinois	8.4
Michigan	8.4
Oklahoma	8.4
Virginia	8.4
Wyoming	8.3
Indiana	8.3
New Jersey	8.3
New Mexico	8.2
Pennsylvania	8.2
New York	8.1
Missouri	8.1
Nevada	8.0
Connecticut	8.0
Rhode Island	7.8
Massachusetts	7.3
Kansas	7.1
Arizona	7.1
Montana	7.1
Nebraska	7.0
Wisconsin	7.0
Utah	6.9
New Hampshire	6.8
California	6.7
Iowa	6.7
Vermont	6.5
Idaho	6.5
Minnesota	6.4
North Dakota	6.3
Maine	6.3
Oregon	6.3
Washington	5.9
Alaska	5.8
South Dakota	5.8

percent of all births

Low birth weight babies weigh less than 2,500 grams (5 pounds,8 ounces). Births to low birth weight babies are based on state of residence, excluding nonresidents of the United States.

SOURCES: U.S. Census Bureau Statistical Abstract of the United States: 2012, Table 89; U.S. National Center for Health Statistics, National Vital Statistics Reports (NVSR), Births: Preliminary Data for 2009, Volume 59, Number 3, December 2010; and earlier reports

http://www.census.gov/compendia/statab/

http://www.cdc.gov/nchs/births.htm

Adult Obesity Rate
(percent in 2011)

The Four Most Populous States
(32.8 percent of U.S. population)

#1 California   #2 Texas   #3 New York   #4 Florida

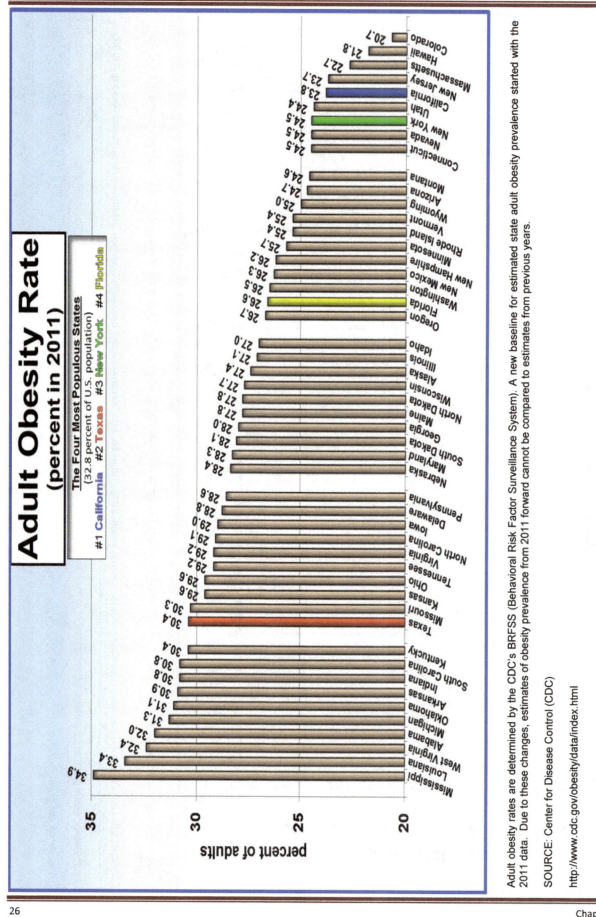

percent of adults

State	Percent
Mississippi	34.9
Louisiana	33.4
West Virginia	32.4
Alabama	32.0
Michigan	31.3
Oklahoma	31.1
Arkansas	30.9
Indiana	30.8
South Carolina	30.8
Kentucky	30.4
Texas	30.4
Missouri	30.3
Kansas	29.6
Ohio	29.6
Tennessee	29.2
Virginia	29.2
North Carolina	29.1
Iowa	29.0
Delaware	28.8
Pennsylvania	28.6
Nebraska	28.4
Maryland	28.3
South Dakota	28.1
Georgia	28.0
Maine	27.8
North Dakota	27.8
Wisconsin	27.7
Alaska	27.4
Illinois	27.1
Idaho	27.0
Oregon	26.7
Florida	26.6
Washington	26.5
New Mexico	26.3
New Hampshire	26.2
Minnesota	25.7
Rhode Island	25.4
Vermont	25.4
Wyoming	25.0
Arizona	24.7
Montana	24.6
Connecticut	24.5
Nevada	24.5
New York	24.5
Utah	24.4
California	23.8
New Jersey	23.7
Massachusetts	22.7
Hawaii	21.8
Colorado	20.7

Adult obesity rates are determined by the CDC's BRFSS (Behavioral Risk Factor Surveillance System). A new baseline for estimated state adult obesity prevalence started with the 2011 data. Due to these changes, estimates of obesity prevalence from 2011 forward cannot be compared to estimates from previous years.

SOURCE: Center for Disease Control (CDC)

http://www.cdc.gov/obesity/data/index.html

Age-Adjusted Cancer Death Rate
(173.2 deaths per 100,000 persons nationally in 2009)

The Four Most Populous States
(32.8 percent of U.S. population)
#1 California   #2 Texas   #3 New York   #4 Florida

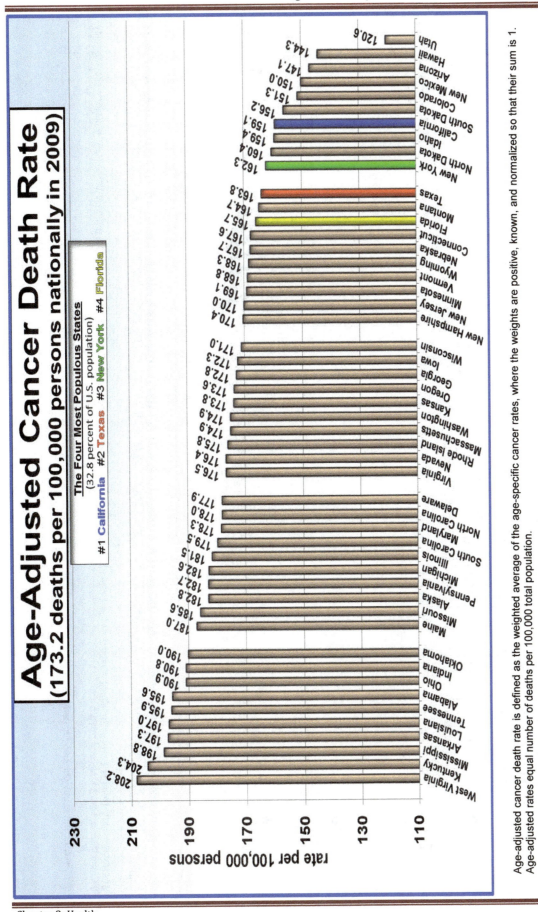

rate per 100,000 persons

West Virginia 208.2
Kentucky 204.3
Mississippi 198.8
Arkansas 197.3
Louisiana 197.0
Tennessee 195.9
Alabama 195.6
Ohio 190.9
Indiana 190.8
Oklahoma 190.0
Maine 187.0
Missouri 185.6
Alaska 182.8
Pennsylvania 182.7
Michigan 182.6
Illinois 181.5
South Carolina 179.5
Maryland 178.3
North Carolina 178.0
Delaware 177.9
Virginia 176.5
Nevada 176.4
Rhode Island 175.8
Massachusetts 174.9
Washington 174.9
Kansas 173.8
Oregon 173.6
Georgia 172.8
Iowa 172.3
Wisconsin 171.0
New Hampshire 170.4
New Jersey 170.0
Minnesota 169.1
Vermont 168.8
Wyoming 168.3
Nebraska 167.7
Connecticut 167.6
Florida 165.7
Montana 164.7
Texas 163.8
New York 162.3
North Dakota 160.4
Idaho 159.4
California 159.1
South Dakota 156.2
Colorado 151.3
New Mexico 150.0
Arizona 147.1
Hawaii 144.3
Utah 120.6

Age-adjusted cancer death rate is defined as the weighted average of the age-specific cancer rates, where the weights are positive, known, and normalized so that their sum is 1. Age-adjusted rates equal number of deaths per 100,000 total population.

SOURCE: Center for Disease Control; National Vital Statistics System, 2009

http://www.cdc.gov/nchs/pressroom/stats_states.htm

Cigarette Smoking by Adults
(20.6 percent nationally in 2009)

The Four Most Populous States
(32.8 percent of U.S. population)
#1 California #2 Texas #3 New York #4 Florida

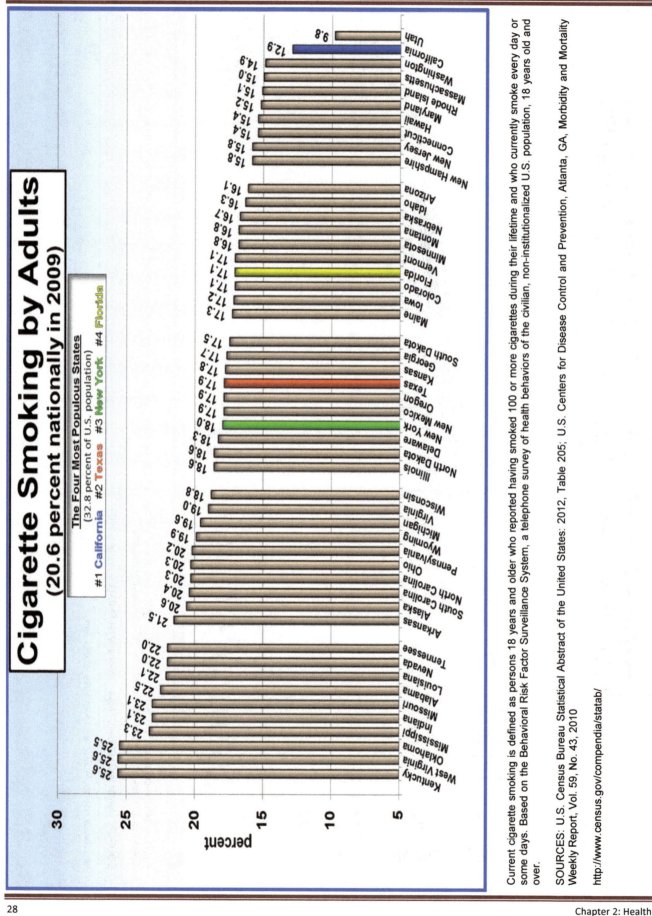

State	Percent
Utah	9.8
California	12.9
Washington	14.9
Massachusetts	15.0
Rhode Island	15.1
Maryland	15.2
Hawaii	15.4
Connecticut	15.4
New Jersey	15.8
New Hampshire	15.8
Arizona	16.1
Idaho	16.3
Nebraska	16.7
Montana	16.8
Minnesota	16.8
Vermont	17.1
Florida	17.1
Colorado	17.1
Iowa	17.2
Maine	17.3
South Dakota	17.5
Georgia	17.7
Kansas	17.8
Texas	17.9
Oregon	17.9
New Mexico	17.9
New York	18.0
Delaware	18.3
North Dakota	18.6
Illinois	18.6
Wisconsin	18.8
Virginia	19.0
Michigan	19.6
Wyoming	19.9
Pennsylvania	20.2
Ohio	20.3
North Carolina	20.3
South Carolina	20.4
Alaska	20.6
Arkansas	21.5
Tennessee	22.0
Nevada	22.0
Louisiana	22.1
Alabama	22.5
Missouri	23.1
Indiana	23.1
Mississippi	23.3
Oklahoma	25.5
West Virginia	25.6
Kentucky	25.6

Current cigarette smoking is defined as persons 18 years and older who reported having smoked 100 or more cigarettes during their lifetime and who currently smoke every day or some days. Based on the Behavioral Risk Factor Surveillance System, a telephone survey of health behaviors of the civilian, non-institutionalized U.S. population, 18 years old and over.

SOURCES: U.S. Census Bureau Statistical Abstract of the United States: 2012, Table 205; U.S. Centers for Disease Control and Prevention, Atlanta, GA, Morbidity and Mortality Weekly Report, Vol. 59, No. 43, 2010

http://www.census.gov/compendia/statab/

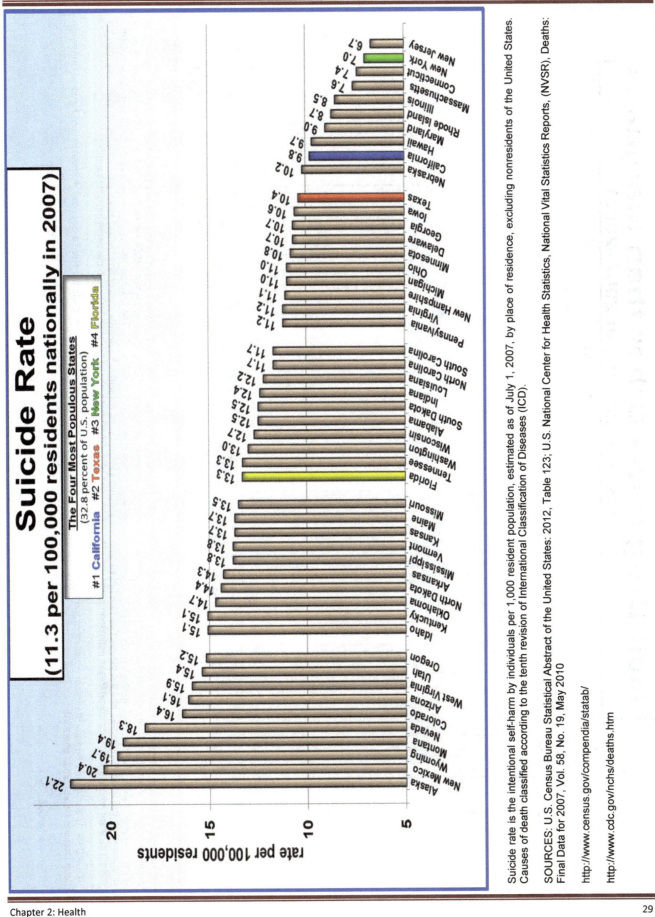

Suicide Rate
(11.3 per 100,000 residents nationally in 2007)

The Four Most Populous States
(32.8 percent of U.S. population)
#1 California   #2 Texas   #3 New York   #4 Florida

State	Rate
Alaska	22.1
New Mexico	20.4
Wyoming	19.7
Montana	19.4
Nevada	18.3
Colorado	16.4
Arizona	16.1
West Virginia	15.9
Utah	15.4
Oregon	15.2
Idaho	15.1
Kentucky	15.1
Oklahoma	14.7
North Dakota	14.4
Arkansas	14.3
Mississippi	13.8
Vermont	13.8
Kansas	13.7
Maine	13.7
Missouri	13.5
Florida	13.3
Tennessee	13.3
Washington	13.0
Wisconsin	12.7
Alabama	12.5
South Dakota	12.5
Indiana	12.4
Louisiana	12.2
North Carolina	11.7
South Carolina	11.7
Pennsylvania	11.2
Virginia	11.2
New Hampshire	11.1
Michigan	11.0
Ohio	11.0
Minnesota	10.8
Delaware	10.7
Georgia	10.7
Iowa	10.6
Texas	10.4
Nebraska	10.2
California	9.8
Hawaii	9.7
Maryland	9.0
Rhode Island	8.7
Illinois	8.5
Massachusetts	7.6
Connecticut	7.4
New York	7.0
New Jersey	6.7

rate per 100,000 residents

Suicide rate is the intentional self-harm by individuals per 1,000 resident population, estimated as of July 1, 2007, by place of residence, excluding nonresidents of the United States. Causes of death classified according to the tenth revision of International Classification of Diseases (ICD).

SOURCES: U.S. Census Bureau Statistical Abstract of the United States: 2012, Table 123; U.S. National Center for Health Statistics, National Vital Statistics Reports, (NVSR), Deaths: Final Data for 2007, Vol. 58, No. 19, May 2010

http://www.census.gov/compendia/statab/

http://www.cdc.gov/nchs/deaths.htm

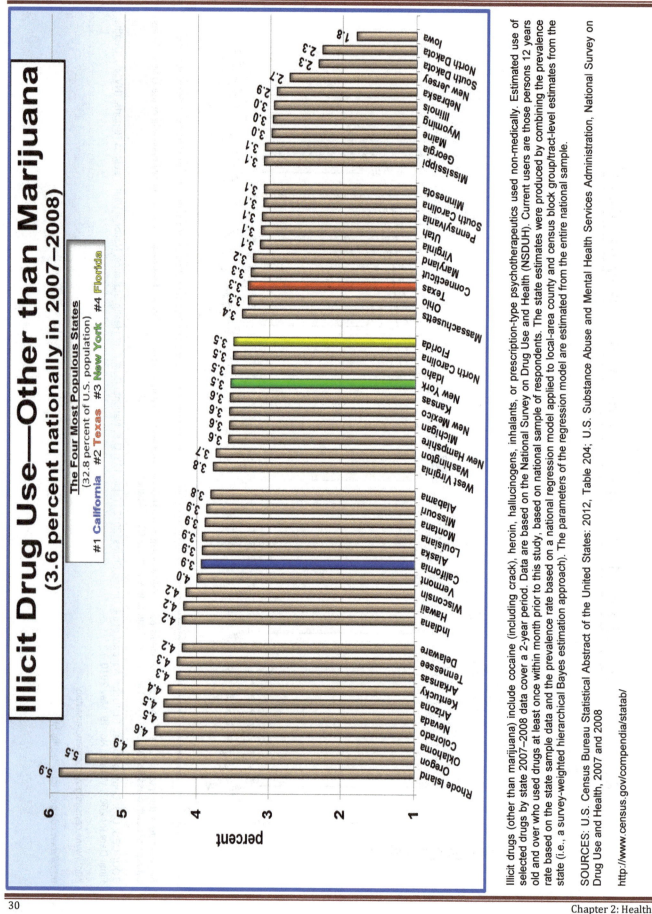

Illicit Drug Use—Other than Marijuana
(3.6 percent nationally in 2007–2008)

The Four Most Populous States
(32.8 percent of U.S. population)
#1 California   #2 Texas   #3 New York   #4 Florida

State	percent
Rhode Island	5.9
Oregon	5.5
Oklahoma	4.9
Colorado	4.6
Nevada	4.5
Arizona	4.5
Kentucky	4.4
Arkansas	4.3
Tennessee	4.2
Delaware	4.2
Indiana	4.2
Hawaii	4.2
Wisconsin	4.0
Vermont	3.9
California	3.9
Alaska	3.9
Louisiana	3.9
Montana	3.9
Missouri	3.8
Alabama	3.8
West Virginia	3.7
Washington	3.6
New Hampshire	3.6
Michigan	3.6
New Mexico	3.6
Kansas	3.5
New York	3.5
Idaho	3.5
North Carolina	3.5
Florida	3.4
Massachusetts	3.4
Ohio	3.3
Texas	3.3
Connecticut	3.2
Maryland	3.1
Virginia	3.1
Utah	3.1
Pennsylvania	3.1
South Carolina	3.1
Minnesota	3.1
Mississippi	3.0
Georgia	3.0
Maine	3.0
Wyoming	2.9
Illinois	2.7
Nebraska	2.3
New Jersey	2.3
South Dakota	1.8
North Dakota	
Iowa	

Illicit drugs (other than marijuana) include cocaine (including crack), heroin, hallucinogens, inhalants, or prescription-type psychotherapeutics used non-medically. Estimated use of selected drugs by state 2007–2008 data cover a 2-year period. Data are based on the National Survey on Drug Use and Health (NSDUH). Current users are those persons 12 years old and over who used drugs at least once within month prior to this study, based on national sample of respondents. The state estimates were produced by combining the prevalence rate based on the state sample data and the prevalence rate based on a national regression model applied to local-area county and census block group/tract-level estimates from the state (i.e., a survey-weighted hierarchical Bayes estimation approach). The parameters of the regression model are estimated from the entire national sample.

SOURCES: U.S. Census Bureau Statistical Abstract of the United States: 2012, Table 204; U.S. Substance Abuse and Mental Health Services Administration, National Survey on Drug Use and Health, 2007 and 2008

http://www.census.gov/compendia/statab/

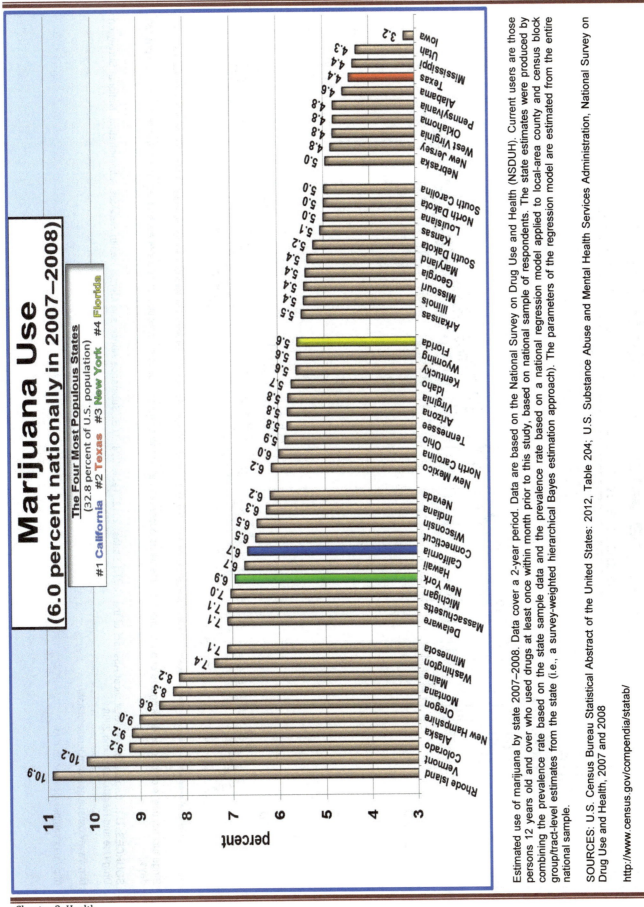

Marijuana Use
(6.0 percent nationally in 2007–2008)

The Four Most Populous States
(32.8 percent of U.S. population)
#1 California #2 Texas #3 New York #4 Florida

State	percent
Rhode Island	10.9
Vermont	10.2
Colorado	9.2
Alaska	9.2
New Hampshire	9.0
Oregon	8.6
Montana	8.3
Maine	8.2
Washington	7.4
Minnesota	7.1
Delaware	7.1
Massachusetts	7.0
Michigan	6.9
New York	6.7
Hawaii	6.7
California	6.5
Connecticut	6.5
Wisconsin	6.3
Indiana	6.2
Nevada	6.2
New Mexico	6.0
North Carolina	5.9
Ohio	5.8
Tennessee	5.8
Arizona	5.8
Virginia	5.7
Idaho	5.6
Kentucky	5.6
Wyoming	5.6
Florida	5.5
Arkansas	5.4
Illinois	5.4
Missouri	5.4
Georgia	5.2
Maryland	5.1
South Dakota	5.0
Kansas	5.0
Louisiana	5.0
North Dakota	5.0
South Carolina	4.8
Nebraska	4.8
New Jersey	4.8
West Virginia	4.6
Oklahoma	4.4
Pennsylvania	4.4
Alabama	4.3
Texas	3.2
Mississippi	
Utah	
Iowa	

Estimated use of marijuana by state 2007–2008. Data cover a 2-year period. Data are based on the National Survey on Drug Use and Health (NSDUH). Current users are those persons 12 years old and over who used drugs at least once within month prior to this study, based on national sample of respondents. The state estimates were produced by combining the prevalence rate based on the state sample data and the prevalence rate based on a national regression model applied to local-area county and census block group/tract-level estimates from the state (i.e., a survey-weighted hierarchical Bayes estimation approach). The parameters of the regression model are estimated from the entire national sample.

SOURCES: U.S. Census Bureau Statistical Abstract of the United States: 2012, Table 204; U.S. Substance Abuse and Mental Health Services Administration, National Survey on Drug Use and Health, 2007 and 2008

http://www.census.gov/compendia/statab/

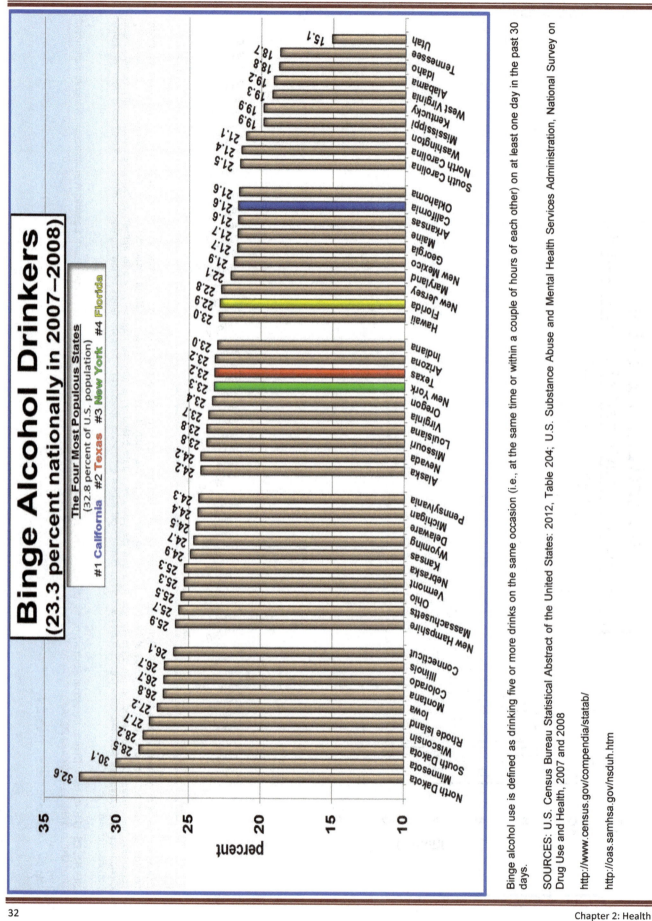

Binge Alcohol Drinkers
(23.3 percent nationally in 2007–2008)

The Four Most Populous States
(32.8 percent of U.S. population)
#1 California   #2 Texas   #3 New York   #4 Florida

State	Percent
North Dakota	32.6
Minnesota	30.1
South Dakota	28.5
Wisconsin	28.2
Rhode Island	27.7
Iowa	27.2
Montana	26.8
Colorado	26.7
Illinois	26.7
Connecticut	26.1
New Hampshire	25.9
Massachusetts	25.7
Ohio	25.5
Vermont	25.3
Nebraska	25.3
Kansas	24.9
Wyoming	24.7
Delaware	24.5
Michigan	24.4
Pennsylvania	24.3
Alaska	24.2
Nevada	24.2
Missouri	23.8
Louisiana	23.8
Virginia	23.7
Oregon	23.4
New York	23.3
Texas	23.2
Arizona	23.2
Indiana	23.0
Hawaii	23.0
Florida	22.9
New Jersey	22.8
Maryland	22.1
New Mexico	21.9
Georgia	21.7
Maine	21.7
Arkansas	21.6
California	21.6
Oklahoma	21.6
South Carolina	21.5
North Carolina	21.4
Washington	21.1
Mississippi	19.9
Kentucky	19.9
West Virginia	19.3
Alabama	19.2
Idaho	18.8
Tennessee	18.7
Utah	15.1

percent

Binge alcohol use is defined as drinking five or more drinks on the same occasion (i.e., at the same time or within a couple of hours of each other) on at least one day in the past 30 days.

SOURCES: U.S. Census Bureau Statistical Abstract of the United States: 2012, Table 204; U.S. Substance Abuse and Mental Health Services Administration, National Survey on Drug Use and Health, 2007 and 2008

http://www.census.gov/compendia/statab/

http://oas.samhsa.gov/nsduh.htm

Chapter 2: Health

Alcohol-Imparied Traffic Fatalities
(31 percent of traffic fatalities nationally in 2010)

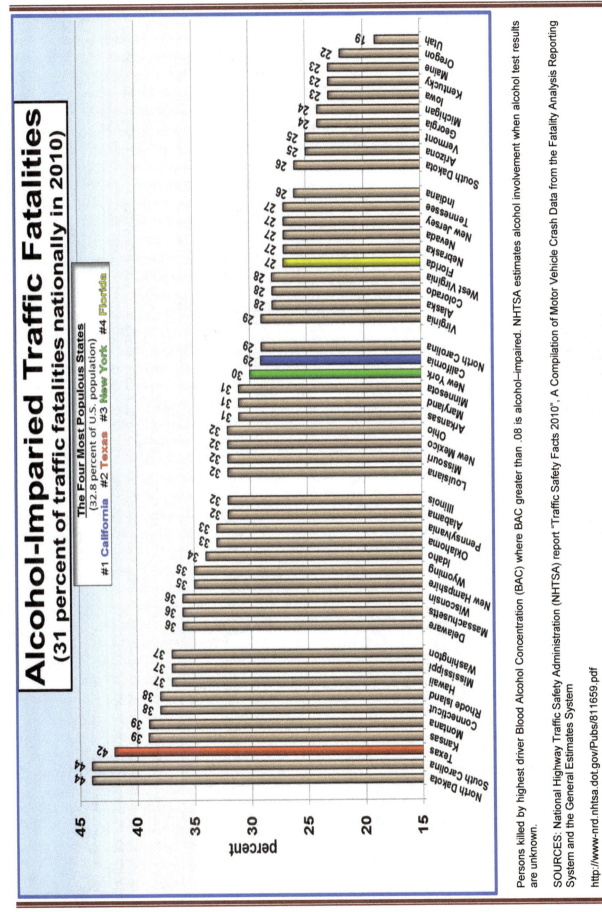

The Four Most Populous States
(32.8 percent of U.S. population)

#1 California   #2 Texas   #3 New York   #4 Florida

State	Percent
North Dakota	44
South Carolina	44
Texas	42
Kansas	39
Montana	39
Connecticut	38
Rhode Island	38
Hawaii	37
Mississippi	37
Washington	37
Delaware	36
Massachusetts	36
Wisconsin	36
New Hampshire	35
Wyoming	35
Idaho	34
Oklahoma	33
Pennsylvania	33
Alabama	32
Illinois	32
Louisiana	32
Missouri	32
New Mexico	32
Ohio	32
Arkansas	31
Maryland	31
Minnesota	31
New York	30
California	29
North Carolina	29
Virginia	29
Alaska	28
Colorado	28
West Virginia	28
Florida	27
Nebraska	27
Nevada	27
New Jersey	27
Tennessee	27
Indiana	26
South Dakota	26
Arizona	25
Vermont	25
Georgia	24
Michigan	24
Iowa	23
Kentucky	23
Maine	23
Oregon	22
Utah	19

Persons killed by highest driver Blood Alcohol Concentration (BAC) where BAC greater than .08 is alcohol–impaired. NHTSA estimates alcohol involvement when alcohol test results are unknown.

SOURCES: National Highway Traffic Safety Administration (NHTSA) report "Traffic Safety Facts 2010", A Compilation of Motor Vehicle Crash Data from the Fatality Analysis Reporting System and the General Estimates System

http://www.www-nrd.nhtsa.dot.gov/Pubs/811659.pdf

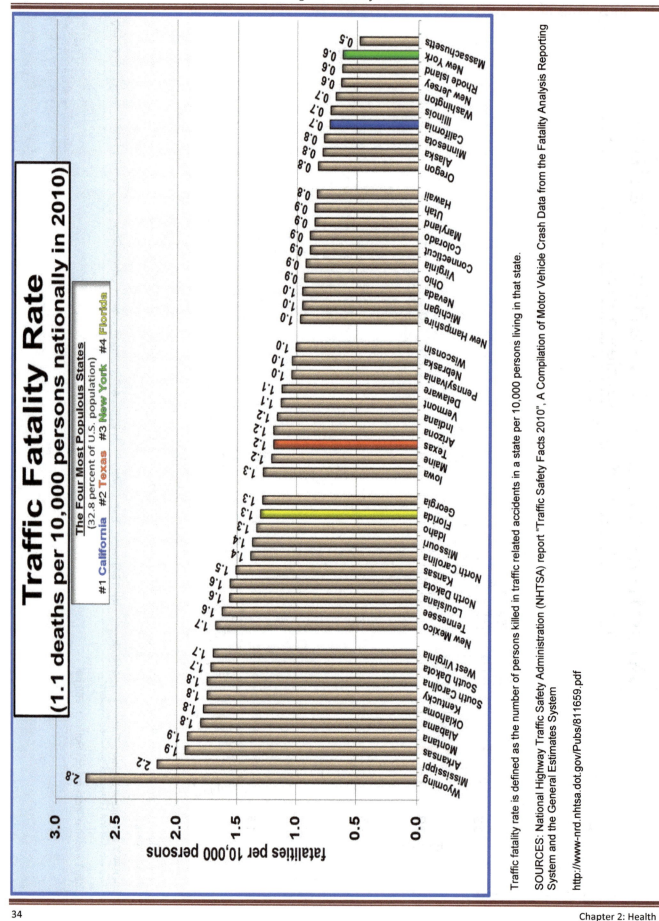

Traffic Fatality Rate
(1.1 deaths per 10,000 persons nationally in 2010)

The Four Most Populous States
(32.8 percent of U.S. population)
#1 California #2 Texas #3 New York #4 Florida

State	fatalities per 10,000 persons
Massachusetts	0.5
New York	0.6
Rhode Island	0.6
New Jersey	0.6
Washington	0.7
Illinois	0.7
California	0.7
Minnesota	0.8
Alaska	0.8
Oregon	0.8
Hawaii	0.8
Utah	0.9
Maryland	0.9
Colorado	0.9
Connecticut	0.9
Virginia	0.9
Ohio	0.9
Nevada	1.0
Michigan	1.0
New Hampshire	1.0
Wisconsin	1.0
Nebraska	1.0
Pennsylvania	1.0
Delaware	1.1
Vermont	1.1
Indiana	1.2
Arizona	1.2
Texas	1.2
Maine	1.2
Iowa	1.3
Georgia	1.3
Florida	1.3
Idaho	1.3
Missouri	1.4
North Carolina	1.4
Kansas	1.5
North Dakota	1.6
Louisiana	1.6
Tennessee	1.6
New Mexico	1.7
West Virginia	1.7
South Dakota	1.7
South Carolina	1.8
Kentucky	1.8
Oklahoma	1.8
Alabama	1.8
Montana	1.9
Arkansas	1.9
Mississippi	2.2
Wyoming	2.8

Traffic fatality rate is defined as the number of persons killed in traffic related accidents in a state per 10,000 persons living in that state.

SOURCES: National Highway Traffic Safety Administration (NHTSA) report "Traffic Safety Facts 2010", A Compilation of Motor Vehicle Crash Data from the Fatality Analysis Reporting System and the General Estimates System

http://www-nrd.nhtsa.dot.gov/Pubs/811659.pdf

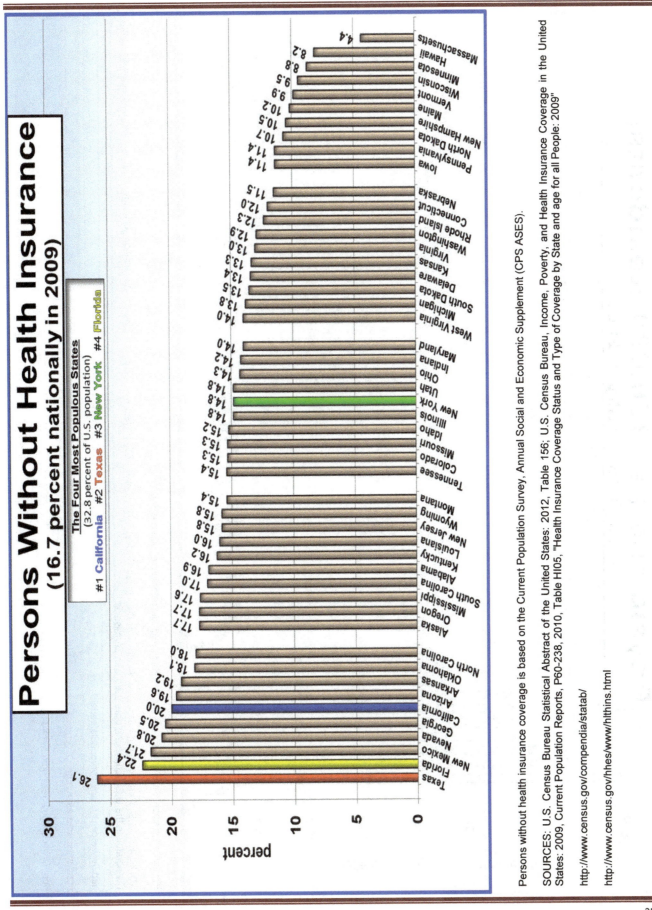

Persons Without Health Insurance
(16.7 percent nationally in 2009)

The Four Most Populous States
(32.8 percent of U.S. population)
#1 California   #2 Texas   #3 New York   #4 Florida

State	percent
Texas	26.1
Florida	22.4
New Mexico	21.7
Nevada	20.8
Georgia	20.5
California	20.0
Arizona	19.6
Arkansas	19.2
Oklahoma	18.1
North Carolina	18.0
Alaska	17.7
Oregon	17.7
Mississippi	17.6
South Carolina	17.0
Alabama	16.9
Kentucky	16.2
Louisiana	16.0
New Jersey	15.8
Wyoming	15.8
Montana	15.4
Tennessee	15.4
Colorado	15.3
Missouri	15.3
Idaho	15.2
Illinois	14.8
New York	14.8
Utah	14.3
Ohio	14.2
Indiana	14.0
Maryland	14.0
West Virginia	13.8
Michigan	13.5
South Dakota	13.4
Delaware	13.3
Kansas	13.0
Virginia	12.9
Washington	12.3
Rhode Island	12.0
Connecticut	11.5
Nebraska	11.4
Iowa	11.4
Pennsylvania	10.7
North Dakota	10.5
New Hampshire	10.2
Maine	9.9
Vermont	9.5
Wisconsin	8.8
Minnesota	8.2
Hawaii	4.4
Massachusetts	

percent

Persons without health insurance coverage is based on the Current Population Survey, Annual Social and Economic Supplement (CPS ASES).

SOURCES: U.S. Census Bureau Statistical Abstract of the United States: 2012, Table 156; U.S. Census Bureau, Income, Poverty, and Health Insurance Coverage in the United States: 2009, Current Population Reports, P60-238, 2010, Table HI05, "Health Insurance Coverage Status and Type of Coverage by State and age for all People: 2009"

http://www.census.gov/compendia/statab/

http://www.census.gov/hhes/www/hlthins.html

Physicians per 100,000 Residents
(273 nationally in 2009)

The Four Most Populous States
(32.8 percent of U.S. population)
#1 California   #2 Texas   #3 New York   #4 Florida

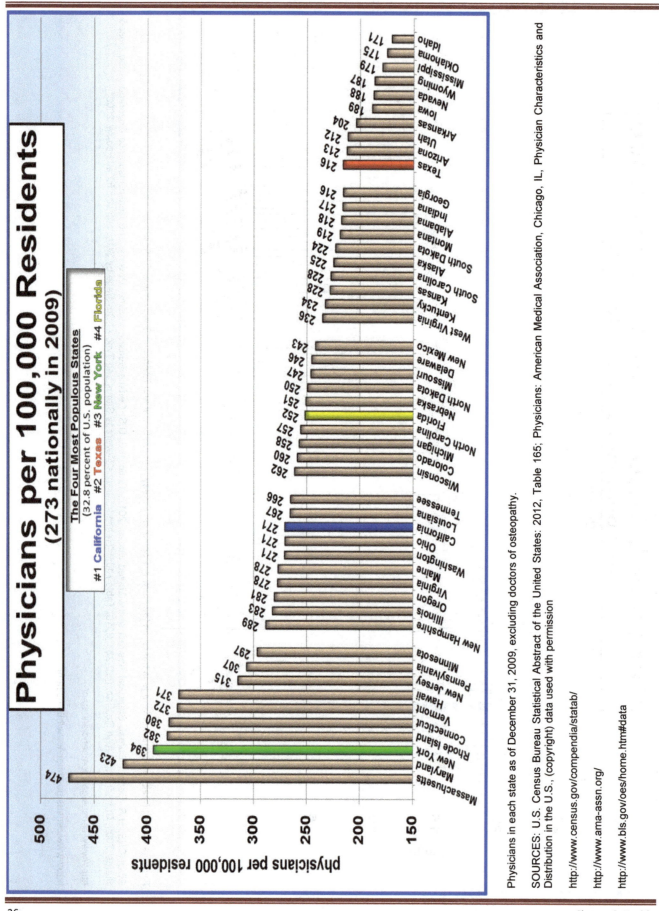

State	physicians per 100,000 residents
Massachusetts	474
Maryland	423
New York	394
Rhode Island	382
Connecticut	380
Vermont	372
Hawaii	371
New Jersey	315
Pennsylvania	307
Minnesota	297
New Hampshire	289
Illinois	283
Oregon	281
Virginia	278
Maine	278
Washington	271
Ohio	271
California	271
Louisiana	267
Tennessee	266
Wisconsin	262
Colorado	260
Michigan	258
North Carolina	257
Florida	252
Nebraska	251
North Dakota	250
Missouri	247
Delaware	246
New Mexico	243
West Virginia	236
Kentucky	234
Kansas	228
South Carolina	228
Alaska	225
South Dakota	224
Montana	219
Alabama	218
Indiana	217
Georgia	216
Texas	216
Arizona	213
Utah	212
Arkansas	204
Iowa	189
Nevada	188
Wyoming	187
Mississippi	179
Oklahoma	175
Idaho	171

Physicians in each state as of December 31, 2009, excluding doctors of osteopathy.

SOURCES: U.S. Census Bureau Statistical Abstract of the United States: 2012, Table 165; Physicians: American Medical Association, Chicago, IL, Physician Characteristics and Distribution in the U.S., (copyright) data used with permission

http://www.census.gov/compendia/statab/

http://www.ama-assn.org/

http://www.bls.gov/oes/home.htm#data

Chapter 3: Lifestyle Overview

Mississippi ranked highest in multiple social categories including: highest proportion of births to unmarried mothers (55 percent), mothers below poverty level (38 percent), and teenage birth rate. One out of six births was to mothers under twenty-one years of age.

Nationally, 4 out of 5 households have Internet access, either in or outside their home, while 9 out of 10 have access in Utah—the highest access rate. Utah also led the nation in volunteerism and charitable contributions of $1,031 per capita.

New York had the highest proportion of Jewish residents while Utah had the highest proportion of Christian residents.

The abortion rate was highest in Delaware in 2008 at 40.0 abortions per 1,000 women followed by New York at 37.8 abortions per 1,000 women. Wyoming had the lowest abortion rate at 0.9 abortions per 1,000 women.

New York attracts the most foreign visitors.

Nationally, 59 percent of eligible voters voted for president in 2012. Minnesota had the highest voter turnout at 76 percent while Hawaii had the lowest at 44 percent. The largest margin of victory for Obama was in Hawaii. Meanwhile, the largest margin of victory for Romney was in Utah.

Over the past decade, over 100 million firearms background checks have been performed nationally, with the highest rate in Utah and the lowest rate in New Jersey.

The annual rate of patents being issued to residents varies twenty-to-one. In Vermont, 107 patents per 100,000 residents were issued compared with only 5 patents per 100,000 residents in Alaska.

The marriage rate was highest in Nevada and New Hampshire and six times the national average. Nevada also had the highest divorce rate—double the national average.

California has led the nation in several metrics. It has the highest population and therefore the most members in the House of Representatives at 53; it led the nation with 100 million annual visits to state parks in 2010, and also had the highest number of same sex households in 2010.

~

Lifestyle Summary Table

States Legend: Highest 10% | Middle 80% | Lowest 10%

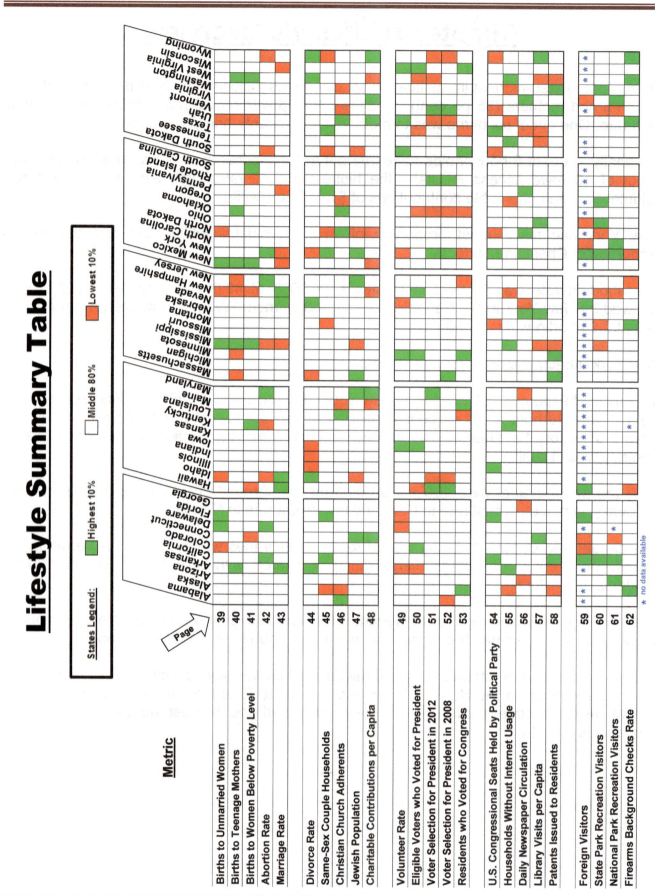

Metric	Page
Births to Unmarried Women	39
Births to Teenage Mothers	40
Births to Women Below Poverty Level	41
Abortion Rate	42
Marriage Rate	43
Divorce Rate	44
Same-Sex Couple Households	45
Christian Church Adherents	46
Jewish Population	47
Charitable Contributions per Capita	48
Volunteer Rate	49
Eligible Voters who Voted for President	50
Voter Selection for President in 2012	51
Voter Selection for President in 2008	52
Residents who Voted for Congress	53
U.S. Congressional Seats Held by Political Party	54
Households Without Internet Usage	55
Daily Newspaper Circulation	56
Library Visits per Capita	57
Patents Issued to Residents	58
Foreign Visitors	59
State Park Recreation Visitors	60
National Park Recreation Visitors	61
Firearms Background Checks Rate	62

* no data available

Chapter 3: Lifestyle Overview

Mississippi ranked highest in multiple social categories including: highest proportion of births to unmarried mothers (55 percent), mothers below poverty level (38 percent), and teenage birth rate. One out of six births was to mothers under twenty-one years of age.

Nationally, 4 out of 5 households have Internet access, either in or outside their home, while 9 out of 10 have access in Utah—the highest access rate. Utah also led the nation in volunteerism and charitable contributions of $1,031 per capita.

New York had the highest proportion of Jewish residents while Utah had the highest proportion of Christian residents.

The abortion rate was highest in Delaware in 2008 at 40.0 abortions per 1,000 women followed by New York at 37.8 abortions per 1,000 women. Wyoming had the lowest abortion rate at 0.9 abortions per 1,000 women.

New York attracts the most foreign visitors.

Nationally, 59 percent of eligible voters voted for president in 2012. Minnesota had the highest voter turnout at 76 percent while Hawaii had the lowest at 44 percent. The largest margin of victory for Obama was in Hawaii. Meanwhile, the largest margin of victory for Romney was in Utah.

Over the past decade, over 100 million firearms background checks have been performed nationally, with the highest rate in Utah and the lowest rate in New Jersey.

The annual rate of patents being issued to residents varies twenty-to-one. In Vermont, 107 patents per 100,000 residents were issued compared with only 5 patents per 100,000 residents in Alaska.

The marriage rate was highest in Nevada and New Hampshire and six times the national average. Nevada also had the highest divorce rate—double the national average.

California has led the nation in several metrics. It has the highest population and therefore the most members in the House of Representatives at 53; it led the nation with 100 million annual visits to state parks in 2010, and also had the highest number of same sex households in 2010.

~

Lifestyle Summary Table

States Legend:

Highest 10% | Middle 80% | Lowest 10%

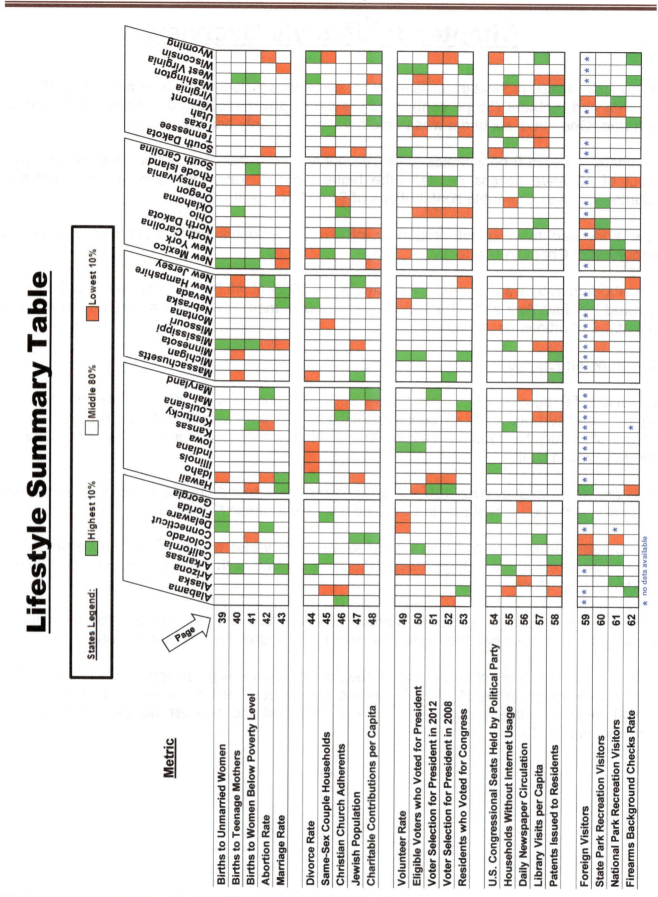

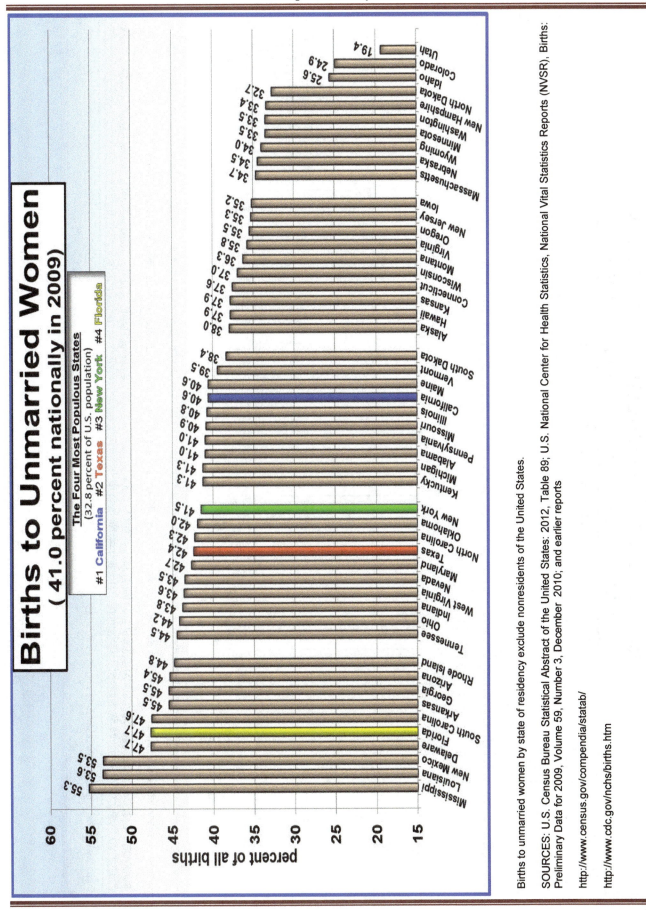

Births to Unmarried Women
(41.0 percent nationally in 2009)

The Four Most Populous States
(32.8 percent of U.S. population)
#1 California #2 Texas #3 New York #4 Florida

percent of all births

Mississippi	55.3
Louisiana	53.6
New Mexico	53.5
Delaware	47.7
Florida	47.7
South Carolina	47.6
Arkansas	45.5
Georgia	45.5
Arizona	45.4
Rhode Island	44.8
Tennessee	44.5
Ohio	44.2
Indiana	43.8
West Virginia	43.6
Nevada	43.5
Maryland	42.7
Texas	42.4
North Carolina	42.3
Oklahoma	42.0
New York	41.5
Kentucky	41.3
Michigan	41.3
Alabama	41.0
Pennsylvania	41.0
Missouri	40.9
Illinois	40.8
California	40.6
Maine	40.6
Vermont	39.5
South Dakota	38.4
Alaska	38.0
Hawaii	37.9
Kansas	37.9
Connecticut	37.6
Wisconsin	37.0
Montana	36.3
Virginia	35.8
Oregon	35.5
New Jersey	35.3
Iowa	35.2
Massachusetts	34.7
Nebraska	34.5
Wyoming	34.0
Minnesota	33.5
Washington	33.5
New Hampshire	33.4
North Dakota	32.7
Idaho	25.6
Colorado	24.9
Utah	19.4

Births to unmarried women by state of residency exclude nonresidents of the United States.

SOURCES: U.S. Census Bureau Statistical Abstract of the United States: 2012, Table 89; U.S. National Center for Health Statistics, National Vital Statistics Reports (NVSR), Births: Preliminary Data for 2009, Volume 59, Number 3, December 2010; and earlier reports

http://www.census.gov/compendia/statab/

http://www.cdc.gov/nchs/births.htm

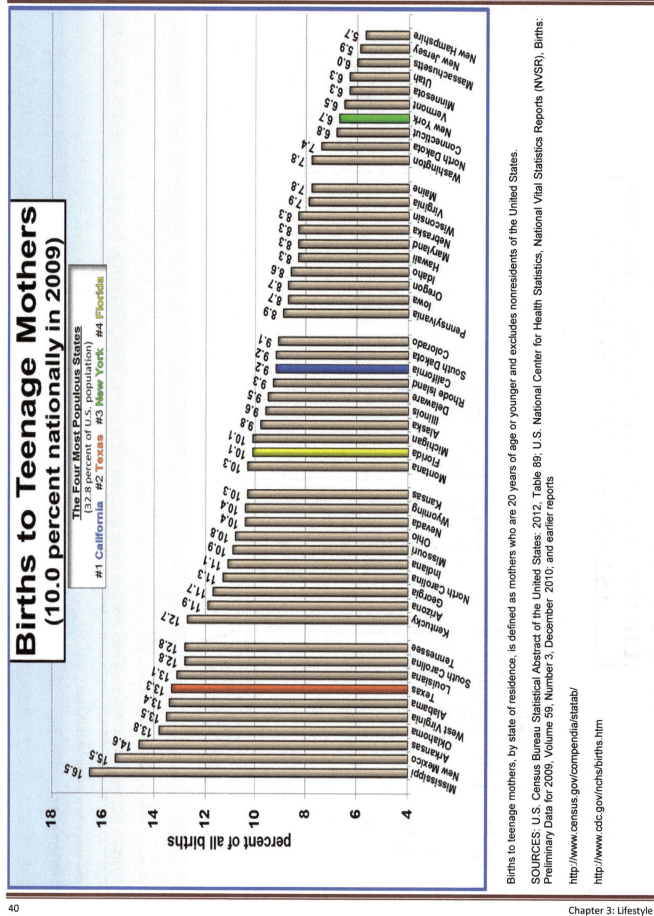

Births to Teenage Mothers
(10.0 percent nationally in 2009)

The Four Most Populous States
(32.8 percent of U.S. population)
#1 California #2 Texas #3 New York #4 Florida

percent of all births

State	Percent
Mississippi	16.5
New Mexico	15.5
Arkansas	14.6
Oklahoma	13.8
West Virginia	13.5
Alabama	13.4
Texas	13.3
Louisiana	13.1
South Carolina	12.8
Tennessee	12.8
Kentucky	12.7
Arizona	11.9
Georgia	11.7
North Carolina	11.3
Indiana	11.1
Missouri	10.9
Ohio	10.8
Nevada	10.4
Wyoming	10.4
Kansas	10.3
Montana	10.3
Florida	10.1
Michigan	10.1
Alaska	9.8
Illinois	9.6
Delaware	9.5
Rhode Island	9.3
California	9.2
South Dakota	9.2
Colorado	9.1
Pennsylvania	8.9
Iowa	8.7
Oregon	8.7
Idaho	8.6
Hawaii	8.3
Maryland	8.3
Nebraska	8.3
Wisconsin	7.9
Virginia	7.8
Maine	7.8
Washington	7.4
North Dakota	6.8
Connecticut	6.7
New York	6.7
Vermont	6.5
Minnesota	6.3
Utah	6.3
Massachusetts	6.0
New Jersey	5.9
New Hampshire	5.7

Births to teenage mothers, by state of residence, is defined as mothers who are 20 years of age or younger and excludes nonresidents of the United States.

SOURCES: U.S. Census Bureau Statistical Abstract of the United States: 2012, Table 89; U.S. National Center for Health Statistics, National Vital Statistics Reports (NVSR), Births: Preliminary Data for 2009, Volume 59, Number 3, December 2010; and earlier reports

http://www.census.gov/compendia/statab/

http://www.cdc.gov/nchs/births.htm

Births to Women Below Poverty Level

(26.6 percent nationally in 2009)

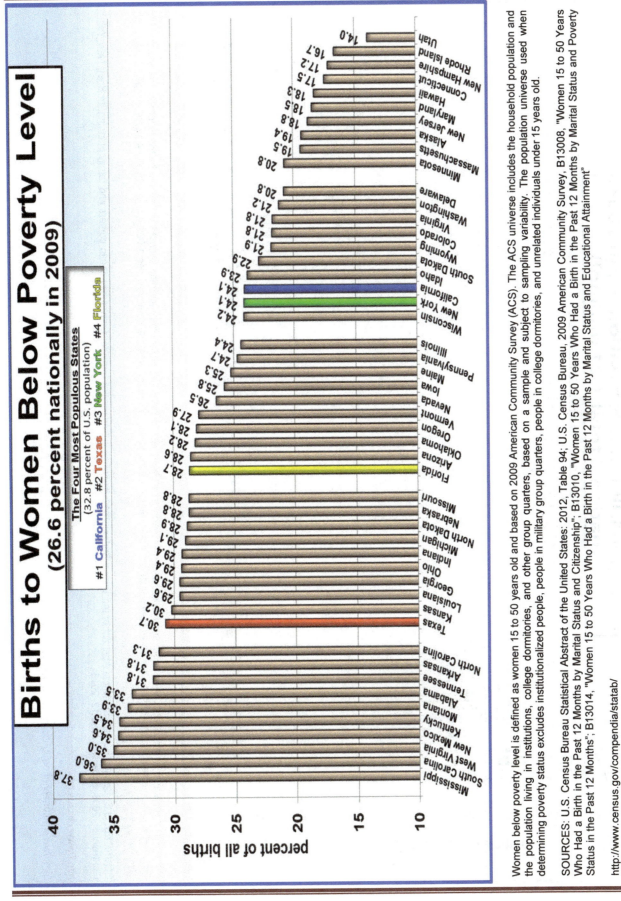

The Four Most Populous States
(32.8 percent of U.S. population)

#1 California #2 Texas #3 New York #4 Florida

State	percent of all births
Mississippi	37.8
South Carolina	36.0
West Virginia	35.0
New Mexico	34.6
Kentucky	34.5
Montana	33.9
Alabama	33.5
Tennessee	31.8
Arkansas	31.8
North Carolina	31.3
Texas	30.7
Kansas	30.2
Louisiana	29.6
Georgia	29.6
Ohio	29.4
Indiana	29.4
Michigan	29.1
North Dakota	28.9
Nebraska	28.8
Missouri	28.8
Florida	28.7
Arizona	28.6
Oklahoma	28.2
Oregon	28.1
Vermont	27.9
Nevada	26.5
Iowa	25.8
Maine	25.3
Pennsylvania	24.7
Illinois	24.4
Wisconsin	24.2
New York	24.1
California	24.1
Idaho	23.9
South Dakota	22.9
Wyoming	21.9
Colorado	21.8
Virginia	21.8
Washington	21.2
Delaware	20.8
Minnesota	20.8
Massachusetts	19.5
Alaska	19.4
New Jersey	18.8
Maryland	18.5
Hawaii	18.3
Connecticut	17.5
New Hampshire	17.2
Rhode Island	16.7
Utah	14.0

Women below poverty level is defined as women 15 to 50 years old and based on 2009 American Community Survey (ACS). The ACS universe includes the household population and the population living in institutions, college dormitories, and other group quarters, based on a sample and subject to sampling variability. The population universe used when determining poverty status excludes institutionalized people, people in military group quarters, people in college dormitories, and unrelated individuals under 15 years old.

SOURCES: U.S. Census Bureau Statistical Abstract of the United States: 2012; Table 94; U.S. Census Bureau, 2009 American Community Survey, B13008, "Women 15 to 50 Years Who Had a Birth in the Past 12 Months by Marital Status and Citizenship", B13010, "Women 15 to 50 Years Who Had a Birth in the Past 12 Months by Marital Status and Educational Attainment"; B13014, "Women 15 to 50 Years Who Had a Birth in the Past 12 Months by Marital Status and Educational Attainment"

http://www.census.gov/compendia/statab/

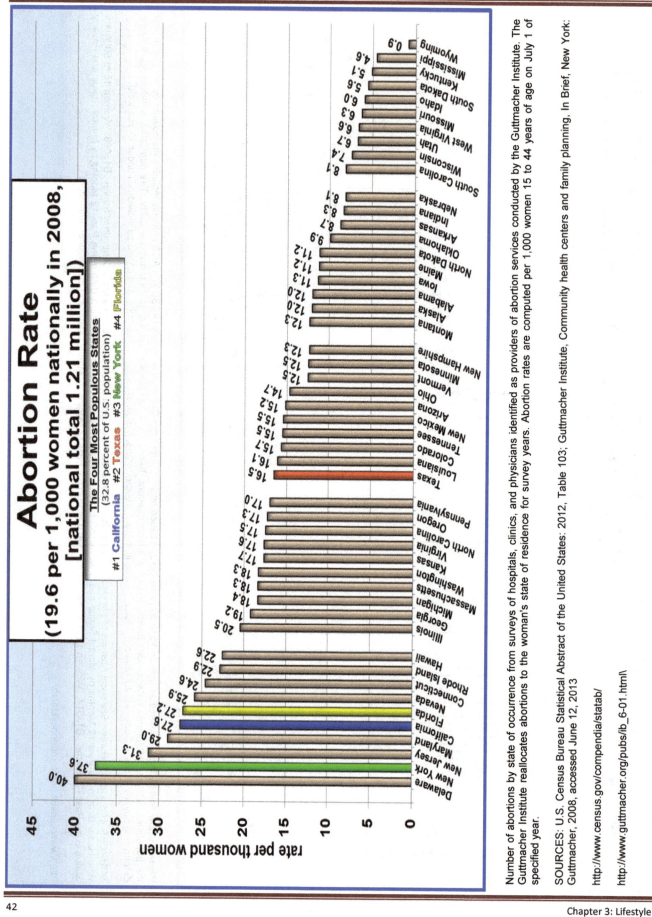

Abortion Rate
(19.6 per 1,000 women nationally in 2008, [national total 1.21 million])

The Four Most Populous States
(32.8 percent of U.S. population)
#1 California #2 Texas #3 New York #4 Florida

rate per thousand women

State	Rate
Delaware	40.0
New York	37.6
New Jersey	31.3
Maryland	29.0
California	27.6
Florida	27.2
Nevada	25.9
Connecticut	24.6
Rhode Island	22.9
Hawaii	22.6
Illinois	20.5
Georgia	19.2
Michigan	18.4
Massachusetts	18.3
Washington	17.7
Kansas	17.6
Virginia	17.5
North Carolina	17.3
Oregon	17.0
Pennsylvania	16.5
Texas	16.1
Louisiana	15.7
Colorado	15.5
Tennessee	15.2
New Mexico	14.7
Arizona	12.5
Ohio	12.5
Vermont	12.3
Minnesota	12.3
New Hampshire	12.3
Montana	12.0
Alaska	12.0
Alabama	11.3
Iowa	11.2
Maine	11.2
North Dakota	9.9
Oklahoma	8.7
Arkansas	8.3
Indiana	8.1
Nebraska	8.1
South Carolina	7.4
Wisconsin	6.7
Utah	6.6
West Virginia	6.3
Missouri	6.0
Idaho	5.6
South Dakota	5.1
Kentucky	4.6
Mississippi	0.9
Wyoming	

Number of abortions by state of occurrence from surveys of hospitals, clinics, and physicians identified as providers of abortion services conducted by the Guttmacher Institute. The Guttmacher Institute reallocates abortions to the woman's state of residence for survey years. Abortion rates are computed per 1,000 women 15 to 44 years of age on July 1 of specified year.

SOURCES: U.S. Census Bureau Statistical Abstract of the United States: 2012, Table 103; Guttmacher Institute, Community health centers and family planning, In Brief, New York: Guttmacher, 2008, accessed June 12, 2013

http://www.census.gov/compendia/statab/

http://www.guttmacher.org/pubs/ib_6-01.html\

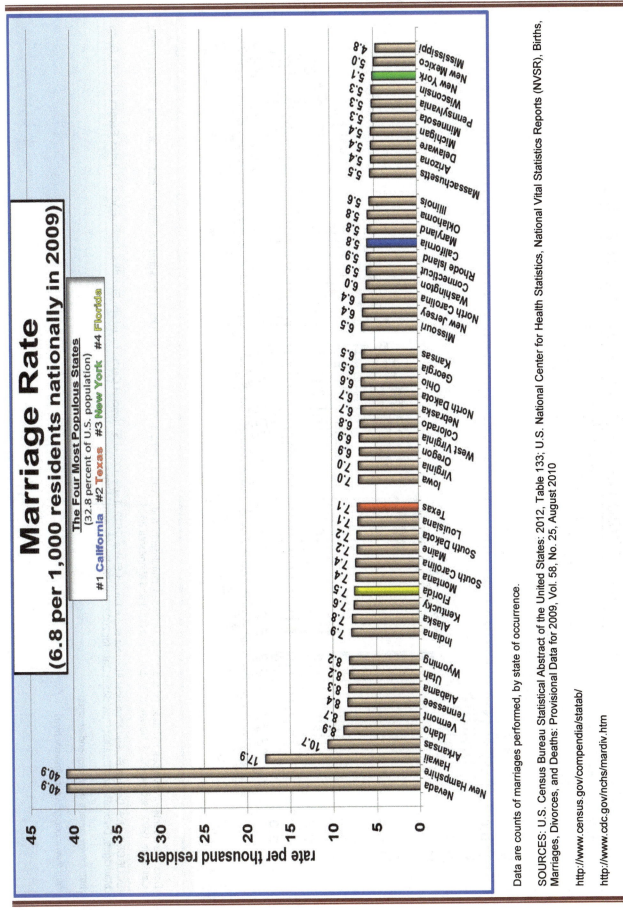

Marriage Rate
(6.8 per 1,000 residents nationally in 2009)

The Four Most Populous States
(32.8 percent of U.S. population)
#1 California   #2 Texas   #3 New York   #4 Florida

rate per thousand residents

State	Rate
Nevada	40.9
New Hampshire	40.9
Hawaii	17.9
Arkansas	10.7
Idaho	8.9
Vermont	8.7
Tennessee	8.4
Alabama	8.3
Utah	8.2
Wyoming	8.2
Indiana	7.9
Alaska	7.8
Kentucky	7.6
Florida	7.5
Montana	7.4
South Carolina	7.4
Maine	7.2
South Dakota	7.2
Louisiana	7.1
Texas	7.1
Iowa	7.0
Virginia	7.0
Oregon	6.9
West Virginia	6.9
Colorado	6.8
Nebraska	6.7
North Dakota	6.7
Ohio	6.6
Georgia	6.5
Kansas	6.5
Missouri	6.5
New Jersey	6.4
North Carolina	6.4
Washington	6.0
Connecticut	5.9
Rhode Island	5.9
California	5.8
Maryland	5.8
Oklahoma	5.8
Illinois	5.6
Massachusetts	5.5
Arizona	5.4
Delaware	5.4
Michigan	5.4
Minnesota	5.3
Pennsylvania	5.3
Wisconsin	5.3
New York	5.1
New Mexico	5.0
Mississippi	4.8

Data are counts of marriages performed, by state of occurrence.

SOURCES: U.S. Census Bureau Statistical Abstract of the United States: 2012, Table 133; U.S. National Center for Health Statistics, National Vital Statistics Reports (NVSR), Births, Marriages, Divorces, and Deaths: Provisional Data for 2009, Vol. 58, No. 25, August 2010

http://www.census.gov/compendia/statab/

http://www.cdc.gov/nchs/mardiv.htm

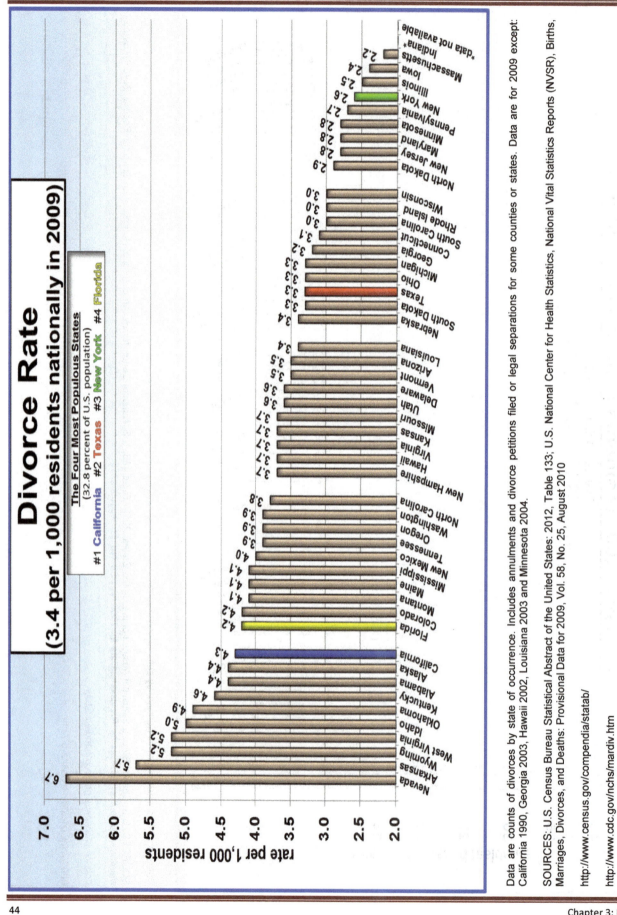

Divorce Rate
(3.4 per 1,000 residents nationally in 2009)

The Four Most Populous States
(32.8 percent of U.S. population)
#1 California   #2 Texas   #3 New York   #4 Florida

rate per 1,000 residents

State	Rate
Nevada	6.7
Arkansas	5.7
Wyoming	5.2
West Virginia	5.2
Idaho	5.0
Oklahoma	4.9
Kentucky	4.6
Alabama	4.4
Alaska	4.4
California	4.3
Florida	4.2
Colorado	4.2
Montana	4.1
Maine	4.1
Mississippi	4.1
New Mexico	4.0
Tennessee	3.9
Oregon	3.9
Washington	3.8
North Carolina	3.8
New Hampshire	3.7
Hawaii	3.7
Virginia	3.7
Kansas	3.7
Missouri	3.7
Utah	3.6
Delaware	3.6
Vermont	3.5
Arizona	3.5
Louisiana	3.4
Nebraska	3.4
South Dakota	3.3
Texas	3.3
Ohio	3.3
Michigan	3.2
Georgia	3.1
Connecticut	3.0
South Carolina	3.0
Rhode Island	3.0
Wisconsin	2.9
North Dakota	2.8
New Jersey	2.8
Maryland	2.7
Minnesota	2.7
Pennsylvania	2.6
New York	2.6
Illinois	2.5
Iowa	2.4
Massachusetts	2.2
Indiana*	*data not available

Data are counts of divorces by state of occurrence. Includes annulments and divorce petitions filed or legal separations for some counties or states. Data are for 2009 except: California 1990, Georgia 2003, Hawaii 2002, Louisiana 2003 and Minnesota 2004.

SOURCES: U.S. Census Bureau Statistical Abstract of the United States: 2012, Table 133; U.S. National Center for Health Statistics, National Vital Statistics Reports (NVSR), Births, Marriages, Divorces, and Deaths: Provisional Data for 2009, Vol. 58, No. 25, August 2010

http://www.census.gov/compendia/statab/

http://www.cdc.gov/nchs/mardiv.htm

Same-Sex Couple Households
(902,000 nationally in 2010)

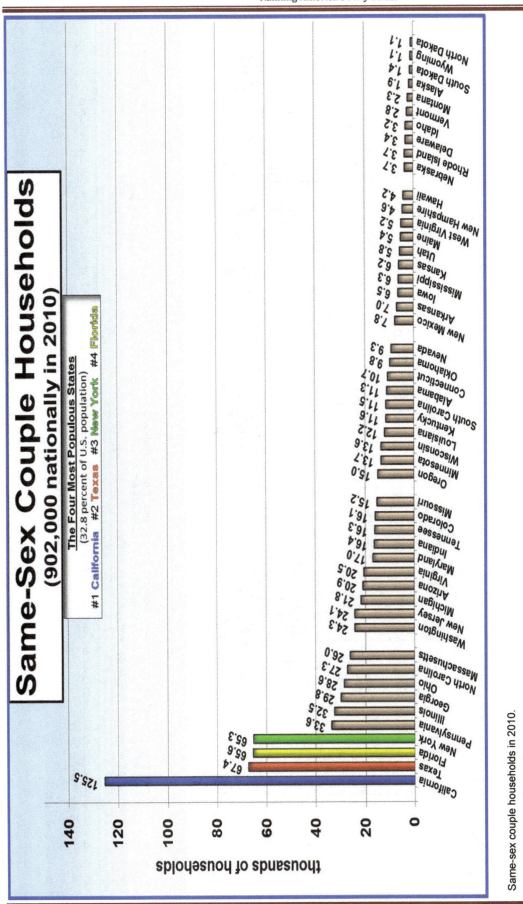

The Four Most Populous States
(32.8 percent of U.S. population)

#1 California   #2 Texas   #3 New York   #4 Florida

State	thousands of households
California	125.5
Texas	67.4
Florida	65.6
New York	65.3
Pennsylvania	33.6
Illinois	32.5
Georgia	29.8
Ohio	28.6
North Carolina	27.3
Massachusetts	26.0
Washington	24.3
New Jersey	24.1
Michigan	21.8
Arizona	20.9
Virginia	20.5
Maryland	17.0
Indiana	16.4
Tennessee	16.3
Colorado	16.1
Missouri	15.2
Oregon	15.0
Minnesota	13.7
Wisconsin	13.6
Louisiana	12.2
Kentucky	11.6
South Carolina	11.5
Alabama	11.3
Connecticut	10.7
Oklahoma	9.8
Nevada	9.3
New Mexico	7.8
Arkansas	7.0
Iowa	6.5
Mississippi	6.3
Kansas	6.2
Utah	5.8
Maine	5.4
West Virginia	5.2
New Hampshire	4.6
Hawaii	4.2
Nebraska	3.7
Rhode Island	3.7
Delaware	3.4
Idaho	3.2
Vermont	2.8
Montana	2.3
Alaska	1.9
South Dakota	1.4
Wyoming	1.1
North Dakota	1.1

Same-sex couple households in 2010.

SOURCE: U.S. Census Bureau; Census 2000 and 2010 Summary File 1 and 2010 American Community Survey

http://www.census.gov/hhes/samesex/

Christian Church Adherents
(47.4 percent of population nationally in 2010)

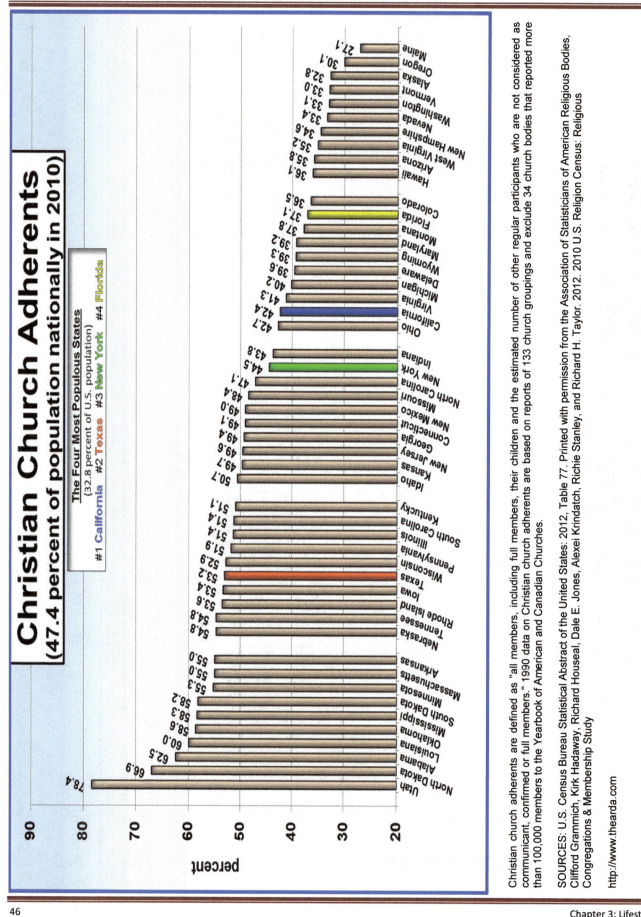

The Four Most Populous States
(32.8 percent of U.S. population)
#1 California   #2 Texas   #3 New York   #4 Florida

State	Percent
Utah	78.4
North Dakota	66.9
Alabama	62.5
Louisiana	60.0
Oklahoma	58.6
Mississippi	58.3
South Dakota	58.2
Minnesota	55.3
Massachusetts	55.0
Arkansas	55.0
Nebraska	54.8
Tennessee	54.8
Rhode Island	53.6
Iowa	53.4
Texas	53.2
Wisconsin	52.9
Pennsylvania	51.9
Illinois	51.4
South Carolina	51.4
Kentucky	51.1
Idaho	50.7
Kansas	49.7
New Jersey	49.6
Georgia	49.4
Connecticut	49.1
New Mexico	49.0
Missouri	48.4
North Carolina	47.1
New York	44.5
Indiana	43.8
Ohio	42.7
California	42.4
Virginia	41.3
Michigan	40.2
Delaware	39.6
Wyoming	39.3
Maryland	39.2
Montana	37.8
Florida	37.1
Colorado	36.5
Hawaii	36.1
Arizona	35.8
West Virginia	35.2
New Hampshire	34.6
Nevada	33.4
Washington	33.1
Vermont	33.0
Alaska	32.8
Oregon	30.1
Maine	27.1

Christian church adherents are defined as "all members, including full members, their children and the estimated number of other regular participants who are not considered as communicant, confirmed or full members." 1990 data on Christian church adherents are based on reports of 133 church groupings and exclude 34 church bodies that reported more than 100,000 members to the Yearbook of American and Canadian Churches.

SOURCES: U.S. Census Bureau Statistical Abstract of the United States: 2012, Table 77. Printed with permission from the Association of Statisticians of American Religious Bodies, Clifford Grammich, Kirk Hadaway, Richard Houseal, Dale E. Jones, Alexei Krindatch, Richie Stanley, and Richard H. Taylor. 2012. 2010 U.S. Religion Census: Religious Congregations & Membership Study

http://www.thearda.com

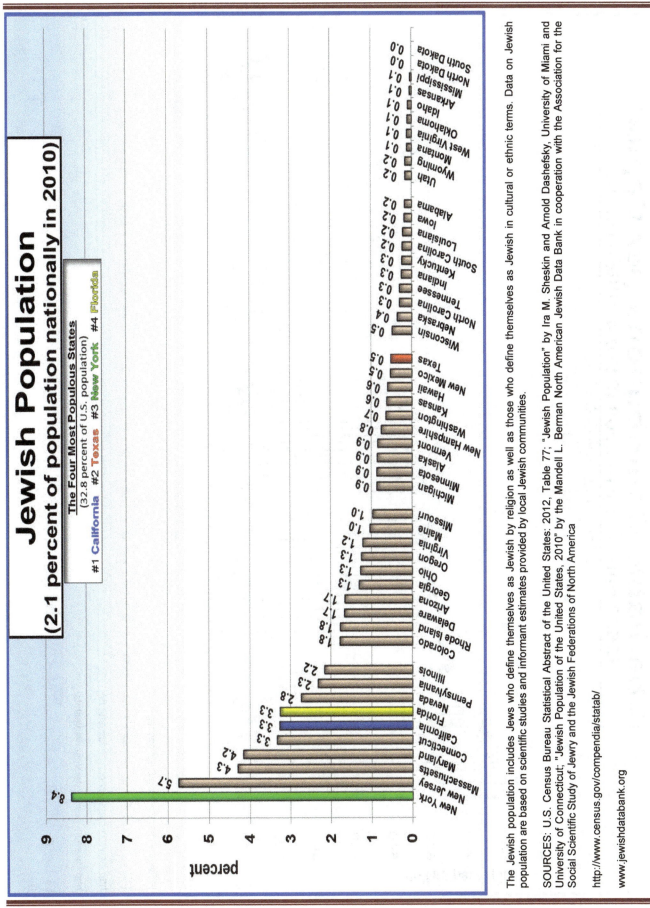

Jewish Population
(2.1 percent of population nationally in 2010)

The Four Most Populous States
(32.8 percent of U.S. population)
#1 California   #2 Texas   #3 New York   #4 Florida

State	percent
New York	8.4
New Jersey	5.7
Massachusetts	4.3
Maryland	4.2
Connecticut	3.3
California	3.3
Florida	3.3
Nevada	2.8
Pennsylvania	2.3
Illinois	2.2
Colorado	1.8
Rhode Island	1.8
Delaware	1.7
Arizona	1.7
Georgia	1.3
Ohio	1.3
Oregon	1.2
Virginia	1.0
Maine	1.0
Missouri	1.0
Michigan	0.9
Minnesota	0.9
Alaska	0.9
Vermont	0.9
New Hampshire	0.8
Washington	0.7
Kansas	0.6
Hawaii	0.6
New Mexico	0.5
Texas	0.5
Wisconsin	0.5
Nebraska	0.4
North Carolina	0.3
Tennessee	0.3
Indiana	0.3
Kentucky	0.3
South Carolina	0.2
Louisiana	0.2
Iowa	0.2
Alabama	0.2
Utah	0.2
Wyoming	0.2
Montana	0.1
West Virginia	0.1
Oklahoma	0.1
Idaho	0.1
Arkansas	0.1
Mississippi	0.1
North Dakota	0.0
South Dakota	0.0

The Jewish population includes Jews who define themselves as Jewish by religion as well as those who define themselves as Jewish in cultural or ethnic terms. Data on Jewish population are based on scientific studies and informant estimates provided by local Jewish communities.

SOURCES: U.S. Census Bureau Statistical Abstract of the United States: 2012, Table 77; "Jewish Population" by Ira M. Sheskin and Arnold Dashefsky, University of Miami and University of Connecticut; "Jewish Population of the United States, 2010" by the Mandell L. Berman North American Jewish Data Bank in cooperation with the Association for the Social Scientific Study of Jewry and the Jewish Federations of North America

http://www.census.gov/compendia/statab/

www.jewishdatabank.org

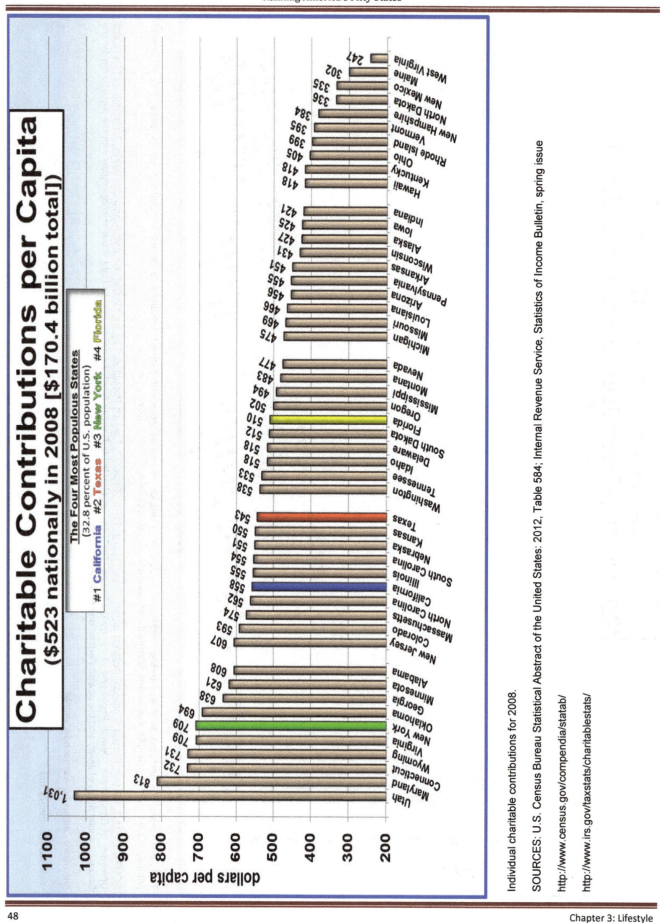

Charitable Contributions per Capita
($523 nationally in 2008 [$170.4 billion total])

The Four Most Populous States
(32.8 percent of U.S. population)
#1 California #2 Texas #3 New York #4 Florida

Utah	1,031
Maryland	813
Connecticut	732
Wyoming	731
Virginia	709
New York	709
Oklahoma	694
Georgia	638
Minnesota	621
Alabama	608
New Jersey	607
Colorado	593
Massachusetts	574
North Carolina	562
California	558
Illinois	555
South Carolina	554
Nebraska	551
Kansas	550
Texas	543
Washington	538
Tennessee	533
Idaho	518
Delaware	518
South Dakota	512
Florida	510
Oregon	502
Mississippi	494
Montana	483
Nevada	477
Michigan	475
Missouri	469
Louisiana	466
Arizona	456
Pennsylvania	455
Arkansas	451
Wisconsin	431
Alaska	427
Iowa	425
Indiana	421
Hawaii	418
Kentucky	418
Ohio	405
Rhode Island	399
Vermont	395
New Hampshire	384
North Dakota	336
New Mexico	335
Maine	302
West Virginia	247

dollars per capita

Individual charitable contributions for 2008.

SOURCES: U.S. Census Bureau Statistical Abstract of the United States: 2012, Table 584; Internal Revenue Service, Statistics of Income Bulletin, spring issue

http://www.census.gov/compendia/statab/

http://www.irs.gov/taxstats/charitablestats/

Volunteer Rate
(26.3 percent of persons nationally in 2010)

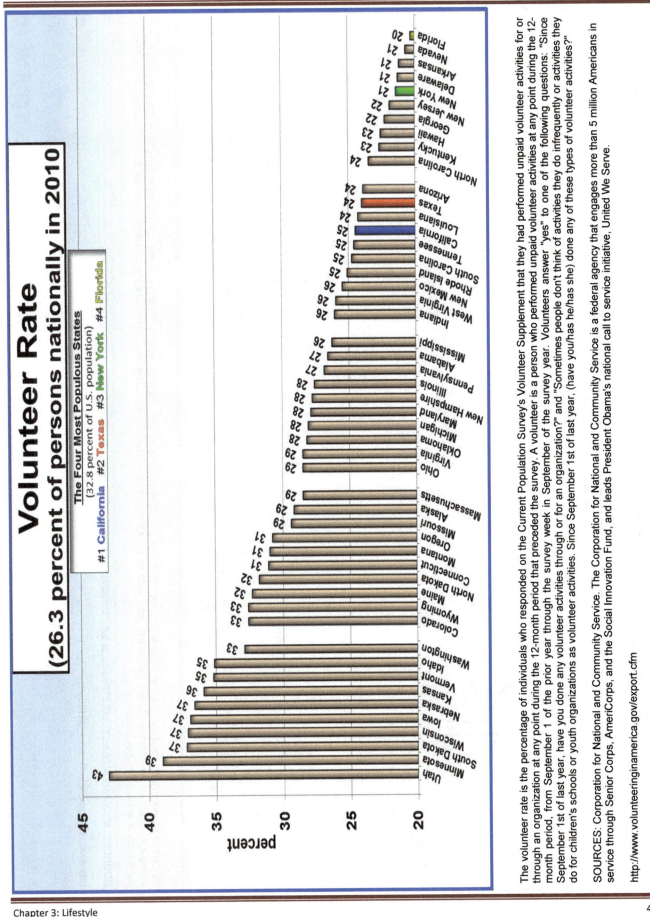

The Four Most Populous States
(32.8 percent of U.S. population)
#1 California #2 Texas #3 New York #4 Florida

State	Percent
Utah	43
Minnesota	39
South Dakota	37
Wisconsin	37
Iowa	37
Nebraska	36
Kansas	35
Vermont	35
Idaho	35
Washington	33
Colorado	33
Wyoming	33
Maine	32
North Dakota	32
Connecticut	31
Montana	31
Oregon	31
Missouri	29
Alaska	29
Massachusetts	29
Ohio	29
Virginia	28
Oklahoma	28
Michigan	28
Maryland	28
New Hampshire	28
Illinois	28
Pennsylvania	27
Alabama	27
Mississippi	26
Indiana	26
West Virginia	26
New Mexico	26
Rhode Island	25
South Carolina	25
Tennessee	25
California	25
Louisiana	24
Texas	24
Arizona	24
North Carolina	24
Kentucky	23
Hawaii	23
Georgia	22
New Jersey	22
New York	21
Delaware	21
Arkansas	21
Nevada	21
Florida	20

The volunteer rate is the percentage of individuals who responded on the Current Population Survey's Volunteer Supplement that they had performed unpaid volunteer activities for or through an organization at any point during the 12-month period that preceded the survey. A volunteer is a person who performed unpaid volunteer activities at any point during the 12-month period, from September 1 of the prior year through the survey week in September of the survey year. Volunteers answer "yes" to one of the following questions: "Since September 1st of last year, have you done any volunteer activities through or for an organization?" and "Sometimes people don't think of activities they do infrequently or activities they do for children's schools or youth organizations as volunteer activities. Since September 1st of last year, (have you/has he/has she) done any of these types of volunteer activities?"

SOURCES: Corporation for National and Community Service. The Corporation for National and Community Service is a federal agency that engages more than 5 million Americans in service through Senior Corps, AmeriCorps, and the Social Innovation Fund, and leads President Obama's national call to service initiative, United We Serve.

http://www.volunteeringinamerica.gov/export.cfm

Eligible Voters who Voted for President
(58.9 percent voted in 2012)

The Four Most Populous States
(32.8 percent of U.S. population)
#1 California #2 Texas #3 New York #4 Florida

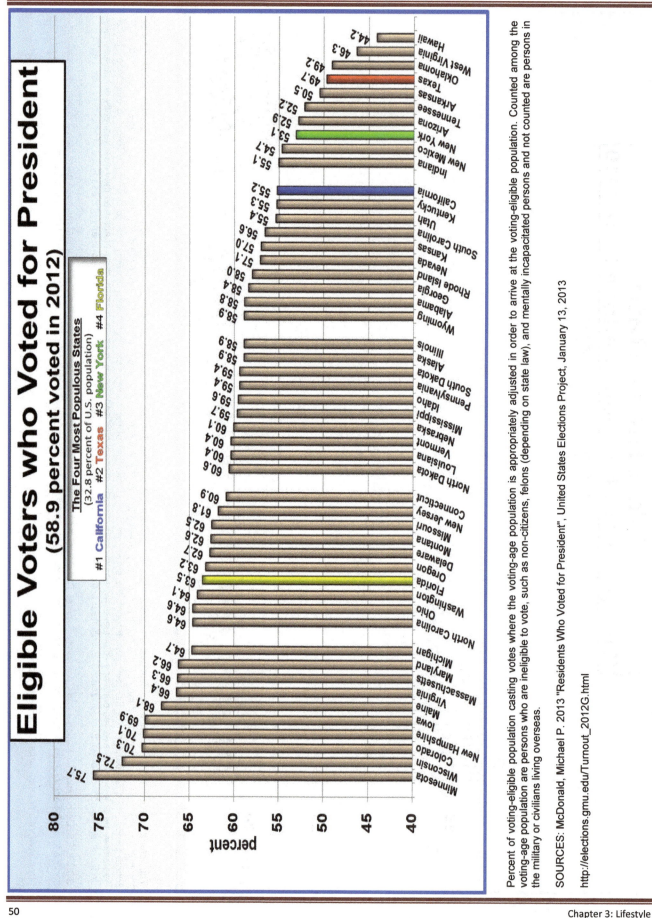

State	Percent
Minnesota	75.7
Wisconsin	72.5
Colorado	70.3
New Hampshire	70.1
Iowa	69.9
Maine	68.1
Virginia	66.4
Massachusetts	66.3
Maryland	66.2
Michigan	64.7
North Carolina	64.6
Ohio	64.6
Washington	64.1
Florida	63.5
Oregon	63.2
Delaware	62.7
Montana	62.6
Missouri	62.5
New Jersey	61.8
Connecticut	60.9
North Dakota	60.6
Louisiana	60.4
Vermont	60.4
Nebraska	60.1
Mississippi	59.7
Idaho	59.6
Pennsylvania	59.4
South Dakota	59.4
Alaska	58.9
Illinois	58.9
Wyoming	58.9
Alabama	58.8
Georgia	58.4
Rhode Island	58.0
Nevada	57.1
Kansas	57.0
South Carolina	56.6
Utah	55.4
Kentucky	55.3
California	55.2
Indiana	55.1
New Mexico	54.7
New York	53.1
Arizona	52.9
Tennessee	52.2
Arkansas	50.5
Texas	49.7
Oklahoma	49.2
West Virginia	46.3
Hawaii	44.2

Percent of voting-eligible population casting votes where the voting-age population is appropriately adjusted in order to arrive at the voting-eligible population. Counted among the voting-age population are persons who are ineligible to vote, such as non-citizens, felons (depending on state law), and mentally incapacitated persons and not counted are persons in the military or civilians living overseas.

SOURCES: McDonald, Michael P. 2013 "Residents Who Voted for President", United States Elections Project, January 13, 2013

http://elections.gmu.edu/Turnout_2012G.html

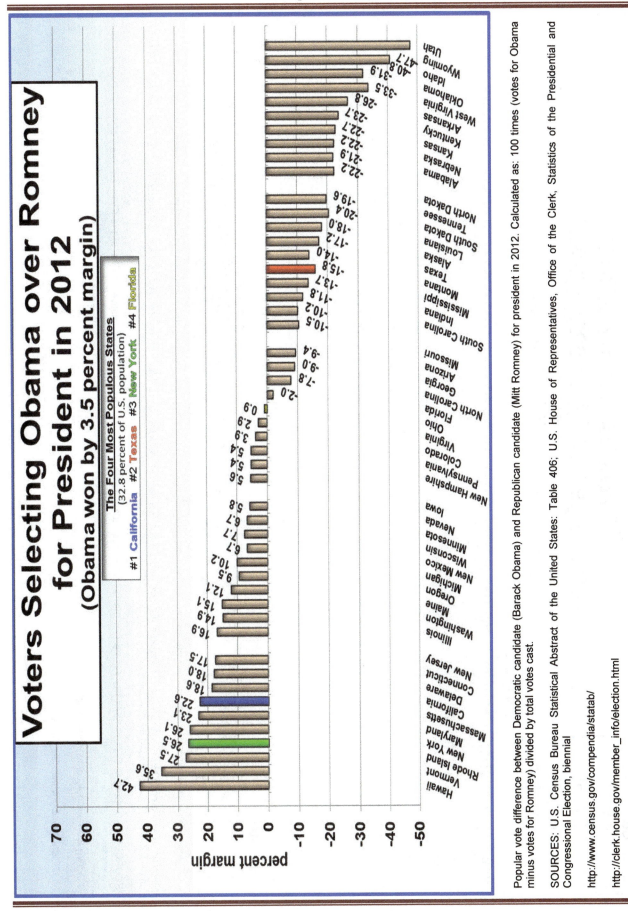

Voters Selecting Obama over Romney for President in 2012
(Obama won by 3.5 percent margin)

The Four Most Populous States
(32.8 percent of U.S. population)
#1 California   #2 Texas   #3 New York   #4 Florida

State	percent margin
Hawaii	42.7
Vermont	35.6
Rhode Island	27.5
New York	26.5
Maryland	26.1
Massachusetts	23.1
California	22.6
Delaware	18.6
Connecticut	18.0
New Jersey	17.5
Illinois	16.9
Washington	14.9
Maine	15.1
Oregon	12.1
Michigan	9.5
New Mexico	10.2
Wisconsin	6.7
Minnesota	7.7
Nevada	6.7
Iowa	5.8
New Hampshire	5.6
Pennsylvania	5.4
Colorado	5.4
Virginia	3.9
Ohio	2.9
Florida	0.9
North Carolina	-2.0
Georgia	-7.8
Arizona	-9.0
Missouri	-9.4
South Carolina	-10.5
Indiana	-11.2
Mississippi	-13.7
Montana	-15.8
Texas	-14.0
Alaska	-17.2
Louisiana	-18.0
South Dakota	-20.4
Tennessee	-19.6
North Dakota	-22.2
Alabama	-21.9
Nebraska	-22.7
Kansas	-22.1
Kentucky	-23.7
Arkansas	-26.8
West Virginia	-33.5
Oklahoma	-31.9
Idaho	-40.8
Wyoming	-47.7
Utah	

Popular vote difference between Democratic candidate (Barack Obama) and Republican candidate (Mitt Romney) for president in 2012. Calculated as: 100 times (votes for Obama minus votes for Romney) divided by total votes cast.

SOURCES: U.S. Census Bureau Statistical Abstract of the United States: Table 406; U.S. House of Representatives, Office of the Clerk, Statistics of the Presidential and Congressional Election, biennial

http://www.census.gov/compendia/statab/

http://clerk.house.gov/member_info/election.html

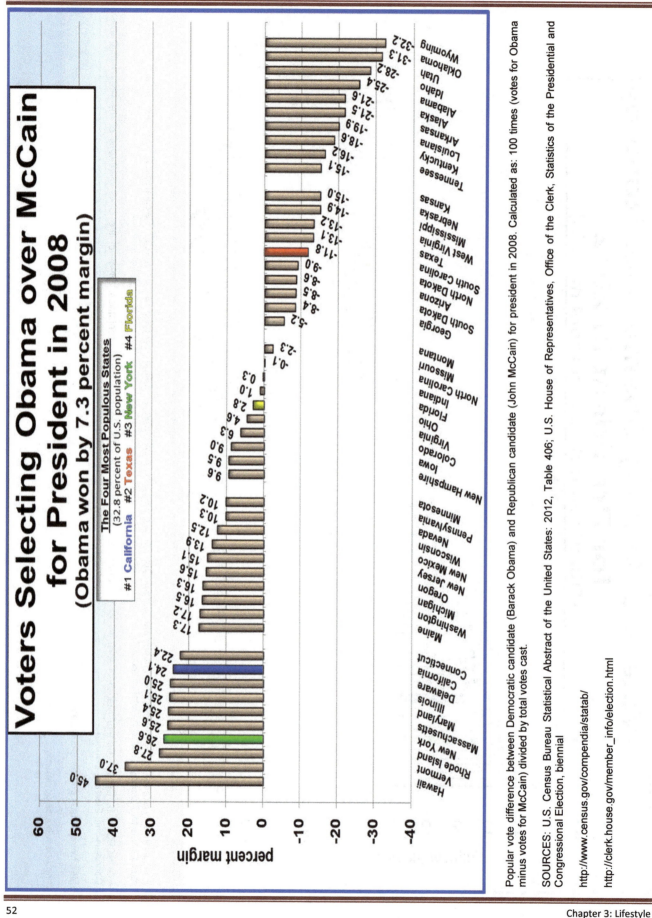

Voters Selecting Obama over McCain for President in 2008
(Obama won by 7.3 percent margin)

The Four Most Populous States
(32.8 percent of U.S. population)
#1 California #2 Texas #3 New York #4 Florida

Hawaii 45.0
Vermont 37.0
Rhode Island 27.8
New York 26.6
Massachusetts 25.6
Maryland 25.4
Illinois 25.1
Delaware 25.0
California 24.1
Connecticut 22.4
Maine 17.3
Washington 17.2
Michigan 16.5
Oregon 16.3
New Jersey 15.6
New Mexico 15.1
Wisconsin 13.9
Nevada 12.5
Pennsylvania 10.3
Minnesota 10.2
New Hampshire 9.6
Iowa 9.5
Colorado 9.0
Virginia 6.3
Ohio 4.6
Florida 2.8
Indiana 1.0
North Carolina 0.3
Missouri -0.1
Montana -2.3
South Dakota -5.2
North Dakota -8.4
Arizona -8.5
Georgia -8.6
South Carolina -9.0
Texas -11.8
West Virginia -13.1
Mississippi -13.2
Nebraska -14.9
Kansas -15.0
Tennessee -15.1
Kentucky -16.2
Louisiana -18.6
Arkansas -19.9
Alabama -21.5
Alaska -21.6
Idaho -25.4
Utah -28.2
Oklahoma -31.3
Wyoming -32.2

percent margin (axis: 60, 50, 40, 30, 20, 10, 0, -10, -20, -30, -40)

Popular vote difference between Democratic candidate (Barack Obama) and Republican candidate (John McCain) for president in 2008. Calculated as: 100 times (votes for Obama minus votes for McCain) divided by total votes cast.

SOURCES: U.S. Census Bureau Statistical Abstract of the United States: 2012, Table 406; U.S. House of Representatives, Office of the Clerk, Statistics of the Presidential and Congressional Election, biennial

http://www.census.gov/compendia/statab/

http://clerk.house.gov/member_info/election.html

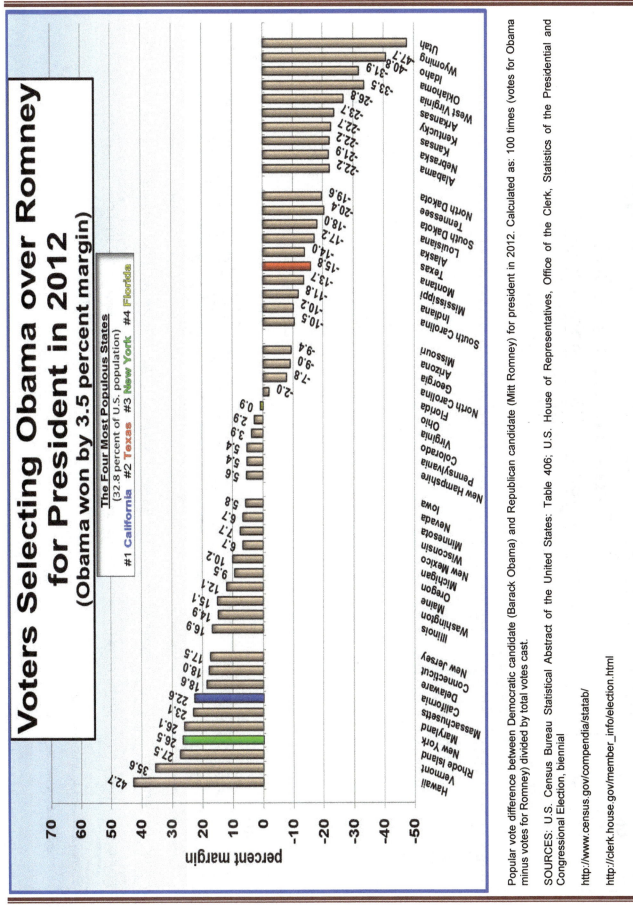

Voters Selecting Obama over Romney for President in 2012
(Obama won by 3.5 percent margin)

The Four Most Populous States
(32.8 percent of U.S. population)
#1 California   #2 Texas   #3 New York   #4 Florida

State	
Hawaii	42.7
Vermont	35.6
Rhode Island	27.5
New York	26.5
Maryland	26.1
Massachusetts	23.1
California	22.6
Delaware	18.6
Connecticut	18.0
New Jersey	17.5
Illinois	16.9
Washington	14.9
Maine	15.1
Oregon	12.1
Michigan	9.5
New Mexico	10.2
Wisconsin	6.7
Minnesota	7.7
Nevada	5.8
Iowa	5.8
New Hampshire	5.6
Pennsylvania	5.4
Colorado	5.4
Virginia	3.9
Ohio	2.9
Florida	0.9
North Carolina	-2.0
Georgia	-7.8
Arizona	-9.0
Missouri	-9.4
South Carolina	-10.5
Indiana	-10.2
Mississippi	-11.8
Montana	-13.7
Texas	-15.8
Alaska	-14.0
Louisiana	-17.2
South Dakota	-18.0
Tennessee	-20.4
North Dakota	-19.6
Alabama	-22.2
Nebraska	-21.9
Kansas	-22.2
Kentucky	-22.7
Arkansas	-23.7
West Virginia	-26.8
Oklahoma	-33.5
Idaho	-31.9
Wyoming	-40.8
Utah	-47.7

percent margin

Popular vote difference between Democratic candidate (Barack Obama) and Republican candidate (Mitt Romney) for president in 2012. Calculated as: 100 times (votes for Obama minus votes for Romney) divided by total votes cast.

SOURCES: U.S. Census Bureau Statistical Abstract of the United States: Table 406; U.S. House of Representatives, Office of the Clerk, Statistics of the Presidential and Congressional Election, biennial

http://www.census.gov/compendia/statab/

http://clerk.house.gov/member_info/election.html

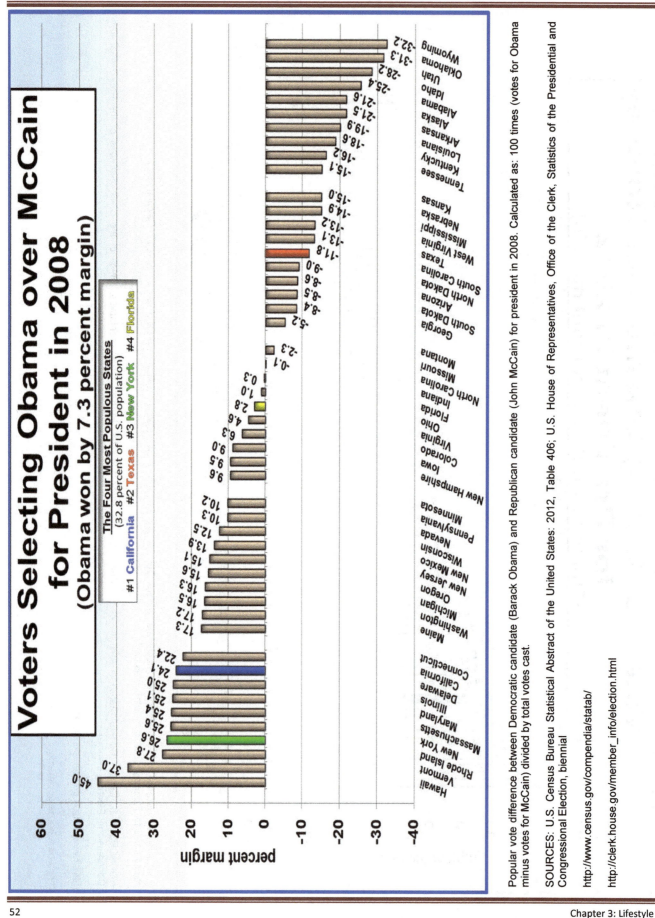

Voters Selecting Obama over McCain for President in 2008

(Obama won by 7.3 percent margin)

The Four Most Populous States
(32.8 percent of U.S. population)
#1 California   #2 Texas   #3 New York   #4 Florida

State	percent margin
Hawaii	45.0
Vermont	37.0
Rhode Island	27.8
New York	26.6
Massachusetts	25.6
Maryland	25.4
Illinois	25.1
Delaware	25.0
California	24.1
Connecticut	22.4
Maine	17.3
Washington	17.2
Michigan	16.3
Oregon	15.6
New Jersey	15.1
New Mexico	13.9
Wisconsin	12.5
Nevada	10.3
Pennsylvania	10.2
Minnesota	10.2
New Hampshire	9.6
Iowa	9.5
Colorado	9.0
Virginia	6.3
Ohio	4.6
Florida	2.8
Indiana	1.0
North Carolina	0.3
Missouri	-0.1
Montana	-2.3
South Dakota	-5.2
Georgia	-8.4
Arizona	-8.5
North Dakota	-8.6
South Carolina	-9.0
Texas	-11.8
West Virginia	-13.1
Mississippi	-13.2
Nebraska	-14.9
Kansas	-15.0
Tennessee	-15.1
Kentucky	-16.2
Louisiana	-18.6
Arkansas	-19.9
Alaska	-21.5
Alabama	-21.6
Idaho	-25.4
Utah	-28.2
Oklahoma	-31.3
Wyoming	-32.2

Popular vote difference between Democratic candidate (Barack Obama) and Republican candidate (John McCain) for president in 2008. Calculated as: 100 times (votes for Obama minus votes for McCain) divided by total votes cast.

SOURCES: U.S. Census Bureau Statistical Abstract of the United States: 2012, Table 406; U.S. House of Representatives, Office of the Clerk, Statistics of the Presidential and Congressional Election, biennial

http://www.census.gov/compendia/statab/

http://clerk.house.gov/member_info/election.html

Residents who Voted for Congress
(37.0 percent of voting age persons nationally in 2010)

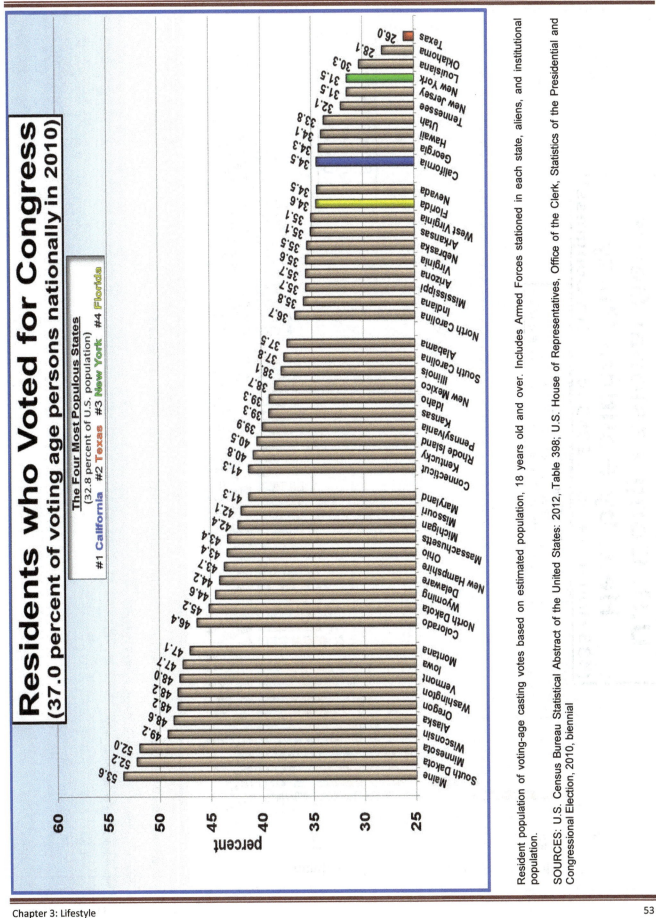

The Four Most Populous States
(32.8 percent of U.S. population)
#1 California   #2 Texas   #3 New York   #4 Florida

State	percent
Maine	53.6
South Dakota	52.2
Minnesota	52.0
Wisconsin	49.2
Alaska	48.6
Oregon	48.2
Washington	48.2
Vermont	48.0
Iowa	47.7
Montana	47.1
Colorado	46.4
North Dakota	45.2
Wyoming	44.6
Delaware	44.2
New Hampshire	43.7
Ohio	43.4
Massachusetts	43.4
Michigan	42.4
Missouri	42.1
Maryland	41.3
Connecticut	41.3
Kentucky	40.8
Rhode Island	40.5
Pennsylvania	39.9
Kansas	39.3
Idaho	39.3
New Mexico	38.7
Illinois	38.1
South Carolina	37.8
Alabama	37.5
North Carolina	36.7
Indiana	35.8
Mississippi	35.7
Arizona	35.7
Virginia	35.6
Nebraska	35.5
Arkansas	35.1
West Virginia	35.1
Florida	34.6
Nevada	34.5
California	34.5
Georgia	34.3
Hawaii	34.1
Utah	33.8
Tennessee	32.1
New Jersey	31.5
New York	31.5
Louisiana	30.3
Oklahoma	28.1
Texas	26.0

Resident population of voting-age casting votes based on estimated population, 18 years old and over. Includes Armed Forces stationed in each state, aliens, and institutional population.

SOURCES: U.S. Census Bureau Statistical Abstract of the United States: 2012, Table 398; U.S. House of Representatives, Office of the Clerk, Statistics of the Presidential and Congressional Election, 2010, biennial

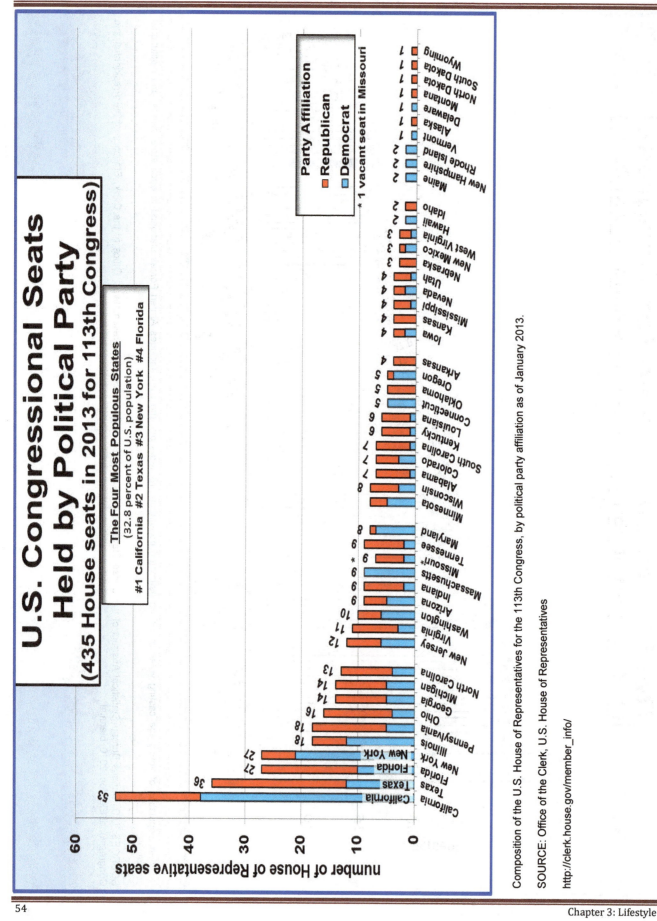

U.S. Congressional Seats Held by Political Party

(435 House seats in 2013 for 113th Congress)

The Four Most Populous States
(32.8 percent of U.S. population)
#1 California #2 Texas #3 New York #4 Florida

Party Affiliation
- ■ Republican
- ■ Democrat

* 1 vacant seat in Missouri

number of House of Representative seats

California	53
Texas	36
Florida	27
New York	27
Illinois	18
Pennsylvania	18
Ohio	16
Georgia	14
Michigan	14
North Carolina	13
New Jersey	12
Virginia	11
Washington	10
Arizona	9
Indiana	9
Massachusetts	9
Missouri*	9 *
Tennessee	9
Maryland	8
Minnesota	8
Wisconsin	8
Alabama	7
Colorado	7
South Carolina	7
Kentucky	6
Louisiana	6
Connecticut	5
Oklahoma	5
Oregon	5
Arkansas	4
Iowa	4
Kansas	4
Mississippi	4
Nevada	4
Utah	4
Nebraska	3
New Mexico	3
West Virginia	3
Hawaii	2
Idaho	2
Maine	2
New Hampshire	2
Rhode Island	2
Vermont	1
Alaska	1
Delaware	1
Montana	1
North Dakota	1
South Dakota	1
Wyoming	1

Composition of the U.S. House of Representatives for the 113th Congress, by political party affiliation as of January 2013.

SOURCE: Office of the Clerk, U.S. House of Representatives

http://clerk.house.gov/member_info/

Households Without Internet Usage
(19.8 percent nationally in 2010)

The Four Most Populous States
(32.8 percent of U.S. population)
#1 California   #2 Texas   #3 New York   #4 Florida

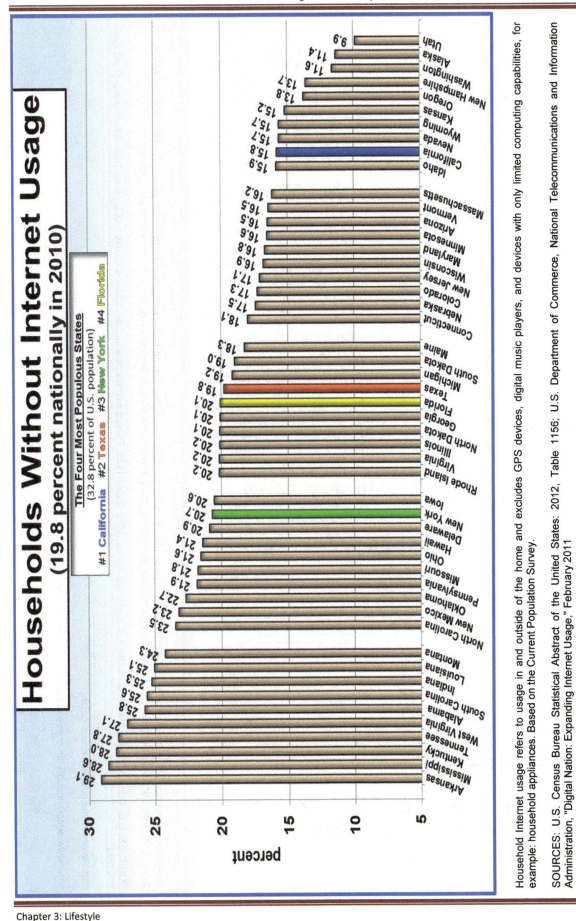

State	percent
Arkansas	29.1
Mississippi	28.6
Kentucky	28.0
Tennessee	27.8
West Virginia	27.1
Alabama	25.8
South Carolina	25.6
Indiana	25.3
Louisiana	25.1
Montana	24.3
North Carolina	23.5
New Mexico	23.2
Oklahoma	22.7
Pennsylvania	21.9
Missouri	21.8
Ohio	21.6
Hawaii	21.4
Delaware	20.9
New York	20.7
Iowa	20.6
Rhode Island	20.2
Virginia	20.2
Illinois	20.2
North Dakota	20.1
Georgia	20.1
Florida	20.1
Texas	19.8
Michigan	19.2
South Dakota	19.0
Maine	18.3
Connecticut	18.1
Nebraska	17.5
Colorado	17.3
New Jersey	17.1
Wisconsin	16.9
Maryland	16.8
Minnesota	16.6
Arizona	16.5
Vermont	16.5
Massachusetts	16.2
Idaho	15.9
California	15.8
Nevada	15.7
Wyoming	15.7
Kansas	15.2
Oregon	13.8
New Hampshire	13.7
Washington	11.6
Alaska	11.4
Utah	9.9

Household Internet usage refers to usage in and outside of the home and excludes GPS devices, digital music players, and devices with only limited computing capabilities, for example: household appliances. Based on the Current Population Survey.

SOURCES: U.S. Census Bureau Statistical Abstract of the United States: 2012, Table 1156; U.S. Department of Commerce, National Telecommunications and Information Administration, "Digital Nation: Expanding Internet Usage," February 2011

http://www.census.gov/compendia/statab/

http://www.ntia.doc.gov/reports.html

Daily Newspaper Circulation
(15.1 per 100 persons nationally in 2009)

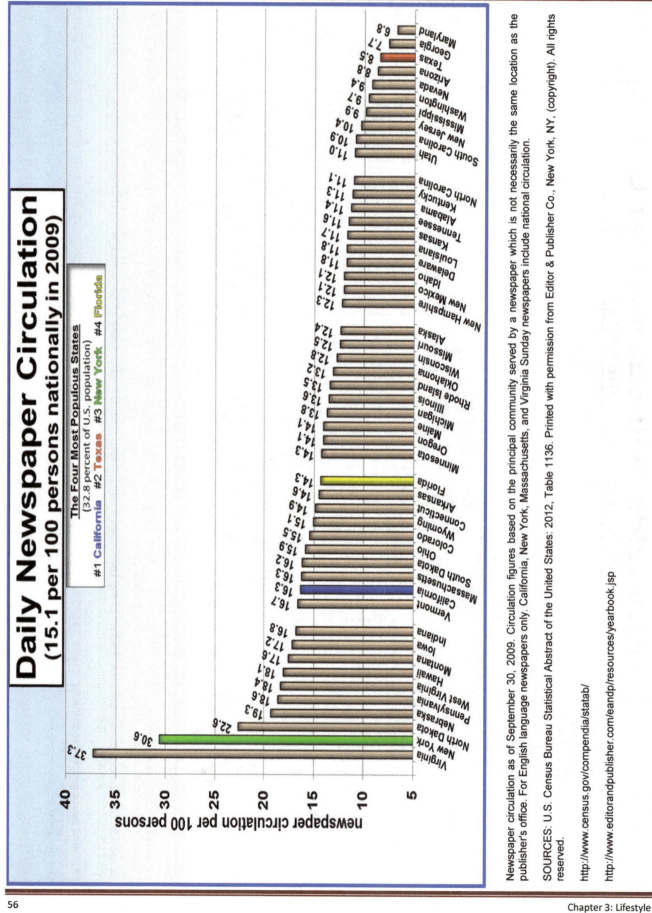

The Four Most Populous States
(32.8 percent of U.S. population)
#1 California   #2 Texas   #3 New York   #4 Florida

State	newspaper circulation per 100 persons
New York	37.3
Virginia	30.6
North Dakota	22.6
Nebraska	19.3
Pennsylvania	18.6
West Virginia	18.4
Hawaii	18.1
Montana	17.6
Iowa	17.2
Indiana	16.8
Vermont	16.7
California	16.3
Massachusetts	16.3
South Dakota	16.2
Ohio	15.9
Colorado	15.5
Wyoming	15.1
Connecticut	14.9
Arkansas	14.6
Florida	14.3
Minnesota	14.3
Oregon	14.1
Maine	14.1
Michigan	13.8
Illinois	13.6
Rhode Island	13.5
Oklahoma	13.2
Wisconsin	12.8
Missouri	12.5
Alaska	12.4
New Hampshire	12.3
New Mexico	12.1
Idaho	12.1
Delaware	11.8
Louisiana	11.7
Kansas	11.6
Tennessee	11.4
Alabama	11.3
Kentucky	11.1
North Carolina	11.0
Utah	10.9
South Carolina	10.4
New Jersey	9.9
Mississippi	9.7
Washington	9.4
Nevada	8.8
Arizona	8.5
Texas	7.7
Georgia	6.8
Maryland	

Newspaper circulation as of September 30, 2009. Circulation figures based on the principal community served by a newspaper which is not necessarily the same location as the publisher's office. For English language newspapers only. California, New York, Massachusetts, and Virginia Sunday newspapers include national circulation.

SOURCES: U.S. Census Bureau Statistical Abstract of the United States: 2012, Table 1136. Printed with permission from Editor & Publisher Co., New York, NY, (copyright). All rights reserved.

http://www.census.gov/compendia/statab/

http://www.editorandpublisher.com/eandp/resources/yearbook.jsp

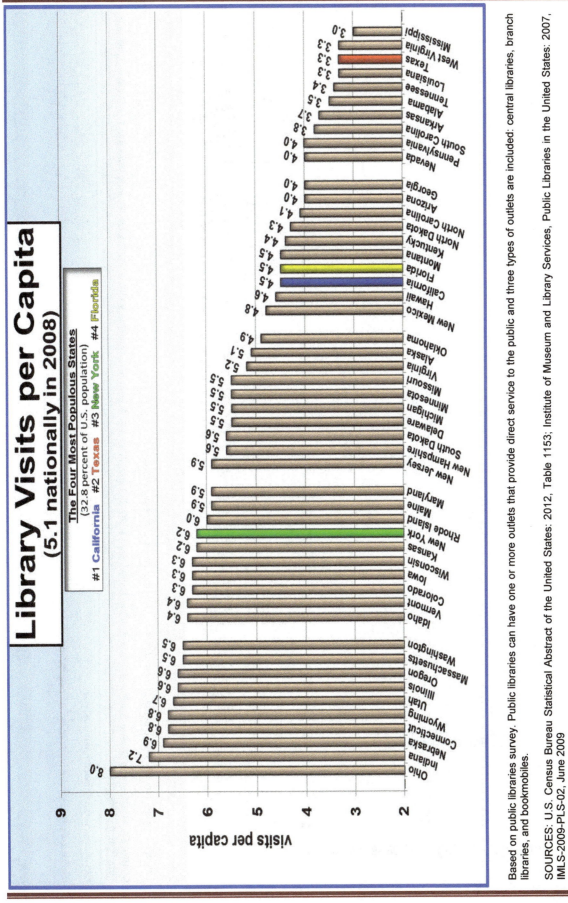

Library Visits per Capita
(5.1 nationally in 2008)

The Four Most Populous States
(32.8 percent of U.S. population)
#1 California #2 Texas #3 New York #4 Florida

State	Visits per capita
Ohio	8.0
Indiana	7.2
Nebraska	6.9
Connecticut	6.8
Wyoming	6.8
Utah	6.7
Illinois	6.6
Oregon	6.6
Massachusetts	6.5
Washington	6.5
Idaho	6.4
Vermont	6.4
Colorado	6.3
Iowa	6.3
Wisconsin	6.3
Kansas	6.2
New York	6.2
Rhode Island	6.0
Maine	5.9
Maryland	5.9
New Jersey	5.9
New Hampshire	5.6
South Dakota	5.6
Delaware	5.5
Michigan	5.5
Minnesota	5.5
Missouri	5.5
Virginia	5.2
Alaska	5.1
Oklahoma	4.9
New Mexico	4.8
Hawaii	4.6
California	4.5
Florida	4.5
Montana	4.5
Kentucky	4.4
North Dakota	4.3
North Carolina	4.1
Arizona	4.0
Georgia	4.0
Nevada	4.0
Pennsylvania	4.0
South Carolina	3.8
Arkansas	3.7
Alabama	3.5
Tennessee	3.4
Louisiana	3.3
Texas	3.3
West Virginia	3.3
Mississippi	3.0

Based on public libraries survey. Public libraries can have one or more outlets that provide direct service to the public and three types of outlets are included: central libraries, branch libraries, and bookmobiles.

SOURCES: U.S. Census Bureau Statistical Abstract of the United States: 2012, Table 1153; Institute of Museum and Library Services, Public Libraries in the United States: 2007, IMLS–2009-PLS-02, June 2009

http://www.census.gov/compendia/statab/

http://harvester.census.gov/imls/pubs/pls/index.asp

Patents Issued to Residents
(39.2 per 100,000 residents nationally in 2010 [121,164 total])

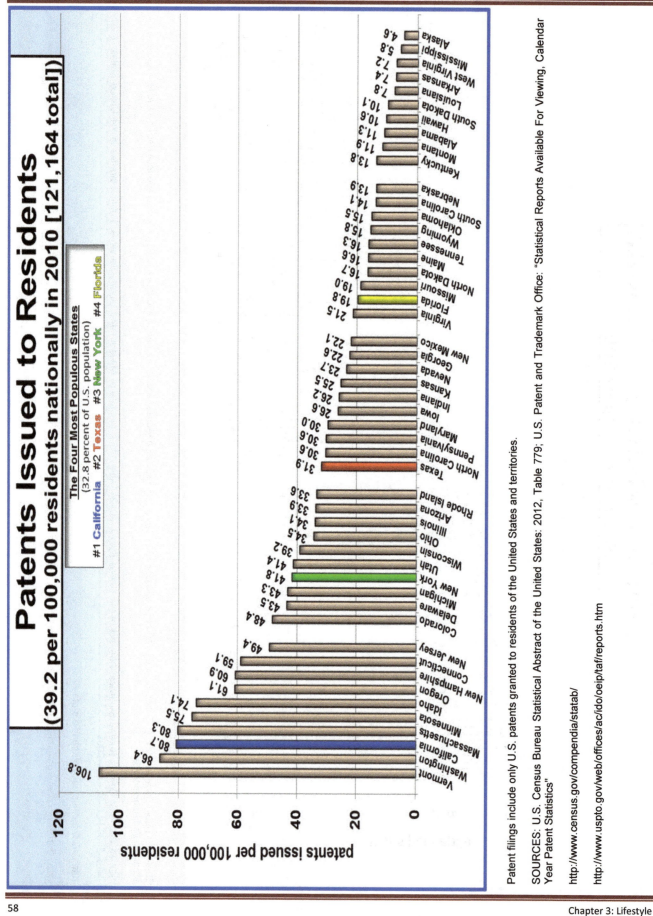

The Four Most Populous States
(32.8 percent of U.S. population)
#1 California #2 Texas #3 New York #4 Florida

patents issued per 100,000 residents

Vermont	106.8
Washington	86.4
California	80.7
Massachusetts	80.3
Minnesota	75.5
Idaho	74.1
Oregon	61.1
New Hampshire	60.9
Connecticut	59.1
New Jersey	49.4
Colorado	48.4
Delaware	43.5
Michigan	43.3
New York	41.8
Utah	41.4
Wisconsin	39.2
Ohio	34.5
Illinois	34.1
Arizona	33.9
Rhode Island	33.6
Texas	31.9
North Carolina	30.6
Pennsylvania	30.6
Maryland	30.0
Iowa	26.9
Indiana	26.2
Kansas	25.5
Nevada	23.7
Georgia	22.6
New Mexico	22.1
Virginia	21.5
Florida	19.8
Missouri	19.0
North Dakota	16.7
Maine	16.6
Tennessee	16.3
Wyoming	15.8
Oklahoma	15.5
South Carolina	14.1
Nebraska	13.9
Kentucky	13.8
Montana	11.9
Alabama	11.3
Hawaii	10.6
South Dakota	10.1
Louisiana	7.8
Arkansas	7.4
West Virginia	7.2
Mississippi	5.8
Alaska	4.6

Patent filings include only U.S. patents granted to residents of the United States and territories.

SOURCES: U.S. Census Bureau Statistical Abstract of the United States: 2012, Table 779; U.S. Patent and Trademark Office: "Statistical Reports Available For Viewing, Calendar Year Patent Statistics"

http://www.census.gov/compendia/statab/

http://www.uspto.gov/web/offices/ac/ido/oeip/taf/reports.htm

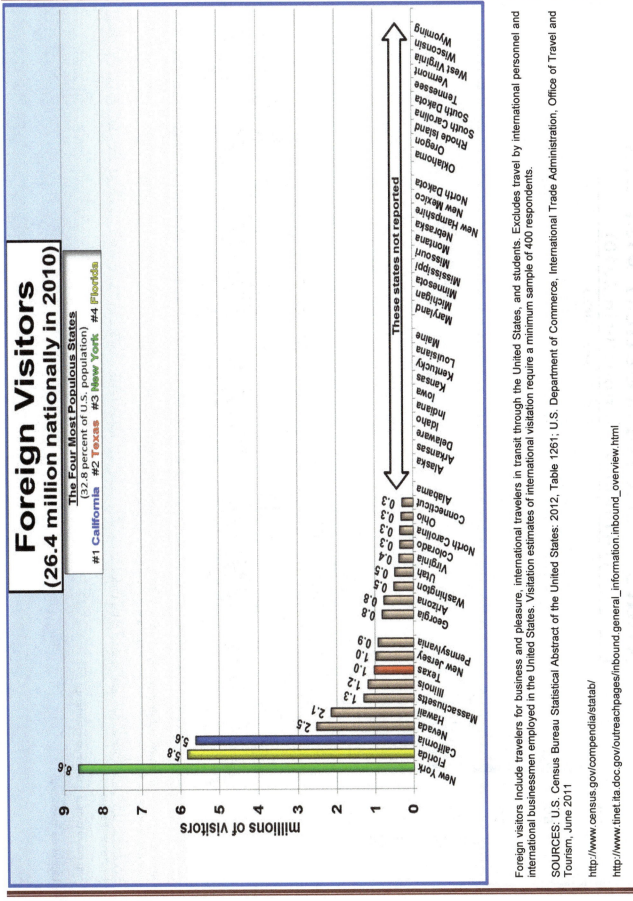

Foreign Visitors
(26.4 million nationally in 2010)

The Four Most Populous States
(32.8 percent of U.S. population)
#1 California   #2 Texas   #3 New York   #4 Florida

millions of visitors

State	Millions
New York	8.6
Florida	5.8
California	5.6
Nevada	2.5
Hawaii	2.1
Massachusetts	1.3
Illinois	1.2
Texas	1.0
New Jersey	1.0
Pennsylvania	0.9
Georgia	0.8
Arizona	0.8
Washington	0.5
Utah	0.5
Virginia	0.4
Colorado	0.3
North Carolina	0.3
Ohio	0.3
Connecticut	0.3

These states not reported

Alabama
Alaska
Arkansas
Delaware
Idaho
Indiana
Iowa
Kansas
Kentucky
Louisiana
Maine
Maryland
Michigan
Minnesota
Mississippi
Missouri
Montana
Nebraska
New Hampshire
New Mexico
North Dakota
Oklahoma
Oregon
Rhode Island
South Carolina
South Dakota
Tennessee
Vermont
West Virginia
Wisconsin
Wyoming

Foreign visitors Include travelers for business and pleasure, international travelers in transit through the United States, and students. Excludes travel by international personnel and international businessmen employed in the United States. Visitation estimates of international visitation require a minimum sample of 400 respondents.

SOURCES: U.S. Census Bureau Statistical Abstract of the United States: 2012, Table 1261; U.S. Department of Commerce, International Trade Administration, Office of Travel and Tourism, June 2011

http://www.census.gov/compendia/statab/

http://www.tinet.ita.doc.gov/outreachpages/inbound.general_information.inbound_overview.html

State Park Recreation Visitors
(741 million nationally in 2010)

The Four Most Populous States
(32.8 percent of U.S. population)
#1 California   #2 Texas   #3 New York   #4 Florida

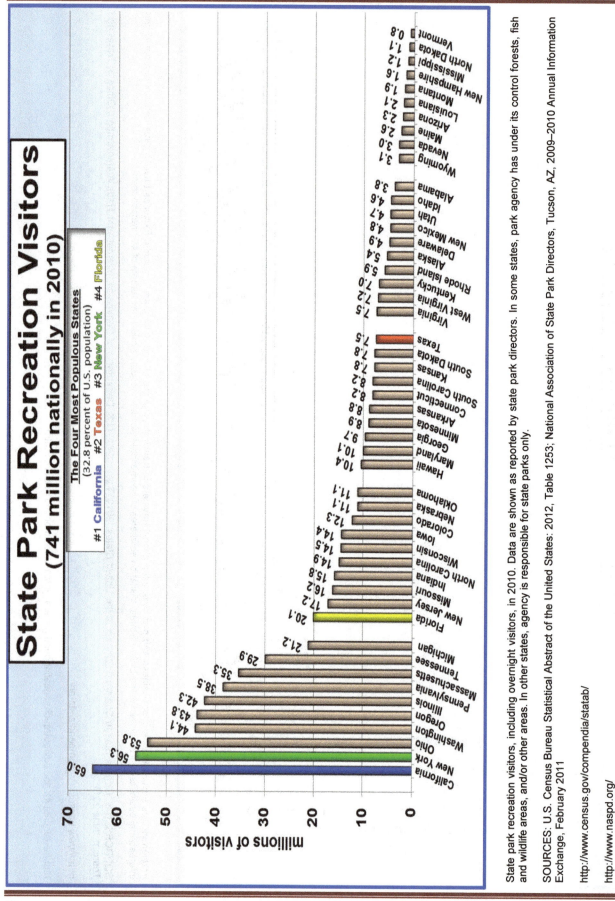

State	millions of visitors
California	65.0
New York	56.3
Ohio	53.8
Washington	44.1
Oregon	43.8
Illinois	42.3
Pennsylvania	38.5
Massachusetts	35.3
Tennessee	29.9
Michigan	21.2
Florida	20.1
New Jersey	17.2
Missouri	16.2
Indiana	15.8
North Carolina	14.9
Wisconsin	14.5
Iowa	14.4
Colorado	12.3
Nebraska	11.1
Oklahoma	11.1
Hawaii	10.4
Maryland	10.1
Georgia	9.7
Minnesota	8.9
Arkansas	8.8
Connecticut	8.2
South Carolina	7.8
Kansas	7.8
South Dakota	7.5
Texas	7.5
Virginia	7.5
West Virginia	7.2
Kentucky	7.0
Rhode Island	5.9
Alaska	5.4
Delaware	4.9
New Mexico	4.8
Utah	4.7
Idaho	4.6
Alabama	3.8
Wyoming	3.1
Nevada	3.0
Maine	2.6
Arizona	2.3
Louisiana	2.1
Montana	1.9
New Hampshire	1.6
Mississippi	1.2
North Dakota	1.1
Vermont	0.8

State park recreation visitors, including overnight visitors, in 2010. Data are shown as reported by state park directors. In some states, park agency has under its control forests, fish and wildlife areas, and/or other areas. In other states, agency is responsible for state parks only.

SOURCES: U.S. Census Bureau Statistical Abstract of the United States: 2012, Table 1253; National Association of State Park Directors, Tucson, AZ, 2009–2010 Annual Information Exchange, February 2011

http://www.census.gov/compendia/statab/

http://www.naspd.org/

Chapter 3: Lifestyle

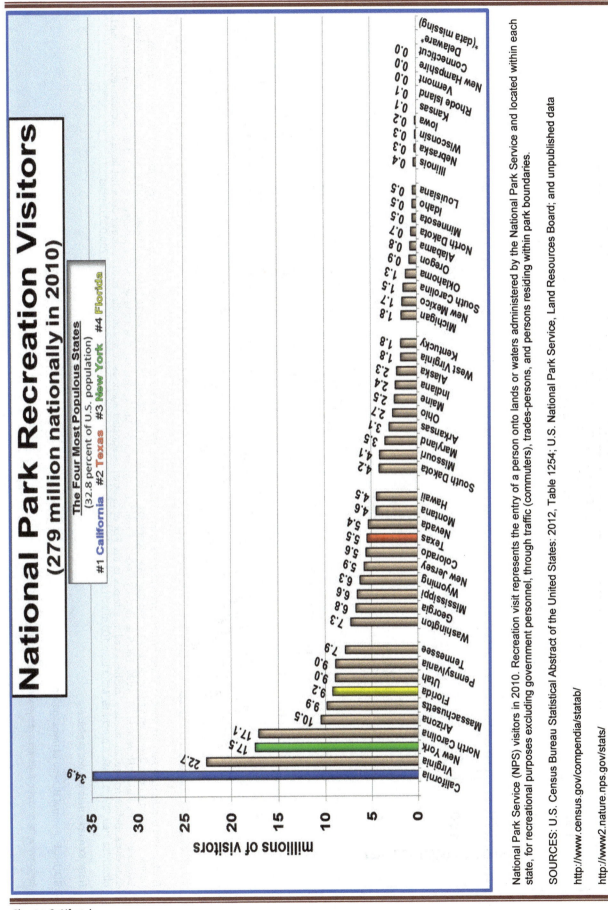

National Park Recreation Visitors
(279 million nationally in 2010)

The Four Most Populous States
(32.8 percent of U.S. population)

#1 California   #2 Texas   #3 New York   #4 Florida

State	Millions of visitors
California	34.9
Virginia	22.7
New York	17.5
North Carolina	17.1
Arizona	10.5
Massachusetts	9.9
Florida	9.2
Utah	9.0
Pennsylvania	9.0
Tennessee	7.9
Washington	7.3
Georgia	6.8
Mississippi	6.6
Wyoming	6.3
New Jersey	5.9
Colorado	5.6
Texas	5.5
Nevada	5.4
Montana	4.6
Hawaii	4.5
South Dakota	4.2
Missouri	4.1
Maryland	3.5
Arkansas	3.1
Ohio	2.7
Maine	2.5
Indiana	2.4
Alaska	2.3
West Virginia	1.8
Kentucky	1.8
Michigan	1.8
New Mexico	1.7
South Carolina	1.5
Oklahoma	1.3
Oregon	0.9
Alabama	0.8
North Dakota	0.7
Minnesota	0.5
Idaho	0.5
Louisiana	0.5
Illinois	0.4
Nebraska	0.3
Wisconsin	0.3
Iowa	0.2
Kansas	0.1
Rhode Island	0.1
Vermont	0.0
New Hampshire	0.0
Connecticut	0.0
Delaware*	0.0
*(data missing)	

National Park Service (NPS) visitors in 2010. Recreation visit represents the entry of a person onto lands or waters administered by the National Park Service and located within each state, for recreational purposes excluding government personnel, through traffic (commuters), trades-persons, and persons residing within park boundaries.

SOURCES: U.S. Census Bureau Statistical Abstract of the United States: 2012, Table 1254; U.S. National Park Service, Land Resources Board; and unpublished data

http://www.census.gov/compendia/statab/

http://www2.nature.nps.gov/stats/

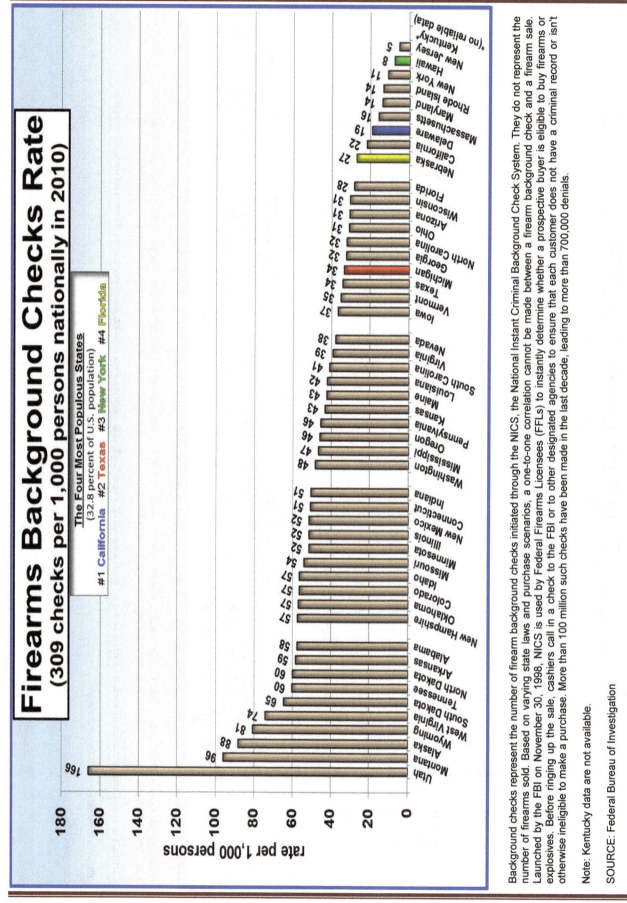

Firearms Background Checks Rate

(309 checks per 1,000 persons nationally in 2010)

The Four Most Populous States
(32.8 percent of U.S. population)

#1 California   #2 Texas   #3 New York   #4 Florida

State	rate per 1,000 persons
Utah	166
Montana	96
Alaska	88
Wyoming	81
West Virginia	74
South Dakota	65
Tennessee	60
North Dakota	60
Arkansas	59
Alabama	58
New Hampshire	57
Oklahoma	57
Colorado	57
Idaho	57
Missouri	54
Minnesota	52
Illinois	52
New Mexico	52
Connecticut	51
Indiana	51
Washington	48
Mississippi	47
Oregon	46
Pennsylvania	46
Kansas	43
Maine	43
Louisiana	42
South Carolina	41
Virginia	39
Nevada	38
Iowa	37
Vermont	35
Texas	34
Michigan	34
Georgia	32
North Carolina	32
Ohio	31
Arizona	31
Wisconsin	31
Florida	28
Nebraska	27
California	22
Delaware	19
Massachusetts	16
Maryland	14
Rhode Island	14
New York	11
Hawaii	8
New Jersey	5
Kentucky*	(no reliable data)

Background checks represent the number of firearm background checks initiated through the NICS, the National Instant Criminal Background Check System. They do not represent the number of firearms sold. Based on varying state laws and purchase scenarios, a one-to-one correlation cannot be made between a firearm background check and a firearm sale. Launched by the FBI on November 30, 1998, NICS is used by Federal Firearms Licensees (FFLs) to instantly determine whether a prospective buyer is eligible to buy firearms or explosives. Before ringing up the sale, cashiers call in a check to the FBI or to other designated agencies to ensure that each customer does not have a criminal record or isn't otherwise ineligible to make a purchase. More than 100 million such checks have been made in the last decade, leading to more than 700,000 denials.

Note: Kentucky data are not available.

SOURCE: Federal Bureau of Investigation

http://www.fbi.gov/about-us/cjis/nics/reports/state-totals_1998-2010

Chapter 4: Education Overview

The pupil-to-teacher ratio in public K-12 classrooms ranged from a low of 11.4-to-1 in North Dakota to a high of 24.1-to-1 in California.

Massachusetts had the highest overall scores for proficiency in 4th and 8th grade math, reading, and science; Mississippi had the lowest. Massachusetts also had the highest percentage of adults with bachelor's degree at 38 percent while West Virginia had the lowest at 17 percent.

Wyoming spent the most for K-12 public education per capita—nearly three times more than Arizona. New Mexico spent 50 percent more per capita than Montana, however, 8th grade students in New Mexico ranked in the bottom fifth for proficiency in math, reading, and science whereas Montana's ranked in the top fifth.

Texas and Mississippi both had a 20 percent high school dropout rate, the highest in the nation, while Wyoming had the lowest dropout rate at 8 percent.

One-in-five college freshmen who attended a college or university out-of-state enrolled in a college or university in New York, Massachusetts, or Pennsylvania. Pennsylvania had the highest net immigration of college freshmen while New Jersey had the lowest. For each college freshmen who entered a college or university in New Jersey from another state, nine left. In contrast, in Utah, five college freshmen entered a college or university in that state for each freshman that left. Over 90 percent of students in Utah chose in-state schools compared with only 41 percent in New Jersey.

~

Education Summary Table

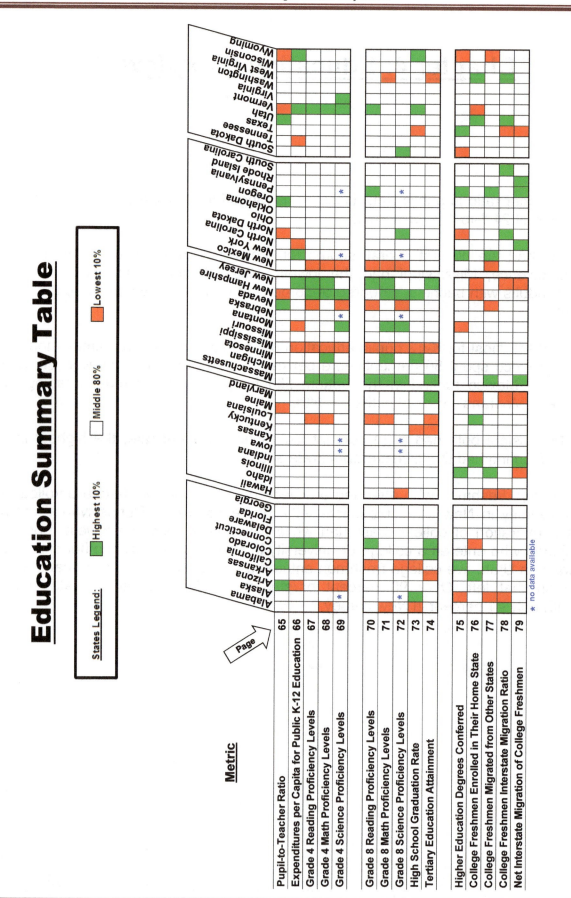

States Legend: ■ Highest 10% ☐ Middle 80% ■ Lowest 10%

Metric	Page
Pupil-to-Teacher Ratio	65
Expenditures per Capita for Public K-12 Education	66
Grade 4 Reading Proficiency Levels	67
Grade 4 Math Proficiency Levels	68
Grade 4 Science Proficiency Levels	69
Grade 8 Reading Proficiency Levels	70
Grade 8 Math Proficiency Levels	71
Grade 8 Science Proficiency Levels	72
High School Graduation Rate	73
Tertiary Education Attainment	74
Higher Education Degrees Conferred	75
College Freshmen Enrolled in Their Home State	76
College Freshmen Migrated from Other States	77
College Freshmen Interstate Migration Ratio	78
Net Interstate Migration of College Freshmen	79

* no data available

Pupil-to-Teacher Ratio
(16.0 nationally in 2011)

The Four Most Populous States
(32.8 percent of U.S. population)
#1 California #2 Texas #3 New York #4 Florida

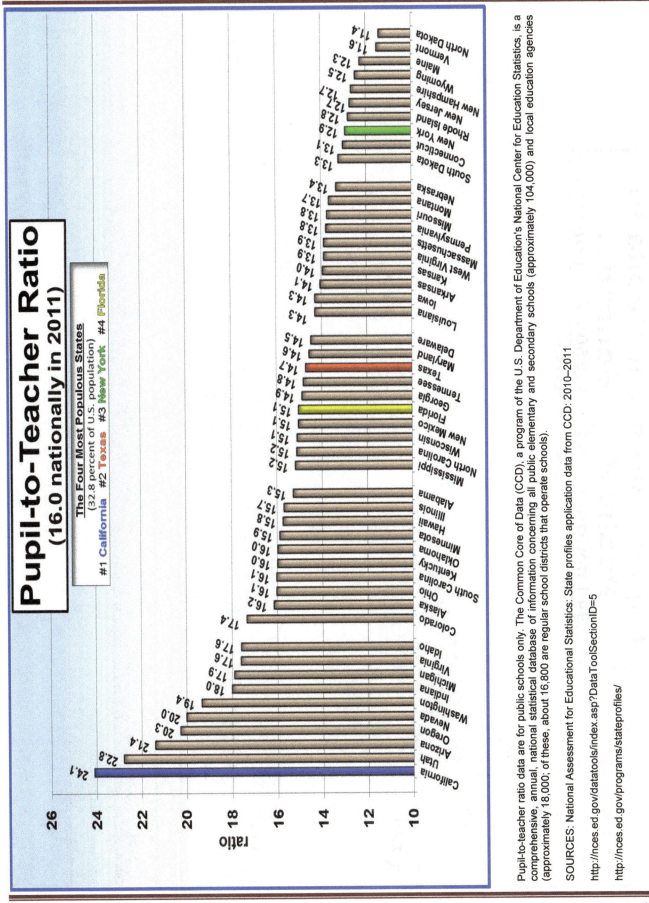

State	Ratio
California	24.1
Utah	22.8
Arizona	21.4
Oregon	20.3
Nevada	20.0
Washington	19.4
Indiana	18.0
Michigan	17.9
Virginia	17.6
Idaho	17.6
Colorado	17.4
Alaska	16.2
Ohio	16.1
South Carolina	16.1
Kentucky	16.0
Oklahoma	16.0
Minnesota	15.9
Hawaii	15.8
Illinois	15.7
Alabama	15.3
Mississippi	15.2
North Carolina	15.2
Wisconsin	15.1
New Mexico	15.1
Florida	14.9
Georgia	14.8
Tennessee	14.7
Texas	14.6
Maryland	14.5
Delaware	14.3
Louisiana	14.3
Iowa	14.1
Arkansas	14.0
Kansas	13.9
West Virginia	13.9
Massachusetts	13.8
Pennsylvania	13.7
Missouri	13.4
Montana	13.4
Nebraska	13.3
South Dakota	13.1
Connecticut	12.9
New York	12.8
Rhode Island	12.7
New Jersey	12.5
New Hampshire	12.3
Wyoming	11.6
Maine	11.4
Vermont	
North Dakota	

Pupil-to-teacher ratio data are for public schools only. The Common Core of Data (CCD), a program of the U.S. Department of Education's National Center for Education Statistics, is a comprehensive, annual, national statistical database of information concerning all public elementary and secondary schools (approximately 104,000) and local education agencies (approximately 18,000; of these, about 16,800 are regular school districts that operate schools).

SOURCES: National Assessment for Educational Statistics: State profiles application data from CCD: 2010–2011

http://nces.ed.gov/datatools/index.asp?DataToolSectionID=5

http://nces.ed.gov/programs/stateprofiles/

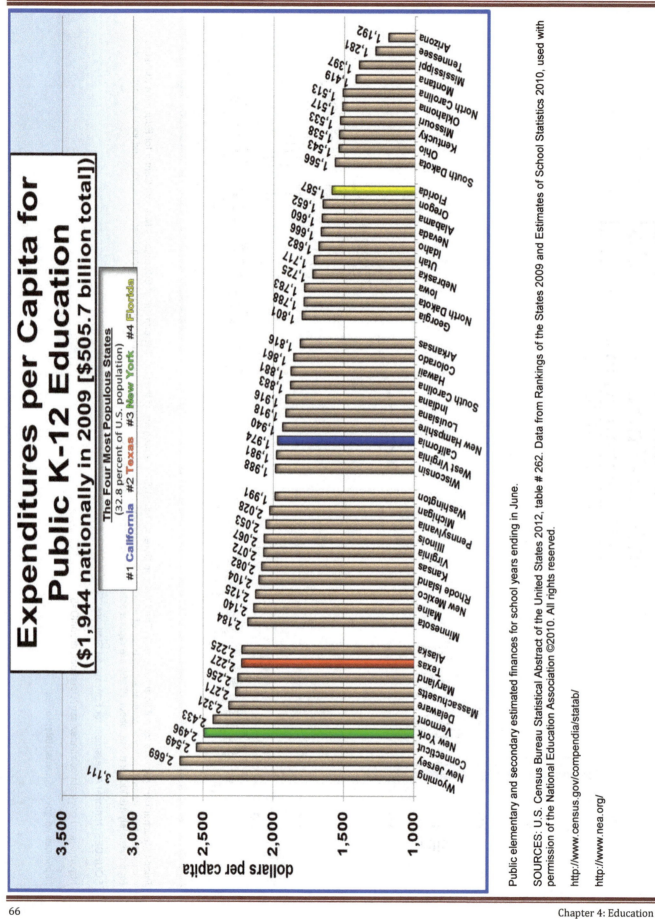

Expenditures per Capita for Public K-12 Education
($1,944 nationally in 2009 [$505.7 billion total])

The Four Most Populous States
(32.8 percent of U.S. population)
#1 California #2 Texas #3 New York #4 Florida

dollars per capita

Wyoming	3,111
New Jersey	2,669
Connecticut	2,549
New York	2,496
Vermont	2,433
Delaware	2,321
Massachusetts	2,271
Maryland	2,256
Texas	2,227
Alaska	2,225
Minnesota	2,184
New Mexico	2,140
Rhode Island	2,125
Kansas	2,104
Virginia	2,082
Illinois	2,072
Pennsylvania	2,067
Michigan	2,053
Washington	2,028
Wisconsin	1,991
West Virginia	1,988
California	1,981
New Hampshire	1,974
Louisiana	1,940
Indiana	1,918
South Carolina	1,916
Hawaii	1,883
Colorado	1,881
Arkansas	1,861
Georgia	1,816
North Dakota	1,801
Iowa	1,788
Nebraska	1,783
Utah	1,725
Idaho	1,717
Nevada	1,682
Alabama	1,666
Oregon	1,660
Florida	1,652
South Dakota	1,587
Ohio	1,566
Kentucky	1,543
Missouri	1,538
Oklahoma	1,533
North Carolina	1,517
Montana	1,513
Mississippi	1,419
Tennessee	1,397
Arizona	1,281
	1,192

Public elementary and secondary estimated finances for school years ending in June.

SOURCES: U.S. Census Bureau Statistical Abstract of the United States 2012, table # 262. Data from Rankings of the States 2009 and Estimates of School Statistics 2010, used with permission of the National Education Association ©2010. All rights reserved.

http://www.census.gov/compendia/statab/

http://www.nea.org/

Grade 4 Reading Proficiency Levels
(average score 33 nationally in 2009)

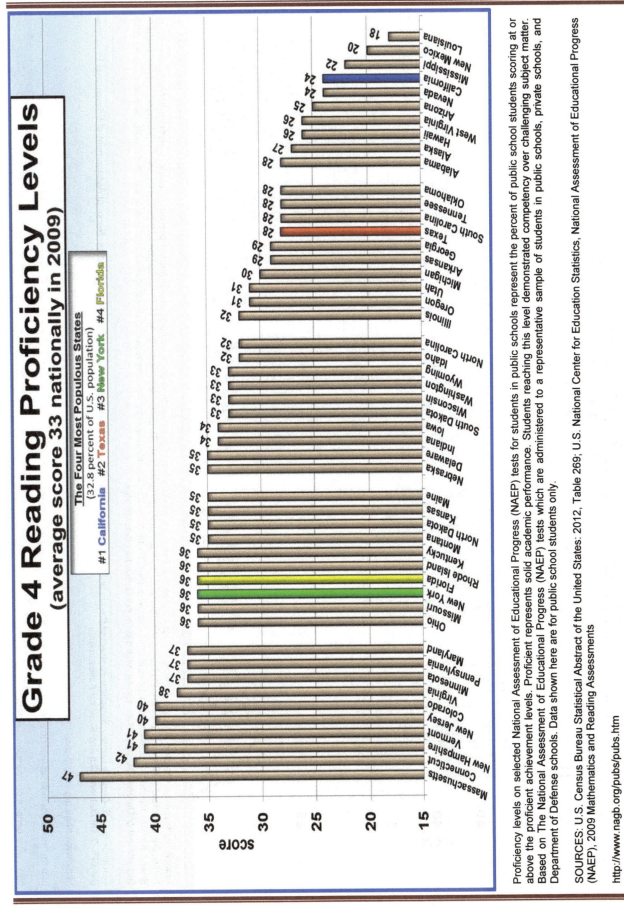

The Four Most Populous States
(32.8 percent of U.S. population)
#1 California #2 Texas #3 New York #4 Florida

State	Score
Massachusetts	47
Connecticut	42
New Hampshire	41
Vermont	41
New Jersey	40
Colorado	40
Virginia	38
Minnesota	37
Pennsylvania	37
Maryland	37
Ohio	36
Missouri	36
New York	36
Florida	36
Rhode Island	36
Kentucky	36
Montana	35
North Dakota	35
Kansas	35
Maine	35
Nebraska	35
Delaware	35
Indiana	34
Iowa	34
South Dakota	33
Wisconsin	33
Washington	33
Wyoming	33
Idaho	32
North Carolina	32
Illinois	32
Oregon	31
Utah	31
Michigan	30
Arkansas	29
Georgia	29
Texas	28
South Carolina	28
Tennessee	28
Oklahoma	28
Alabama	28
Alaska	27
Hawaii	26
West Virginia	26
Arizona	25
Nevada	24
California	24
Mississippi	22
New Mexico	20
Louisiana	18

Proficiency levels on selected National Assessment of Educational Progress (NAEP) tests for students in public schools represent the percent of public school students scoring at or above the proficient achievement levels. Proficient represents solid academic performance. Students reaching this level demonstrated competency over challenging subject matter. Based on The National Assessment of Educational Progress (NAEP) tests which are administered to a representative sample of students in public schools, private schools, and Department of Defense schools. Data shown here are for public school students only.

SOURCES: U.S. Census Bureau Statistical Abstract of the United States: 2012, Table 269; U.S. National Center for Education Statistics, National Assessment of Educational Progress (NAEP), 2009 Mathematics and Reading Assessments

http://www.nagb.org/pubs/pubs.htm

http://nces.ed.gov/nationsreportcard/

http://www.census.gov/compendia/statab/

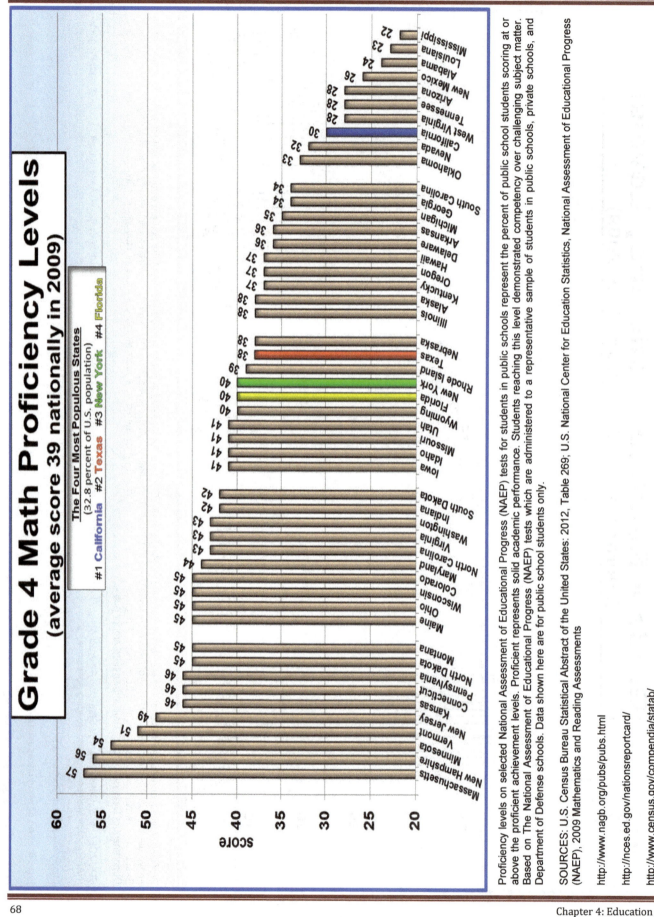

Grade 4 Math Proficiency Levels
(average score 39 nationally in 2009)

The Four Most Populous States
(32.8 percent of U.S. population)
#1 California   #2 Texas   #3 New York   #4 Florida

State	Score
Massachusetts	57
New Hampshire	56
Minnesota	56
Vermont	54
New Jersey	51
Kansas	49
Connecticut	46
Pennsylvania	46
North Dakota	46
Montana	45
Maine	45
Ohio	45
Wisconsin	45
Colorado	45
Maryland	44
North Carolina	43
Virginia	43
Washington	43
Indiana	42
South Dakota	42
Iowa	41
Idaho	41
Missouri	41
Utah	41
Wyoming	40
Florida	40
New York	40
Rhode Island	39
Texas	38
Nebraska	38
Illinois	38
Alaska	38
Kentucky	37
Oregon	37
Hawaii	37
Delaware	36
Arkansas	36
Michigan	35
Georgia	34
South Carolina	34
Oklahoma	33
Nevada	32
California	30
West Virginia	28
Tennessee	28
Arizona	28
New Mexico	26
Alabama	24
Louisiana	23
Mississippi	22

Proficiency levels on selected National Assessment of Educational Progress (NAEP) tests for students in public schools represent the percent of public school students scoring at or above the proficient achievement levels. Proficient represents solid academic performance. Students reaching this level demonstrated competency over challenging subject matter. Based on The National Assessment of Educational Progress (NAEP) tests which are administered to a representative sample of students in public schools, private schools, and Department of Defense schools. Data shown here are for public school students only.

SOURCES: U.S. Census Bureau Statistical Abstract of the United States: 2012, Table 269; U.S. National Center for Education Statistics, National Assessment of Educational Progress (NAEP), 2009 Mathematics and Reading Assessments

http://www.nagb.org/pubs/pubs.html

http://nces.ed.gov/nationsreportcard/

http://www.census.gov/compendia/statab/

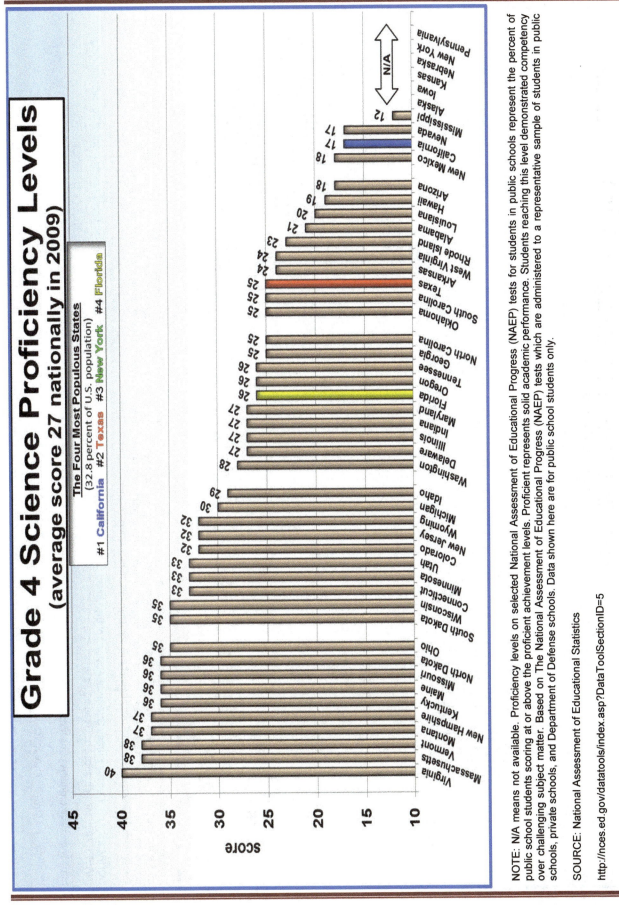

Grade 4 Science Proficiency Levels
(average score 27 nationally in 2009)

The Four Most Populous States
(32.8 percent of U.S. population)
#1 California #2 Texas #3 New York #4 Florida

State	Score
Virginia	40
Massachusetts	38
Vermont	38
Montana	37
New Hampshire	37
Kentucky	36
Maine	36
Missouri	36
North Dakota	36
Ohio	35
South Dakota	35
Wisconsin	35
Connecticut	33
Minnesota	33
Utah	33
Colorado	32
New Jersey	32
Wyoming	32
Michigan	30
Idaho	29
Washington	28
Delaware	27
Illinois	27
Indiana	27
Maryland	27
Florida	26
Oregon	26
Tennessee	26
Georgia	25
North Carolina	25
Oklahoma	25
South Carolina	25
Texas	25
Arkansas	24
West Virginia	24
Rhode Island	23
Alabama	21
Louisiana	20
Hawaii	19
Arizona	18
New Mexico	18
California	17
Nevada	17
Mississippi	12
Alaska	N/A
Iowa	N/A
Kansas	N/A
Nebraska	N/A
New York	N/A
Pennsylvania	N/A

score

NOTE: N/A means not available. Proficiency levels on selected National Assessment of Educational Progress (NAEP) tests for students in public schools represent the percent of public school students scoring at or above the proficient achievement levels. Proficient represents solid academic performance. Students reaching this level demonstrated competency over challenging subject matter. Based on The National Assessment of Educational Progress (NAEP) tests which are administered to a representative sample of students in public schools, private schools, and Department of Defense schools. Data shown here are for public school students only.

SOURCE: National Assessment of Educational Statistics

http://nces.ed.gov/datatools/index.asp?DataToolSectionID=5

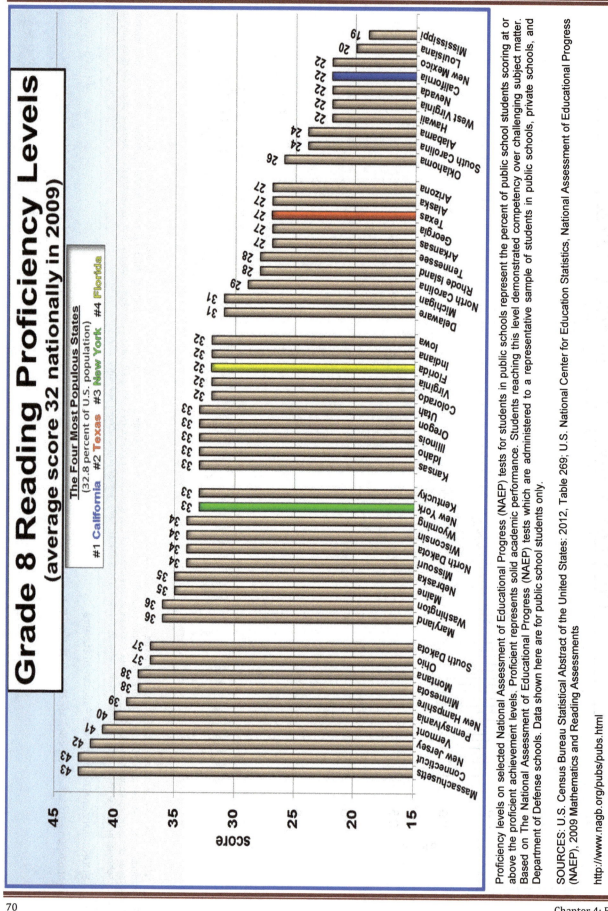

Grade 8 Reading Proficiency Levels
(average score 32 nationally in 2009)

The Four Most Populous States
(32.8 percent of U.S. population)
#1 California #2 Texas #3 New York #4 Florida

State	Score
Massachusetts	43
Connecticut	43
New Jersey	42
Vermont	41
Pennsylvania	40
New Hampshire	39
Minnesota	38
Montana	38
Ohio	37
South Dakota	37
Maryland	36
Washington	36
Maine	35
Nebraska	35
Missouri	34
North Dakota	34
Wisconsin	34
Wyoming	34
New York	33
Kentucky	33
Kansas	33
Idaho	33
Illinois	33
Oregon	33
Utah	33
Colorado	32
Virginia	32
Florida	32
Indiana	32
Iowa	32
Delaware	31
Michigan	31
North Carolina	29
Rhode Island	28
Tennessee	28
Arkansas	27
Georgia	27
Texas	27
Alaska	27
Arizona	27
Oklahoma	26
South Carolina	24
Alabama	24
Hawaii	22
West Virginia	22
Nevada	22
California	22
New Mexico	22
Louisiana	20
Mississippi	19

Proficiency levels on selected National Assessment of Educational Progress (NAEP) tests for students in public schools represent the percent of public school students scoring at or above the proficient achievement levels. Proficient represents solid academic performance. Students reaching this level demonstrated competency over challenging subject matter. Based on The National Assessment of Educational Progress (NAEP) tests which are administered to a representative sample of students in public schools, private schools, and Department of Defense schools. Data shown here are for public school students only.

SOURCES: U.S. Census Bureau Statistical Abstract of the United States: 2012, Table 269; U.S. National Center for Education Statistics, National Assessment of Educational Progress (NAEP), 2009 Mathematics and Reading Assessments

http://www.nagb.org/pubs/pubs.html

http://nces.ed.gov/nationsreportcard/

http://www.census.gov/compendia/statab/

Grade 8 Math Proficiency Levels
(average score 34 nationally in 2009)

The Four Most Populous States
(32.8 percent of U.S. population)
#1 California   #2 Texas   #3 New York   #4 Florida

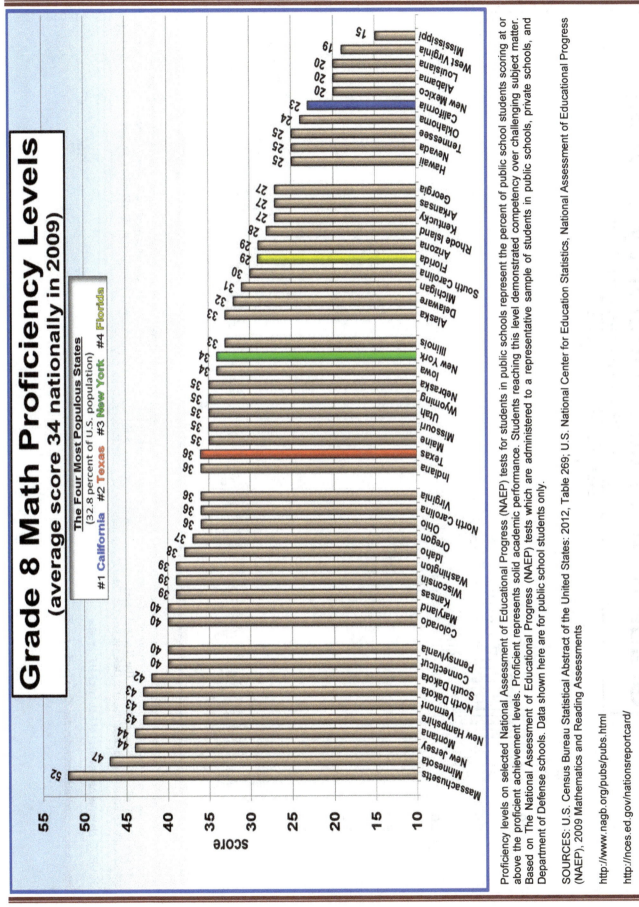

State	Score
Massachusetts	52
Minnesota	47
New Jersey	44
Montana	44
New Hampshire	43
Vermont	43
North Dakota	43
South Dakota	42
Connecticut	40
Pennsylvania	40
Colorado	40
Maryland	40
Kansas	39
Wisconsin	39
Washington	39
Idaho	38
Oregon	37
Ohio	36
North Carolina	36
Virginia	36
Indiana	36
Texas	36
Maine	35
Missouri	35
Utah	35
Wyoming	35
Nebraska	35
Iowa	34
New York	34
Illinois	33
Alaska	33
Delaware	32
Michigan	31
South Carolina	30
Florida	29
Arizona	29
Rhode Island	28
Kentucky	27
Arkansas	27
Georgia	27
Hawaii	25
Nevada	25
Tennessee	25
Oklahoma	24
California	23
New Mexico	20
Alabama	20
Louisiana	20
West Virginia	19
Mississippi	15

Proficiency levels on selected National Assessment of Educational Progress (NAEP) tests for students in public schools represent the percent of public school students scoring at or above the proficient achievement levels. Proficient represents solid academic performance. Students reaching this level demonstrated competency over challenging subject matter. Based on The National Assessment of Educational Progress (NAEP) tests which are administered to a representative sample of students in public schools, private schools, and Department of Defense schools. Data shown here are for public school students only.

SOURCES: U.S. Census Bureau Statistical Abstract of the United States: 2012, Table 269; U.S. National Center for Education Statistics, National Assessment of Educational Progress (NAEP), 2009 Mathematics and Reading Assessments

http://www.nagb.org/pubs/pubs.html

http://nces.ed.gov/nationsreportcard/

http://www.census.gov/compendia/statab/

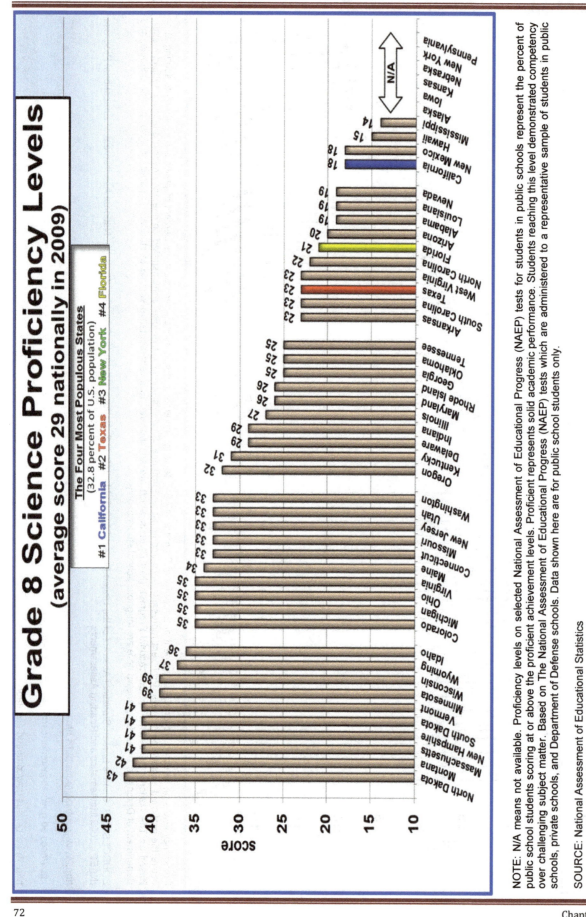

Grade 8 Science Proficiency Levels
(average score 29 nationally in 2009)

The Four Most Populous States
(32.8 percent of U.S. population)
#1 California   #2 Texas   #3 New York   #4 Florida

State	Score
North Dakota	43
Montana	42
Massachusetts	41
New Hampshire	41
South Dakota	41
Vermont	41
Minnesota	39
Wisconsin	39
Wyoming	37
Idaho	36
Colorado	35
Michigan	35
Ohio	35
Virginia	35
Maine	34
Connecticut	33
Missouri	33
New Jersey	33
Utah	33
Washington	33
Oregon	32
Kentucky	31
Delaware	29
Indiana	29
Illinois	27
Maryland	26
Rhode Island	26
Georgia	25
Oklahoma	25
Tennessee	25
Arkansas	23
South Carolina	23
Texas	23
West Virginia	23
North Carolina	22
Florida	21
Arizona	20
Alabama	19
Louisiana	19
Nevada	19
California	18
New Mexico	18
Hawaii	15
Mississippi	14
Alaska	N/A
Iowa	N/A
Kansas	N/A
Nebraska	N/A
New York	N/A
Pennsylvania	N/A

NOTE: N/A means not available. Proficiency levels on selected National Assessment of Educational Progress (NAEP) tests for students in public schools represent the percent of public school students scoring at or above the proficient achievement levels. Proficient represents solid academic performance. Students reaching this level demonstrated competency over challenging subject matter. Based on The National Assessment of Educational Progress (NAEP) tests which are administered to a representative sample of students in public schools, private schools, and Department of Defense schools. Data shown here are for public school students only.

SOURCE: National Assessment of Educational Statistics

http://nces.ed.gov/datatools/index.asp?DataToolSectionID=5

High School Graduation Rate
(85.3 percent nationally in 2009)

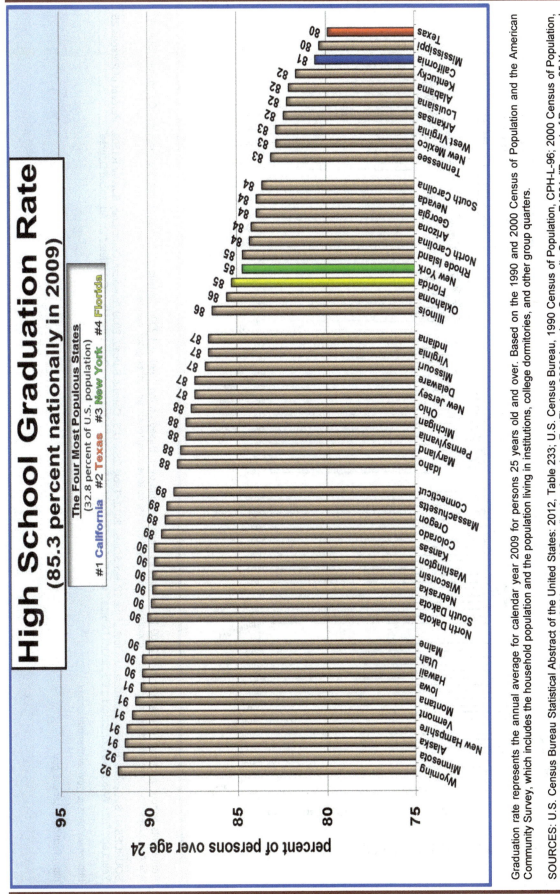

The Four Most Populous States
(32.8 percent of U.S. population)
#1 California   #2 Texas   #3 New York   #4 Florida

percent of persons over age 24

Texas	80
Mississippi	80
California	81
Kentucky	82
Alabama	82
Louisiana	82
Arkansas	82
West Virginia	83
New Mexico	83
Tennessee	83
South Carolina	84
Nevada	84
Georgia	84
Arizona	84
North Carolina	84
Rhode Island	85
New York	85
Florida	85
Oklahoma	86
Illinois	86
Indiana	87
Virginia	87
Missouri	87
Delaware	87
New Jersey	87
Ohio	88
Michigan	88
Pennsylvania	88
Maryland	88
Idaho	88
Connecticut	89
Massachusetts	89
Oregon	89
Colorado	89
Kansas	90
Washington	90
Wisconsin	90
Nebraska	90
South Dakota	90
North Dakota	90
Maine	90
Utah	90
Hawaii	90
Iowa	91
Montana	91
Vermont	91
New Hampshire	91
Alaska	91
Minnesota	92
Wyoming	92

Graduation rate represents the annual average for calendar year 2009 for persons 25 years old and over. Based on the 1990 and 2000 Census of Population and the American Community Survey, which includes the household population and the population living in institutions, college dormitories, and other group quarters.

SOURCES: U.S. Census Bureau Statistical Abstract of the United States: 2012, Table 233; U.S. Census Bureau, 1990 Census of Population, CPH-L-96; 2000 Census of Population, P37. "Sex by Educational Attainment for the Population 25 Years and Over," using American FactFinder; 2009 American Community Survey, R1501, "Percent of Persons 25 Years and Over Who Have Completed High School (Includes Equivalency)"

http://factfinder.census.gov

http://www.census.gov/compendia/statab/

http://www.census.gov/population/www/socdemo/educ-attn.html

Tertiary Education Attainment
(27.9 percent nationally in 2009)

The Four Most Populous States
(32.8 percent of U.S. population)
#1 California #2 Texas #3 New York #4 Florida

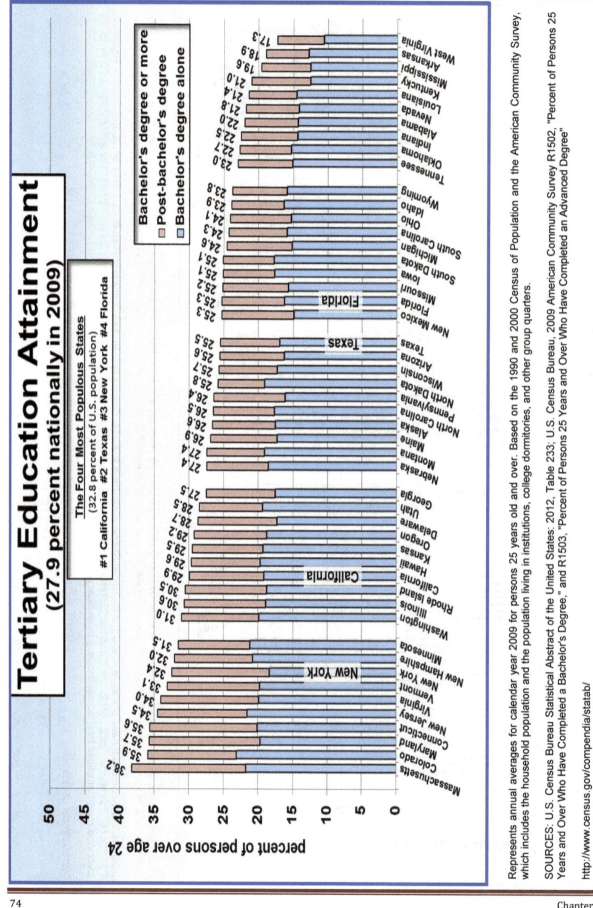

Legend:
- Bachelor's degree or more
- Post-bachelor's degree
- Bachelor's degree alone

Y-axis: percent of persons over age 24

Data values (percent of persons over age 24):
- Massachusetts 38.2
- Colorado 35.9
- Maryland 35.7
- Connecticut 35.6
- New Jersey 34.5
- Virginia 34.0
- Vermont 33.1
- New York 32.4
- New Hampshire 32.0
- Minnesota 31.5
- Washington 31.0
- Illinois 30.6
- Rhode Island 30.5
- California 29.9
- Hawaii 29.6
- Kansas 29.5
- Oregon 29.2
- Delaware 28.7
- Utah 28.5
- Georgia 27.5
- Nebraska 27.4
- Montana 27.4
- Maine 26.9
- Alaska 26.6
- North Carolina 26.5
- Pennsylvania 26.4
- North Dakota 25.8
- Wisconsin 25.7
- Arizona 25.6
- Texas 25.5
- New Mexico 25.3
- Florida 25.3
- Missouri 25.2
- Iowa 25.1
- South Dakota 25.1
- Michigan 24.6
- South Carolina 24.3
- Ohio 24.1
- Idaho 23.9
- Wyoming 23.8
- Tennessee 23.0
- Oklahoma 22.7
- Indiana 22.5
- Alabama 22.0
- Nevada 21.8
- Louisiana 21.4
- Kentucky 21.0
- Mississippi 19.6
- Arkansas 18.9
- West Virginia 17.3

Represents annual averages for calendar year 2009 for persons 25 years old and over. Based on the 1990 and 2000 Census of Population and the American Community Survey, which includes the household population and the population living in institutions, college dormitories, and other group quarters.

SOURCES: U.S. Census Bureau Statistical Abstract of the United States: 2012, Table 233; U.S. Census Bureau, 2009 American Community Survey R1502, "Percent of Persons 25 Years and Over Who Have Completed a Bachelor's Degree," and R1503, "Percent of Persons 25 Years and Over Who Have Completed an Advanced Degree"

http://www.census.gov/compendia/statab/

http://factfinder.census.gov

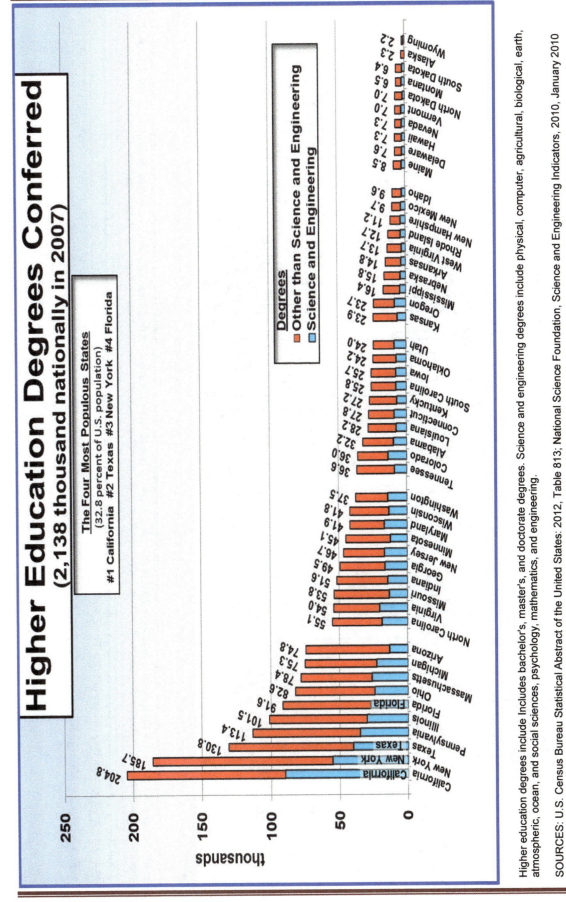

Higher Education Degrees Conferred
(2,138 thousand nationally in 2007)

The Four Most Populous States
(32.8 percent of U.S. population)
#1 California #2 Texas #3 New York #4 Florida

Degrees
- Other than Science and Engineering
- Science and Engineering

California	204.8
New York	185.7
Texas	130.8
Pennsylvania	113.4
Illinois	101.5
Florida	91.6
Ohio	82.6
Massachusetts	78.4
Michigan	75.3
Arizona	74.8
North Carolina	55.1
Virginia	54.0
Missouri	53.8
Indiana	51.6
Georgia	49.5
New Jersey	46.7
Minnesota	45.1
Maryland	41.9
Wisconsin	41.8
Washington	37.5
Tennessee	36.6
Colorado	36.0
Alabama	32.2
Louisiana	28.2
Connecticut	27.8
Kentucky	27.2
South Carolina	25.8
Iowa	25.7
Oklahoma	24.2
Utah	24.0
Kansas	23.9
Oregon	23.7
Mississippi	16.4
Nebraska	15.8
Arkansas	14.8
West Virginia	13.7
Rhode Island	12.7
New Hampshire	11.2
New Mexico	9.7
Idaho	9.6
Maine	8.5
Delaware	7.6
Hawaii	7.3
Nevada	7.3
Vermont	7.0
North Dakota	7.0
Montana	6.5
South Dakota	6.4
Alaska	2.3
Wyoming	2.2

thousands

Higher education degrees include Includes bachelor's, master's, and doctorate degrees. Science and engineering degrees include physical, computer, agricultural, biological, earth, atmospheric, ocean, and social sciences, psychology, mathematics, and engineering.

SOURCES: U.S. Census Bureau Statistical Abstract of the United States: 2012, Table 813; National Science Foundation, Science and Engineering Indicators, 2010, January 2010

http://www.census.gov/compendia/statab/

http://www.nsf.gov/statistics/seind10

College Freshmen Enrolled in Their Home State

(74.3 percent nationally in 2008)

The Four Most Populous States
(32.8 percent of U.S. population)
#1 California #2 Texas #3 New York #4 Florida

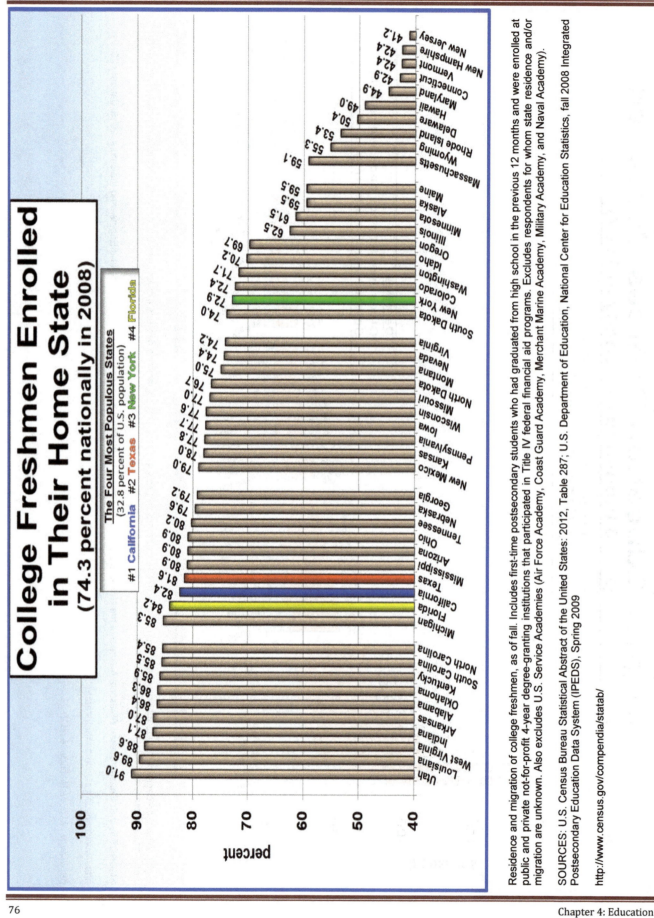

State	Percent
Utah	91.0
Louisiana	89.6
West Virginia	88.6
Indiana	87.1
Arkansas	87.0
Alabama	86.4
Oklahoma	86.3
Kentucky	85.9
South Carolina	85.5
North Carolina	85.4
Michigan	85.3
Florida	84.2
California	82.4
Texas	81.6
Mississippi	80.9
Arizona	80.9
Ohio	80.2
Tennessee	79.6
Nebraska	79.2
Georgia	
New Mexico	79.0
Kansas	78.0
Pennsylvania	77.8
Iowa	77.7
Wisconsin	77.6
Missouri	77.0
North Dakota	76.7
Montana	75.0
Nevada	74.4
Virginia	74.2
South Dakota	74.0
New York	72.9
Colorado	72.4
Washington	71.7
Idaho	70.2
Oregon	69.7
Illinois	62.5
Minnesota	61.5
Alaska	59.5
Maine	59.5
Massachusetts	59.1
Wyoming	55.3
Rhode Island	53.4
Delaware	50.4
Hawaii	49.0
Maryland	44.9
Connecticut	42.9
Vermont	42.4
New Hampshire	42.4
New Jersey	41.2

percent

Residence and migration of college freshmen, as of fall. Includes first-time postsecondary students who had graduated from high school in the previous 12 months and were enrolled at public and private not-for-profit 4-year degree-granting institutions that participated in Title IV federal financial aid programs. Excludes respondents for whom state residence and/or migration are unknown. Also excludes U.S. Service Academies (Air Force Academy, Coast Guard Academy, Merchant Marine Academy, Military Academy, and Naval Academy).

SOURCES: U.S. Census Bureau Statistical Abstract of the United States: 2012, Table 287; U.S. Department of Education, National Center for Education Statistics, fall 2008 Integrated Postsecondary Education Data System (IPEDS), Spring 2009

http://www.census.gov/compendia/statab/

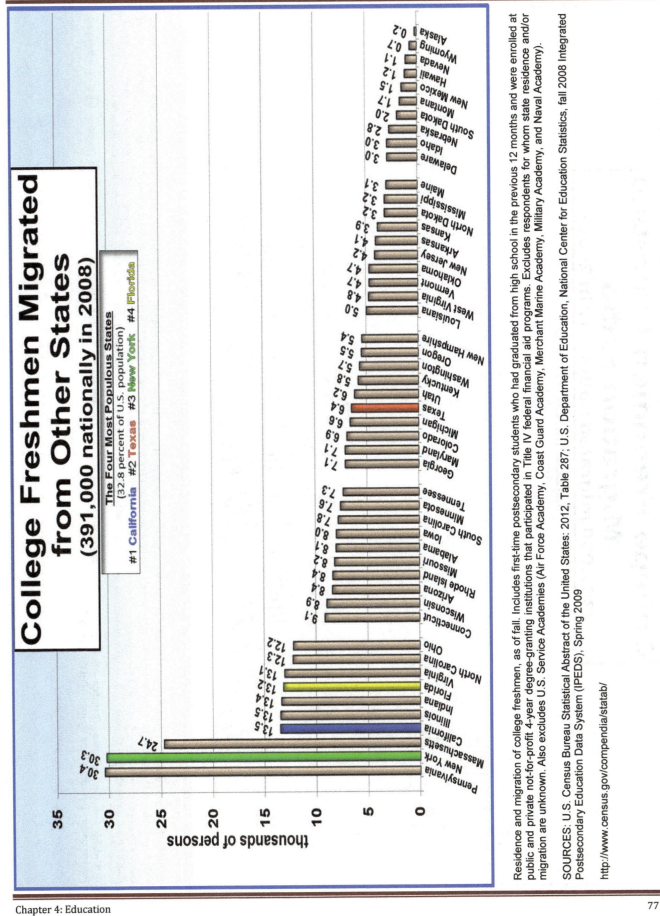

College Freshmen Migrated from Other States

(391,000 nationally in 2008)

The Four Most Populous States
(32.8 percent of U.S. population)
#1 California   #2 Texas   #3 New York   #4 Florida

State	thousands of persons
Pennsylvania	30.4
New York	30.3
Massachusetts	24.7
California	13.5
Illinois	13.5
Indiana	13.4
Florida	13.2
Virginia	13.1
North Carolina	12.3
Ohio	12.2
Connecticut	9.1
Wisconsin	8.9
Arizona	8.4
Rhode Island	8.4
Missouri	8.2
Alabama	8.1
Iowa	8.0
South Carolina	7.8
Minnesota	7.6
Tennessee	7.3
Georgia	7.1
Maryland	7.1
Colorado	6.9
Michigan	6.6
Texas	6.4
Utah	6.2
Kentucky	5.8
Washington	5.7
Oregon	5.5
New Hampshire	5.4
Louisiana	5.0
West Virginia	4.8
Vermont	4.7
Oklahoma	4.7
New Jersey	4.2
Arkansas	4.1
Kansas	3.9
North Dakota	3.2
Mississippi	3.2
Maine	3.1
Delaware	3.0
Idaho	3.0
Nebraska	2.8
South Dakota	2.0
Montana	1.7
New Mexico	1.5
Hawaii	1.2
Nevada	1.1
Wyoming	0.7
Alaska	0.2

Residence and migration of college freshmen, as of fall. Includes first-time postsecondary students who had graduated from high school in the previous 12 months and were enrolled at public and private not-for-profit 4-year degree-granting institutions that participated in Title IV federal financial aid programs. Excludes respondents for whom state residence and/or migration are unknown. Also excludes U.S. Service Academies (Air Force Academy, Coast Guard Academy, Merchant Marine Academy, Military Academy, and Naval Academy).

SOURCES: U.S. Census Bureau Statistical Abstract of the United States: 2012, Table 287; U.S. Department of Education, National Center for Education Statistics, fall 2008 Integrated Postsecondary Education Data System (IPEDS), Spring 2009

http://www.census.gov/compendia/statab/

College Freshmen Interstate Migration Ratio
(391,000 migrated nationally in 2008)

The Four Most Populous States
(32.8 percent of U.S. population)
#1 California   #2 Texas   #3 New York   #4 Florida

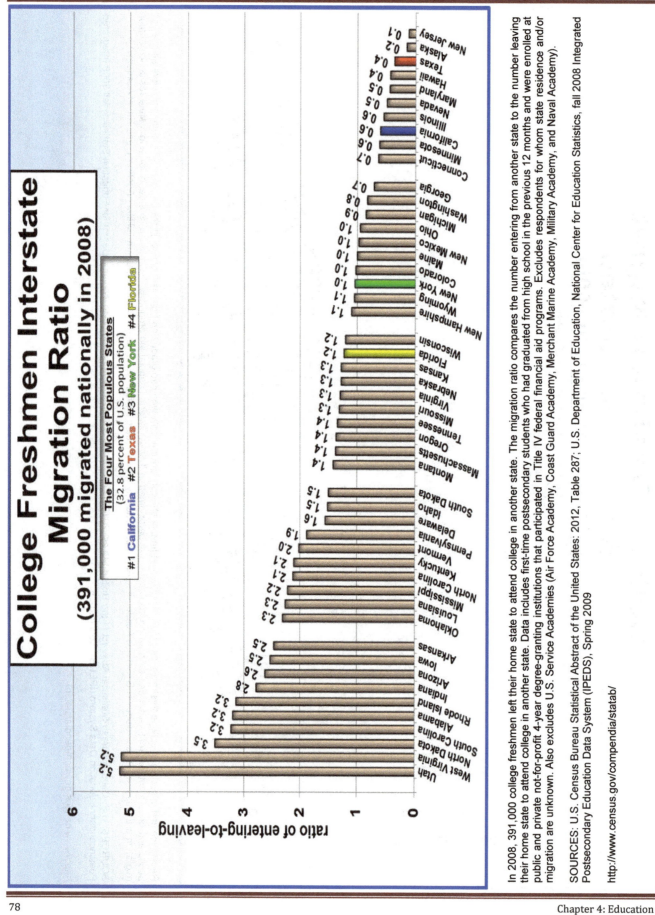

ratio of entering-to-leaving

State	Ratio
Utah	5.2
West Virginia	5.2
North Dakota	3.5
South Carolina	3.2
Alabama	3.2
Rhode Island	2.8
Indiana	2.6
Arizona	2.5
Iowa	2.5
Arkansas	2.3
Oklahoma	2.3
Louisiana	2.2
Mississippi	2.1
North Carolina	2.1
Kentucky	2.0
Vermont	1.9
Pennsylvania	1.6
Delaware	1.5
Idaho	1.5
South Dakota	1.4
Montana	1.4
Massachusetts	1.4
Oregon	1.3
Tennessee	1.3
Missouri	1.3
Virginia	1.3
Nebraska	1.2
Kansas	1.2
Florida	1.2
Wisconsin	1.1
New Hampshire	1.1
Wyoming	1.0
New York	1.0
Colorado	1.0
Maine	1.0
New Mexico	0.9
Ohio	0.8
Michigan	0.7
Washington	0.7
Georgia	0.7
Connecticut	0.6
Minnesota	0.6
California	0.6
Illinois	0.5
Nevada	0.5
Maryland	0.4
Hawaii	0.4
Texas	0.2
Alaska	0.1
New Jersey	0.1

In 2008, 391,000 college freshmen left their home state to attend college in another state. The migration ratio compares the number entering from another state to the number leaving their home state to attend college in another state. Data includes first-time postsecondary students who had graduated from high school in the previous 12 months and were enrolled at public and private not-for-profit 4-year degree-granting institutions that participated in Title IV federal financial aid programs. Excludes respondents for whom state residence and/or migration are unknown. Also excludes U.S. Service Academies (Air Force Academy, Coast Guard Academy, Merchant Marine Academy, Military Academy, and Naval Academy).

SOURCES: U.S. Census Bureau Statistical Abstract of the United States: 2012, Table 287; U.S. Department of Education, National Center for Education Statistics, fall 2008 Integrated Postsecondary Education Data System (IPEDS), Spring 2009

http://www.census.gov/compendia/statab/

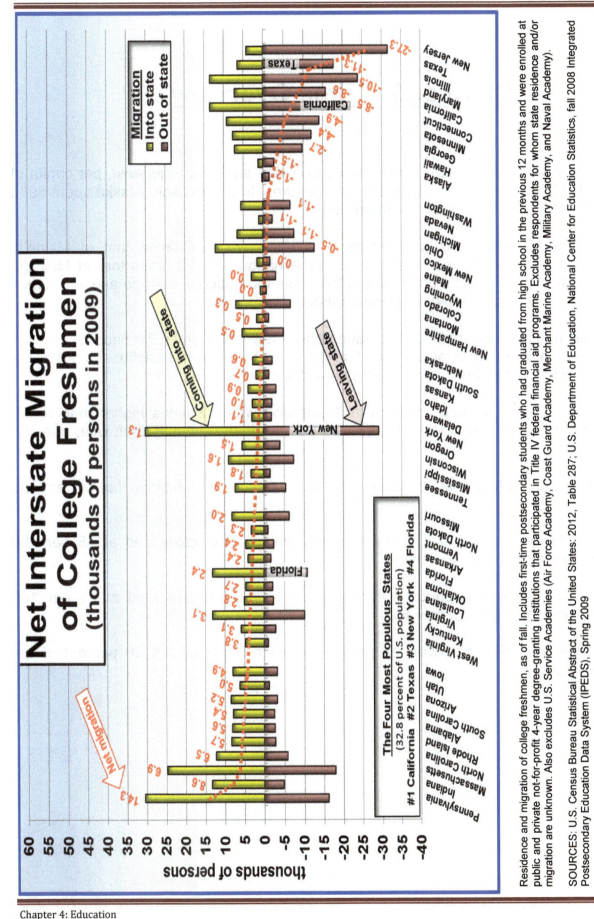

Net Interstate Migration of College Freshmen
(thousands of persons in 2009)

The Four Most Populous States
(32.8 percent of U.S. population)
#1 California #2 Texas #3 New York #4 Florida

Residence and migration of college freshmen, as of fall. Includes first-time postsecondary students who had graduated from high school in the previous 12 months and were enrolled at public and private not-for-profit 4-year degree-granting institutions that participated in Title IV federal financial aid programs. Excludes respondents for whom state residence and/or migration are unknown. Also excludes U.S. Service Academies (Air Force Academy, Coast Guard Academy, Merchant Marine Academy, Military Academy, and Naval Academy).

SOURCES: U.S. Census Bureau Statistical Abstract of the United States: 2012, Table 287; U.S. Department of Education, National Center for Education Statistics, fall 2008 Integrated Postsecondary Education Data System (IPEDS), Spring 2009

http://www.census.gov/compendia/statab/

Chapter 5: Crime Overview

Maine had the lowest violent crime and incarceration rate and spent the least, per capita of any state at $397 for criminal justice related expenditures. In comparison, Alaska spent $980 per capita on criminal justice—the most of any state.

Nevada had the highest violent crime rate in 2010. It was 5.5 times that of Maine's. Louisiana's incarceration rate was the highest in the nation and 5.3 times that of Maine's. Louisiana also had the highest murder rate at 2.4 times the national average and 13.7 times that of New Hampshire, which had the lowest murder rate.

Massachusetts had the highest child abuse and neglect rate at 2.7 times the national average and 18.5 times that of Pennsylvania, which had the lowest rate. In Massachusetts, a child is 15 times more likely to be abused or neglected than for a car to be stolen.

The highest property crime rate occurred in Texas and was 2.2 times higher than South Dakota's property crime rate. South Dakota also has the lowest identify theft rate, one-fifth the rate in Florida.

California motor vehicle theft rate was the highest in the nation and 5.8 times that of Vermont, the lowest.

Delaware had the highest annual incoming state criminal court case load at 45 per 100 residents, 6.5 times the national average.

New Jersey had the highest annual incoming state civil court case load at 81 per 100 residents, 3.0 times the national average.

Texas executed 464 prisoners over the past 35 years and constitutes 38 percent of the nation's executions.

~

Crime Summary Table

States Legend:
■ Highest 10% □ Middle 80% ■ Lowest 10%

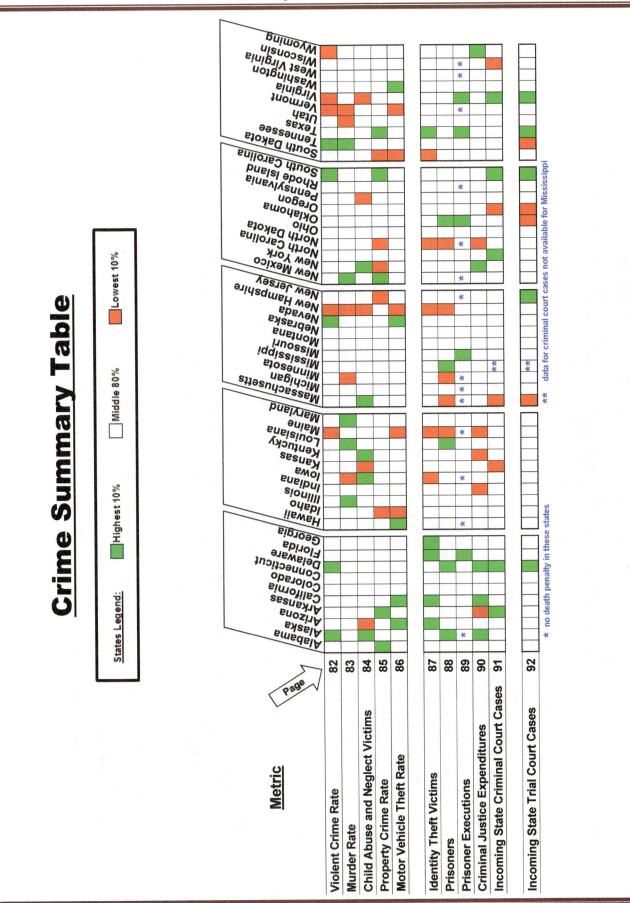

Violent Crime Rate
(406 per 100,000 persons nationally in 2010)

The Four Most Populous States
(32.8 percent of U.S. population)
#1 California #2 Texas #3 New York #4 Florida

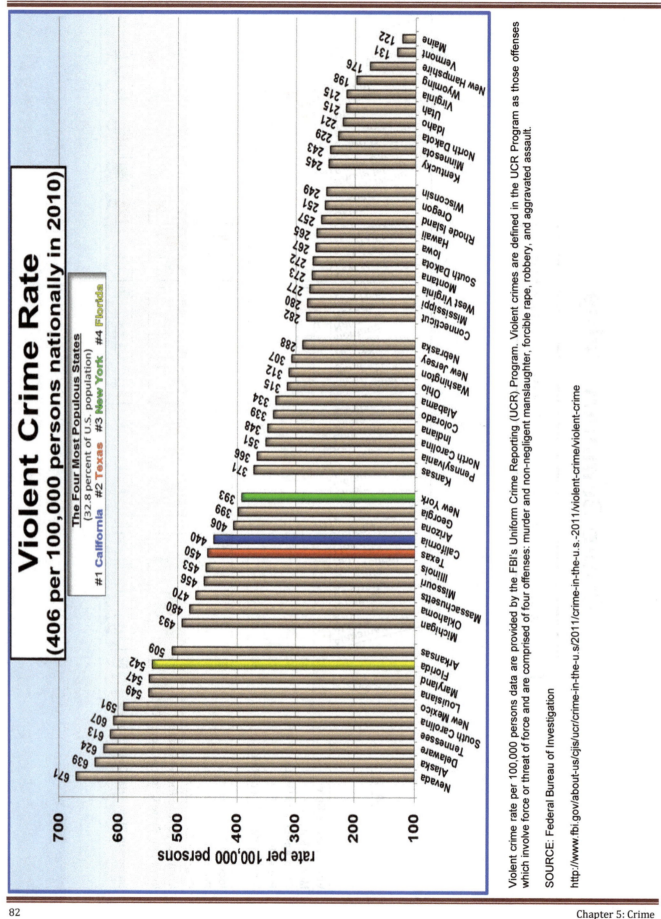

State	Rate
Nevada	671
Alaska	639
Delaware	624
Tennessee	613
South Carolina	607
New Mexico	591
Louisiana	549
Maryland	547
Florida	542
Arkansas	509
Michigan	493
Oklahoma	480
Massachusetts	470
Missouri	456
Illinois	453
Texas	450
California	440
Arizona	406
Georgia	399
New York	393
Kansas	371
Pennsylvania	366
North Carolina	351
Indiana	348
Colorado	339
Alabama	334
Ohio	315
Washington	312
New Jersey	307
Nebraska	288
Connecticut	282
Mississippi	280
West Virginia	277
Montana	273
South Dakota	272
Iowa	267
Hawaii	265
Rhode Island	257
Oregon	251
Wisconsin	249
Kentucky	245
Minnesota	243
North Dakota	229
Idaho	221
Utah	215
Virginia	215
Wyoming	198
New Hampshire	176
Vermont	131
Maine	122

rate per 100,000 persons

Violent crime rate per 100,000 persons data are provided by the FBI's Uniform Crime Reporting (UCR) Program. Violent crimes are defined in the UCR Program as those offenses which involve force or threat of force and are comprised of four offenses: murder and non-negligent manslaughter, forcible rape, robbery, and aggravated assault.

SOURCE: Federal Bureau of Investigation

http://www.fbi.gov/about-us/cjis/ucr/crime-in-the-u.s/2011/crime-in-the-u.s.-2011/violent-crime/violent-crime

Crime Summary Table

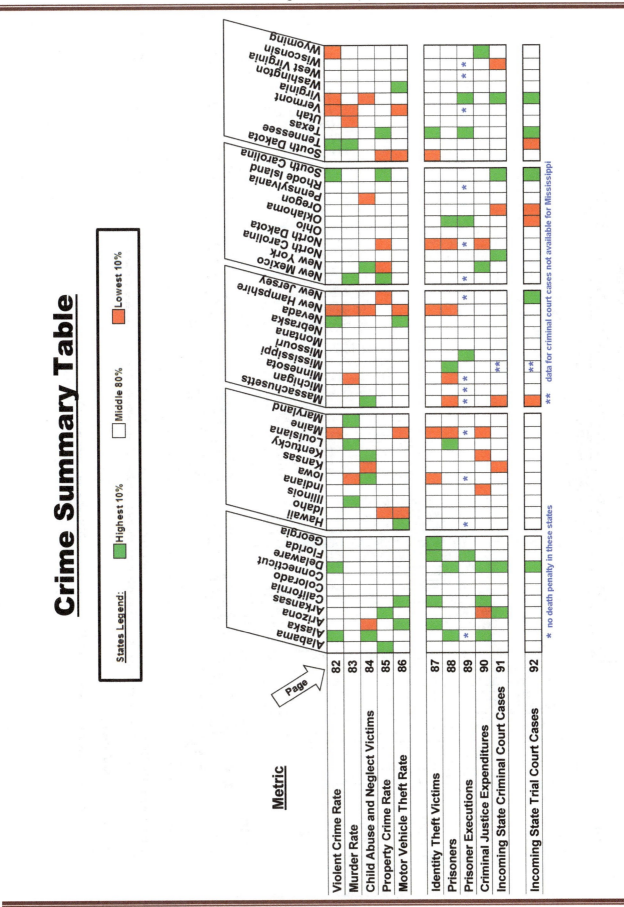

States Legend: ▇ Highest 10%   ☐ Middle 80%   ▇ Lowest 10%

Violent Crime Rate
(406 per 100,000 persons nationally in 2010)

The Four Most Populous States
(32.8 percent of U.S. population)
#1 California   #2 Texas   #3 New York   #4 Florida

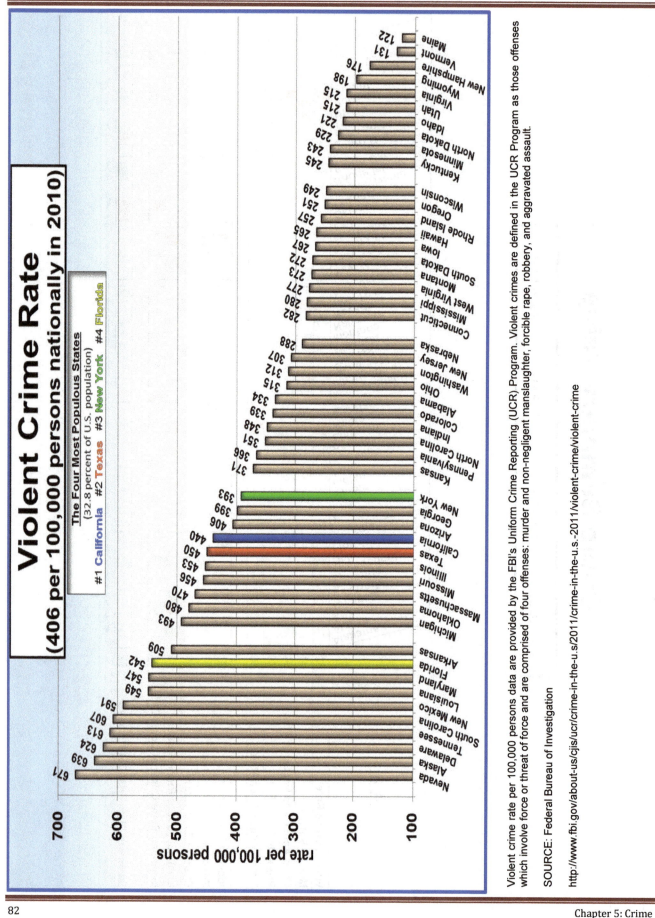

State	rate per 100,000 persons
Nevada	671
Alaska	639
Delaware	624
Tennessee	613
South Carolina	607
New Mexico	591
Louisiana	549
Maryland	547
Florida	542
Arkansas	509
Michigan	493
Oklahoma	480
Massachusetts	470
Missouri	456
Illinois	453
Texas	450
California	440
Arizona	406
Georgia	399
New York	393
Kansas	371
Pennsylvania	366
North Carolina	351
Indiana	348
Colorado	339
Alabama	334
Ohio	315
Washington	312
New Jersey	307
Nebraska	288
Connecticut	282
Mississippi	280
West Virginia	277
Montana	273
South Dakota	272
Iowa	267
Hawaii	265
Rhode Island	257
Oregon	251
Wisconsin	249
Kentucky	245
Minnesota	243
North Dakota	229
Idaho	221
Utah	215
Virginia	215
Wyoming	198
New Hampshire	176
Vermont	131
Maine	122

Violent crime rate per 100,000 persons data are provided by the FBI's Uniform Crime Reporting (UCR) Program. Violent crimes are defined in the UCR Program as those offenses which involve force or threat of force and are comprised of four offenses: murder and non-negligent manslaughter, forcible rape, robbery, and aggravated assault.

SOURCE: Federal Bureau of Investigation

http://www.fbi.gov/about-us/cjis/ucr/crime-in-the-u.s/2011/crime-in-the-u.s.-2011/violent-crime/violent-crime

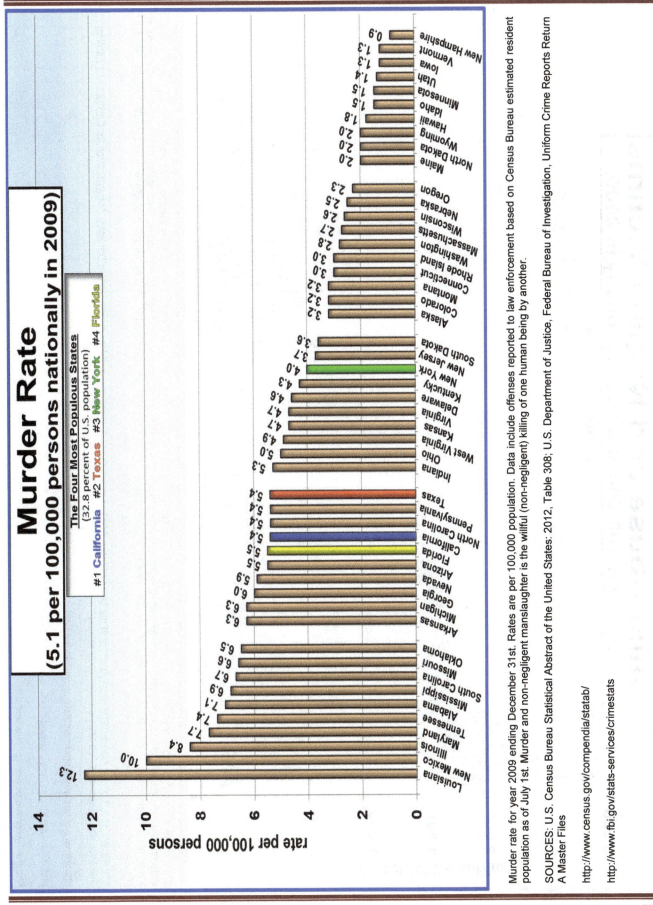

Murder Rate
(5.1 per 100,000 persons nationally in 2009)

The Four Most Populous States
(32.8 percent of U.S. population)
#1 California   #2 Texas   #3 New York   #4 Florida

State	rate per 100,000 persons
Louisiana	12.3
New Mexico	10.0
Illinois	8.4
Maryland	7.7
Tennessee	7.4
Alabama	7.1
Mississippi	6.9
South Carolina	6.7
Missouri	6.6
Oklahoma	6.5
Arkansas	6.3
Michigan	6.3
Georgia	6.0
Nevada	5.9
Arizona	5.5
Florida	5.5
California	5.4
North Carolina	5.4
Pennsylvania	5.4
Texas	5.4
Indiana	5.3
Ohio	5.0
West Virginia	4.9
Kansas	4.7
Virginia	4.7
Delaware	4.6
Kentucky	4.3
New York	4.0
New Jersey	3.7
South Dakota	3.6
Alaska	3.2
Colorado	3.2
Montana	3.2
Connecticut	3.0
Rhode Island	3.0
Washington	2.8
Massachusetts	2.7
Wisconsin	2.6
Nebraska	2.5
Oregon	2.3
Maine	2.0
North Dakota	2.0
Wyoming	2.0
Hawaii	1.8
Idaho	1.5
Minnesota	1.5
Utah	1.4
Iowa	1.3
Vermont	1.3
New Hampshire	0.9

Murder rate for year 2009 ending December 31st. Rates are per 100,000 population. Data include offenses reported to law enforcement based on Census Bureau estimated resident population as of July 1st. Murder and non-negligent manslaughter is the willful (non-negligent) killing of one human being by another.

SOURCES: U.S. Census Bureau Statistical Abstract of the United States: 2012, Table 308; U.S. Department of Justice, Federal Bureau of Investigation, Uniform Crime Reports Return A Master Files

http://www.census.gov/compendia/statab/

http://www.fbi.gov/stats-services/crimestats

Child Abuse and Neglect Victims
(1,010 per 100,000 children nationally in 2009)

The Four Most Populous States
(32.8 percent of U.S. population)
#1 California   #2 Texas   #3 New York   #4 Florida

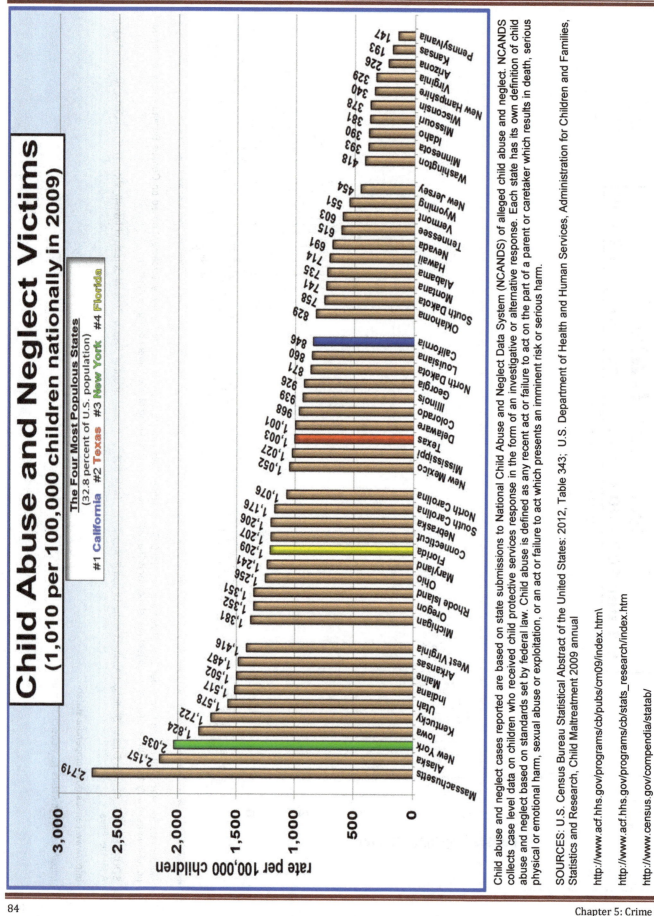

rate per 100,000 children

State	Rate
Massachusetts	2,719
Alaska	2,157
New York	2,035
Iowa	1,824
Kentucky	1,722
Utah	1,578
Indiana	1,517
Maine	1,502
Arkansas	1,487
West Virginia	1,416
Michigan	1,381
Oregon	1,352
Rhode Island	1,351
Ohio	1,256
Maryland	1,241
Florida	1,209
Connecticut	1,207
Nebraska	1,206
South Carolina	1,176
North Carolina	1,076
New Mexico	1,052
Mississippi	1,027
Texas	1,003
Delaware	1,001
Colorado	968
Illinois	939
Georgia	926
North Dakota	871
Louisiana	860
California	846
Oklahoma	829
South Dakota	758
Montana	741
Alabama	735
Hawaii	714
Nevada	691
Tennessee	615
Vermont	603
Wyoming	551
New Jersey	454
Washington	418
Minnesota	393
Idaho	390
Missouri	381
Wisconsin	378
New Hampshire	340
Virginia	329
Arizona	226
Kansas	193
Pennsylvania	147

Child abuse and neglect cases reported are based on state submissions to National Child Abuse and Neglect Data System (NCANDS) of alleged child abuse and neglect. NCANDS collects case level data on children who received child protective services response in the form of an investigative or alternative response. Each state has its own definition of child abuse and neglect based on standards set by federal law. Child abuse is defined as any recent act or failure to act on the part of a parent or caretaker which results in death, serious physical or emotional harm, sexual abuse or exploitation, or an act or failure to act which presents an imminent risk or serious harm.

SOURCES: U.S. Census Bureau Statistical Abstract of the United States: 2012, Table 343; U.S. Department of Health and Human Services, Administration for Children and Families, Statistics and Research, Child Maltreatment 2009 annual

http://www.acf.hhs.gov/programs/cb/pubs/cm09/index.htm\

http://www.acf.hhs.gov/programs/cb/stats_research/index.htm

http://www.census.gov/compendia/statab/

Property Crime Rate
(3,072 per 100,000 persons nationally in 2009)

The Four Most Populous States
(32.8 percent of U.S. population)
#1 California #2 Texas #3 New York #4 Florida

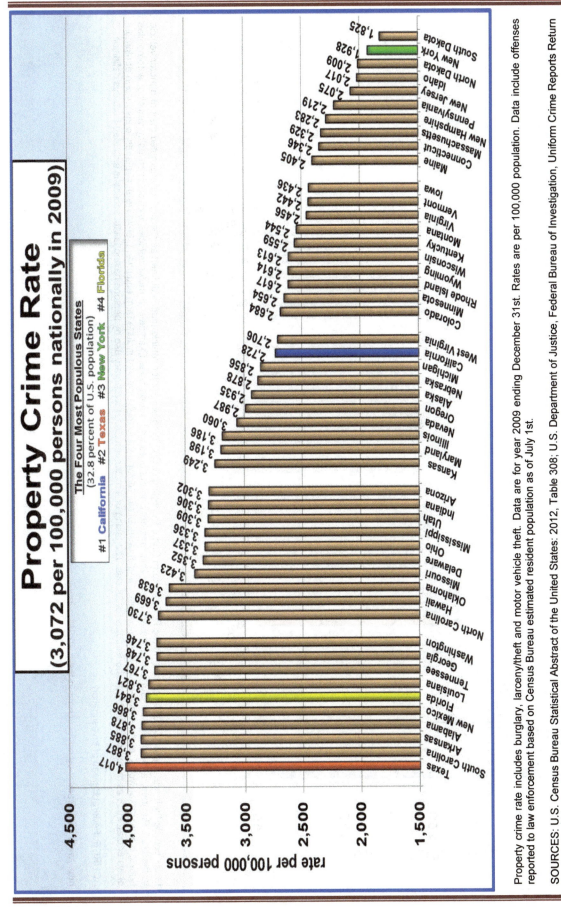

State	Rate
Texas	4,017
South Carolina	3,887
Arkansas	3,885
Alabama	3,878
New Mexico	3,866
Florida	3,841
Louisiana	3,821
Tennessee	3,767
Georgia	3,748
Washington	3,746
North Carolina	3,730
Hawaii	3,669
Oklahoma	3,638
Missouri	3,423
Delaware	3,352
Ohio	3,337
Mississippi	3,336
Utah	3,309
Indiana	3,306
Arizona	3,302
Kansas	3,249
Maryland	3,198
Illinois	3,186
Nevada	3,060
Oregon	2,987
Alaska	2,935
Nebraska	2,878
Michigan	2,856
California	2,728
West Virginia	2,706
Colorado	2,684
Minnesota	2,654
Rhode Island	2,617
Wyoming	2,614
Wisconsin	2,613
Kentucky	2,559
Montana	2,544
Virginia	2,456
Vermont	2,442
Iowa	2,436
Maine	2,405
Connecticut	2,346
Massachusetts	2,329
New Hampshire	2,283
Pennsylvania	2,219
New Jersey	2,075
Idaho	2,017
North Dakota	2,009
New York	1,928
South Dakota	1,825

rate per 100,000 persons

Property crime rate includes burglary, larceny/theft and motor vehicle theft. Data are for year 2009 ending December 31st. Rates are per 100,000 population. Data include offenses reported to law enforcement based on Census Bureau estimated resident population as of July 1st.

SOURCES: U.S. Census Bureau Statistical Abstract of the United States: 2012, Table 308; U.S. Department of Justice, Federal Bureau of Investigation, Uniform Crime Reports Return A Master Files

http://www.census.gov/compendia/statab/

http://www.fbi.gov/stats-services/crimestats

Motor Vehicle Theft Rate
(240 per 100,000 persons nationally in 2010)

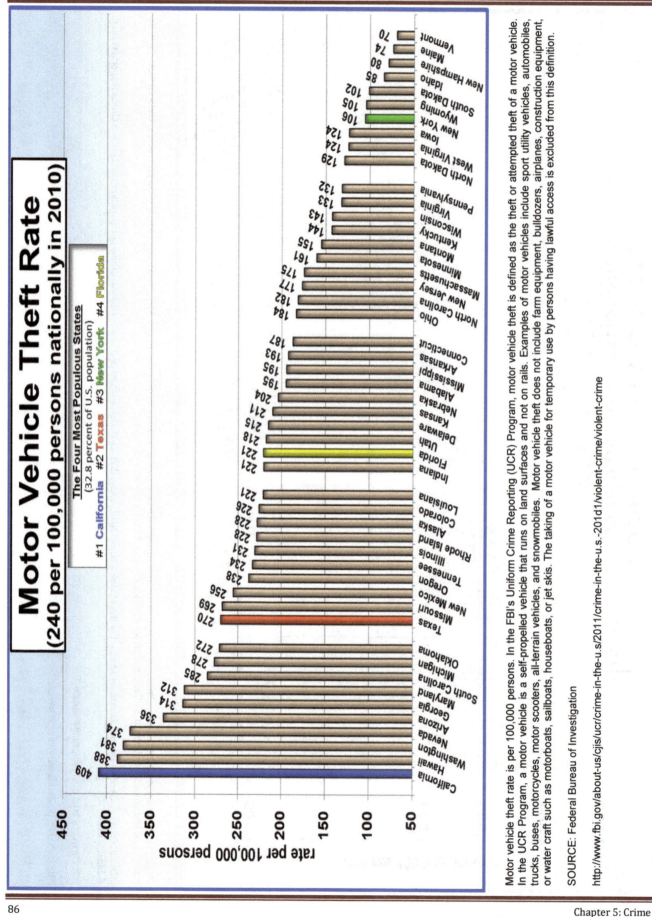

The Four Most Populous States
(32.8 percent of U.S. population)
#1 California   #2 Texas   #3 New York   #4 Florida

State	Rate
California	409
Hawaii	388
Washington	381
Nevada	374
Arizona	336
Georgia	314
Maryland	312
South Carolina	285
Michigan	278
Oklahoma	272
Texas	270
Missouri	269
New Mexico	256
Oregon	238
Tennessee	234
Illinois	231
Rhode Island	228
Alaska	228
Colorado	226
Louisiana	221
Indiana	221
Florida	221
Utah	218
Delaware	215
Kansas	211
Nebraska	204
Alabama	195
Mississippi	195
Arkansas	193
Connecticut	187
Ohio	184
North Carolina	182
New Jersey	177
Massachusetts	175
Minnesota	161
Montana	155
Kentucky	144
Wisconsin	143
Virginia	133
Pennsylvania	132
North Dakota	129
West Virginia	124
Iowa	124
New York	106
Wyoming	105
South Dakota	102
Idaho	85
New Hampshire	80
Maine	74
Vermont	70

rate per 100,000 persons

Motor vehicle theft rate is per 100,000 persons. In the FBI's Uniform Crime Reporting (UCR) Program, motor vehicle theft is defined as the theft or attempted theft of a motor vehicle. In the UCR Program, a motor vehicle is a self-propelled vehicle that runs on land surfaces and not on rails. Examples of motor vehicles include sport utility vehicles, automobiles, trucks, buses, motorcycles, motor scooters, all-terrain vehicles, and snowmobiles. Motor vehicle theft does not include farm equipment, bulldozers, airplanes, construction equipment, or water craft such as motorboats, sailboats, houseboats, or jet skis. The taking of a motor vehicle for temporary use by persons having lawful access is excluded from this definition.

SOURCE: Federal Bureau of Investigation

http://www.fbi.gov/about-us/cjis/ucr/crime-in-the-u.s/2011/crime-in-the-u.s.-201d1/violent-crime/violent-crime

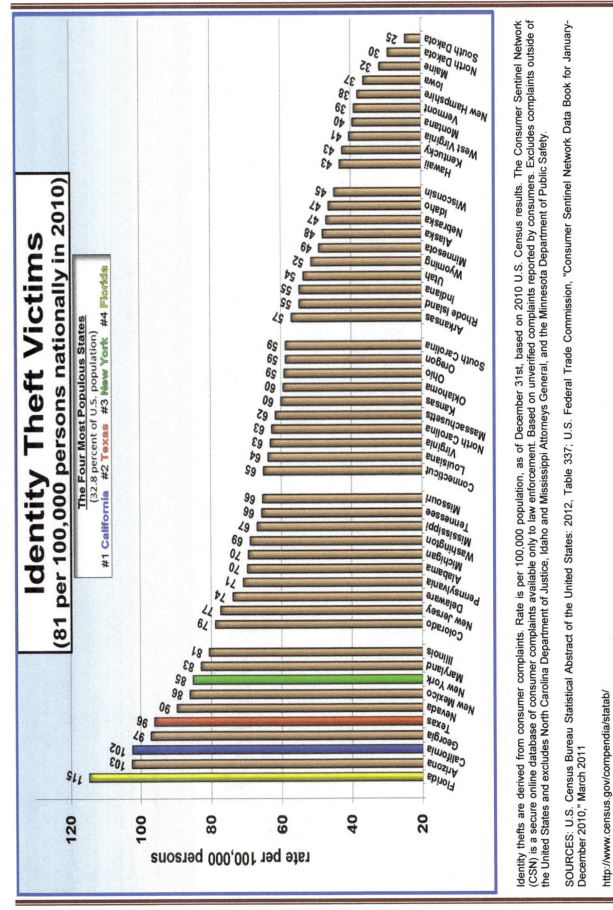

Identity Theft Victims
(81 per 100,000 persons nationally in 2010)

The Four Most Populous States
(32.8 percent of U.S. population)
#1 California #2 Texas #3 New York #4 Florida

rate per 100,000 persons

State	Rate
Florida	115
Arizona	103
California	102
Georgia	97
Texas	96
Nevada	90
New Mexico	86
New York	85
Maryland	83
Illinois	81
Colorado	79
New Jersey	77
Delaware	74
Pennsylvania	71
Alabama	70
Michigan	70
Washington	69
Mississippi	67
Tennessee	66
Missouri	66
Connecticut	65
Louisiana	64
Virginia	63
North Carolina	63
Massachusetts	62
Kansas	60
Oklahoma	60
Ohio	59
Oregon	59
South Carolina	59
Arkansas	57
Rhode Island	55
Indiana	55
Utah	54
Wyoming	52
Minnesota	49
Alaska	48
Nebraska	47
Idaho	47
Wisconsin	45
Hawaii	43
Kentucky	43
West Virginia	41
Montana	40
Vermont	39
New Hampshire	38
Iowa	37
Maine	32
North Dakota	30
South Dakota	25

Identity thefts are derived from consumer complaints. Rate is per 100,000 population, as of December 31st, based on 2010 U.S. Census results. The Consumer Sentinel Network (CSN) is a secure online database of consumer complaints available only to law enforcement. Based on unverified complaints reported by consumers. Excludes complaints outside of the United States and excludes North Carolina Department of Justice, Idaho and Mississippi Attorneys General, and the Minnesota Department of Public Safety.

SOURCES: U.S. Census Bureau Statistical Abstract of the United States: 2012, Table 337; U.S. Federal Trade Commission, "Consumer Sentinel Network Data Book for January-December 2010," March 2011

http://www.census.gov/compendia/statab/

http://www.ftc.gov/sentinel/reports.shtml

Prisoners
(523 per 100,000 persons nationally in 2009)

The Four Most Populous States
(32.8 percent of U.S. population)
#1 California #2 Texas #3 New York #4 Florida

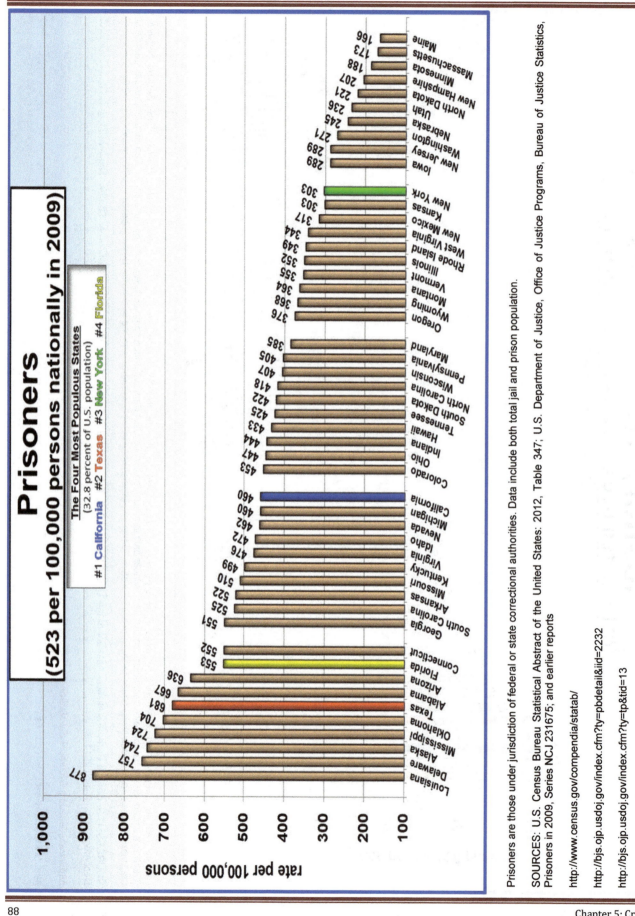

State	rate per 100,000 persons
Louisiana	877
Delaware	757
Alaska	744
Mississippi	724
Oklahoma	704
Texas	681
Alabama	667
Arizona	636
Florida	553
Connecticut	552
Georgia	551
South Carolina	525
Arkansas	522
Missouri	510
Kentucky	499
Virginia	476
Idaho	472
Nevada	462
Michigan	460
California	460
Colorado	453
Ohio	447
Indiana	444
Hawaii	433
Tennessee	425
South Dakota	422
North Carolina	418
Wisconsin	407
Pennsylvania	405
Maryland	385
Oregon	376
Wyoming	368
Montana	364
Vermont	355
Illinois	352
Rhode Island	349
West Virginia	344
New Mexico	317
Kansas	303
New York	303
Iowa	289
New Jersey	289
Washington	271
Nebraska	245
Utah	236
North Dakota	221
New Hampshire	207
Minnesota	188
Massachusetts	173
Maine	166

Prisoners are those under jurisdiction of federal or state correctional authorities. Data include both total jail and prison population.

SOURCES: U.S. Census Bureau Statistical Abstract of the United States: 2012, Table 347; U.S. Department of Justice, Office of Justice Programs, Bureau of Justice Statistics, Prisoners in 2009, Series NCJ 231675; and earlier reports

http://www.census.gov/compendia/statab/

http://bjs.ojp.usdoj.gov/index.cfm?ty=pbdetail&iid=2232

http://bjs.ojp.usdoj.gov/index.cfm?ty=tp&tid=13

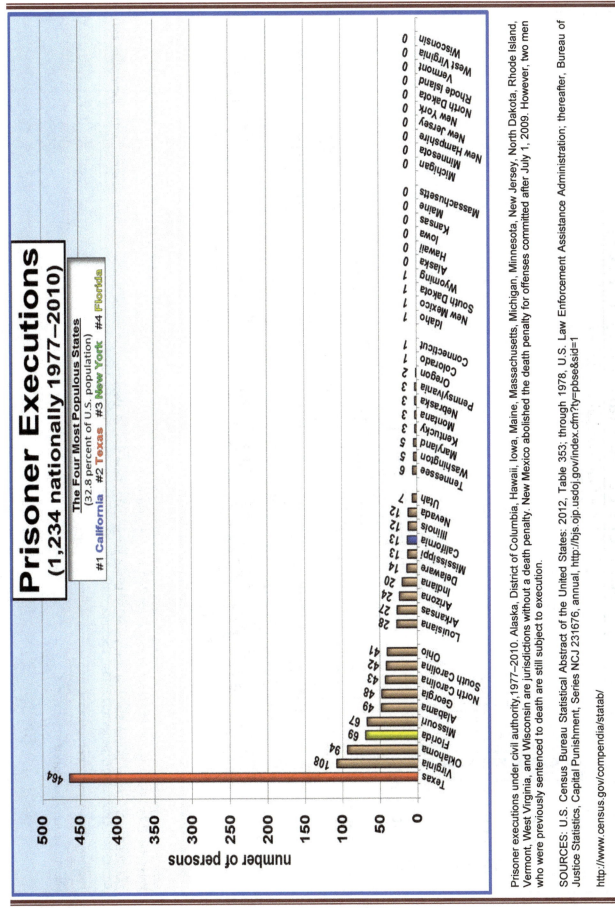

Prisoner Executions
(1,234 nationally 1977–2010)

The Four Most Populous States
(32.8 percent of U.S. population)
#1 California   #2 Texas   #3 New York   #4 Florida

number of persons

Texas	464
Virginia	108
Oklahoma	94
Florida	69
Missouri	67
Alabama	49
Georgia	48
North Carolina	43
South Carolina	42
Ohio	41
Louisiana	28
Arkansas	27
Arizona	24
Indiana	20
Delaware	14
Mississippi	13
California	13
Illinois	12
Nevada	12
Utah	7
Tennessee	6
Washington	5
Maryland	5
Kentucky	3
Montana	3
Nebraska	3
Pennsylvania	3
Oregon	2
Colorado	1
Connecticut	1
Idaho	1
New Mexico	1
South Dakota	1
Wyoming	1
Alaska	0
Hawaii	0
Iowa	0
Kansas	0
Maine	0
Massachusetts	0
Michigan	0
Minnesota	0
New Hampshire	0
New Jersey	0
New York	0
North Dakota	0
Rhode Island	0
Vermont	0
West Virginia	0
Wisconsin	0

Prisoner executions under civil authority,1977–2010. Alaska, District of Columbia, Hawaii, Iowa, Maine, Massachusetts, Michigan, Minnesota, New Jersey, North Dakota, Rhode Island, Vermont, West Virginia, and Wisconsin are jurisdictions without a death penalty. New Mexico abolished the death penalty for offenses committed after July 1, 2009. However, two men who were previously sentenced to death are still subject to execution.

SOURCES: U.S. Census Bureau Statistical Abstract of the United States: 2012, Table 353; through 1978, U.S. Law Enforcement Assistance Administration; thereafter, Bureau of Justice Statistics, Capital Punishment, Series NCJ 231676, annual, http://bjs.ojp.usdoj.gov/index.cfm?ty=pbse&sid=1

http://www.census.gov/compendia/statab/

http://bjs.gov/index.cfm?ty=pbdetail&iid=2215

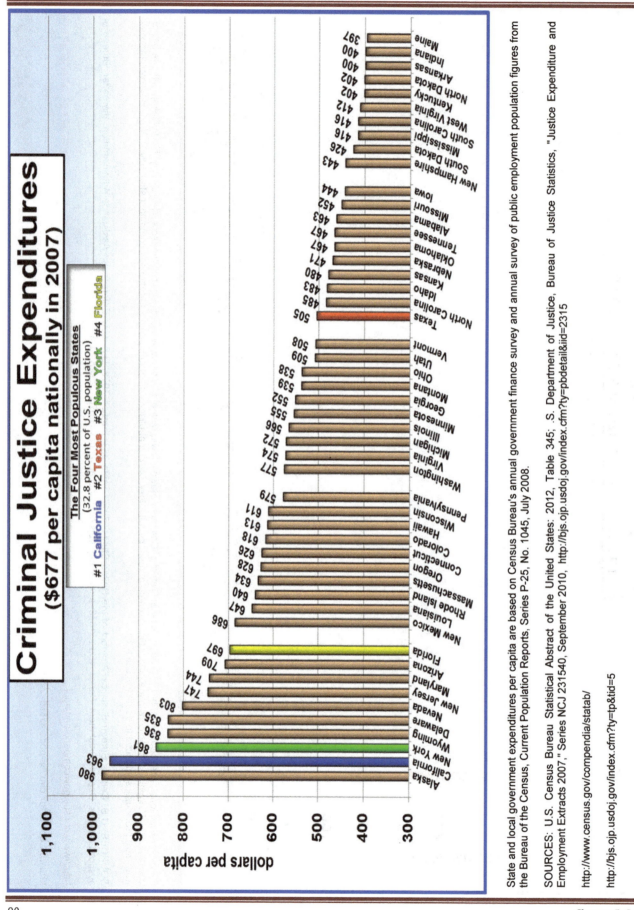

Criminal Justice Expenditures
($677 per capita nationally in 2007)

The Four Most Populous States
(32.8 percent of U.S. population)
#1 California   #2 Texas   #3 New York   #4 Florida

State	dollars per capita
Alaska	980
California	963
New York	861
Wyoming	836
Delaware	835
Nevada	803
New Jersey	747
Maryland	744
Arizona	709
Florida	697
New Mexico	686
Louisiana	647
Rhode Island	640
Massachusetts	634
Oregon	628
Connecticut	626
Colorado	618
Hawaii	613
Wisconsin	611
Pennsylvania	579
Washington	577
Virginia	574
Michigan	572
Illinois	566
Minnesota	555
Georgia	552
Montana	539
Ohio	538
Utah	509
Vermont	508
Texas	505
North Carolina	485
Idaho	483
Kansas	480
Nebraska	471
Oklahoma	467
Tennessee	467
Alabama	463
Missouri	452
Iowa	444
New Hampshire	443
South Dakota	426
Mississippi	416
South Carolina	416
West Virginia	412
Kentucky	402
North Dakota	402
Arkansas	400
Indiana	400
Maine	397

State and local government expenditures per capita are based on Census Bureau's annual government finance survey and annual survey of public employment population figures from the Bureau of the Census, Current Population Reports, Series P-25, No. 1045, July 2008.

SOURCES: U.S. Census Bureau Statistical Abstract of the United States: 2012, Table 345; S. Department of Justice, Bureau of Justice Statistics, "Justice Expenditure and Employment Extracts 2007," Series NCJ 231540, September 2010, http://bjs.ojp.usdoj.gov/index.cfm?ty=pbdetail&iid=2315

http://www.census.gov/compendia/statab/

http://bjs.ojp.usdoj.gov/index.cfm?ty=tp&tid=5

Incoming State Criminal Court Cases
(6,887 per 100,000 persons nationally in 2009)

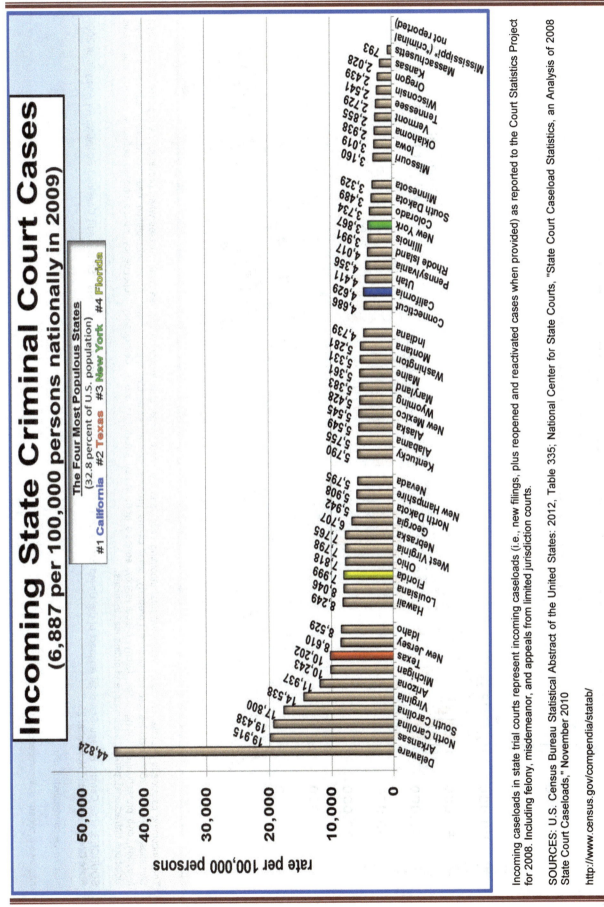

The Four Most Populous States
(32.8 percent of U.S. population)
#1 California   #2 Texas   #3 New York   #4 Florida

rate per 100,000 persons

State	Rate
Delaware	44,824
Arkansas	19,915
North Carolina	19,438
South Carolina	17,800
Virginia	14,538
Arizona	11,937
Michigan	10,243
Texas	10,202
New Jersey	8,610
Idaho	8,529
Hawaii	8,249
Louisiana	8,046
Florida	7,999
Ohio	7,818
West Virginia	7,798
Nebraska	7,765
Georgia	6,707
North Dakota	5,942
New Hampshire	5,908
Nevada	5,795
Kentucky	5,790
Alabama	5,755
Alaska	5,549
New Mexico	5,545
Wyoming	5,428
Maryland	5,383
Maine	5,361
Washington	5,331
Montana	5,281
Indiana	4,739
Connecticut	4,686
California	4,629
Utah	4,411
Pennsylvania	4,356
Rhode Island	4,017
Illinois	3,991
New York	3,867
Colorado	3,734
South Dakota	3,489
Minnesota	3,329
Missouri	3,160
Iowa	3,019
Oklahoma	2,938
Vermont	2,855
Tennessee	2,729
Wisconsin	2,541
Oregon	2,439
Kansas	2,028
Massachusetts	793
Mississippi: ("criminal not reported)	

Incoming caseloads in state trial courts represent incoming caseloads (i.e., new filings, plus reopened and reactivated cases when provided) as reported to the Court Statistics Project for 2008. Including felony, misdemeanor, and appeals from limited jurisdiction courts.

SOURCES: U.S. Census Bureau Statistical Abstract of the United States: 2012, Table 335; National Center for State Courts, "State Court Caseload Statistics, an Analysis of 2008 State Court Caseloads," November 2010

http://www.census.gov/compendia/statab/

http://www.courtstatistics.org

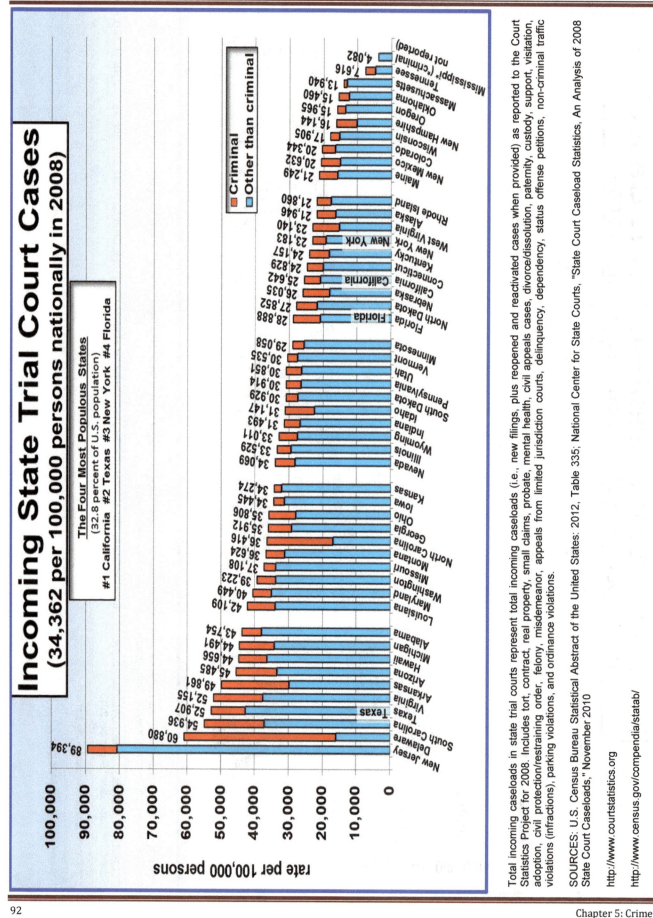

Incoming State Trial Court Cases
(34,362 per 100,000 persons nationally in 2008)

The Four Most Populous States
(32.8 percent of U.S. population)
#1 California #2 Texas #3 New York #4 Florida

Legend: ■ Criminal ■ Other than criminal

rate per 100,000 persons

New Jersey	89,394
Delaware	60,880
South Carolina	54,936
Texas	52,907
Virginia	52,155
Arkansas	49,861
Arizona	45,485
Hawaii	44,656
Michigan	44,491
Alabama	43,754
Louisiana	42,109
Maryland	40,449
Washington	39,223
Missouri	37,108
Montana	36,624
North Carolina	36,416
Georgia	35,912
Ohio	35,806
Iowa	34,445
Kansas	34,274
Nevada	34,069
Illinois	33,529
Wyoming	33,011
Indiana	31,493
Idaho	31,147
South Dakota	30,929
Pennsylvania	30,914
Utah	30,851
Vermont	30,535
Minnesota	29,058
Florida	28,888
North Dakota	27,852
Nebraska	26,035
California	25,642
Connecticut	24,829
Kentucky	24,157
New York	23,183
West Virginia	23,140
Alaska	21,946
Rhode Island	21,860
Maine	21,249
New Mexico	20,632
Colorado	20,344
Wisconsin	17,905
New Hampshire	16,144
Oregon	15,965
Oklahoma	15,460
Massachusetts	13,940
Tennessee	7,616
Mississippi ("criminal" not reported)	4,082

Total incoming caseloads in state trial courts represent total incoming caseloads (i.e., new filings, plus reopened and reactivated cases when provided) as reported to the Court Statistics Project for 2008. Includes tort, contract, real property, small claims, probate, mental health, civil appeals cases, divorce/dissolution, paternity, custody, support, visitation, adoption, civil protection/restraining order, felony, misdemeanor, appeals from limited jurisdiction courts, delinquency, dependency, status offense petitions, non-criminal traffic violations (infractions), parking violations, and ordinance violations.

SOURCES: U.S. Census Bureau Statistical Abstract of the United States: 2012, Table 335; National Center for State Courts, "State Court Caseload Statistics, An Analysis of 2008 State Court Caseloads," November 2010

http://www.courtstatistics.org

http://www.census.gov/compendia/statab/

Chapter 6: Environment Overview

Texas averaged 3.6 major disasters each year over the past sixty years, the highest number in the nation. Meanwhile, Rhode Island averaged only one every 6.7 years. Texas also experienced the highest number of wildfire declarations in this period—two per year—whereas 22 states declared none. Major disasters and fire emergency declarations are those officially declared by the President of the United States in accordance with federal law under the Stafford Act.

Texas and California ranked highest for the most flood disasters over the past sixty years, averaging one every 15 months. Both Texas and Florida experienced the highest number of storm disasters—averaging one every 15 months—while 7 states declared none over the same period. Texas and Arizona had the hottest summers, averaging 83 degrees Fahrenheit compared with Alaska which had the coldest at 54 degrees. Texas emitted 11.7 percent of the nations' carbon dioxide, the highest percentage. Vermont emitted .01 percent, the least of any state.

Alaska released the most toxic chemicals—3.5 times as much as Texas, the second highest emitter. Alaska recorded the lowest air temperature since 1885 at 80 degrees Fahrenheit below zero while the highest was 134 degrees in California.

Both Alaska and North Dakota have the coldest winters, averaging 12 degrees Fahrenheit, whereas Hawaii has the hottest, averaging 72 degrees. Hawaii also has the largest annual rainfall while Alaska has the largest annual frozen precipitation. Juneau, Alaska has the most cloudy days and the highest relative humidity while Phoenix, Arizona has the least. However, Arizona has the worst air quality while Montana has the best.

California experienced the most earthquake major disaster declarations over the past sixty years, averaging one every five years, whereas 41 states declared none. Los Angeles, California had the lowest total degree days while Duluth, Minnesota had the highest. Total degree days provides a relative measure of the annual energy requirement to heat and cool to 65 degrees Fahrenheit, calculated by adding the difference in degrees, between the average daily temperature and 65 degrees—whether above or below—for each day during a 365 day period.

~

Environment Summary Table

States Legend: ■ Highest 10% □ Middle 80% ■ Lowest 10%

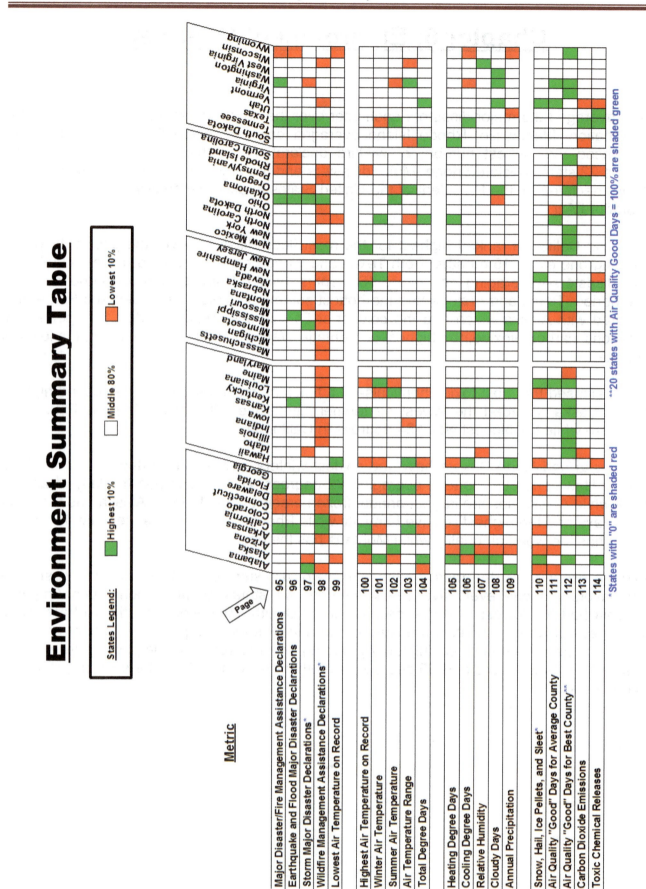

Metric	Page
Major Disaster/Fire Management Assistance Declarations	95
Earthquake and Flood Major Disaster Declarations	96
Storm Major Disaster Declarations*	97
Wildfire Management Assistance Declarations*	98
Lowest Air Temperature on Record	99
Highest Air Temperature on Record	100
Winter Air Temperature	101
Summer Air Temperature	102
Air Temperature Range	103
Total Degree Days	104
Heating Degree Days	105
Cooling Degree Days	106
Relative Humidity	107
Cloudy Days	108
Annual Precipitation	109
Snow, Hail, Ice Pellets, and Sleet*	110
Air Quality "Good" Days for Average County	111
Air Quality "Good" Days for Best County**	112
Carbon Dioxide Emissions	113
Toxic Chemical Releases	114

*States with "0" are shaded red

**20 states with Air Quality Good Days = 100% are shaded green

Major Disaster/Fire Management Assistance Declarations

(2,588 nationally, 1953–2012)

The Four Most Populous States
(32.8 percent of U.S. population)
#1 California   #2 Texas   #3 New York   #4 Florida

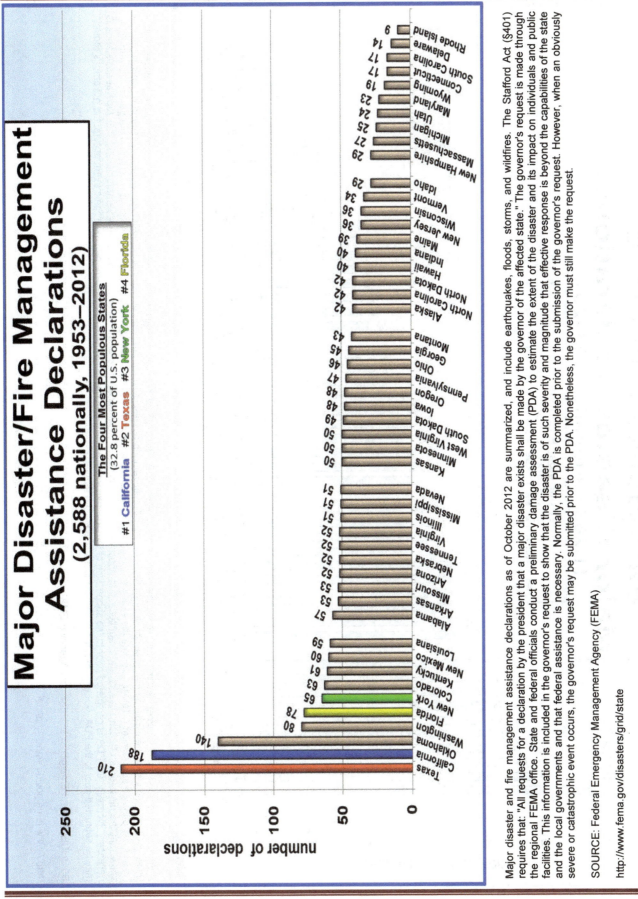

number of declarations

Texas	210
California	188
Oklahoma	140
Washington	80
Florida	78
New York	65
Colorado	63
Kentucky	61
New Mexico	60
Louisiana	59
Alabama	57
Arkansas	53
Missouri	53
Arizona	52
Nebraska	52
Tennessee	52
Virginia	52
Illinois	51
Mississippi	51
Nevada	51
Kansas	50
Minnesota	50
West Virginia	50
South Dakota	49
Iowa	48
Oregon	48
Pennsylvania	47
Ohio	46
Georgia	45
Montana	43
Alaska	42
North Carolina	42
North Dakota	42
Hawaii	40
Indiana	40
Maine	39
New Jersey	36
Wisconsin	36
Vermont	34
Idaho	29
New Hampshire	29
Massachusetts	27
Michigan	25
Utah	24
Maryland	23
Wyoming	19
Connecticut	17
South Carolina	17
Delaware	14
Rhode Island	9

Major disaster and fire management assistance declarations as of October 2012 are summarized, and include earthquakes, floods, storms, and wildfires. The Stafford Act (§401) requires that: "All requests for a declaration by the president that a major disaster exists shall be made by the governor of the affected state." The governor's request is made through the regional FEMA office. State and federal officials conduct a preliminary damage assessment (PDA) to estimate the extent of the disaster and its impact on individuals and public facilities. This information is included in the governor's request to show that the disaster is of such severity and magnitude that effective response is beyond the capabilities of the state and the local governments and that federal assistance is necessary. Normally, the PDA is completed prior to the submission of the governor's request. However, when an obviously severe or catastrophic event occurs, the governor's request may be submitted prior to the PDA. Nonetheless, the governor must still make the request.

SOURCE: Federal Emergency Management Agency (FEMA)

http://www.fema.gov/disasters/grid/state

Earthquake and Flood Major Disaster Declarations

(1,266 nationally, 1953–2012)

The Four Most Populous States
(32.8 percent of U.S. population)
#1 California #2 Texas #3 New York #4 Florida

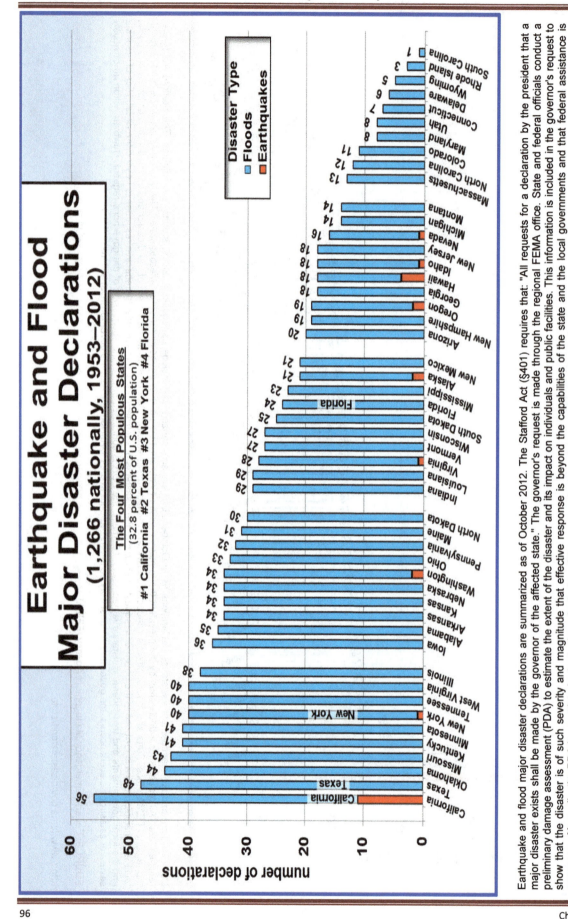

Disaster Type
- Floods
- Earthquakes

number of declarations

California	56
Texas	48
Oklahoma	44
Missouri	43
Kentucky	41
Minnesota	41
New York	40
Tennessee	40
West Virginia	40
Illinois	38
Iowa	36
Alabama	35
Arkansas	34
Kansas	34
Nebraska	34
Washington	34
Ohio	33
Pennsylvania	32
Maine	31
North Dakota	30
Indiana	29
Louisiana	29
Virginia	28
Vermont	27
Wisconsin	27
South Dakota	25
Florida	24
Mississippi	23
Alaska	21
New Mexico	21
Arizona	20
New Hampshire	19
Oregon	19
Georgia	18
Hawaii	18
Idaho	18
New Jersey	18
Nevada	16
Michigan	14
Montana	14
Massachusetts	13
North Carolina	12
Colorado	11
Maryland	8
Utah	8
Connecticut	7
Delaware	6
Wyoming	5
Rhode Island	3
South Carolina	1

Earthquake and flood major disaster declarations are summarized as of October 2012. The Stafford Act (§401) requires that: "All requests for a declaration by the president that a major disaster exists shall be made by the governor of the affected state." The governor's request is made through the regional FEMA office. State and federal officials conduct a preliminary damage assessment (PDA) to estimate the extent of the disaster and its impact on individuals and public facilities. This information is included in the governor's request to show that the disaster is of such severity and magnitude that effective response is beyond the capabilities of the state and the local governments and that federal assistance is necessary. Normally, the PDA is completed prior to the submission of the governor's request. However, when an obviously severe or catastrophic event occurs, the governor's request may be submitted prior to the PDA. Nonetheless, the governor must still make the request.

SOURCE: Federal Emergency Management Agency (FEMA)

http://www.fema.gov/disasters/grid/state

Storm Major Disaster Declarations
(637 nationally, 1953–2012)

The Four Most Populous States
(32.8 percent of U.S. population)
#1 California #2 Texas #3 New York #4 Florida

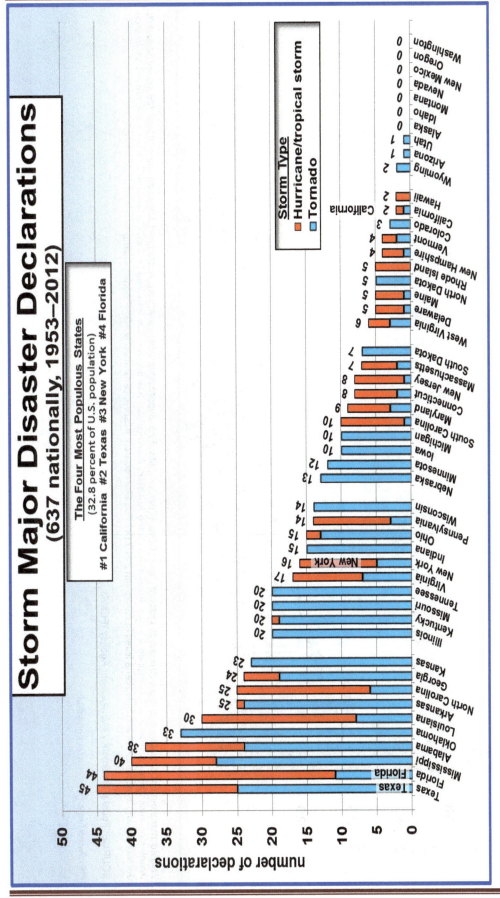

Storm Type
- Hurricane/tropical storm
- Tornado

number of declarations

Major disaster declarations due to storms are summarized as of October 2012. The Stafford Act (§401) requires that: "All requests for a declaration by the president that a major disaster exists shall be made by the governor of the affected state." The governor's request is made through the regional FEMA office. State and federal officials conduct a preliminary damage assessment (PDA) to estimate the extent of the disaster and its impact on individuals and public facilities. This information is included in the governor's request to show that the disaster is of such severity and magnitude that effective response is beyond the capabilities of the state and the local governments and that federal assistance is necessary. Normally, the PDA is completed prior to the submission of the governor's request. However, when an obviously severe or catastrophic event occurs, the governor's request may be submitted prior to the PDA. Nonetheless, the governor must still make the request.

SOURCE: Federal Emergency Management Agency (FEMA)

http://www.fema.gov/disasters/grid/state

Wildfire Management Assistance Declarations
(630 nationally, 1953–2012)

The Four Most Populous States
(32.8 percent of U.S. population)
#1 California #2 Texas #3 New York #4 Florida

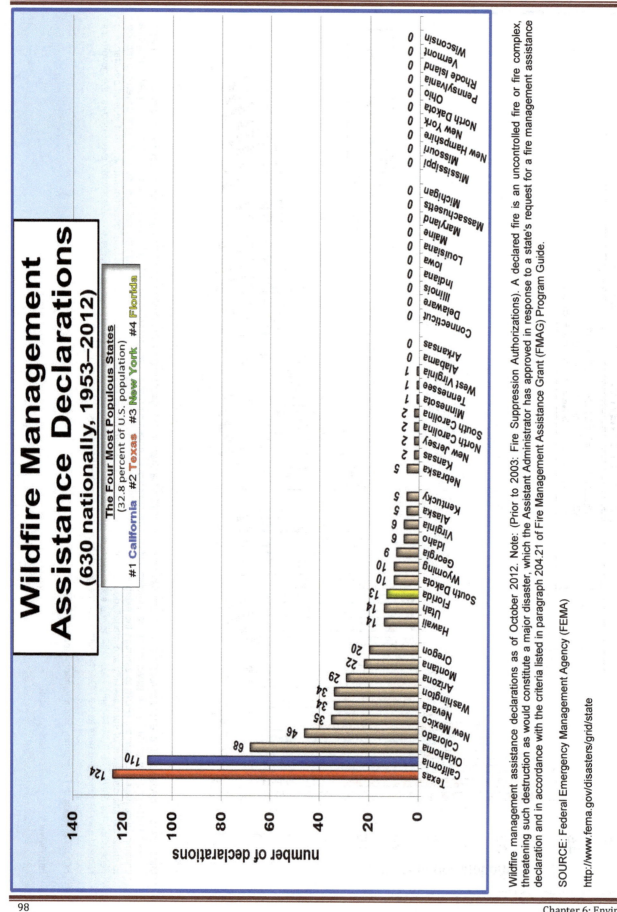

number of declarations

State	Declarations
Texas	124
California	110
Oklahoma	68
Colorado	46
New Mexico	35
Nevada	34
Washington	34
Arizona	29
Montana	22
Oregon	20
Hawaii	14
Utah	14
Florida	13
South Dakota	10
Wyoming	10
Georgia	9
Idaho	9
Virginia	9
Alaska	5
Kentucky	5
Nebraska	5
Kansas	2
New Jersey	2
North Carolina	2
South Carolina	2
Minnesota	1
Tennessee	1
West Virginia	1
Alabama	0
Arkansas	0
Connecticut	0
Delaware	0
Illinois	0
Indiana	0
Iowa	0
Louisiana	0
Maine	0
Maryland	0
Massachusetts	0
Michigan	0
Mississippi	0
Missouri	0
New Hampshire	0
New York	0
North Dakota	0
Ohio	0
Pennsylvania	0
Rhode Island	0
Vermont	0
Wisconsin	0

Wildfire management assistance declarations as of October 2012. Note: (Prior to 2003: Fire Suppression Authorizations). A declared fire is an uncontrolled fire or fire complex, threatening such destruction as would constitute a major disaster, which the Assistant Administrator has approved in response to a state's request for a fire management assistance declaration and in accordance with the criteria listed in paragraph 204.21 of Fire Management Assistance Grant (FMAG) Program Guide.

SOURCE: Federal Emergency Management Agency (FEMA)

http://www.fema.gov/disasters/grid/state

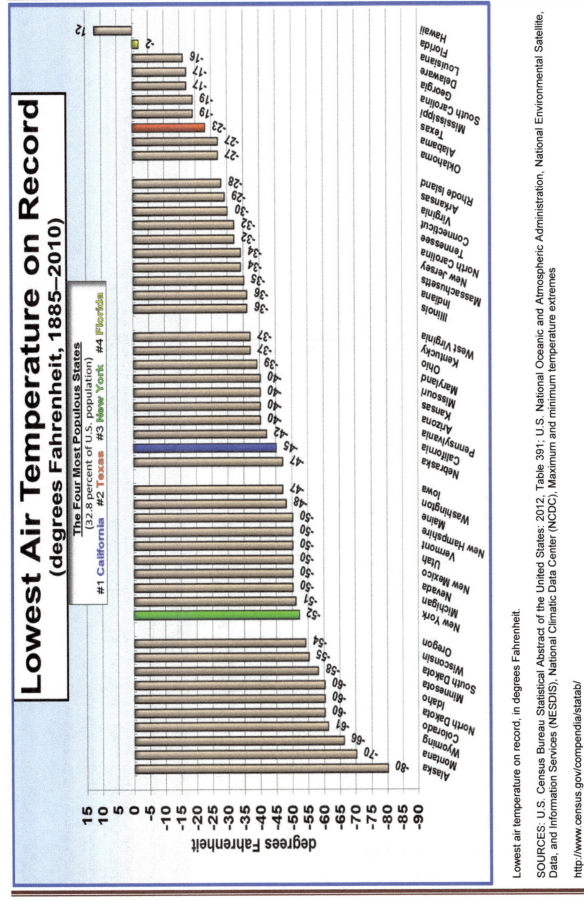

Lowest Air Temperature on Record
(degrees Fahrenheit, 1885–2010)

The Four Most Populous States
(32.8 percent of U.S. population)
#1 California   #2 Texas   #3 New York   #4 Florida

Lowest air temperature on record, in degrees Fahrenheit.

SOURCES: U.S. Census Bureau Statistical Abstract of the United States: 2012, Table 391; U.S. National Oceanic and Atmospheric Administration, National Environmental Satellite, Data, and Information Services (NESDIS), National Climatic Data Center (NCDC), Maximum and minimum temperature extremes

http://www.census.gov/compendia/statab/

http://www.ncdc.noaa.gov/extremes/scec/searchrecs.php

Highest Air Temperature on Record
(degrees Fahrenheit, 1885–2010)

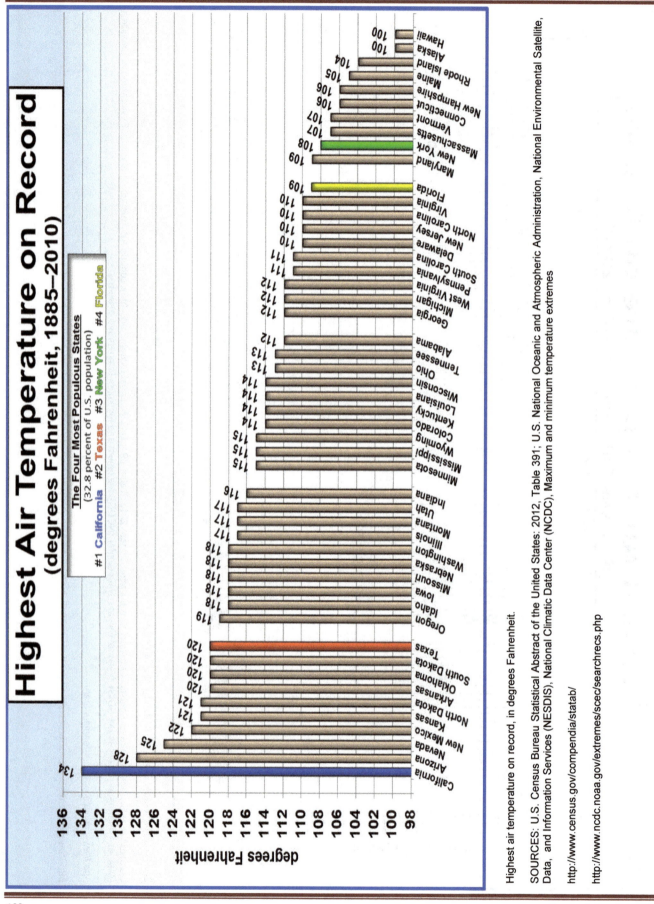

The Four Most Populous States
(32.8 percent of U.S. population)
#1 California #2 Texas #3 New York #4 Florida

State	°F
California	134
Arizona	128
Nevada	125
New Mexico	122
Kansas	121
North Dakota	121
Arkansas	120
Oklahoma	120
South Dakota	120
Texas	120
Oregon	119
Idaho	118
Iowa	118
Missouri	118
Nebraska	118
Washington	118
Illinois	117
Montana	117
Utah	117
Indiana	116
Minnesota	115
Mississippi	115
Wyoming	115
Colorado	114
Kentucky	114
Louisiana	114
Wisconsin	114
Ohio	113
Tennessee	113
Alabama	112
Georgia	112
Michigan	112
West Virginia	112
Pennsylvania	111
South Carolina	111
Delaware	110
New Jersey	110
North Carolina	110
Virginia	110
Florida	109
Maryland	109
New York	108
Massachusetts	107
Vermont	107
Connecticut	106
New Hampshire	106
Maine	105
Rhode Island	104
Alaska	100
Hawaii	100

degrees Fahrenheit

Highest air temperature on record, in degrees Fahrenheit.

SOURCES: U.S. Census Bureau Statistical Abstract of the United States: 2012, Table 391; U.S. National Oceanic and Atmospheric Administration, National Environmental Satellite, Data, and Information Services (NESDIS), National Climatic Data Center (NCDC), Maximum and minimum temperature extremes

http://www.census.gov/compendia/statab/

http://www.ncdc.noaa.gov/extremes/scec/searchrecs.php

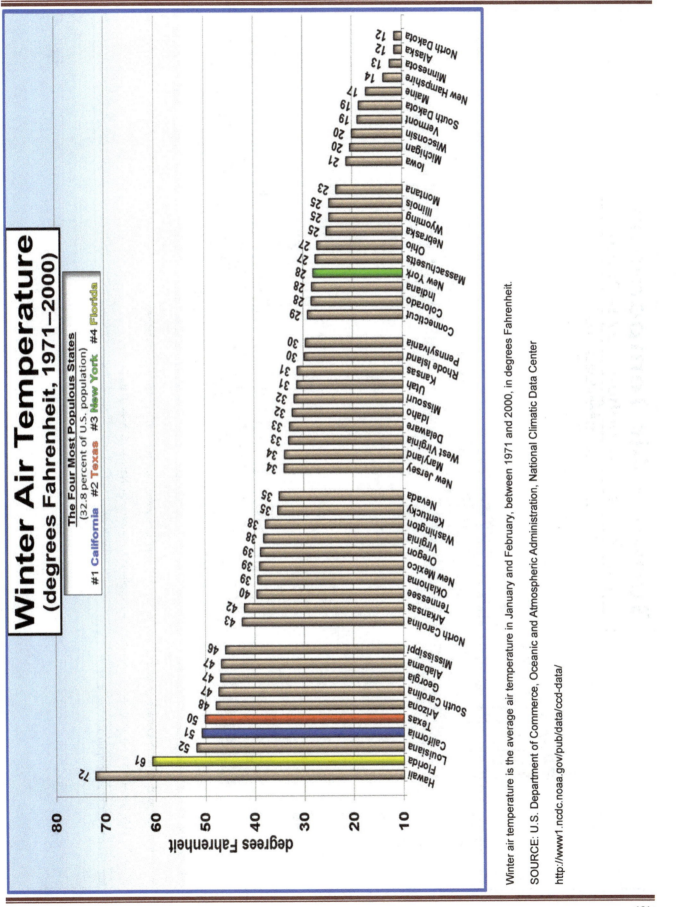

Winter Air Temperature
(degrees Fahrenheit, 1971–2000)

The Four Most Populous States
(32.8 percent of U.S. population)

#1 California   #2 Texas   #3 New York   #4 Florida

State	degrees Fahrenheit
Hawaii	72
Florida	61
Louisiana	52
California	51
Texas	50
Arizona	48
South Carolina	47
Georgia	47
Alabama	47
Mississippi	46
North Carolina	43
Arkansas	42
Tennessee	40
Oklahoma	39
New Mexico	39
Oregon	39
Virginia	38
Washington	38
Kentucky	35
Nevada	35
New Jersey	34
Maryland	34
West Virginia	33
Delaware	33
Idaho	32
Missouri	32
Utah	31
Kansas	31
Rhode Island	30
Pennsylvania	30
Connecticut	29
Colorado	28
Indiana	28
New York	28
Massachusetts	27
Ohio	27
Nebraska	25
Wyoming	25
Illinois	25
Montana	23
Iowa	21
Michigan	20
Wisconsin	20
Vermont	19
South Dakota	19
Maine	17
New Hampshire	14
Minnesota	13
Alaska	12
North Dakota	12

Winter air temperature is the average air temperature in January and February, between 1971 and 2000, in degrees Fahrenheit.

SOURCE: U.S. Department of Commerce, Oceanic and Atmospheric Administration, National Climatic Data Center

http://www1.ncdc.noaa.gov/pub/data/ccd-data/

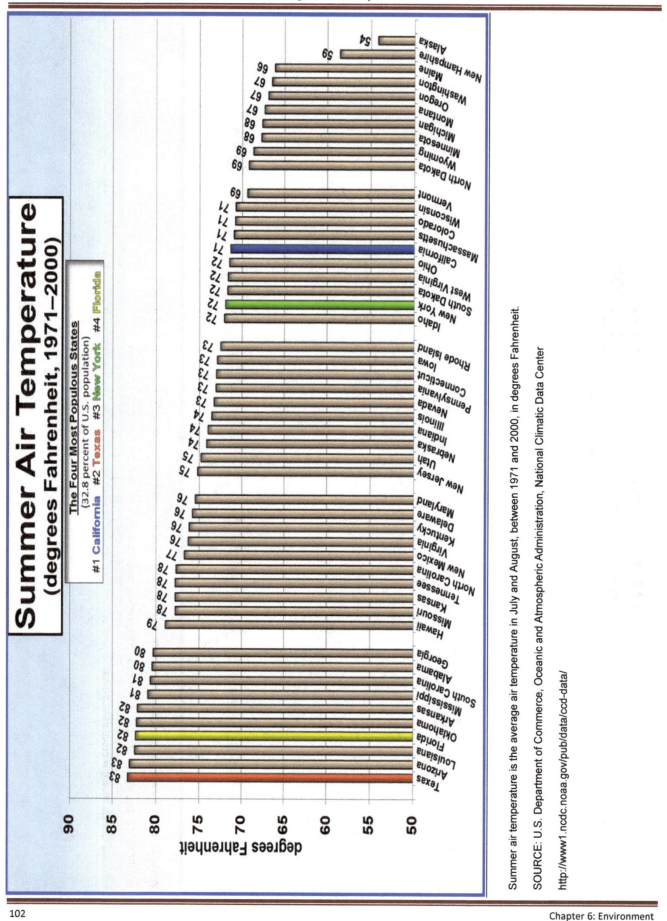

Summer Air Temperature
(degrees Fahrenheit, 1971–2000)

The Four Most Populous States
(32.8 percent of U.S. population)
#1 California #2 Texas #3 New York #4 Florida

State	degrees Fahrenheit
Texas	83
Arizona	83
Louisiana	82
Florida	82
Oklahoma	82
Arkansas	82
Mississippi	81
South Carolina	81
Alabama	80
Georgia	80
Hawaii	79
Missouri	78
Kansas	78
Tennessee	78
North Carolina	77
New Mexico	76
Virginia	76
Kentucky	76
Delaware	76
Maryland	76
New Jersey	75
Utah	75
Nebraska	74
Indiana	74
Illinois	74
Nevada	73
Pennsylvania	73
Connecticut	73
Iowa	73
Rhode Island	73
Idaho	72
New York	72
South Dakota	72
West Virginia	72
Ohio	72
California	71
Massachusetts	71
Colorado	71
Wisconsin	71
Vermont	69
North Dakota	69
Wyoming	69
Minnesota	68
Michigan	68
Montana	67
Oregon	67
Washington	67
Maine	66
New Hampshire	59
Alaska	54

Summer air temperature is the average air temperature in July and August, between 1971 and 2000, in degrees Fahrenheit.

SOURCE: U.S. Department of Commerce, Oceanic and Atmospheric Administration, National Climatic Data Center

http://www1.ncdc.noaa.gov/pub/data/ccd-data/

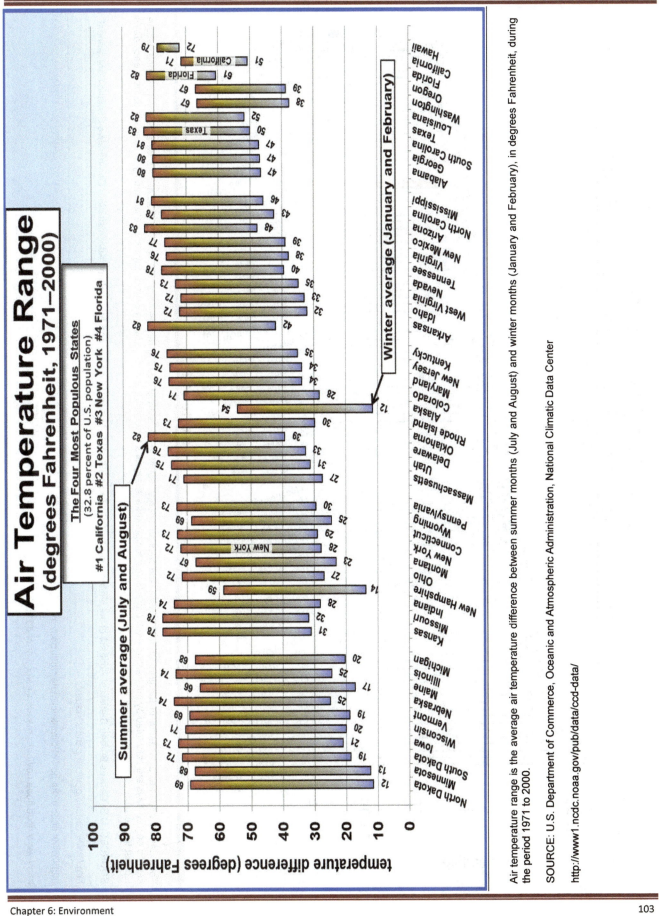

Air Temperature Range
(degrees Fahrenheit, 1971–2000)

The Four Most Populous States
(32.8 percent of U.S. population)
#1 California #2 Texas #3 New York #4 Florida

Summer average (July and August)

Winter average (January and February)

Air temperature range is the average air temperature difference between summer months (July and August) and winter months (January and February), in degrees Fahrenheit, during the period 1971 to 2000.

SOURCE: U.S. Department of Commerce, Oceanic and Atmospheric Administration, National Climatic Data Center

http://www1.ncdc.noaa.gov/pub/data/ccd-data/

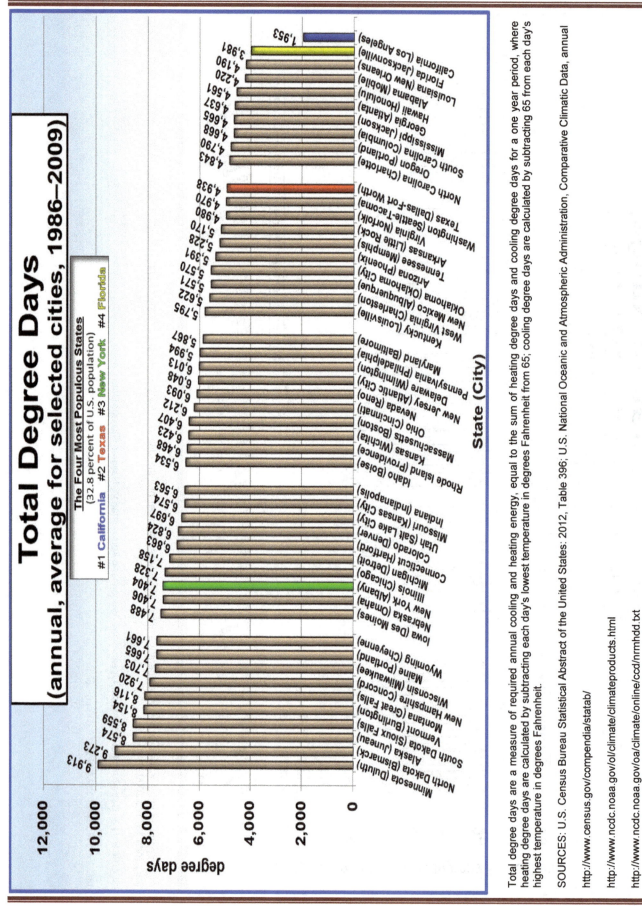

Total Degree Days
(annual, average for selected cities, 1986–2009)

The Four Most Populous States
(32.8 percent of U.S. population)
#1 California   #2 Texas   #3 New York   #4 Florida

State (City)	degree days
California (Los Angeles)	1,953
Florida (Jacksonville)	3,981
Louisiana (New Orleans)	4,190
Alabama (Mobile)	4,220
Hawaii (Honolulu)	4,561
Georgia (Atlanta)	4,637
Mississippi (Jackson)	4,665
South Carolina (Columbia)	4,668
Oregon (Portland)	4,790
North Carolina (Charlotte)	4,843
Texas (Dallas-Fort Worth)	4,938
Washington (Seattle-Tacoma)	4,970
Virginia (Norfolk)	4,980
Arkansas (Little Rock)	5,170
Tennessee (Memphis)	5,228
Arizona (Phoenix)	5,391
Oklahoma (Oklahoma City)	5,570
New Mexico (Albuquerque)	5,571
West Virginia (Charleston)	5,622
Kentucky (Louisville)	5,795
Maryland (Baltimore)	5,887
Pennsylvania (Philadelphia)	5,994
Delaware (Wilmington)	6,013
New Jersey (Atlantic City)	6,048
Nevada (Reno)	6,093
Ohio (Cincinnati)	6,212
Massachusetts (Boston)	6,407
Kansas (Wichita)	6,423
Rhode Island (Providence)	6,468
Idaho (Boise)	6,534
Indiana (Indianapolis)	6,563
Missouri (Kansas City)	6,574
Utah (Salt Lake City)	6,697
Colorado (Denver)	6,824
Connecticut (Hartford)	6,863
Michigan (Detroit)	7,158
Illinois (Chicago)	7,328
New York (Albany)	7,404
Nebraska (Omaha)	7,406
Iowa (Des Moines)	7,488
Wyoming (Cheyenne)	7,661
Maine (Portland)	7,665
Wisconsin (Milwaukee)	7,703
New Hampshire (Concord)	7,920
Montana (Great Falls)	8,116
Vermont (Burlington)	8,154
South Dakota (Sioux Falls)	8,559
Alaska (Juneau)	8,574
North Dakota (Bismarck)	9,273
Minnesota (Duluth)	9,913

Total degree days are a measure of required annual cooling and heating energy, equal to the sum of heating degree days and cooling degree days for a one year period, where heating degree days are calculated by subtracting each day's lowest temperature in degrees Fahrenheit from 65; cooling degree days are calculated by subtracting 65 from each day's highest temperature in degrees Fahrenheit.

SOURCES: U.S. Census Bureau Statistical Abstract of the United States: 2012, Table 396; U.S. National Oceanic and Atmospheric Administration, Comparative Climatic Data, annual

http://www.census.gov/compendia/statab/

http://www.ncdc.noaa.gov/ol/climate/climateproducts.html

http://www.ncdc.noaa.gov/oa/climate/online/ccd/nrmhdd.txt

Heating Degree Days

(annual, average for selected cities, 1986–2009)

The Four Most Populous States
(32.8 percent of U.S. population)
#1 California #2 Texas #3 New York #4 Florida

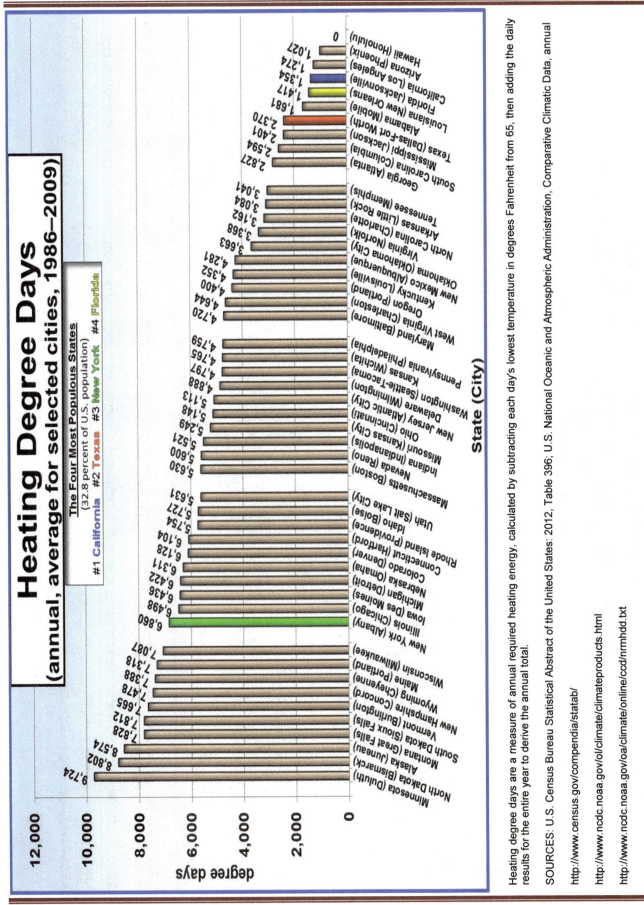

State (City)

Hawaii (Honolulu) 0
Arizona (Phoenix) 1,027
California (Los Angeles) 1,274
Florida (Jacksonville) 1,354
Louisiana (New Orleans) 1,417
Alabama (Mobile) 1,681
Texas (Dallas–Fort Worth) 2,370
Mississippi (Jackson) 2,401
South Carolina (Columbia) 2,594
Georgia (Atlanta) 2,827
Tennessee (Memphis) 3,041
Arkansas (Little Rock) 3,084
North Carolina (Charlotte) 3,162
Virginia (Norfolk) 3,368
Oklahoma (Oklahoma City) 3,663
New Mexico (Albuquerque) 4,281
Kentucky (Louisville) 4,352
Oregon (Portland) 4,400
West Virginia (Charleston) 4,644
Maryland (Baltimore) 4,720
Pennsylvania (Philadelphia) 4,759
Kansas (Wichita) 4,765
Washington (Seattle–Tacoma) 4,797
Delaware (Wilmington) 4,888
New Jersey (Atlantic City) 5,113
Ohio (Cincinnati) 5,148
Missouri (Kansas City) 5,249
Indiana (Indianapolis) 5,521
Nevada (Reno) 5,600
Massachusetts (Boston) 5,630
Utah (Salt Lake City) 5,631
Idaho (Boise) 5,727
Rhode Island (Providence) 5,754
Connecticut (Hartford) 6,104
Colorado (Denver) 6,128
Nebraska (Omaha) 6,311
Michigan (Detroit) 6,422
Iowa (Des Moines) 6,436
Illinois (Chicago) 6,498
New York (Albany) 6,860
Wisconsin (Milwaukee) 7,087
Maine (Portland) 7,318
Wyoming (Cheyenne) 7,388
New Hampshire (Concord) 7,478
Vermont (Burlington) 7,665
South Dakota (Sioux Falls) 7,812
Montana (Great Falls) 7,828
Alaska (Juneau) 8,574
North Dakota (Bismarck) 8,802
Minnesota (Duluth) 9,724

degree days — 0, 2,000, 4,000, 6,000, 8,000, 10,000, 12,000

Heating degree days are a measure of annual required heating energy, calculated by subtracting each day's lowest temperature in degrees Fahrenheit from 65, then adding the daily results for the entire year to derive the annual total.

SOURCES: U.S. Census Bureau Statistical Abstract of the United States: 2012, Table 396; U.S. National Oceanic and Atmospheric Administration, Comparative Climatic Data, annual

http://www.census.gov/compendia/statab/

http://www.ncdc.noaa.gov/ol/climate/climateproducts.html

http://www.ncdc.noaa.gov/oa/climate/online/ccd/nrmhdd.txt

Cooling Degree Days
(annual, average for selected cities, 1986–2009)

The Four Most Populous States
(32.8 percent of U.S. population)
#1 California #2 Texas #3 New York #4 Florida

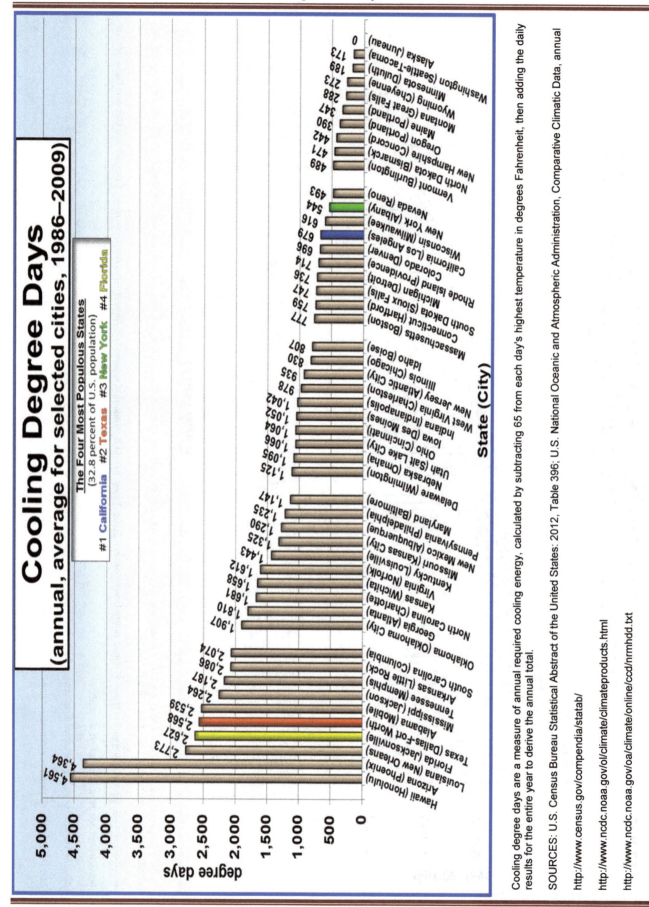

State (City)

State (City)	degree days
Hawaii (Honolulu)	4,561
Arizona (Phoenix)	4,364
Louisiana (New Orleans)	2,773
Florida (Jacksonville)	2,627
Texas (Dallas-Fort Worth)	2,568
Alabama (Mobile)	2,539
Mississippi (Jackson)	2,264
Tennessee (Memphis)	2,187
Arkansas (Little Rock)	2,086
South Carolina (Columbia)	2,074
Oklahoma (Oklahoma City)	1,907
Georgia (Atlanta)	1,810
North Carolina (Charlotte)	1,681
Kansas (Wichita)	1,658
Virginia (Norfolk)	1,612
Kentucky (Louisville)	1,443
Missouri (Kansas City)	1,325
New Mexico (Albuquerque)	1,290
Pennsylvania (Philadelphia)	1,235
Maryland (Baltimore)	1,147
Delaware (Wilmington)	1,125
Nebraska (Omaha)	1,095
Utah (Salt Lake City)	1,066
Ohio (Cincinnati)	1,064
Iowa (Des Moines)	1,052
Indiana (Indianapolis)	1,042
West Virginia (Charleston)	978
New Jersey (Atlantic City)	935
Illinois (Chicago)	830
Idaho (Boise)	807
Massachusetts (Boston)	777
Connecticut (Hartford)	759
South Dakota (Sioux Falls)	747
Michigan (Detroit)	736
Rhode Island (Providence)	714
Colorado (Denver)	696
California (Los Angeles)	679
Wisconsin (Milwaukee)	616
New York (Albany)	544
Nevada (Reno)	493
Vermont (Burlington)	489
North Dakota (Bismarck)	471
New Hampshire (Concord)	442
Oregon (Portland)	390
Maine (Portland)	347
Montana (Great Falls)	288
Wyoming (Cheyenne)	273
Minnesota (Duluth)	189
Washington (Seattle-Tacoma)	173
Alaska (Juneau)	0

Cooling degree days are a measure of annual required cooling energy, calculated by subtracting 65 from each day's highest temperature in degrees Fahrenheit, then adding the daily results for the entire year to derive the annual total.

SOURCES: U.S. Census Bureau Statistical Abstract of the United States: 2012, Table 396; U.S. National Oceanic and Atmospheric Administration, Comparative Climatic Data, annual

http://www.census.gov/compendia/statab/

http://www.ncdc.noaa.gov/oll/climate/climateproducts.html

http://www.ncdc.noaa.gov/oa/climate/online/ccd/nrmhdd.txt

Relative Humidity
(annual, average afternoon for selected cities, 1986–2009)

The Four Most Populous States
(32.8 percent of U.S. population)
#1 California #2 Texas #3 New York #4 Florida

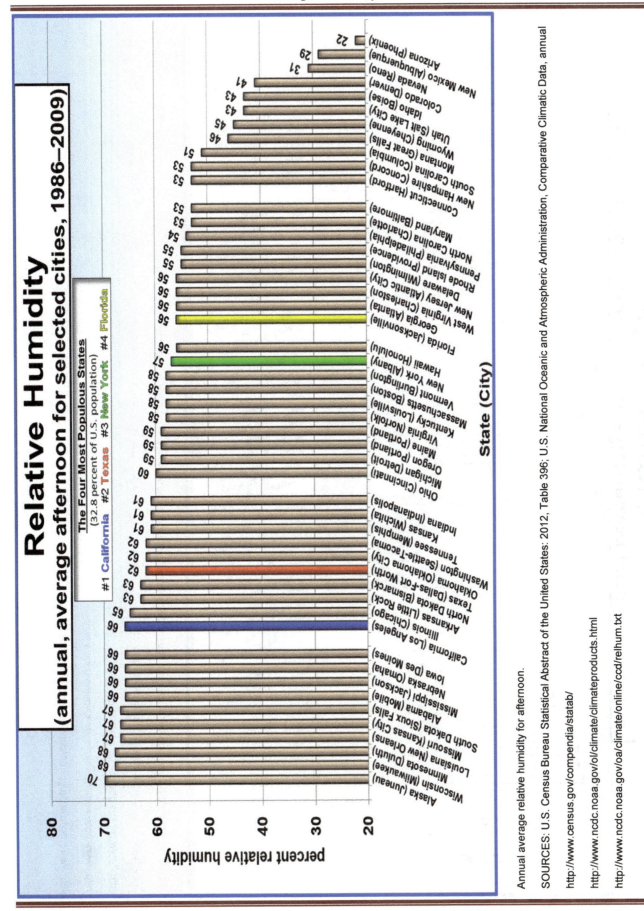

percent relative humidity

State (City)

State (City)	Value
Arizona (Phoenix)	22
New Mexico (Albuquerque)	29
Nevada (Reno)	31
Colorado (Denver)	41
Idaho (Boise)	43
Utah (Salt Lake City)	43
Wyoming (Cheyenne)	45
Montana (Great Falls)	46
South Carolina (Columbia)	51
New Hampshire (Concord)	53
Connecticut (Hartford)	53
Maryland (Baltimore)	53
North Carolina (Charlotte)	53
Pennsylvania (Philadelphia)	54
Rhode Island (Providence)	55
Delaware (Wilmington)	55
New Jersey (Atlantic City)	56
West Virginia (Charleston)	56
Georgia (Atlanta)	56
Florida (Jacksonville)	56
Hawaii (Honolulu)	56
New York (Albany)	57
Vermont (Burlington)	58
Massachusetts (Boston)	58
Kentucky (Louisville)	58
Virginia (Norfolk)	58
Maine (Portland)	59
Oregon (Portland)	59
Michigan (Detroit)	59
Ohio (Cincinnati)	60
Indiana (Indianapolis)	61
Kansas (Wichita)	61
Tennessee (Memphis)	61
Washington (Seattle-Tacoma)	62
Oklahoma (Oklahoma City)	62
Texas (Dallas-Fort Worth)	62
North Dakota (Bismarck)	63
Arkansas (Little Rock)	63
Illinois (Chicago)	65
California (Los Angeles)	66
Iowa (Des Moines)	66
Nebraska (Omaha)	66
Mississippi (Jackson)	66
Alabama (Mobile)	66
South Dakota (Sioux Falls)	67
Missouri (Kansas City)	67
Louisiana (New Orleans)	67
Minnesota (Duluth)	68
Wisconsin (Milwaukee)	68
Alaska (Juneau)	70

Annual average relative humidity for afternoon.

SOURCES: U.S. Census Bureau Statistical Abstract of the United States: 2012, Table 396; U.S. National Oceanic and Atmospheric Administration, Comparative Climatic Data, annual

http://www.census.gov/compendia/statab/

http://www.ncdc.noaa.gov/ol/climate/climateproducts.html

http://www.ncdc.noaa.gov/oa/climate/online/ccd/relhum.txt

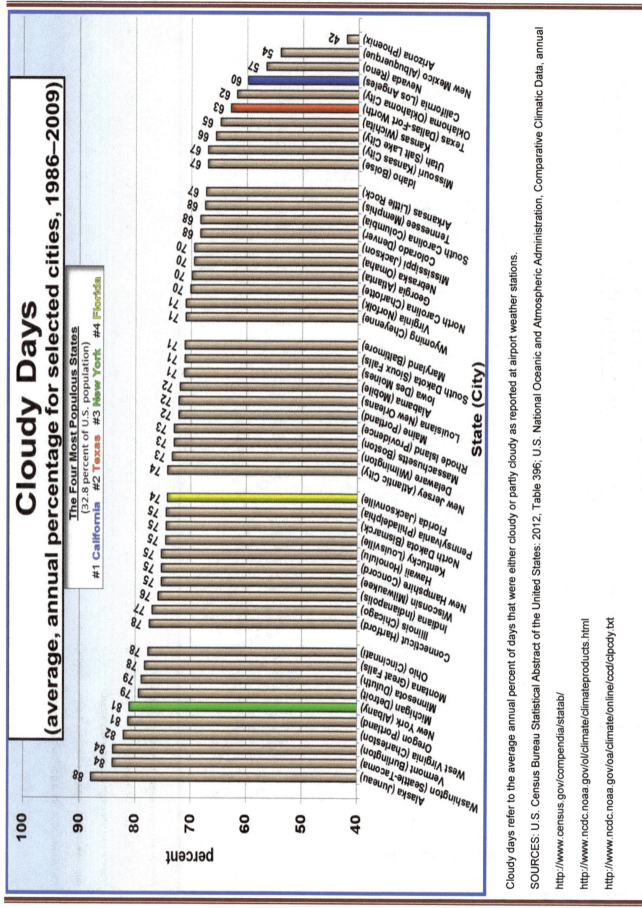

Cloudy Days
(average, annual percentage for selected cities, 1986–2009)

The Four Most Populous States
(32.8 percent of U.S. population)
#1 California   #2 Texas   #3 New York   #4 Florida

State (City)

State (City)	percent
Arizona (Phoenix)	42
New Mexico (Albuquerque)	54
Nevada (Reno)	57
California (Los Angeles)	60
Oklahoma (Oklahoma City)	62
Texas (Dallas–Fort Worth)	63
Kansas (Wichita)	65
Utah (Salt Lake City)	66
Missouri (Kansas City)	67
Idaho (Boise)	67
Arkansas (Little Rock)	67
Tennessee (Memphis)	68
South Carolina (Columbia)	68
Colorado (Denver)	68
Mississippi (Jackson)	70
Nebraska (Omaha)	70
Georgia (Atlanta)	70
North Carolina (Charlotte)	71
Virginia (Norfolk)	71
Wyoming (Cheyenne)	71
Maryland (Baltimore)	71
South Dakota (Sioux Falls)	71
Iowa (Des Moines)	72
Alabama (Mobile)	72
Louisiana (New Orleans)	72
Maine (Portland)	73
Rhode Island (Providence)	73
Massachusetts (Boston)	74
Delaware (Wilmington)	74
New Jersey (Atlantic City)	74
Florida (Jacksonville)	75
Pennsylvania (Philadelphia)	75
North Dakota (Bismarck)	75
Kentucky (Louisville)	75
Hawaii (Honolulu)	75
New Hampshire (Concord)	76
Wisconsin (Milwaukee)	77
Indiana (Indianapolis)	78
Illinois (Chicago)	78
Connecticut (Hartford)	78
Ohio (Cincinnati)	79
Montana (Great Falls)	79
Minnesota (Duluth)	81
Michigan (Detroit)	81
New York (Albany)	82
Oregon (Portland)	84
West Virginia (Charleston)	84
Vermont (Burlington)	88
Washington (Seattle–Tacoma)	88
Alaska (Juneau)	88

percent

Cloudy days refer to the average annual percent of days that were either cloudy or partly cloudy as reported at airport weather stations.

SOURCES: U.S. Census Bureau Statistical Abstract of the United States: 2012, Table 396; U.S. National Oceanic and Atmospheric Administration, Comparative Climatic Data, annual

http://www.census.gov/compendia/statab/

http://www.ncdc.noaa.gov/ol/climate/climateproducts.html

http://www.ncdc.noaa.gov/oa/climate/online/ccd/clpcdy.txt

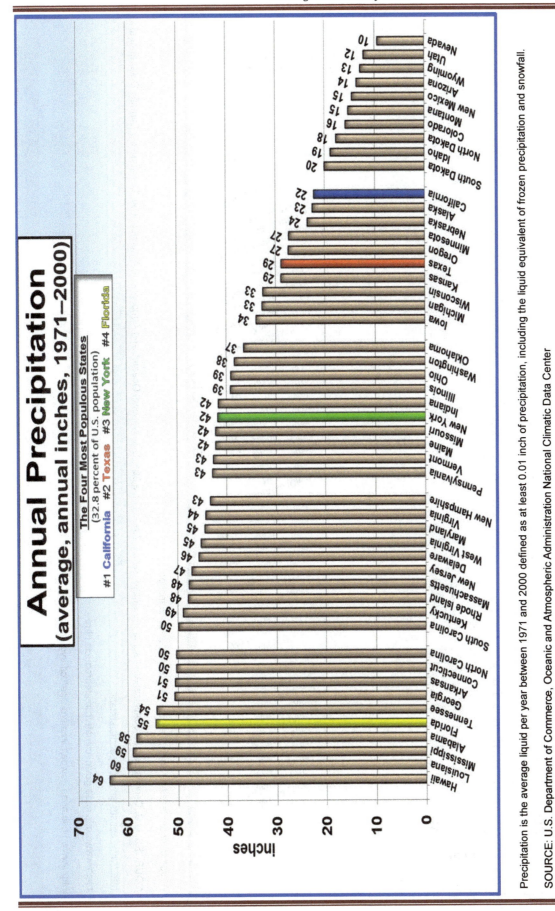

Annual Precipitation
(average, annual inches, 1971–2000)

The Four Most Populous States
(32.8 percent of U.S. population)
#1 California   #2 Texas   #3 New York   #4 Florida

State	Inches
Hawaii	64
Louisiana	60
Mississippi	59
Alabama	58
Florida	55
Tennessee	54
Georgia	51
Arkansas	51
Connecticut	50
North Carolina	50
South Carolina	50
Kentucky	49
Rhode Island	48
Massachusetts	48
New Jersey	47
Delaware	46
West Virginia	45
Maryland	45
Virginia	44
New Hampshire	43
Pennsylvania	43
Vermont	43
Maine	42
Missouri	42
New York	42
Indiana	42
Illinois	39
Ohio	39
Washington	38
Oklahoma	37
Iowa	34
Michigan	33
Wisconsin	33
Kansas	29
Texas	29
Oregon	27
Minnesota	27
Nebraska	24
Alaska	23
California	22
South Dakota	20
Idaho	19
North Dakota	18
Colorado	16
Montana	15
New Mexico	15
Arizona	14
Wyoming	13
Utah	12
Nevada	10

inches

Precipitation is the average liquid per year between 1971 and 2000 defined as at least 0.01 inch of precipitation, including the liquid equivalent of frozen precipitation and snowfall.

SOURCE: U.S. Department of Commerce, Oceanic and Atmospheric Administration National Climatic Data Center

http://ols.nndc.noaa.gov/plolstore/plsql/olstore.prodspecific?prodnum=C00095-PUB-A0001

Snow, Hail, Ice Pellets, and Sleet
(annual, average inches for selected cities, 1960–2008)

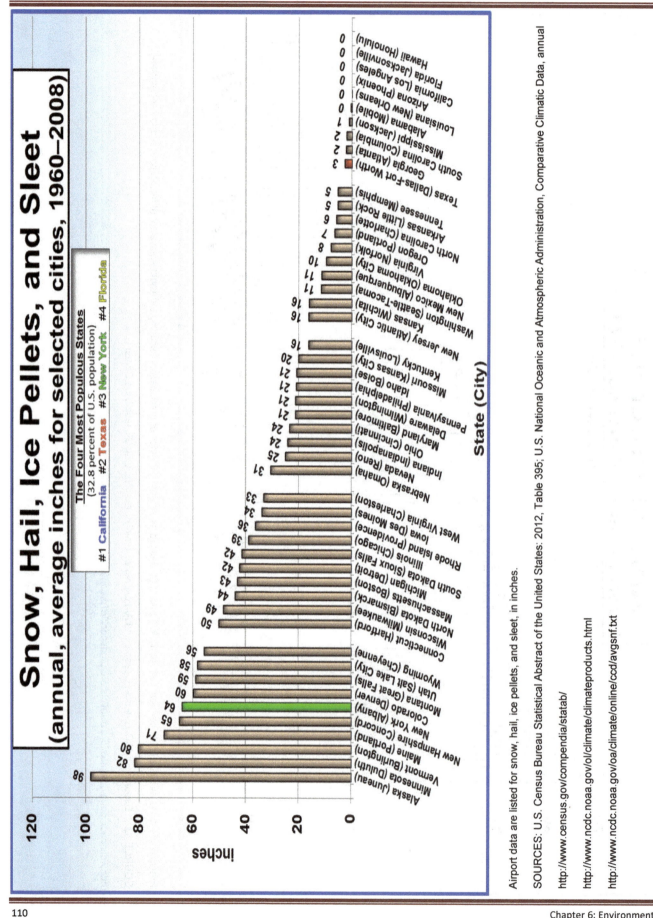

The Four Most Populous States
(32.8 percent of U.S. population)

#1 California #2 Texas #3 New York #4 Florida

Alaska (Juneau) 98
Minnesota (Duluth) 82
Vermont (Burlington) 80
Maine (Portland) 71
New Hampshire (Concord) 65
New York (Albany) 64
Colorado (Denver) 60
Montana (Great Falls) 59
Utah (Salt Lake City) 58
Wyoming (Cheyenne) 56
Connecticut (Hartford) 50
Wisconsin (Milwaukee) 49
North Dakota (Bismarck) 44
Massachusetts (Boston) 43
Michigan (Detroit) 42
South Dakota (Sioux Falls) 42
Illinois (Chicago) 39
Rhode Island (Providence) 36
Iowa (Des Moines) 34
West Virginia (Charleston) 33
Nebraska (Omaha) 31
Nevada (Reno) 25
Indiana (Indianapolis) 24
Ohio (Cincinnati) 24
Maryland (Baltimore) 21
Delaware (Wilmington) 21
Pennsylvania (Philadelphia) 21
Idaho (Boise) 21
Missouri (Kansas City) 20
Kentucky (Louisville) 16
New Jersey (Atlantic City) 16
Kansas (Wichita) 16
Washington (Seattle-Tacoma) 11
New Mexico (Albuquerque) 11
Oklahoma (Oklahoma City) 10
Virginia (Norfolk) 8
Oregon (Portland) 7
North Carolina (Charlotte) 6
Arkansas (Little Rock) 5
Tennessee (Memphis) 5
Texas (Dallas-Fort Worth) 3
Georgia (Atlanta) 2
South Carolina (Columbia) 2
Mississippi (Jackson) 1
Alabama (Mobile) 1
Louisiana (New Orleans) 0
Arizona (Phoenix) 0
California (Los Angeles) 0
Florida (Jacksonville) 0
Hawaii (Honolulu) 0

State (City)

Inches

Airport data are listed for snow, hail, ice pellets, and sleet, in inches.

SOURCES: U.S. Census Bureau Statistical Abstract of the United States: 2012, Table 395; U.S. National Oceanic and Atmospheric Administration, Comparative Climatic Data, annual

http://www.census.gov/compendia/statab/

http://www.ncdc.noaa.gov/ol/climate/climateproducts.html

http://www.ncdc.noaa.gov/oa/climate/online/ccd/avgsnf.txt

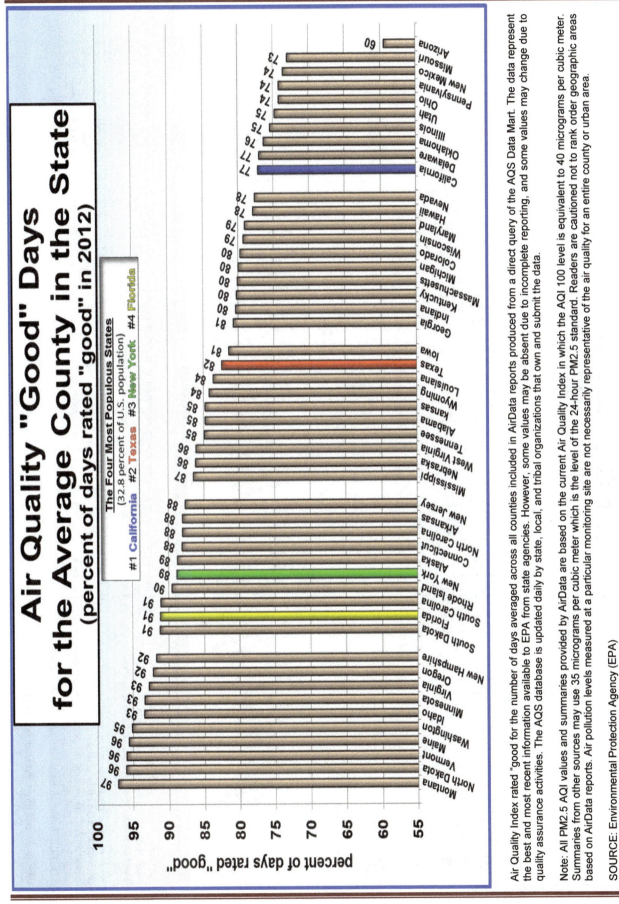

Air Quality "Good" Days for the Average County in the State

(percent of days rated "good" in 2012)

The Four Most Populous States
(32.8 percent of U.S. population)
#1 California #2 Texas #3 New York #4 Florida

State	Percent
Montana	97
North Dakota	96
Vermont	96
Maine	96
Washington	95
Idaho	93
Minnesota	93
Virginia	93
Oregon	92
New Hampshire	92
South Dakota	91
Florida	91
South Carolina	91
Rhode Island	90
New York	89
Alaska	89
Connecticut	88
North Carolina	88
Arkansas	88
New Jersey	88
Mississippi	87
Nebraska	86
West Virginia	86
Tennessee	85
Alabama	85
Kansas	85
Wyoming	84
Louisiana	84
Texas	82
Iowa	81
Georgia	81
Indiana	80
Kentucky	80
Massachusetts	80
Michigan	80
Colorado	79
Wisconsin	79
Maryland	78
Hawaii	78
Nevada	78
California	77
Delaware	77
Oklahoma	76
Illinois	75
Utah	75
Ohio	74
Pennsylvania	74
New Mexico	74
Missouri	73
Arizona	60

percent of days rated "good"

Air Quality Index rated "good for the number of days averaged across all counties included in AirData reports produced from a direct query of the AQS Data Mart. The data represent the best and most recent information available to EPA from state agencies. However, some values may be absent due to incomplete reporting, and some values may change due to quality assurance activities. The AQS database is updated daily by state, local, and tribal organizations that own and submit the data.

Note: All PM2.5 AQI values and summaries provided by AirData are based on the current Air Quality Index in which the AQI 100 level is equivalent to 40 micrograms per cubic meter. Summaries from other sources may use 35 micrograms per cubic meter which is the level of the 24-hour PM2.5 standard. Readers are cautioned not to rank order geographic areas based on AirData reports. Air pollution levels measured at a particular monitoring site are not necessarily representative of the air quality for an entire county or urban area.

SOURCE: Environmental Protection Agency (EPA)

http://www.epa.gov/airdata/ad_rep_aqi.html

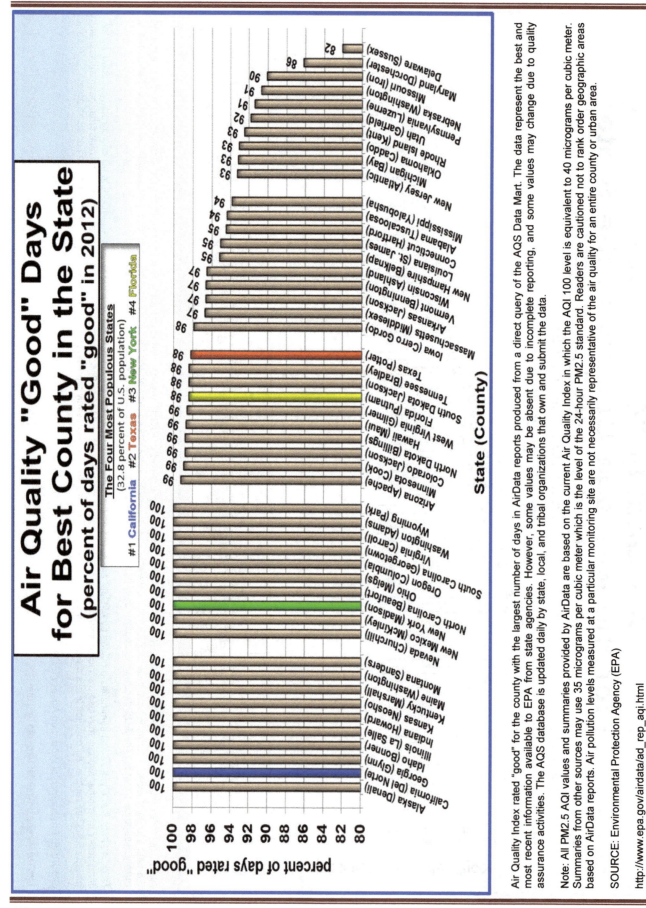

Air Quality "Good" Days for Best County in the State
(percent of days rated "good" in 2012)

The Four Most Populous States
(32.8 percent of U.S. population)
#1 California #2 Texas #3 New York #4 Florida

State (County):
- Alaska (Denali) — 100
- California (Del Norte) — 100
- Georgia (Glynn) — 100
- Idaho (Bonner) — 100
- Illinois (La Salle) — 100
- Indiana (Howard) — 100
- Kansas (Neosho) — 100
- Kentucky (Marshall) — 100
- Maine (Washington) — 100
- Montana (Sanders) — 100
- Nevada (Churchill) — 100
- New Mexico (McKinley) — 100
- North Carolina (Beaufort) — 100
- Ohio (Meigs) — 100
- Oregon (Columbia) — 100
- South Carolina (Georgetown) — 100
- Virginia (Carroll) — 100
- Washington (Adams) — 100
- Wyoming (Park) — 100
- Arizona (Apache) — 99
- Minnesota (Cook) — 99
- Colorado (Jackson) — 99
- North Dakota (Billings) — 99
- Hawaii (Maui) — 99
- West Virginia (Gilmer) — 99
- Florida (Putnam) — 99
- South Dakota (Jackson) — 99
- Tennessee (Bradley) — 98
- Texas (Potter) — 98
- Iowa (Cerro Gordo) — 98
- Massachusetts (Middlesex) — 98
- Arkansas (Jackson) — 97
- Vermont (Bennington) — 97
- Wisconsin (Ashland) — 97
- New Hampshire (Belknap) — 97
- Louisiana (St. James) — 95
- Connecticut (Hartford) — 95
- Alabama (Tuscaloosa) — 95
- Mississippi (Yalobusha) — 94
- New Jersey (Atlantic) — 94
- Michigan (Bay) — 93
- Oklahoma (Caddo) — 93
- Rhode Island (Kent) — 93
- Utah (Garfield) — 93
- Pennsylvania (Luzerne) — 92
- Nebraska (Washington) — 91
- Missouri (Iron) — 91
- Maryland (Dorchester) — 90
- Delaware (Sussex) — 86
- Delaware (Sussex) — 82

percent of days rated "good"

Air Quality Index rated "good" for the county with the largest number of days in AirData reports produced from a direct query of the AQS Data Mart. The data represent the best and most recent information available to EPA from state agencies. However, some values may be absent due to incomplete reporting, and some values may change due to quality assurance activities. The AQS database is updated daily by state, local, and tribal organizations that own and submit the data.

Note: All PM2.5 AQI values and summaries provided by AirData are based on the current Air Quality Index in which the AQI 100 level is equivalent to 40 micrograms per cubic meter. Summaries from other sources may use 35 micrograms per cubic meter which is the level of the 24-hour PM2.5 standard. Readers are cautioned not to rank order geographic areas based on AirData reports. Air pollution levels measured at a particular monitoring site are not necessarily representative of the air quality for an entire county or urban area.

SOURCE: Environmental Protection Agency (EPA)

http://www.epa.gov/airdata/ad_rep_aqi.html

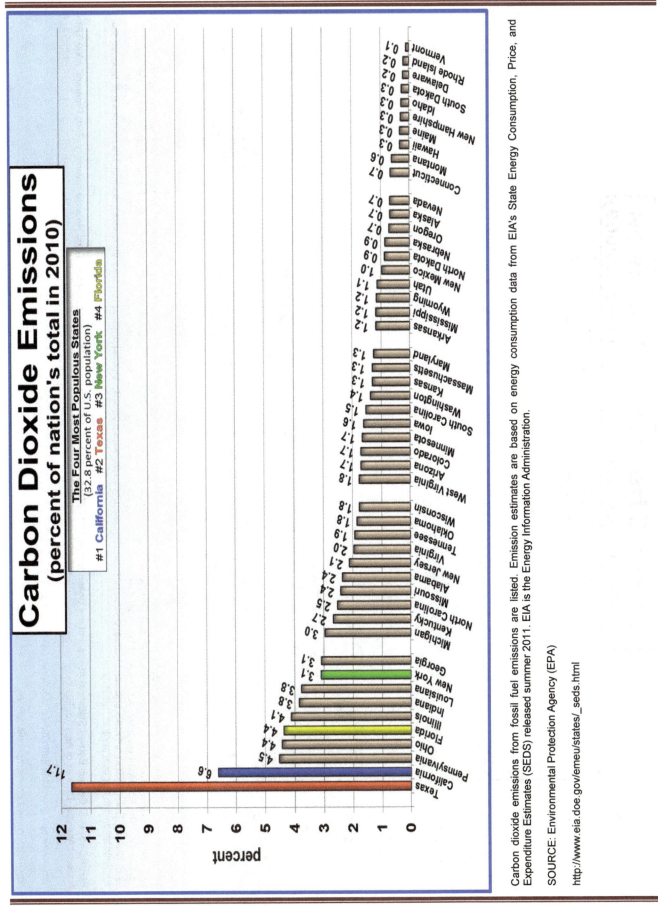

Carbon Dioxide Emissions
(percent of nation's total in 2010)

The Four Most Populous States
(32.8 percent of U.S. population)
#1 California   #2 Texas   #3 New York   #4 Florida

State	percent
Texas	11.7
California	6.6
Pennsylvania	4.5
Ohio	4.4
Florida	4.4
Illinois	4.1
Indiana	3.8
Louisiana	3.8
New York	3.1
Georgia	3.1
Michigan	3.0
Kentucky	2.7
North Carolina	2.5
Missouri	2.4
Alabama	2.4
New Jersey	2.1
Virginia	2.0
Tennessee	1.9
Oklahoma	1.8
Wisconsin	1.8
West Virginia	1.8
Arizona	1.7
Colorado	1.7
Minnesota	1.6
Iowa	1.5
South Carolina	1.4
Washington	1.3
Kansas	1.3
Massachusetts	1.3
Maryland	1.2
Arkansas	1.2
Mississippi	1.2
Wyoming	1.1
Utah	1.0
New Mexico	0.9
North Dakota	0.9
Nebraska	0.7
Oregon	0.7
Alaska	0.7
Nevada	0.6
Connecticut	0.3
Montana	0.3
Hawaii	0.3
Maine	0.3
New Hampshire	0.3
Idaho	0.2
South Dakota	0.2
Delaware	0.1
Rhode Island	
Vermont	

Carbon dioxide emissions from fossil fuel emissions are listed. Emission estimates are based on energy consumption data from EIA's State Energy Consumption, Price, and Expenditure Estimates (SEDS) released summer 2011. EIA is the Energy Information Administration.

SOURCE: Environmental Protection Agency (EPA)

http://www.eia.doe.gov/emeu/states/_seds.html

Toxic Chemical Releases
(3,386 million pounds nationally in 2009)

The Four Most Populous States
(32.8 percent of U.S. population)
#1 California   #2 Texas   #3 New York   #4 Florida

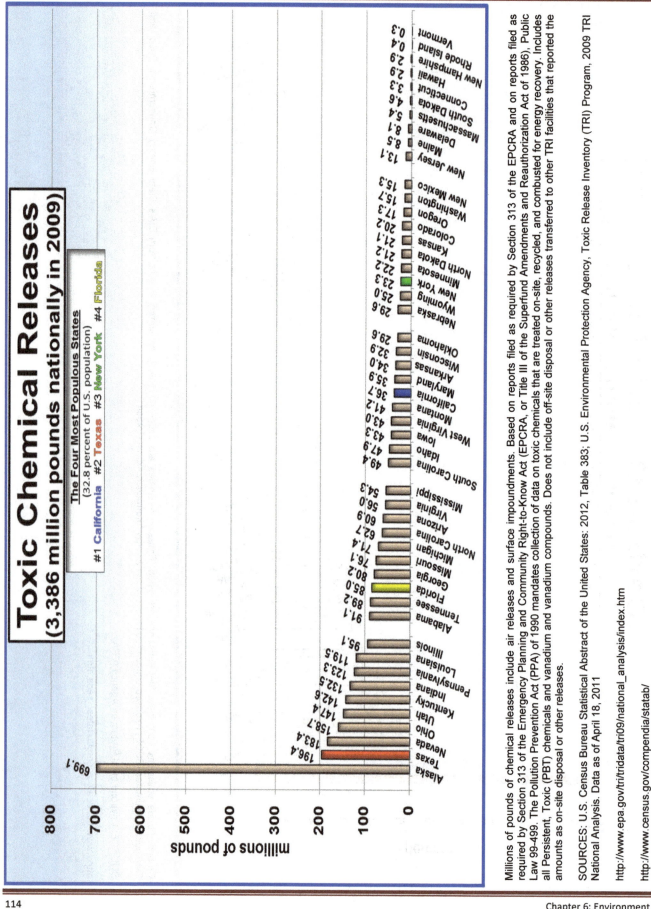

State	Value
Alaska	699.1
Texas	196.4
Nevada	183.4
Ohio	158.7
Utah	147.4
Kentucky	142.6
Indiana	132.5
Pennsylvania	123.3
Louisiana	119.5
Illinois	95.1
Alabama	91.1
Tennessee	89.2
Florida	85.0
Georgia	80.2
Missouri	76.1
Michigan	71.4
North Carolina	62.7
Arizona	60.9
Virginia	56.0
Mississippi	54.3
South Carolina	49.4
Idaho	47.9
Iowa	43.3
West Virginia	43.0
Montana	41.2
California	36.7
Maryland	35.9
Arkansas	34.0
Wisconsin	32.9
Oklahoma	29.6
Nebraska	29.6
Wyoming	25.0
New York	23.3
Minnesota	22.2
North Dakota	21.2
Kansas	21.1
Colorado	20.2
Oregon	17.3
Washington	15.7
New Mexico	15.3
New Jersey	13.1
Maine	8.5
Delaware	8.1
Massachusetts	5.4
South Dakota	4.6
Connecticut	3.3
Hawaii	2.9
New Hampshire	2.9
Rhode Island	0.4
Vermont	0.3

millions of pounds

Millions of pounds of chemical releases include air releases and surface impoundments. Based on reports filed as required by Section 313 of the EPCRA and on reports filed as required by Section 313 of the Emergency Planning and Community Right-to-Know Act (EPCRA, or Title III of the Superfund Amendments and Reauthorization Act of 1986), Public Law 99-499. The Pollution Prevention Act (PPA) of 1990 mandates collection of data on toxic chemicals that are treated on-site, recycled, and combusted for energy recovery. Includes all Persistent, Toxic (PBT) chemicals and vanadium and vanadium compounds. Does not include off-site disposal or other releases transferred to other TRI facilities that reported the amounts as on-site disposal or other releases.

SOURCES: U.S. Census Bureau Statistical Abstract of the United States: 2012, Table 383; U.S. Environmental Protection Agency, Toxic Release Inventory (TRI) Program, 2009 TRI National Analysis. Data as of April 18, 2011

http://www.epa.gov/tri/tridata/tri09/national_analysis/index.htm

http://www.census.gov/compendia/statab/

Chapter 7: Resources Overview

Alaska comprises 22.6 percent of the nation's land area and is double the size of Texas and 570 times larger than Rhode Island, the smallest state.

Texas had the largest proved reserves of crude oil at 24.2 percent, and natural gas at 29.5 percent; Montana had the most demonstrated coal reserves with 24.5 percent of the nation's total. Texas also led with 8.9 percent of the livestock market.

California led all states with 16.5 percent of the crops market. Both California and Alaska had the same amount of forest land, a combined total representing 19.8 percent of the nation's total, of which approximately 85 percent is federal land.

Wyoming used the most energy per capita, five times the amount used by New York.

Washington led by producing 10 percent of the nation's renewable energy.

Vermont produced 74 percent of its electricity by nuclear power while 19 states have no nuclear power generation.

~

Resources Summary Table

States Legend: ■ Highest 10% □ Middle 80% ■ Lowest 10%

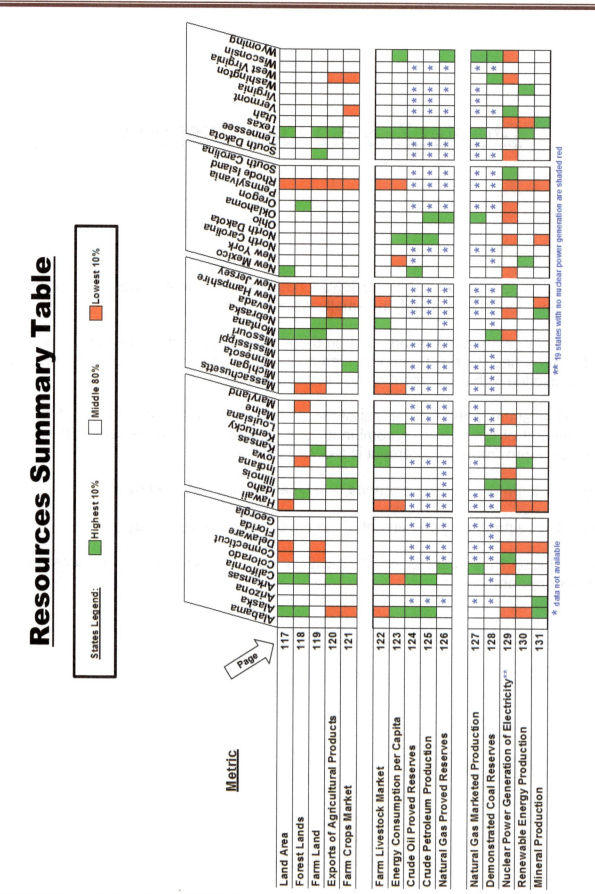

* data not available

** 19 states with no nuclear power generation are shaded red

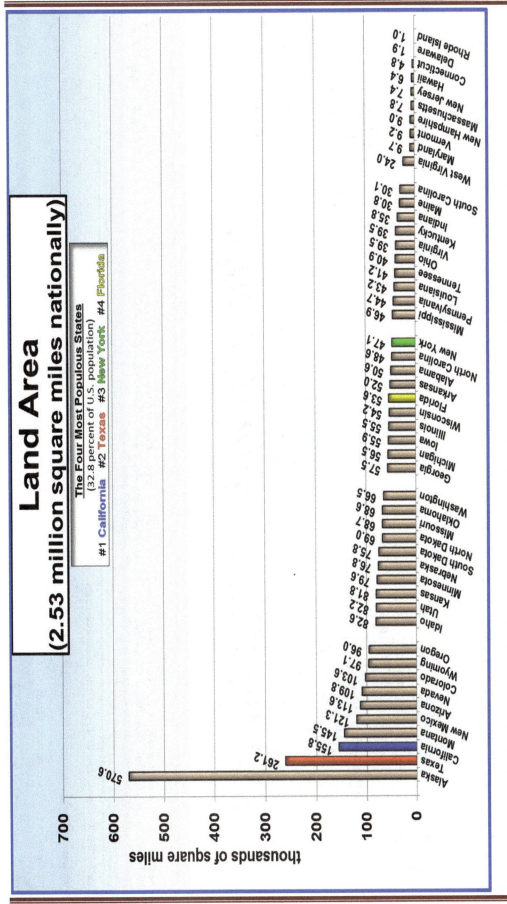

Land Area
(2.53 million square miles nationally)

The Four Most Populous States
(32.8 percent of U.S. population)
#1 California #2 Texas #3 New York #4 Florida

thousands of square miles

Alaska	570.6
Texas	261.2
California	155.8
Montana	145.5
New Mexico	121.3
Arizona	113.6
Nevada	109.8
Colorado	103.6
Wyoming	97.1
Oregon	96.0
Idaho	82.6
Utah	82.2
Kansas	81.8
Minnesota	79.6
Nebraska	76.8
South Dakota	75.8
North Dakota	69.0
Missouri	68.7
Oklahoma	68.6
Washington	66.5
Georgia	57.5
Michigan	56.5
Iowa	55.9
Illinois	55.5
Wisconsin	54.2
Florida	53.6
Arkansas	52.0
Alabama	50.6
North Carolina	48.6
New York	47.1
Mississippi	46.9
Pennsylvania	44.7
Louisiana	43.2
Tennessee	41.2
Ohio	40.9
Virginia	39.5
Kentucky	39.5
Indiana	35.8
Maine	30.8
South Carolina	30.1
West Virginia	24.0
Maryland	9.7
Vermont	9.2
New Hampshire	9.0
Massachusetts	7.8
New Jersey	7.4
Hawaii	6.4
Connecticut	4.8
Delaware	1.9
Rhode Island	1.0

State area data are extracted from the 2010 TIGER/Line Shapefiles product. The area measurements, in square meters and square miles, are for statistical purposes only.

SOURCE: U.S. Census Bureau

http://www.census.gov

Forest Lands

(percent of 246 million acres nationally in 2010)

The Four Most Populous States
(32.8 percent of U.S. population)
#1 California #2 Texas #3 New York #4 Florida

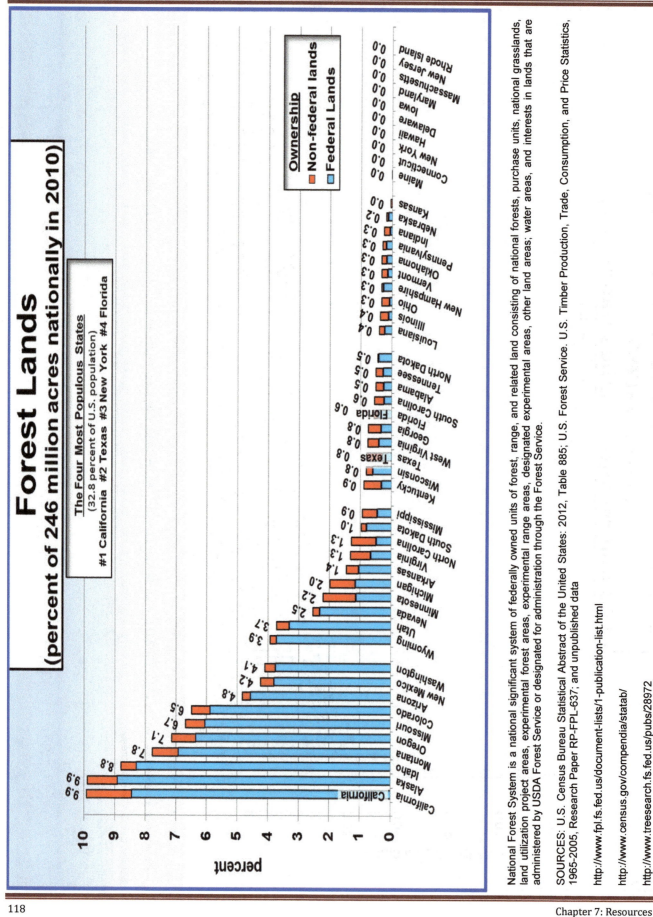

Ownership
- Non-federal lands
- Federal Lands

State	Percent
California	9.9
Alaska	9.9
Idaho	8.8
Montana	7.8
Oregon	7.1
Missouri	6.7
Colorado	6.5
Arizona	4.8
New Mexico	4.2
Washington	4.1
Wyoming	3.9
Utah	3.7
Nevada	2.5
Minnesota	2.2
Michigan	2.0
Arkansas	1.4
Virginia	1.3
North Carolina	1.3
South Dakota	1.0
Mississippi	0.9
Kentucky	0.9
Wisconsin	0.8
Texas	0.8
West Virginia	0.8
Georgia	0.8
Florida	0.6
South Carolina	0.6
Alabama	0.5
Tennessee	0.5
North Dakota	0.5
Louisiana	0.4
Illinois	0.4
Ohio	0.3
New Hampshire	0.3
Vermont	0.3
Oklahoma	0.3
Pennsylvania	0.3
Indiana	0.2
Nebraska	0.2
Kansas	0.0
Maine	0.0
Connecticut	0.0
New York	0.0
Hawaii	0.0
Delaware	0.0
Iowa	0.0
Maryland	0.0
Massachusetts	0.0
New Jersey	0.0
Rhode Island	0.0

National Forest System is a national significant system of federally owned units of forest, range, and related land consisting of national forests, purchase units, national grasslands, land utilization project areas, experimental forest areas, experimental range areas, designated experimental areas, other land areas; water areas, and interests in lands that are administered by USDA Forest Service or designated for administration through the Forest Service.

SOURCES: U.S. Census Bureau Statistical Abstract of the United States: 2012, Table 885; U.S. Forest Service. U.S. Timber Production, Trade, Consumption, and Price Statistics, 1965-2005, Research Paper RP-FPL-637; and unpublished data

http://www.fpl.fs.fed.us/document-lists/1-publication-list.html

http://www.census.gov/compendia/statab/

http://www.treesearch.fs.fed.us/pubs/28972

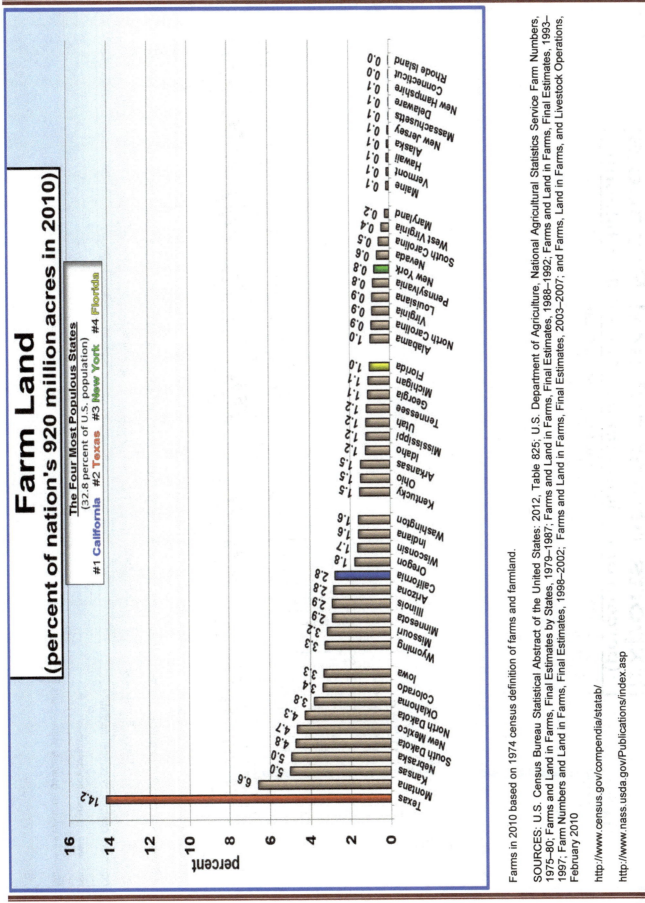

Farm Land
(percent of nation's 920 million acres in 2010)

The Four Most Populous States
(32.8 percent of U.S. population)
#1 California   #2 Texas   #3 New York   #4 Florida

State	Percent
Texas	14.2
Montana	6.6
Kansas	5.0
Nebraska	5.0
South Dakota	4.8
New Mexico	4.7
North Dakota	4.3
Oklahoma	3.8
Colorado	3.3
Iowa	3.3
Wyoming	3.3
Missouri	3.2
Minnesota	2.9
Illinois	2.9
Arizona	2.8
California	2.8
Oregon	1.8
Wisconsin	1.7
Indiana	1.6
Washington	1.6
Kentucky	1.5
Ohio	1.5
Arkansas	1.5
Idaho	1.2
Mississippi	1.2
Utah	1.2
Tennessee	1.1
Georgia	1.1
Michigan	1.0
Florida	1.0
Alabama	1.0
North Carolina	0.9
Virginia	0.9
Louisiana	0.9
Pennsylvania	0.8
New York	0.8
Nevada	0.6
South Carolina	0.5
West Virginia	0.4
Maryland	0.2
Maine	0.1
Vermont	0.1
Hawaii	0.1
Alaska	0.1
New Jersey	0.1
Massachusetts	0.1
Delaware	0.1
New Hampshire	0.1
Connecticut	0.0
Rhode Island	0.0

Farms in 2010 based on 1974 census definition of farms and farmland.

SOURCES: U.S. Census Bureau Statistical Abstract of the United States: 2012, Table 825; U.S. Department of Agriculture, National Agricultural Statistics Service Farm Numbers, 1975–80; Farms and Land in Farms, Final Estimates by States, 1979–1987; Farms and Land in Farms, Final Estimates, 1988–1992; Farms and Land in Farms, Final Estimates, 1993–1997; Farm Numbers and Land in Farms, Final Estimates, 1998–2002; Farms and Land in Farms, Final Estimates, 2003–2007; and Farms, Land in Farms, and Livestock Operations, February 2010

http://www.census.gov/compendia/statab/

http://www.nass.usda.gov/Publications/index.asp

Exports of Agricultural Products
(percent of national total in 2009 [$96.6 billion])

The Four Most Populous States
(32.8 percent of U.S. population)
#1 California   #2 Texas   #3 New York   #4 Florida

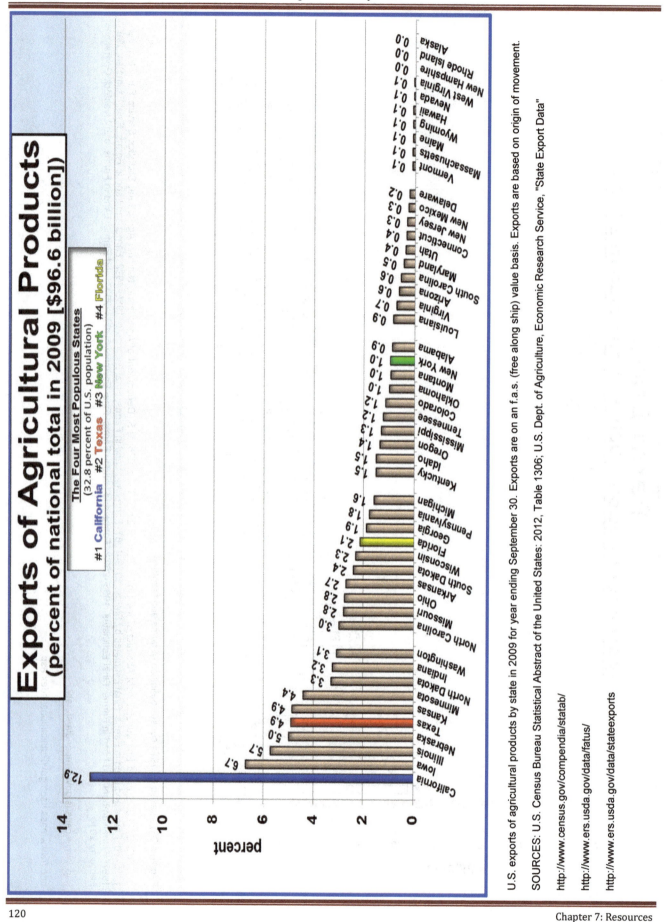

California 12.9
Iowa 6.7
Illinois 5.7
Nebraska 5.0
Texas 4.9
Kansas 4.9
Minnesota 4.4
North Dakota 3.3
Indiana 3.2
Washington 3.1
North Carolina 3.0
Missouri 2.8
Ohio 2.8
Arkansas 2.7
South Dakota 2.4
Wisconsin 2.3
Florida 2.1
Georgia 1.9
Pennsylvania 1.8
Michigan 1.6
Kentucky 1.5
Idaho 1.5
Oregon 1.4
Mississippi 1.3
Tennessee 1.2
Colorado 1.2
Oklahoma 1.0
Montana 1.0
New York 1.0
Alabama 0.9
Louisiana 0.9
Virginia 0.7
Arizona 0.6
South Carolina 0.6
Maryland 0.5
Utah 0.4
Connecticut 0.4
New Jersey 0.3
New Mexico 0.2
Delaware 0.2
Vermont 0.1
Massachusetts 0.1
Maine 0.1
Wyoming 0.1
Hawaii 0.1
Nevada 0.1
West Virginia 0.1
New Hampshire 0.0
Rhode Island 0.0
Alaska 0.0

percent

U.S. exports of agricultural products by state in 2009 for year ending September 30. Exports are on an f.a.s. (free along ship) value basis. Exports are based on origin of movement.

SOURCES: U.S. Census Bureau Statistical Abstract of the United States: 2012, Table 1306; U.S. Dept. of Agriculture, Economic Research Service, "State Export Data"

http://www.census.gov/compendia/statab/

http://www.ers.usda.gov/data/fatus/

http://www.ers.usda.gov/data/stateexports

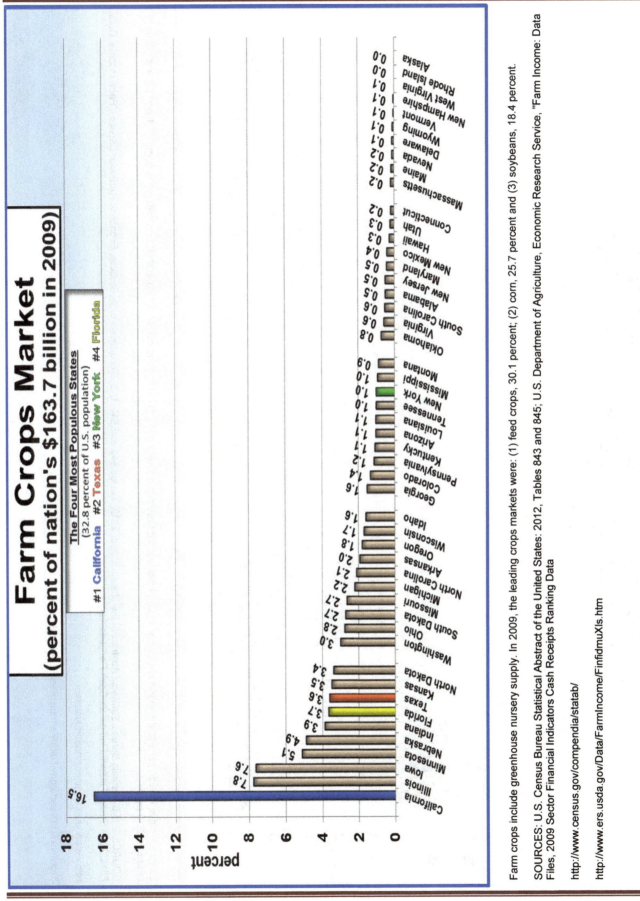

Farm Crops Market
(percent of nation's $163.7 billion in 2009)

The Four Most Populous States
(32.8 percent of U.S. population)
#1 California #2 Texas #3 New York #4 Florida

State	Percent
California	16.5
Illinois	7.8
Iowa	7.6
Minnesota	5.1
Nebraska	4.9
Indiana	3.9
Florida	3.7
Texas	3.6
Kansas	3.5
North Dakota	3.4
Washington	3.0
Ohio	2.8
South Dakota	2.7
Missouri	2.7
Michigan	2.2
North Carolina	2.1
Arkansas	2.0
Oregon	1.8
Wisconsin	1.7
Idaho	1.6
Georgia	1.6
Colorado	1.4
Pennsylvania	1.2
Kentucky	1.1
Arizona	1.1
Louisiana	1.1
Tennessee	1.0
New York	1.0
Mississippi	1.0
Montana	0.9
Oklahoma	0.8
Virginia	0.6
South Carolina	0.6
Alabama	0.5
New Jersey	0.5
Maryland	0.5
New Mexico	0.4
Hawaii	0.3
Utah	0.3
Connecticut	0.2
Massachusetts	0.2
Maine	0.2
Nevada	0.1
Delaware	0.1
Wyoming	0.1
Vermont	0.1
New Hampshire	0.1
West Virginia	0.1
Rhode Island	0.0
Alaska	0.0

Farm crops include greenhouse nursery supply. In 2009, the leading crops markets were: (1) feed crops, 30.1 percent; (2) corn, 25.7 percent and (3) soybeans, 18.4 percent.

SOURCES: U.S. Census Bureau Statistical Abstract of the United States: 2012, Tables 843 and 845; U.S. Department of Agriculture, Economic Research Service, "Farm Income: Data Files, 2009 Sector Financial Indicators Cash Receipts Ranking Data

http://www.census.gov/compendia/statab/

http://www.ers.usda.gov/Data/FarmIncome/FinfidmuXls.htm

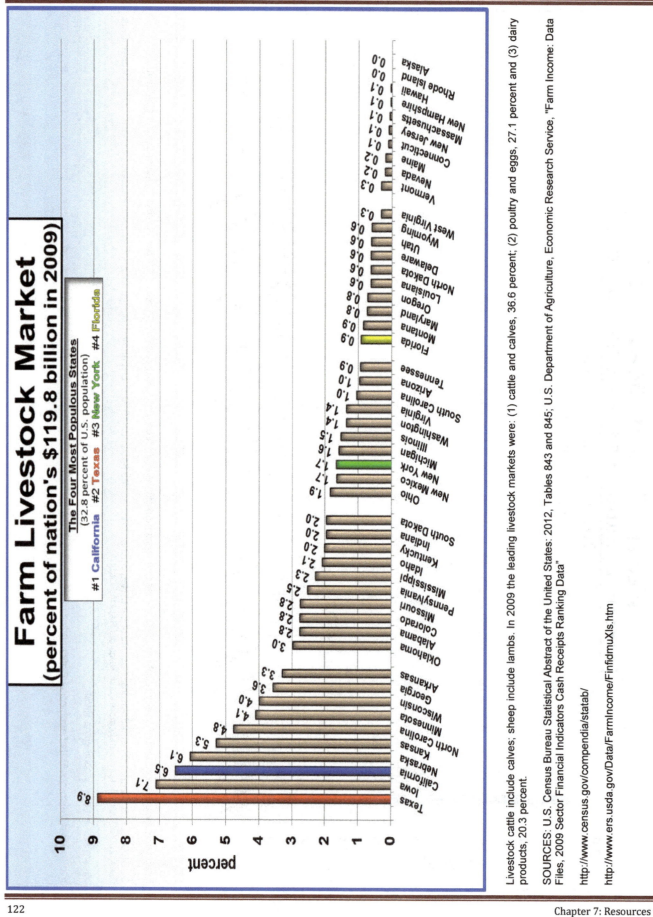

Farm Livestock Market
(percent of nation's $119.8 billion in 2009)

The Four Most Populous States
(32.8 percent of U.S. population)

#1 California   #2 Texas   #3 New York   #4 Florida

State	Percent
Texas	8.9
Iowa	7.1
California	6.5
Nebraska	6.1
Kansas	5.3
North Carolina	4.8
Minnesota	4.1
Wisconsin	4.0
Georgia	3.6
Arkansas	3.3
Oklahoma	3.0
Alabama	2.8
Colorado	2.8
Missouri	2.8
Pennsylvania	2.5
Mississippi	2.3
Idaho	2.1
Kentucky	2.0
Indiana	2.0
South Dakota	2.0
Ohio	1.9
New Mexico	1.7
New York	1.7
Michigan	1.6
Illinois	1.5
Washington	1.4
Virginia	1.4
South Carolina	1.0
Arizona	1.0
Tennessee	0.9
Florida	0.9
Montana	0.9
Maryland	0.8
Oregon	0.8
Louisiana	0.6
North Dakota	0.6
Delaware	0.6
Utah	0.6
Wyoming	0.6
West Virginia	0.3
Vermont	0.3
Nevada	0.2
Maine	0.2
Connecticut	0.1
New Jersey	0.1
Massachusetts	0.1
New Hampshire	0.1
Hawaii	0.1
Rhode Island	0.0
Alaska	0.0

Livestock cattle include calves; sheep include lambs. In 2009 the leading livestock markets were: (1) cattle and calves, 36.6 percent; (2) poultry and eggs, 27.1 percent and (3) dairy products, 20.3 percent.

SOURCES: U.S. Census Bureau Statistical Abstract of the United States: 2012, Tables 843 and 845; U.S. Department of Agriculture, Economic Research Service, "Farm Income: Data Files, 2009 Sector Financial Indicators Cash Receipts Ranking Data"

http://www.census.gov/compendia/statab/

http://www.ers.usda.gov/Data/FarmIncome/FinfidmuXls.htm

Energy Consumption per Capita
(327 million BTUs per capita nationally in 2008)

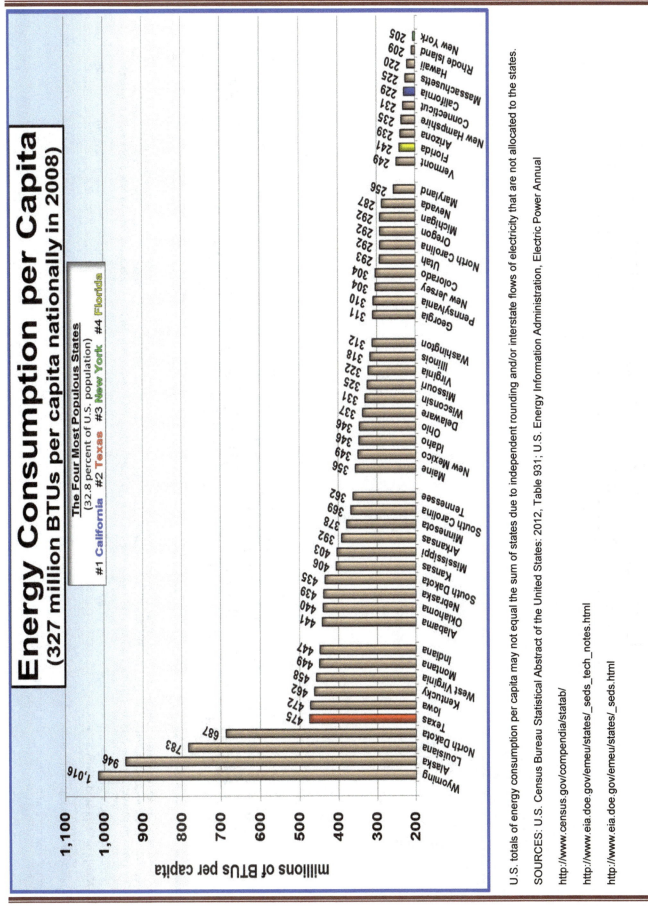

The Four Most Populous States
(32.8 percent of U.S. population)
#1 California   #2 Texas   #3 New York   #4 Florida

State	millions of BTUs per capita
Wyoming	1,016
Alaska	946
Louisiana	783
North Dakota	687
Texas	475
Iowa	472
Kentucky	462
West Virginia	458
Montana	449
Indiana	447
Alabama	441
Oklahoma	440
Nebraska	439
South Dakota	435
Kansas	406
Mississippi	403
Arkansas	392
Minnesota	378
South Carolina	369
Tennessee	362
New Mexico	356
Maine	349
Idaho	346
Ohio	346
Delaware	337
Wisconsin	331
Missouri	325
Virginia	322
Illinois	318
Washington	312
Georgia	311
Pennsylvania	310
New Jersey	304
Colorado	304
Utah	293
North Carolina	292
Oregon	292
Michigan	292
Nevada	287
Maryland	256
Vermont	249
Florida	241
Arizona	239
New Hampshire	235
Connecticut	231
California	229
Massachusetts	225
Hawaii	220
Rhode Island	209
New York	205

U.S. totals of energy consumption per capita may not equal the sum of states due to independent rounding and/or interstate flows of electricity that are not allocated to the states.

SOURCES: U.S. Census Bureau Statistical Abstract of the United States: 2012, Table 931; U.S. Energy Information Administration, Electric Power Annual

http://www.census.gov/compendia/statab/

http://www.eia.doe.gov/emeu/states/_seds_tech_notes.html

http://www.eia.doe.gov/emeu/states/_seds.html

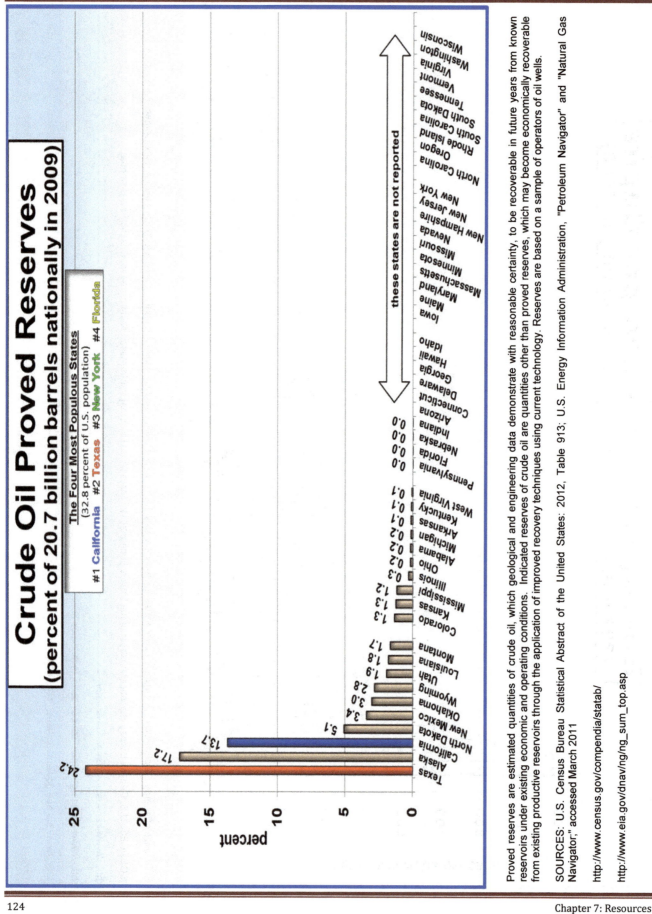

Crude Oil Proved Reserves
(percent of 20.7 billion barrels nationally in 2009)

The Four Most Populous States
(32.8 percent of U.S. population)
#1 California #2 Texas #3 New York #4 Florida

percent

Texas	24.2
Alaska	17.2
California	13.7
North Dakota	5.1
New Mexico	3.4
Oklahoma	3.0
Wyoming	2.8
Utah	1.9
Louisiana	1.8
Montana	1.7
Colorado	1.3
Kansas	1.3
Mississippi	1.2
Illinois	0.3
Ohio	0.2
Alabama	0.2
Michigan	0.2
Arkansas	0.1
Kentucky	0.1
West Virginia	0.1
Pennsylvania	0.0
Florida	0.0
Nebraska	0.0
Indiana	0.0

these states are not reported

Arizona, Connecticut, Delaware, Georgia, Hawaii, Idaho, Iowa, Maine, Maryland, Massachusetts, Minnesota, Missouri, Nevada, New Hampshire, New Jersey, New York, North Carolina, Oregon, Rhode Island, South Carolina, South Dakota, Tennessee, Vermont, Virginia, Washington, Wisconsin

Proved reserves are estimated quantities of crude oil, which geological and engineering data demonstrate with reasonable certainty, to be recoverable in future years from known reservoirs under existing economic and operating conditions. Indicated reserves of crude oil are quantities other than proved reserves, which may become economically recoverable from existing productive reservoirs through the application of improved recovery techniques using current technology. Reserves are based on a sample of operators of oil wells.

SOURCES: U.S. Census Bureau Statistical Abstract of the United States: 2012, Table 913; U.S. Energy Information Administration, "Petroleum Navigator" and "Natural Gas Navigator," accessed March 2011

http://www.census.gov/compendia/statab/

http://www.eia.gov/dnav/ng/ng_sum_top.asp

Crude Petroleum Production
(percent of 2.0 billion barrels nationally in 2010)

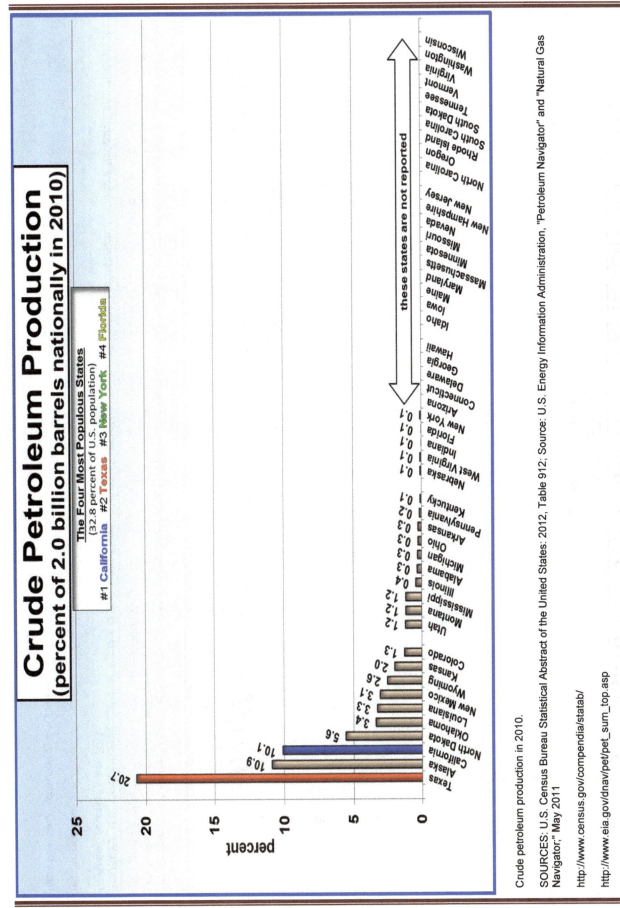

The Four Most Populous States
(32.8 percent of U.S. population)
#1 California   #2 Texas   #3 New York   #4 Florida

State	percent
Texas	20.7
Alaska	10.9
California	10.1
North Dakota	5.6
Oklahoma	3.4
Louisiana	3.3
New Mexico	3.1
Wyoming	2.6
Kansas	2.0
Colorado	1.3
Utah	1.2
Montana	1.2
Mississippi	1.2
Illinois	0.4
Alabama	0.3
Michigan	0.3
Ohio	0.3
Arkansas	0.3
Pennsylvania	0.2
Kentucky	0.1
Nebraska	0.1
West Virginia	0.1
Indiana	0.1
Florida	0.1
New York	0.1

these states are not reported: Arizona, Connecticut, Delaware, Georgia, Hawaii, Idaho, Iowa, Maine, Maryland, Massachusetts, Minnesota, Missouri, Nevada, New Hampshire, New Jersey, North Carolina, Oregon, Rhode Island, South Carolina, South Dakota, Tennessee, Vermont, Virginia, Washington, Wisconsin

Crude petroleum production in 2010.

SOURCES: U.S. Census Bureau Statistical Abstract of the United States: 2012, Table 912; Source: U.S. Energy Information Administration, "Petroleum Navigator" and "Natural Gas Navigator," May 2011

http://www.census.gov/compendia/statab/

http://www.eia.gov/dnav/pet/pet_sum_top.asp

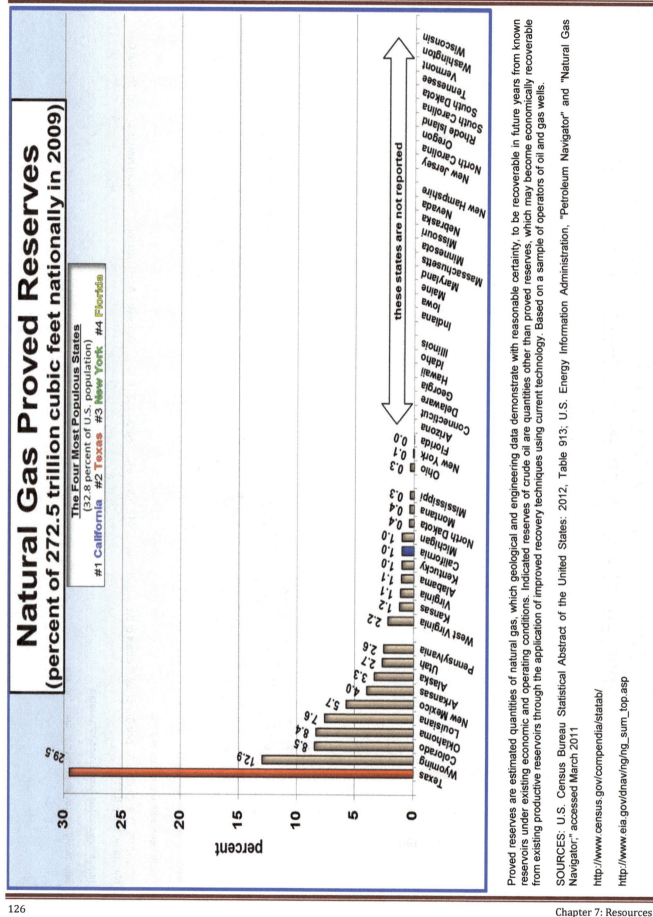

Natural Gas Proved Reserves
(percent of 272.5 trillion cubic feet nationally in 2009)

The Four Most Populous States
(32.8 percent of U.S. population)
#1 California #2 Texas #3 New York #4 Florida

these states are not reported

State	percent
Texas	29.5
Wyoming	12.9
Colorado	8.5
Oklahoma	8.4
Louisiana	7.6
New Mexico	5.7
Arkansas	4.0
Alaska	3.3
Utah	2.7
Pennsylvania	2.6
West Virginia	2.2
Kansas	1.2
Virginia	1.1
Alabama	1.1
Kentucky	1.0
California	1.0
Michigan	1.0
North Dakota	0.4
Montana	0.4
Mississippi	0.3
Ohio	0.3
New York	0.1
Florida	0.0

Arizona, Connecticut, Delaware, Georgia, Hawaii, Idaho, Illinois, Indiana, Iowa, Maine, Maryland, Massachusetts, Minnesota, Missouri, Nebraska, Nevada, New Hampshire, New Jersey, North Carolina, Oregon, Rhode Island, South Carolina, South Dakota, Tennessee, Vermont, Washington, Wisconsin

Proved reserves are estimated quantities of natural gas, which geological and engineering data demonstrate with reasonable certainty, to be recoverable in future years from known reservoirs under existing economic and operating conditions. Indicated reserves of crude oil are quantities other than proved reserves, which may become economically recoverable from existing productive reservoirs through the application of improved recovery techniques using current technology. Based on a sample of operators of oil and gas wells.

SOURCES: U.S. Census Bureau Statistical Abstract of the United States: 2012, Table 913; U.S. Energy Information Administration, "Petroleum Navigator" and "Natural Gas Navigator," accessed March 2011

http://www.census.gov/compendia/statab/

http://www.eia.gov/dnav/ng/ng_sum_top.asp

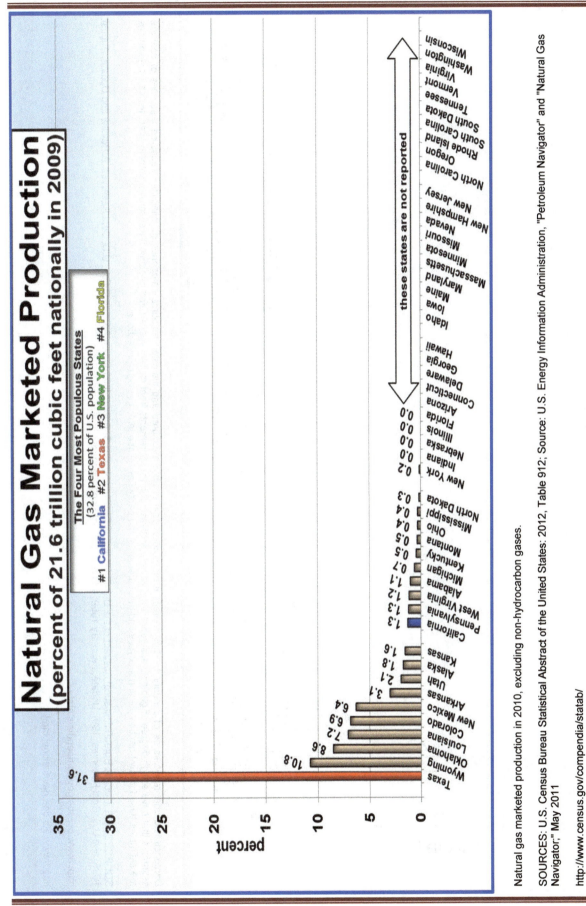

Natural Gas Marketed Production
(percent of 21.6 trillion cubic feet nationally in 2009)

The Four Most Populous States
(32.8 percent of U.S. population)
#1 California #2 Texas #3 New York #4 Florida

Texas — 31.6
Wyoming — 10.8
Oklahoma — 8.6
Louisiana — 7.2
Colorado — 6.9
New Mexico — 6.4
Arkansas — 3.1
Utah — 2.1
Alaska — 1.8
Kansas — 1.6
California — 1.3
Pennsylvania — 1.3
West Virginia — 1.2
Alabama — 1.1
Michigan — 0.7
Kentucky — 0.5
Montana — 0.5
Ohio — 0.4
Mississippi — 0.4
North Dakota — 0.3
New York — 0.2
Indiana — 0.0
Nebraska — 0.0
Illinois — 0.0
Florida — 0.0

Arizona
Connecticut
Delaware
Georgia
Hawaii
Idaho
Iowa
Maine
Maryland
Massachusetts
Minnesota
Missouri
Nevada
New Hampshire
New Jersey
North Carolina
Oregon
Rhode Island
South Carolina
South Dakota
Tennessee
Vermont
Virginia
Washington
Wisconsin

these states are not reported

percent

Natural gas marketed production in 2010, excluding non-hydrocarbon gases.

SOURCES: U.S. Census Bureau Statistical Abstract of the United States: 2012, Table 912; Source: U.S. Energy Information Administration, "Petroleum Navigator" and "Natural Gas Navigator," May 2011

http://www.census.gov/compendia/statab/

http://www.eia.gov/dnav/pet/pet_sum_top.asp

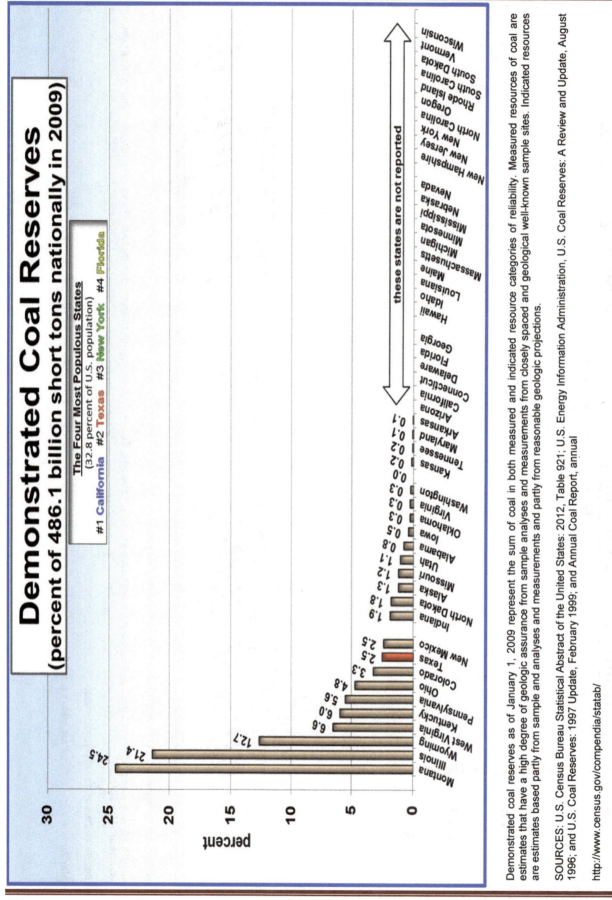

Demonstrated Coal Reserves
(percent of 486.1 billion short tons nationally in 2009)

The Four Most Populous States
(32.8 percent of U.S. population)
#1 California #2 Texas #3 New York #4 Florida

percent

Montana	24.5
Illinois	21.4
Wyoming	12.7
West Virginia	6.6
Kentucky	6.0
Pennsylvania	5.6
Ohio	4.8
Colorado	3.3
Texas	2.5
New Mexico	2.5
Indiana	1.9
North Dakota	1.8
Alaska	1.3
Missouri	1.2
Utah	1.1
Alabama	0.8
Iowa	0.5
Oklahoma	0.3
Virginia	0.3
Washington	0.3
Kansas	0.0
Tennessee	0.2
Maryland	0.1
Arkansas	0.1

these states are not reported

Arizona
California
Connecticut
Delaware
Florida
Georgia
Hawaii
Idaho
Louisiana
Maine
Massachusetts
Michigan
Minnesota
Mississippi
Nebraska
Nevada
New Hampshire
New Jersey
New York
North Carolina
Oregon
Rhode Island
South Carolina
South Dakota
Vermont
Wisconsin

Demonstrated coal reserves as of January 1, 2009 represent the sum of coal in both measured and indicated resource categories of reliability. Measured resources of coal are estimates that have a high degree of geologic assurance from sample analyses and measurements from closely spaced and geological well-known sample sites. Indicated resources are estimates based partly from sample and analyses and measurements and partly from reasonable geologic projections.

SOURCES: U.S. Census Bureau Statistical Abstract of the United States: 2012, Table 921; U.S. Energy Information Administration, U.S. Coal Reserves: A Review and Update, August 1996; and U.S. Coal Reserves: 1997 Update, February 1999; and Annual Coal Report, annual

http://www.census.gov/compendia/statab/

http://www.eia.doe.gov/fuelcoal.html

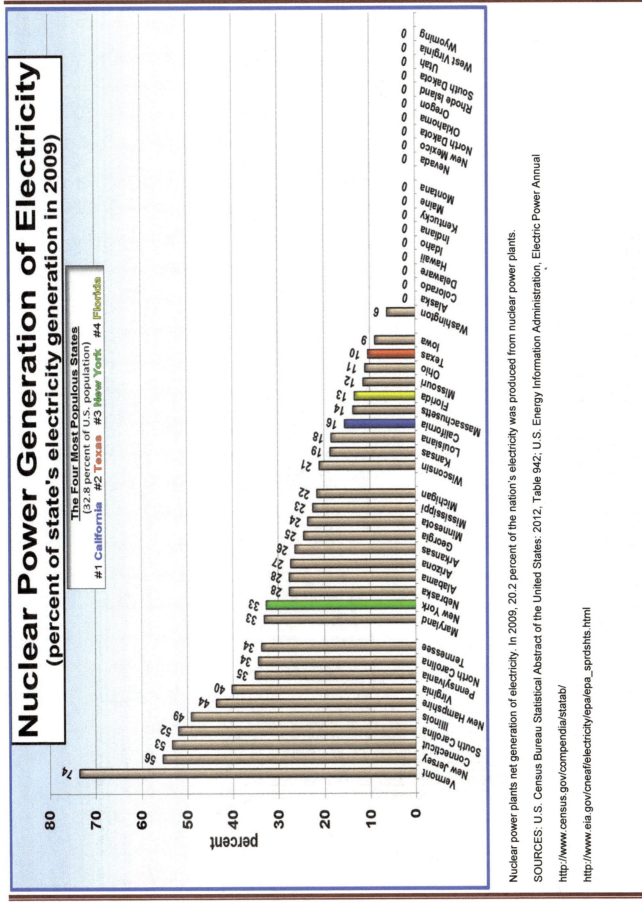

Nuclear Power Generation of Electricity
(percent of state's electricity generation in 2009)

The Four Most Populous States
(32.8 percent of U.S. population)
#1 California   #2 Texas   #3 New York   #4 Florida

State	percent
Vermont	74
New Jersey	56
Connecticut	53
South Carolina	52
Illinois	49
New Hampshire	44
Virginia	40
Pennsylvania	35
North Carolina	34
Tennessee	34
Maryland	33
New York	33
Nebraska	28
Alabama	28
Arizona	27
Arkansas	26
Georgia	25
Minnesota	24
Mississippi	23
Michigan	22
Wisconsin	21
Kansas	19
Louisiana	18
California	16
Massachusetts	14
Florida	13
Missouri	12
Ohio	11
Texas	10
Iowa	9
Washington	9
Alaska	0
Colorado	0
Delaware	0
Hawaii	0
Idaho	0
Indiana	0
Kentucky	0
Maine	0
Montana	0
Nevada	0
New Mexico	0
North Dakota	0
Oklahoma	0
Oregon	0
Rhode Island	0
South Dakota	0
Utah	0
West Virginia	0
Wyoming	0

Nuclear power plants net generation of electricity. In 2009, 20.2 percent of the nation's electricity was produced from nuclear power plants.

SOURCES: U.S. Census Bureau Statistical Abstract of the United States: 2012, Table 942; U.S. Energy Information Administration, Electric Power Annual

http://www.census.gov/compendia/statab/

http://www.eia.gov/cneaf/electricity/epa/epa_sprdshts.html

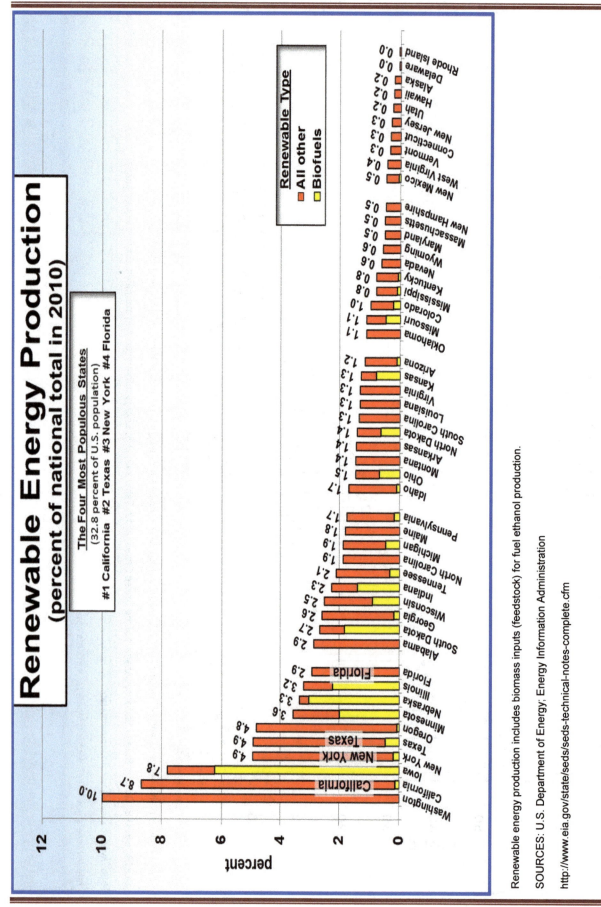

Renewable Energy Production
(percent of national total in 2010)

The Four Most Populous States
(32.8 percent of U.S. population)
#1 California #2 Texas #3 New York #4 Florida

Renewable Type
- All other
- Biofuels

Washington	10.0
California	8.7
Iowa	7.8
New York	4.9
Texas	4.9
Oregon	4.8
Minnesota	3.6
Nebraska	3.3
Illinois	3.2
Florida	2.9
Alabama	2.9
South Dakota	2.7
Georgia	2.6
Wisconsin	2.5
Indiana	2.3
Tennessee	2.1
North Carolina	1.9
Michigan	1.9
Maine	1.8
Pennsylvania	1.7
Idaho	1.7
Ohio	1.5
Montana	1.4
Arkansas	1.4
North Dakota	1.4
South Carolina	1.3
Louisiana	1.3
Virginia	1.3
Kansas	1.3
Arizona	1.2
Oklahoma	1.1
Missouri	1.1
Colorado	1.0
Mississippi	0.8
Kentucky	0.8
Nevada	0.6
Wyoming	0.6
Maryland	0.5
Massachusetts	0.5
New Hampshire	0.5
New Mexico	0.5
West Virginia	0.4
Vermont	0.3
Connecticut	0.3
New Jersey	0.3
Utah	0.2
Hawaii	0.2
Alaska	0.2
Delaware	0.0
Rhode Island	0.0

percent

Renewable energy production includes biomass inputs (feedstock) for fuel ethanol production.

SOURCES: U.S. Department of Energy; Energy Information Administration

http://www.eia.gov/state/seds/seds-technical-notes-complete.cfm

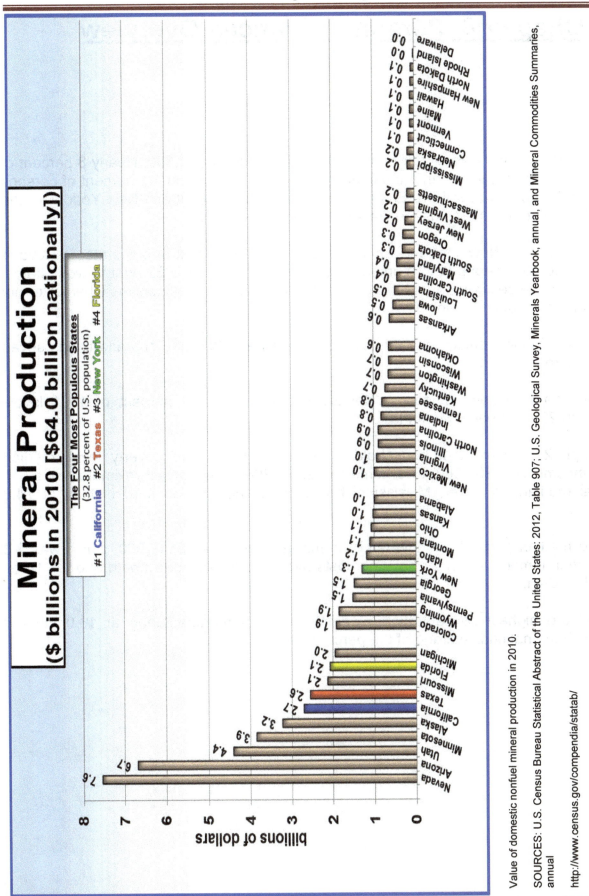

Mineral Production
($ billions in 2010 [$64.0 billion nationally])

The Four Most Populous States
(32.8 percent of U.S. population)
#1 California   #2 Texas   #3 New York   #4 Florida

State	billions of dollars
Nevada	7.6
Arizona	6.7
Utah	4.4
Minnesota	3.9
Alaska	3.2
California	2.7
Texas	2.6
Missouri	2.1
Florida	2.1
Michigan	2.0
Colorado	1.9
Wyoming	1.9
Pennsylvania	1.5
Georgia	1.5
New York	1.3
Idaho	1.2
Montana	1.1
Ohio	1.1
Kansas	1.0
Alabama	1.0
New Mexico	1.0
Virginia	1.0
Illinois	0.9
North Carolina	0.9
Indiana	0.8
Tennessee	0.8
Kentucky	0.7
Washington	0.7
Wisconsin	0.7
Oklahoma	0.6
Arkansas	0.6
Iowa	0.5
Louisiana	0.5
South Carolina	0.4
Maryland	0.4
South Dakota	0.3
Oregon	0.3
New Jersey	0.2
West Virginia	0.2
Massachusetts	0.2
Mississippi	0.2
Nebraska	0.2
Connecticut	0.1
Vermont	0.1
Maine	0.1
Hawaii	0.1
New Hampshire	0.1
North Dakota	0.1
Rhode Island	0.0
Delaware	0.0

Value of domestic nonfuel mineral production in 2010.

SOURCES: U.S. Census Bureau Statistical Abstract of the United States: 2012, Table 907; U.S. Geological Survey, Minerals Yearbook, annual, and Mineral Commodities Summaries, annual

http://www.census.gov/compendia/statab/

http://minerals.er.usgs.gov/minerals/pubs/mcs/

Chapter 8: Personal Finances Overview

Connecticut led the nation with a per capita personal income of $54,000. Nearly 8 percent of households in Connecticut had an annual income over $200,000, and 1.1 percent of persons had a net worth above $2.0 million. Employee wages in Connecticut and New York were the highest in the nation and 1.7 times the wages in South Dakota.

One-in-four workers in New York were union members—the highest of any state. In Nevada 15 percent of workers belonged to a union—the highest of any of the 22 right to work states. A right to work state secures the right of employees to decide for themselves whether or not to join or financially support a union.

Nevada had the highest bankruptcy rate at 11.5 filings per 1,000 persons and it was seven times Alaska's rate.

In 2010, single-family home prices in Nevada had risen to 126 percent of 1991 levels compared with 289 percent in Montana.

In Mississippi, 21.9 percent of households were at or below the poverty level, median household income was $36,000, and home values in 2009 were at approximately one-half the national median. However, Mississippi home ownership ranked third highest at 74.8 percent.

In 2009, the median price of a single-family home in Hawaii was $518,000, which was 2.8 times the national median. Renter housing costs averaged $1,293 per month and 1.5 times the national median.

Indiana had the highest concentration of employment in manufacturing at 16.0 percent compared with the national average of 8.9 percent.

~

Personal Finances Summary Table

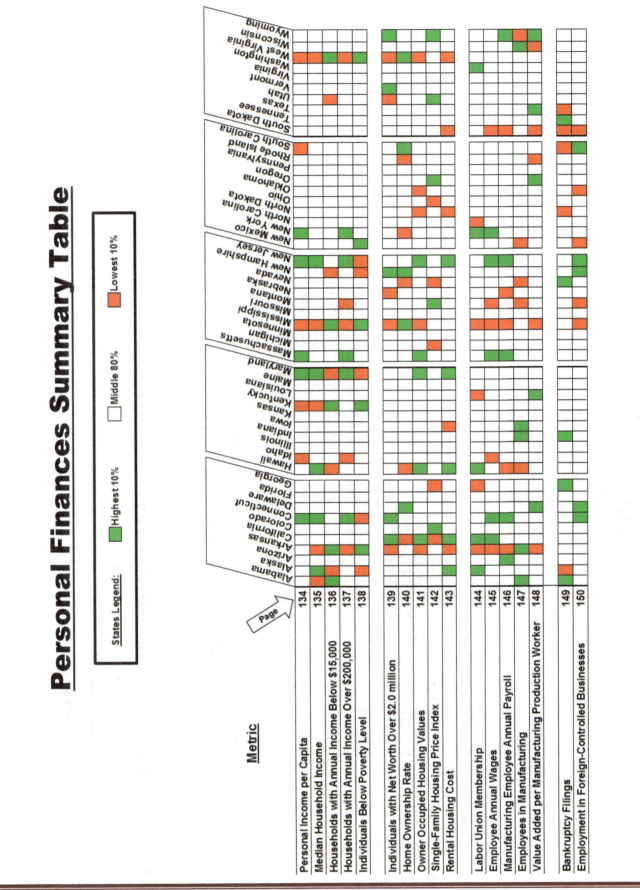

Personal Income per Capita
($39.9 thousand nationally in 2010)

The Four Most Populous States
(32.8 percent of U.S. population)
#1 California   #2 Texas   #3 New York   #4 Florida

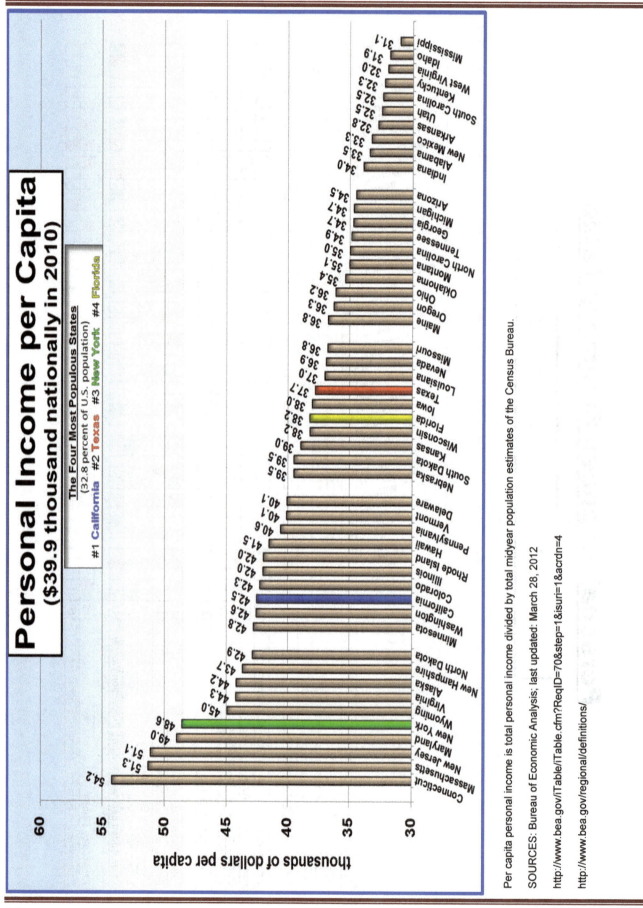

State	thousands of dollars per capita
Connecticut	54.2
Massachusetts	51.3
New Jersey	51.1
Maryland	49.0
New York	48.6
Wyoming	45.0
Virginia	44.3
Alaska	44.2
New Hampshire	43.7
North Dakota	42.9
Minnesota	42.8
Washington	42.6
California	42.5
Colorado	42.3
Illinois	42.0
Rhode Island	42.0
Hawaii	41.5
Pennsylvania	40.6
Vermont	40.1
Delaware	40.1
Nebraska	39.5
South Dakota	39.0
Kansas	38.2
Wisconsin	38.2
Florida	38.0
Iowa	37.7
Texas	37.0
Louisiana	36.9
Nevada	36.8
Missouri	36.8
Maine	36.3
Oregon	36.2
Ohio	35.4
Oklahoma	35.1
Montana	35.0
North Carolina	34.9
Tennessee	34.7
Georgia	34.7
Michigan	34.5
Arizona	34.0
Indiana	33.5
Alabama	33.3
New Mexico	32.8
Arkansas	32.5
Utah	32.5
South Carolina	32.3
Kentucky	32.0
West Virginia	31.9
Idaho	31.1
Mississippi	

Per capita personal income is total personal income divided by total midyear population estimates of the Census Bureau.

SOURCES: Bureau of Economic Analysis; last updated: March 28, 2012

http://www.bea.gov/iTable/iTable.cfm?ReqID=70&step=1&isuri=1&acrdn=4

http://www.bea.gov/regional/definitions/

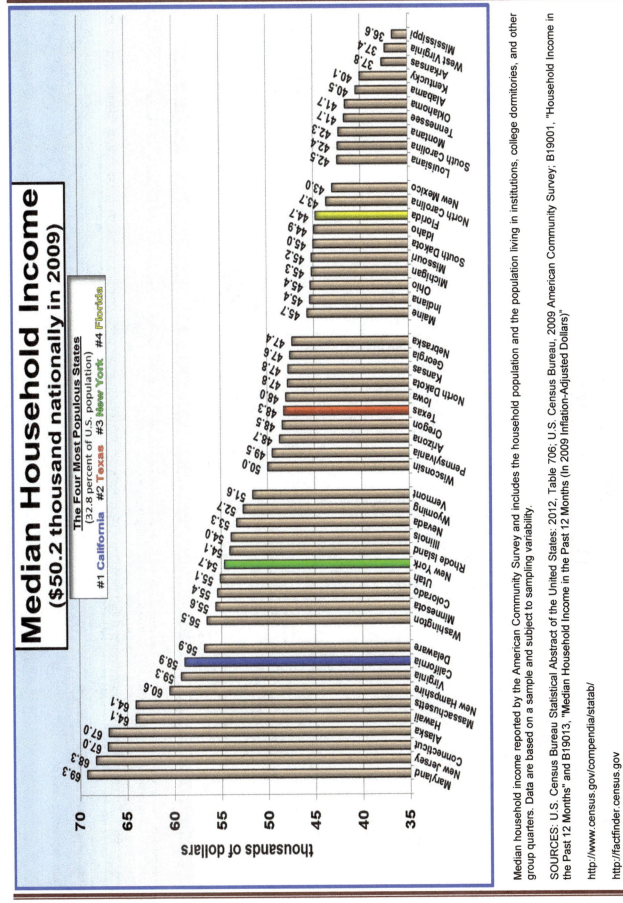

Median Household Income
($50.2 thousand nationally in 2009)

The Four Most Populous States
(32.8 percent of U.S. population)
#1 California   #2 Texas   #3 New York   #4 Florida

Maryland	69.3
New Jersey	68.3
Connecticut	67.0
Alaska	67.0
Hawaii	64.1
Massachusetts	64.1
New Hampshire	60.6
Virginia	59.3
California	58.9
Delaware	56.9
Washington	56.5
Minnesota	55.6
Colorado	55.4
Utah	55.1
New York	54.7
Rhode Island	54.1
Illinois	54.0
Nevada	53.3
Wyoming	52.7
Vermont	51.6
Wisconsin	50.0
Pennsylvania	49.5
Arizona	48.7
Oregon	48.5
Texas	48.3
Iowa	48.0
North Dakota	47.8
Kansas	47.8
Georgia	47.6
Nebraska	47.4
Maine	45.7
Indiana	45.4
Ohio	45.4
Michigan	45.3
Missouri	45.2
South Dakota	45.0
Idaho	44.9
Florida	44.7
North Carolina	43.7
New Mexico	43.0
Louisiana	42.5
South Carolina	42.4
Montana	42.3
Tennessee	41.7
Oklahoma	41.7
Alabama	40.5
Kentucky	40.1
Arkansas	37.8
West Virginia	37.4
Mississippi	36.6

thousands of dollars

Median household income reported by the American Community Survey and includes the household population and the population living in institutions, college dormitories, and other group quarters. Data are based on a sample and subject to sampling variability.

SOURCES: U.S. Census Bureau Statistical Abstract of the United States: 2012, Table 706; U.S. Census Bureau, 2009 American Community Survey; B19001, "Household Income in the Past 12 Months" and B19013, "Median Household Income in the Past 12 Months (In 2009 Inflation-Adjusted Dollars)"

http://www.census.gov/compendia/statab/

http://factfinder.census.gov

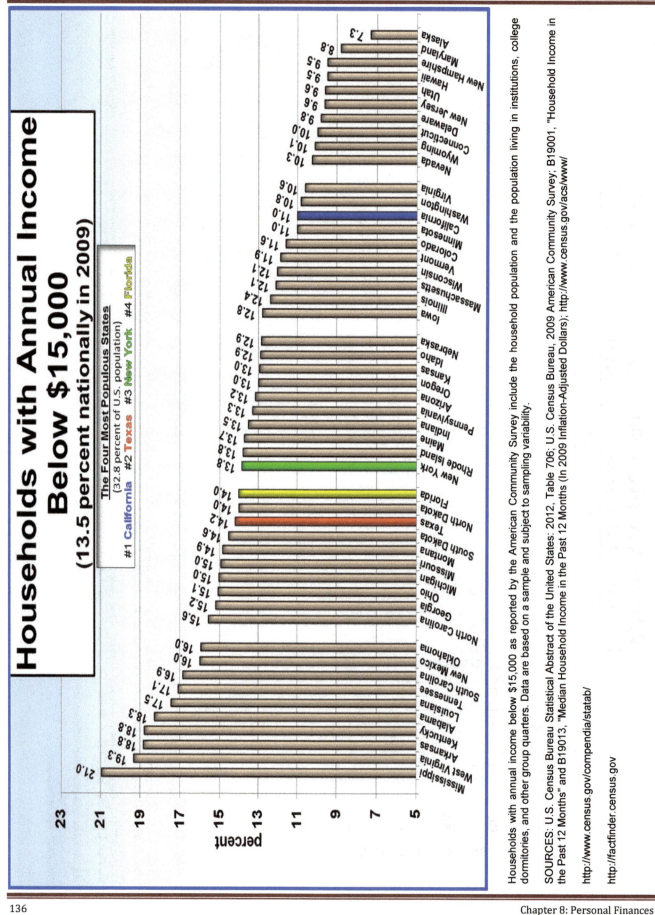

Households with Annual Income Below $15,000

(13.5 percent nationally in 2009)

The Four Most Populous States
(32.8 percent of U.S. population)
#1 California   #2 Texas   #3 New York   #4 Florida

State	Percent
Alaska	7.3
Maryland	8.8
New Hampshire	9.5
Hawaii	9.5
Utah	9.6
New Jersey	9.6
Delaware	9.8
Connecticut	10.0
Wyoming	10.1
Nevada	10.3
Virginia	10.6
Washington	10.8
California	11.0
Minnesota	11.0
Colorado	11.6
Vermont	11.9
Wisconsin	12.1
Massachusetts	12.1
Illinois	12.4
Iowa	12.8
Nebraska	12.9
Idaho	12.9
Kansas	13.0
Oregon	13.0
Arizona	13.2
Pennsylvania	13.3
Indiana	13.5
Maine	13.7
Rhode Island	13.8
New York	13.8
Florida	14.0
North Dakota	14.0
Texas	14.2
South Dakota	14.6
Montana	14.9
Missouri	15.0
Michigan	15.0
Ohio	15.1
Georgia	15.2
North Carolina	15.6
Oklahoma	16.0
New Mexico	16.0
South Carolina	16.9
Tennessee	17.1
Louisiana	17.5
Alabama	18.3
Kentucky	18.8
Arkansas	18.8
West Virginia	19.3
Mississippi	21.0

percent

Households with annual income below $15,000 as reported by the American Community Survey include the household population and the population living in institutions, college dormitories, and other group quarters. Data are based on a sample and subject to sampling variability.

SOURCES: U.S. Census Bureau Statistical Abstract of the United States: 2012, Table 706; U.S. Census Bureau, 2009 American Community Survey; B19001, "Household Income in the Past 12 Months" and B19013, "Median Household Income in the Past 12 Months (In 2009 Inflation-Adjusted Dollars); http://www.census.gov/acs/www/

http://www.census.gov/compendia/statab/

http://factfinder.census.gov

Households with Annual Income Over $200,000

(3.9 percent nationally in 2009)

The Four Most Populous States
(32.8 percent of U.S. population)
#1 California   #2 Texas   #3 New York   #4 Florida

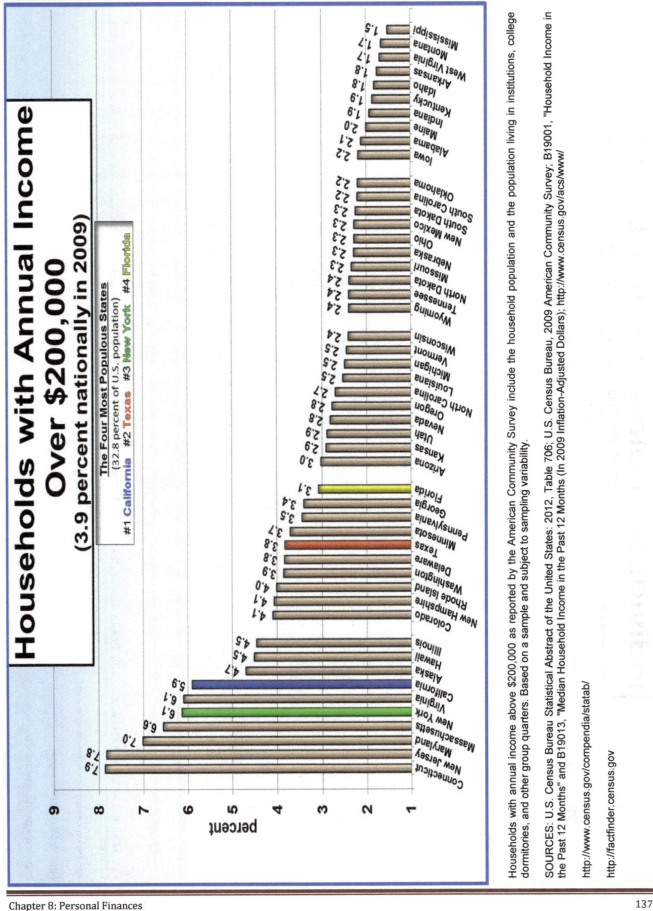

State	Percent
Connecticut	7.9
New Jersey	7.8
Maryland	7.0
Massachusetts	6.6
New York	6.1
Virginia	6.1
California	5.9
Alaska	4.7
Hawaii	4.5
Illinois	4.5
Colorado	4.1
New Hampshire	4.1
Rhode Island	4.0
Washington	3.9
Delaware	3.8
Texas	3.8
Minnesota	3.7
Pennsylvania	3.5
Georgia	3.4
Florida	3.1
Arizona	3.0
Kansas	2.9
Utah	2.9
Nevada	2.8
Oregon	2.8
North Carolina	2.7
Louisiana	2.5
Michigan	2.5
Vermont	2.5
Wisconsin	2.4
Wyoming	2.4
Tennessee	2.4
North Dakota	2.4
Missouri	2.3
Nebraska	2.3
Ohio	2.3
New Mexico	2.3
South Dakota	2.3
South Carolina	2.2
Oklahoma	2.2
Iowa	2.2
Alabama	2.1
Maine	2.0
Indiana	1.9
Kentucky	1.9
Idaho	1.8
Arkansas	1.8
West Virginia	1.7
Montana	1.7
Mississippi	1.5

Households with annual income above $200,000 as reported by the American Community Survey include the household population and the population living in institutions, college dormitories, and other group quarters. Based on a sample and subject to sampling variability.

SOURCES: U.S. Census Bureau Statistical Abstract of the United States: 2012, Table 706; U.S. Census Bureau, 2009 American Community Survey; B19001, "Household Income in the Past 12 Months" and B19013, "Median Household Income in the Past 12 Months (In 2009 Inflation-Adjusted Dollars); http://www.census.gov/acs/www/

http://www.census.gov/compendia/statab/

http://factfinder.census.gov

Individuals Below Poverty Level
(14.3 percent nationally in 2009)

The Four Most Populous States
(32.8 percent of U.S. population)

#1 California #2 Texas #3 New York #4 Florida

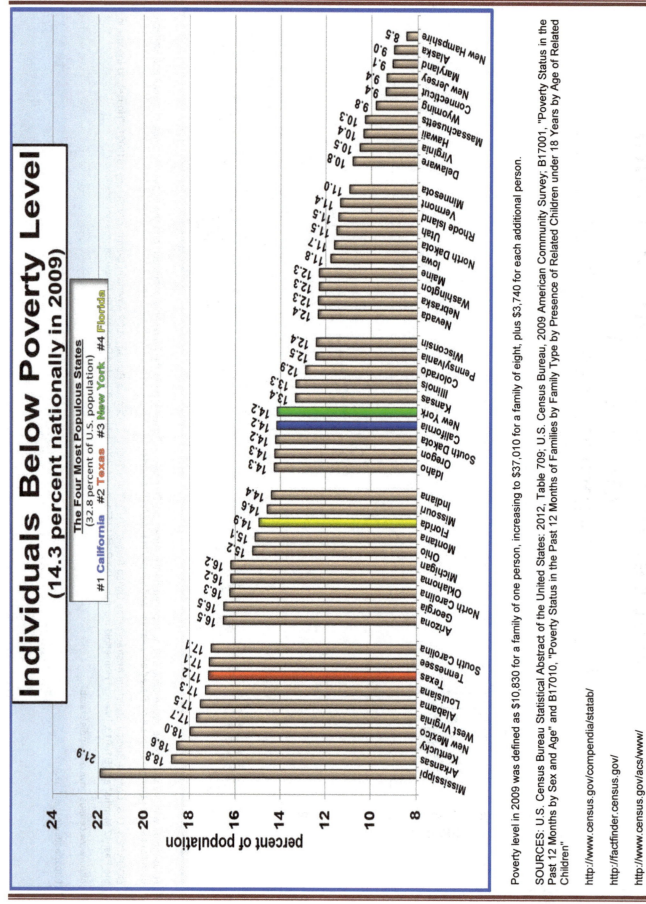

percent of population

New Hampshire 8.5
Alaska 9.0
Maryland 9.1
New Jersey 9.4
Connecticut 9.4
Wyoming 9.8
Massachusetts 10.3
Hawaii 10.4
Virginia 10.5
Delaware 10.8
Minnesota 11.0
Vermont 11.4
Rhode Island 11.5
Utah 11.5
North Dakota 11.7
Iowa 11.8
Maine 12.3
Washington 12.3
Nebraska 12.3
Nevada 12.4
Wisconsin 12.4
Pennsylvania 12.5
Colorado 12.9
Illinois 13.3
Kansas 13.4
New York 14.2
California 14.2
South Dakota 14.2
Oregon 14.3
Idaho 14.3
Indiana 14.4
Missouri 14.6
Florida 14.9
Montana 15.1
Ohio 15.2
Michigan 16.2
Oklahoma 16.2
North Carolina 16.3
Georgia 16.5
Arizona 16.5
South Carolina 17.1
Tennessee 17.1
Texas 17.2
Louisiana 17.3
Alabama 17.5
West Virginia 17.7
New Mexico 18.0
Kentucky 18.6
Arkansas 18.8
Mississippi 21.9

Poverty level in 2009 was defined as $10,830 for a family of one person, increasing to $37,010 for a family of eight, plus $3,740 for each additional person.

SOURCES: U.S. Census Bureau Statistical Abstract of the United States: 2012, Table 709; U.S. Census Bureau, 2009 American Community Survey; B17001, "Poverty Status in the Past 12 Months by Sex and Age" and B17010, "Poverty Status in the Past 12 Months of Families by Family Type by Presence of Related Children under 18 Years by Age of Related Children"

http://www.census.gov/compendia/statab/

http://factfinder.census.gov/

http://www.census.gov/acs/www/

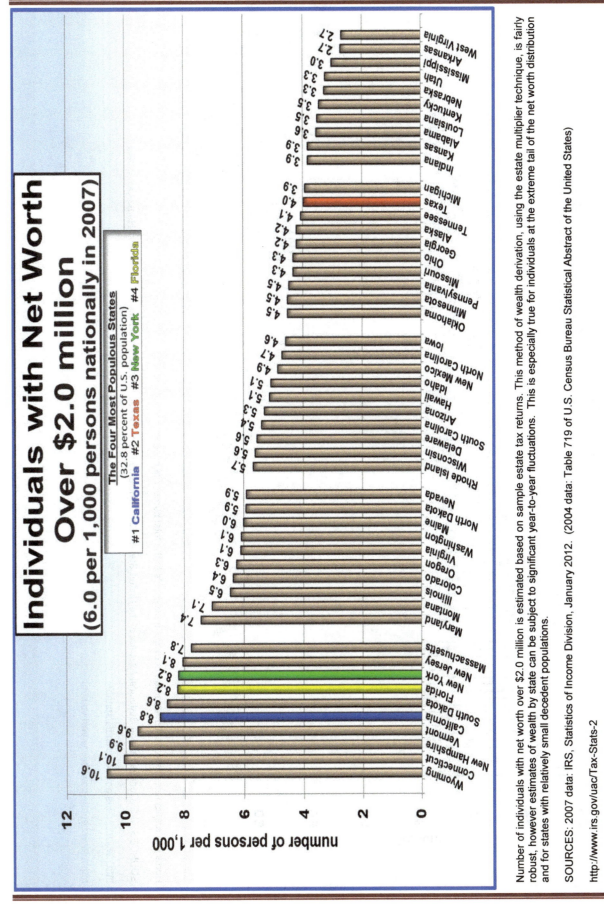

Individuals with Net Worth Over $2.0 million

(6.0 per 1,000 persons nationally in 2007)

The Four Most Populous States
(32.8 percent of U.S. population)
#1 California   #2 Texas   #3 New York   #4 Florida

State	number of persons per 1,000
Wyoming	10.6
Connecticut	10.1
New Hampshire	9.9
Vermont	9.6
California	8.8
South Dakota	8.6
Florida	8.2
New York	8.2
New Jersey	8.1
Massachusetts	7.8
Maryland	7.4
Montana	7.1
Illinois	6.5
Colorado	6.4
Oregon	6.3
Virginia	6.1
Washington	6.1
Maine	6.0
North Dakota	5.9
Nevada	5.9
Rhode Island	5.7
Wisconsin	5.6
Delaware	5.6
South Carolina	5.4
Arizona	5.3
Hawaii	5.1
Idaho	5.1
New Mexico	4.9
North Carolina	4.7
Iowa	4.6
Oklahoma	4.5
Minnesota	4.5
Pennsylvania	4.5
Missouri	4.3
Ohio	4.3
Georgia	4.2
Alaska	4.2
Tennessee	4.1
Texas	4.0
Michigan	3.9
Indiana	3.9
Kansas	3.9
Alabama	3.6
Louisiana	3.5
Kentucky	3.5
Nebraska	3.3
Utah	3.3
Mississippi	3.0
Arkansas	2.7
West Virginia	2.7

number of persons per 1,000

Number of individuals with net worth over $2.0 million is estimated based on sample estate tax returns. This method of wealth derivation, using the estate multiplier technique, is fairly robust, however estimates of wealth by state can be subject to significant year-to-year fluctuations. This is especially true for individuals at the extreme tail of the net worth distribution and for states with relatively small decedent populations.

SOURCES: 2007 data: IRS, Statistics of Income Division, January 2012. (2004 data: Table 719 of U.S. Census Bureau Statistical Abstract of the United States)

http://www.irs.gov/uac/Tax-Stats-2

Home Ownership Rate

(66.9 percent of households nationally in 2010)

The Four Most Populous States
(32.8 percent of U.S. population)

#1 California   #2 Texas   #3 New York   #4 Florida

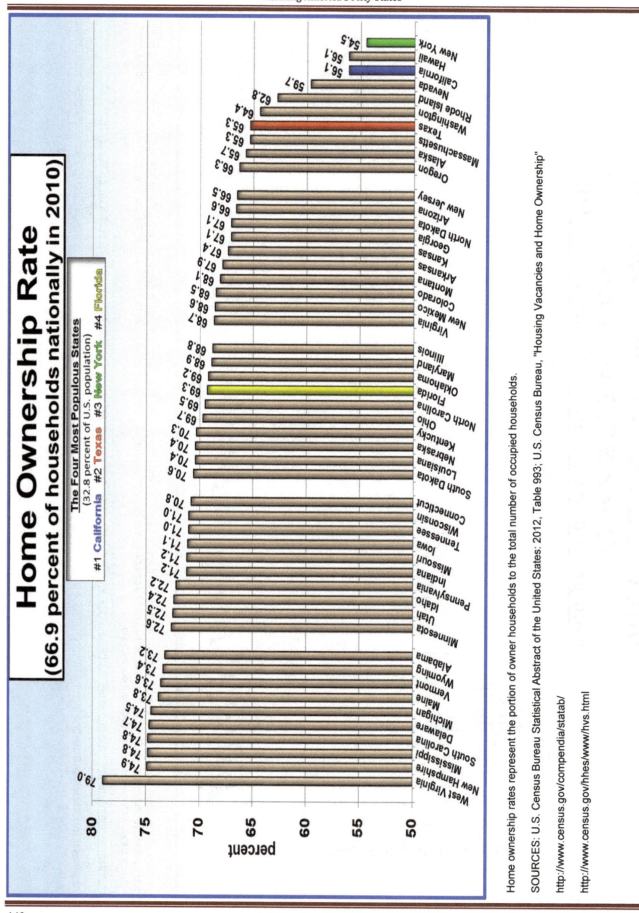

State	Percent
West Virginia	79.0
New Hampshire	74.9
Mississippi	74.8
South Carolina	74.8
Delaware	74.7
Michigan	74.5
Maine	73.8
Vermont	73.6
Wyoming	73.4
Alabama	73.2
Minnesota	72.6
Utah	72.5
Idaho	72.4
Pennsylvania	72.2
Indiana	71.2
Missouri	71.2
Iowa	71.1
Tennessee	71.0
Wisconsin	71.0
Connecticut	70.8
South Dakota	70.6
Louisiana	70.4
Nebraska	70.4
Kentucky	70.3
Ohio	69.7
North Carolina	69.5
Florida	69.3
Oklahoma	69.2
Maryland	68.9
Illinois	68.8
Virginia	68.7
New Mexico	68.6
Colorado	68.5
Montana	68.1
Arkansas	67.9
Kansas	67.4
Georgia	67.1
North Dakota	67.1
Arizona	66.6
New Jersey	66.5
Oregon	66.3
Alaska	65.7
Massachusetts	65.3
Texas	65.3
Washington	64.4
Rhode Island	62.8
Nevada	59.7
California	56.1
Hawaii	56.1
New York	54.5

percent

Home ownership rates represent the portion of owner households to the total number of occupied households.

SOURCES: U.S. Census Bureau Statistical Abstract of the United States: 2012, Table 993; U.S. Census Bureau, "Housing Vacancies and Home Ownership"

http://www.census.gov/compendia/statab/

http://www.census.gov/hhes/www/hvs.html

Owner Occupied Housing Values
(median home value $185.2 thousand nationally in 2009)

The Four Most Populous States
(32.8 percent of U.S. population)
#1 California #2 Texas #3 New York #4 Florida

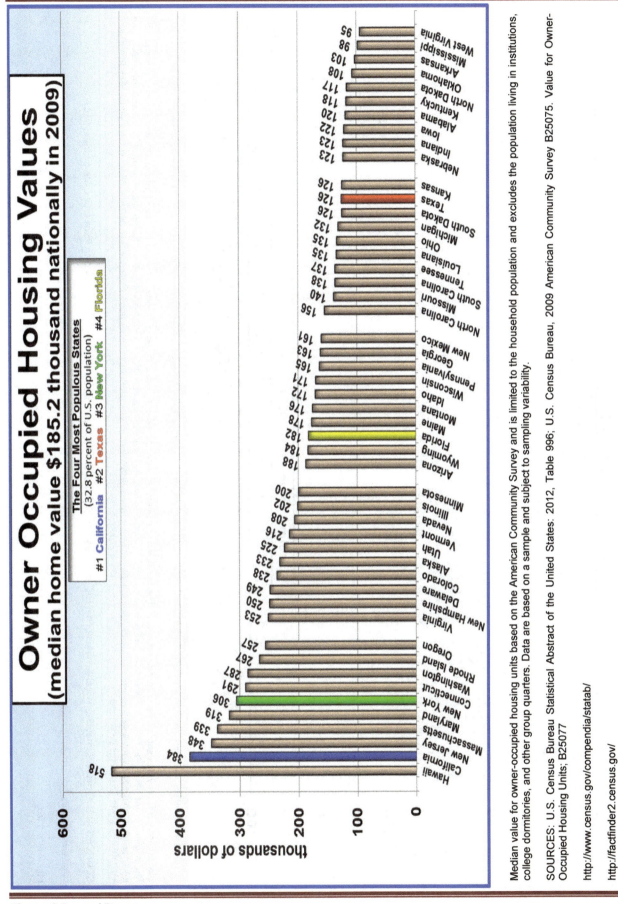

thousands of dollars

Hawaii	518
California	384
New Jersey	348
Massachusetts	339
Maryland	319
New York	306
Connecticut	291
Washington	287
Rhode Island	267
Oregon	257
Virginia	253
New Hampshire	250
Delaware	249
Colorado	238
Alaska	233
Utah	225
Vermont	216
Nevada	208
Illinois	202
Minnesota	200
Arizona	188
Wyoming	184
Florida	182
Maine	178
Montana	176
Idaho	172
Wisconsin	171
Pennsylvania	165
Georgia	163
New Mexico	161
North Carolina	156
Missouri	140
South Carolina	138
Tennessee	137
Louisiana	135
Ohio	135
Michigan	132
South Dakota	126
Texas	126
Kansas	126
Nebraska	123
Indiana	123
Iowa	122
Alabama	120
Kentucky	118
North Dakota	117
Oklahoma	108
Arkansas	103
Mississippi	98
West Virginia	95

Median value for owner-occupied housing units based on the American Community Survey and is limited to the household population and excludes the population living in institutions, college dormitories, and other group quarters. Data are based on a sample and subject to sampling variability.

SOURCES: U.S. Census Bureau Statistical Abstract of the United States: 2012, Table 996; U.S. Census Bureau, 2009 American Community Survey B25075. Value for Owner-Occupied Housing Units; B25077

http://www.census.gov/compendia/statab/

http://factfinder2.census.gov/

Single-Family Housing Price Index
(national average 185.7 in 2010)

The Four Most Populous States
(32.8 percent of U.S. population)
#1 California #2 Texas #3 New York #4 Florida

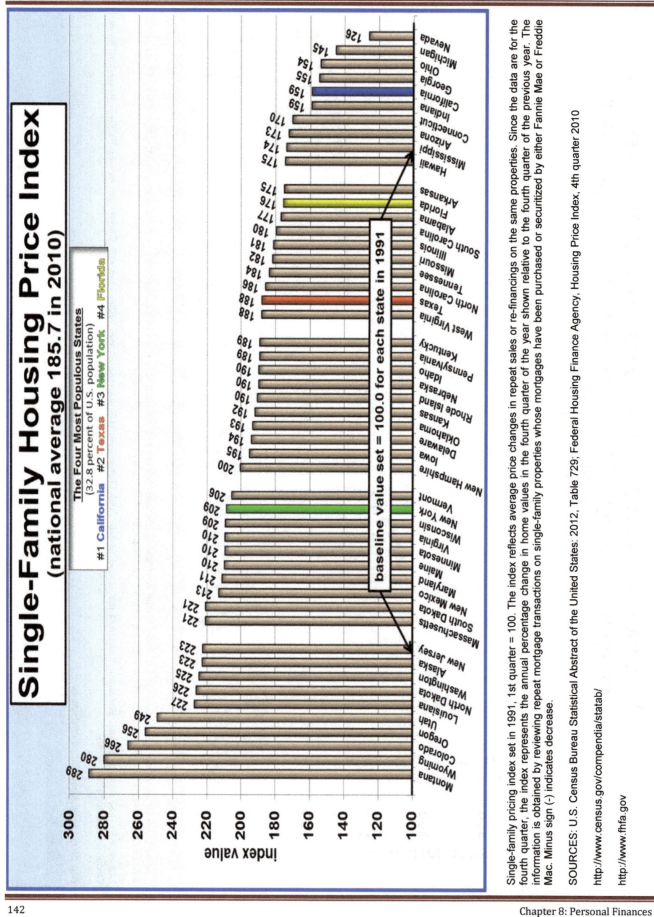

State	Index value
Montana	289
Wyoming	280
Colorado	266
Oregon	256
Utah	249
Louisiana	227
North Dakota	226
Washington	225
Alaska	223
New Jersey	223
Massachusetts	221
South Dakota	221
New Mexico	213
Maryland	211
Maine	210
Minnesota	210
Virginia	210
Wisconsin	209
New York	209
Vermont	206
New Hampshire	200
Iowa	195
Delaware	194
Oklahoma	193
Kansas	192
Rhode Island	190
Nebraska	190
Idaho	190
Pennsylvania	189
Kentucky	189
West Virginia	188
Texas	188
North Carolina	186
Tennessee	184
Missouri	182
Illinois	181
South Carolina	180
Alabama	177
Florida	176
Arkansas	175
Hawaii	175
Mississippi	174
Arizona	173
Connecticut	170
Indiana	159
California	159
Georgia	155
Ohio	154
Michigan	145
Nevada	126

baseline value set = 100.0 for each state in 1991

Single-family pricing index set in 1991, 1st quarter = 100. The index reflects average price changes in repeat sales or re-financings on the same properties. Since the data are for the fourth quarter, the index represents the annual percentage change in home values in the fourth quarter of the year shown relative to the fourth quarter of the previous year. The information is obtained by reviewing repeat mortgage transactions on single-family properties whose mortgages have been purchased or securitized by either Fannie Mae or Freddie Mac. Minus sign (-) indicates decrease.

SOURCES: U.S. Census Bureau Statistical Abstract of the United States: 2012, Table 729; Federal Housing Finance Agency, Housing Price Index, 4th quarter 2010

http://www.census.gov/compendia/statab/

http://www.fhfa.gov

Rental Housing Cost

($842 median rental cost per month nationally in 2009)

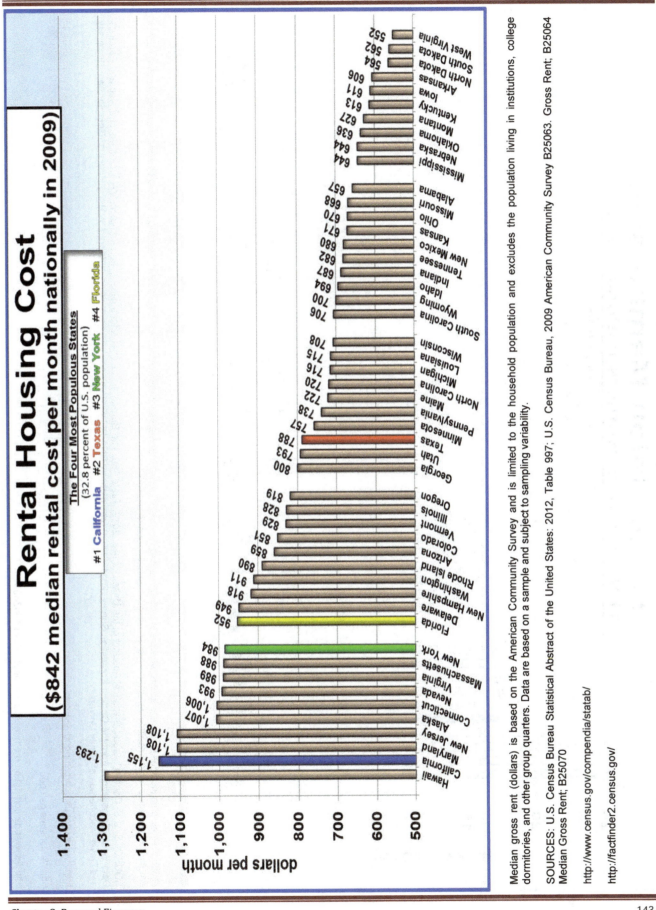

The Four Most Populous States
(32.8 percent of U.S. population)
#1 California #2 Texas #3 New York #4 Florida

State	dollars per month
Hawaii	1,293
California	1,155
Maryland	1,108
New Jersey	1,108
Alaska	1,007
Connecticut	1,006
Nevada	993
Virginia	989
Massachusetts	988
New York	984
Florida	952
Delaware	949
New Hampshire	918
Washington	911
Rhode Island	890
Arizona	859
Colorado	851
Vermont	829
Illinois	828
Oregon	819
Georgia	800
Utah	793
Texas	788
Minnesota	757
Pennsylvania	738
Maine	722
North Carolina	720
Michigan	716
Louisiana	715
Wisconsin	708
South Carolina	706
Wyoming	700
Idaho	694
Indiana	687
Tennessee	682
New Mexico	680
Kansas	671
Ohio	670
Missouri	668
Alabama	657
Mississippi	644
Nebraska	644
Oklahoma	636
Montana	627
Kentucky	613
Iowa	611
Arkansas	606
North Dakota	564
South Dakota	562
West Virginia	552

Median gross rent (dollars) is based on the American Community Survey and is limited to the household population and excludes the population living in institutions, college dormitories, and other group quarters. Data are based on a sample and subject to sampling variability.

SOURCES: U.S. Census Bureau Statistical Abstract of the United States: 2012, Table 997; U.S. Census Bureau, 2009 American Community Survey B25063. Gross Rent; B25064 Median Gross Rent; B25070

http://www.census.gov/compendia/statab/

http://factfinder2.census.gov/

Labor Union Membership
(11.9 percent of workers nationally in 2010)

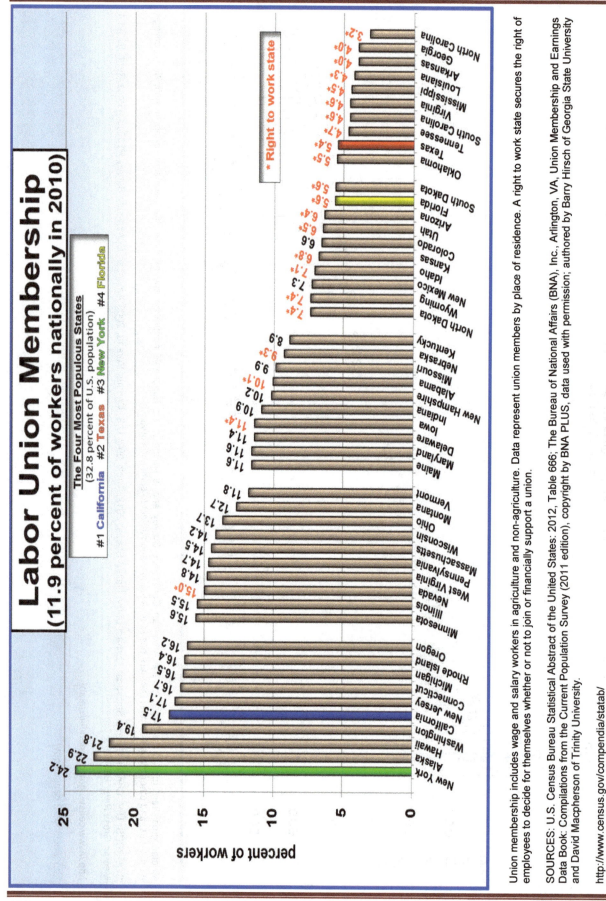

The Four Most Populous States
(32.8 percent of U.S. population)
#1 California #2 Texas #3 New York #4 Florida

* Right to work state

State	percent of workers
New York	24.2
Alaska	22.9
Hawaii	21.8
Washington	19.4
California	17.5
New Jersey	17.1
Connecticut	16.7
Michigan	16.5
Rhode Island	16.4
Oregon	16.2
Minnesota	15.6
Illinois	15.5
Nevada	15.0*
Pennsylvania	14.8
West Virginia	14.7
Massachusetts	14.5
Wisconsin	14.2
Ohio	13.7
Montana	12.7
Vermont	11.8
Maine	11.6
Maryland	11.6
Delaware	11.4*
Iowa	10.9
Indiana	10.2
New Hampshire	10.1*
Alabama	9.9
Missouri	9.3*
Nebraska	8.9
Kentucky	
North Dakota	7.4*
Wyoming	7.4*
New Mexico	7.3
Idaho	7.1*
Kansas	6.8*
Colorado	6.6
Utah	6.5*
Arizona	6.4*
Florida	5.6*
South Dakota	5.6*
Oklahoma	5.5*
Texas	5.4*
Tennessee	4.7*
South Carolina	4.6*
Virginia	4.6*
Mississippi	4.5*
Louisiana	4.3*
Arkansas	4.0*
Georgia	4.0*
North Carolina	3.2*

Union membership includes wage and salary workers in agriculture and non-agriculture. Data represent union members by place of residence. A right to work state secures the right of employees to decide for themselves whether or not to join or financially support a union.

SOURCES: U.S. Census Bureau Statistical Abstract of the United States: 2012, Table 666; The Bureau of National Affairs (BNA), Inc., Arlington, VA, Union Membership and Earnings Data Book: Compilations from the Current Population Survey (2011 edition), copyright by BNA PLUS, data used with permission; authored by Barry Hirsch of Georgia State University and David Macpherson of Trinity University.

http://www.census.gov/compendia/statab/

http://unionstats.gsu.edu

http://www.bna.com/union-membership-earnings-p12884903659/

Employee Annual Wages
($45.6 thousand nationally in 2009)

The Four Most Populous States
(32.8 percent of U.S. population)
#1 California   #2 Texas   #3 New York   #4 Florida

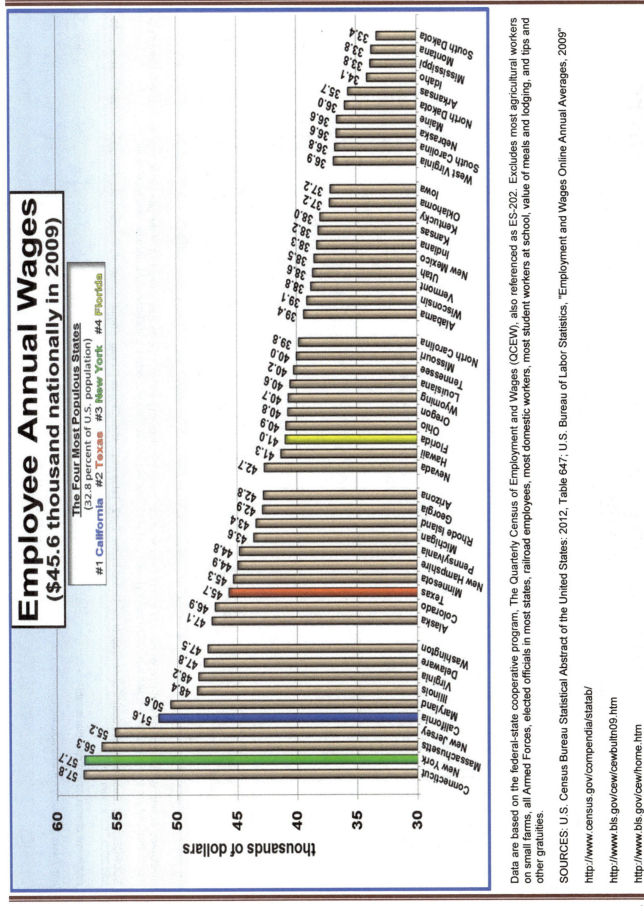

State	thousands of dollars
Connecticut	57.8
New York	57.7
Massachusetts	56.3
New Jersey	55.2
California	51.6
Maryland	50.6
Illinois	48.4
Virginia	48.2
Delaware	47.8
Washington	47.5
Alaska	47.1
Colorado	46.9
Texas	45.7
Minnesota	45.3
New Hampshire	44.9
Pennsylvania	44.8
Michigan	43.6
Rhode Island	43.4
Georgia	42.9
Arizona	42.8
Nevada	42.7
Hawaii	41.3
Florida	41.0
Ohio	40.9
Oregon	40.8
Wyoming	40.7
Louisiana	40.6
Tennessee	40.2
Missouri	40.0
North Carolina	39.8
Alabama	39.4
Wisconsin	39.1
Vermont	38.8
Utah	38.6
New Mexico	38.5
Indiana	38.3
Kansas	38.2
Kentucky	38.0
Oklahoma	37.2
Iowa	37.2
West Virginia	36.9
South Carolina	36.8
Nebraska	36.6
Maine	36.6
North Dakota	36.0
Arkansas	35.7
Idaho	34.1
Mississippi	33.8
Montana	33.8
South Dakota	33.4

Data are based on the federal-state cooperative program, The Quarterly Census of Employment and Wages (QCEW), also referenced as ES-202. Excludes most agricultural workers on small farms, all Armed Forces, elected officials in most states, railroad employees, most domestic workers, most student workers at school, value of meals and lodging, and tips and other gratuities.

SOURCES: U.S. Census Bureau Statistical Abstract of the United States: 2012, Table 647; U.S. Bureau of Labor Statistics, "Employment and Wages Online Annual Averages, 2009"

http://www.census.gov/compendia/statab/

http://www.bls.gov/cew/cewbultn09.htm

http://www.bls.gov/cew/home.htm

Manufacturing Employee Annual Payroll
($48.3 thousand nationally in 2009)

The Four Most Populous States
(32.8 percent of U.S. population)
#1 California   #2 Texas   #3 New York   #4 Florida

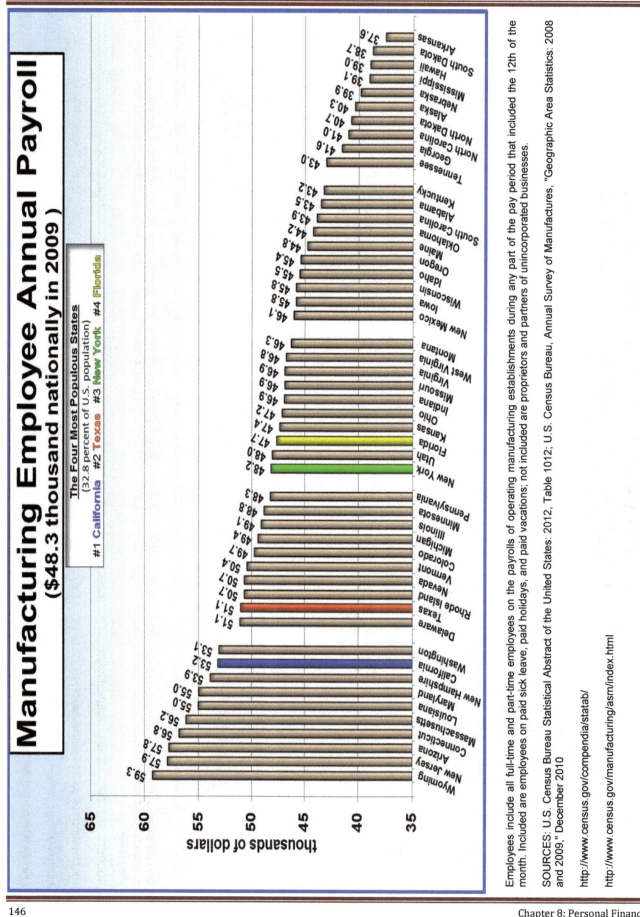

thousands of dollars

Wyoming	59.3
New Jersey	57.9
Arizona	57.8
Connecticut	56.8
Massachusetts	56.2
Louisiana	55.0
Maryland	55.0
New Hampshire	53.9
California	53.2
Washington	53.1
Delaware	51.1
Texas	51.1
Rhode Island	50.7
Nevada	50.7
Vermont	50.4
Colorado	49.7
Michigan	49.4
Illinois	49.1
Minnesota	48.8
Pennsylvania	48.3
New York	48.2
Utah	48.0
Florida	47.7
Kansas	47.4
Ohio	47.2
Indiana	46.9
Missouri	46.9
Virginia	46.9
West Virginia	46.8
Montana	46.3
New Mexico	46.1
Iowa	45.8
Wisconsin	45.8
Idaho	45.5
Oregon	45.4
Maine	44.8
Oklahoma	44.2
South Carolina	43.9
Alabama	43.5
Kentucky	43.2
Tennessee	43.0
Georgia	41.6
North Carolina	41.0
North Dakota	40.7
Alaska	40.3
Nebraska	39.9
Mississippi	39.1
Hawaii	39.0
South Dakota	38.7
Arkansas	37.6

Employees include all full-time and part-time employees on the payrolls of operating manufacturing establishments during any part of the pay period that included the 12th of the month. Included are employees on paid sick leave, paid holidays, and paid vacations; not included are proprietors and partners of unincorporated businesses.

SOURCES: U.S. Census Bureau Statistical Abstract of the United States: 2012, Table 1012; U.S. Census Bureau, Annual Survey of Manufactures, "Geographic Area Statistics: 2008 and 2009," December 2010

http://www.census.gov/compendia/statab/

http://www.census.gov/manufacturing/asm/index.html

Employees in Manufacturing
(8.9 percent of all employees nationally in 2010)

The Four Most Populous States
(32.8 percent of U.S. population)
#1 California #2 Texas #3 New York #4 Florida

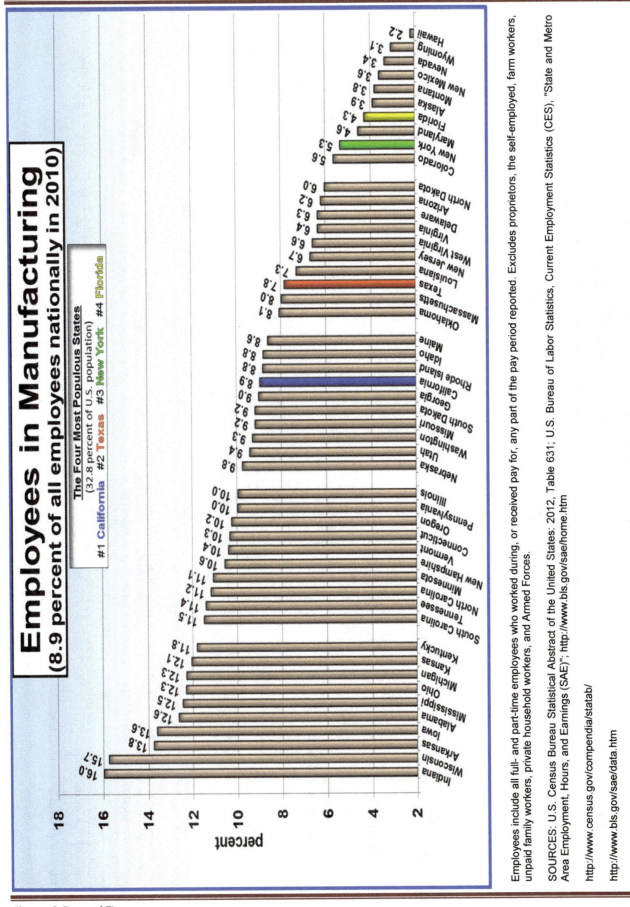

State	Percent
Indiana	16.0
Wisconsin	15.7
Arkansas	13.8
Iowa	13.6
Alabama	12.6
Mississippi	12.5
Ohio	12.3
Michigan	12.3
Kansas	12.1
Kentucky	11.8
South Carolina	11.5
Tennessee	11.4
North Carolina	11.2
Minnesota	11.1
New Hampshire	10.6
Vermont	10.4
Connecticut	10.3
Oregon	10.2
Pennsylvania	10.0
Illinois	10.0
Nebraska	9.8
Utah	9.4
Washington	9.3
Missouri	9.2
South Dakota	9.2
Georgia	9.0
California	8.9
Rhode Island	8.8
Idaho	8.8
Maine	8.6
Oklahoma	8.1
Massachusetts	8.0
Texas	7.8
Louisiana	7.3
New Jersey	6.7
West Virginia	6.6
Virginia	6.4
Delaware	6.3
Arizona	6.2
North Dakota	6.0
Colorado	5.6
New York	5.3
Maryland	4.6
Florida	4.3
Alaska	3.9
Montana	3.8
New Mexico	3.6
Nevada	3.4
Wyoming	3.1
Hawaii	2.2

percent

Employees include all full- and part-time employees who worked during, or received pay for, any part of the pay period reported. Excludes proprietors, the self-employed, farm workers, unpaid family workers, private household workers, and Armed Forces.

SOURCES: U.S. Census Bureau Statistical Abstract of the United States: 2012, Table 631; U.S. Bureau of Labor Statistics, Current Employment Statistics (CES), "State and Metro Area Employment, Hours, and Earnings (SAE)"; http://www.bls.gov/sae/home.htm

http://www.census.gov/compendia/statab/

http://www.bls.gov/sae/data.htm

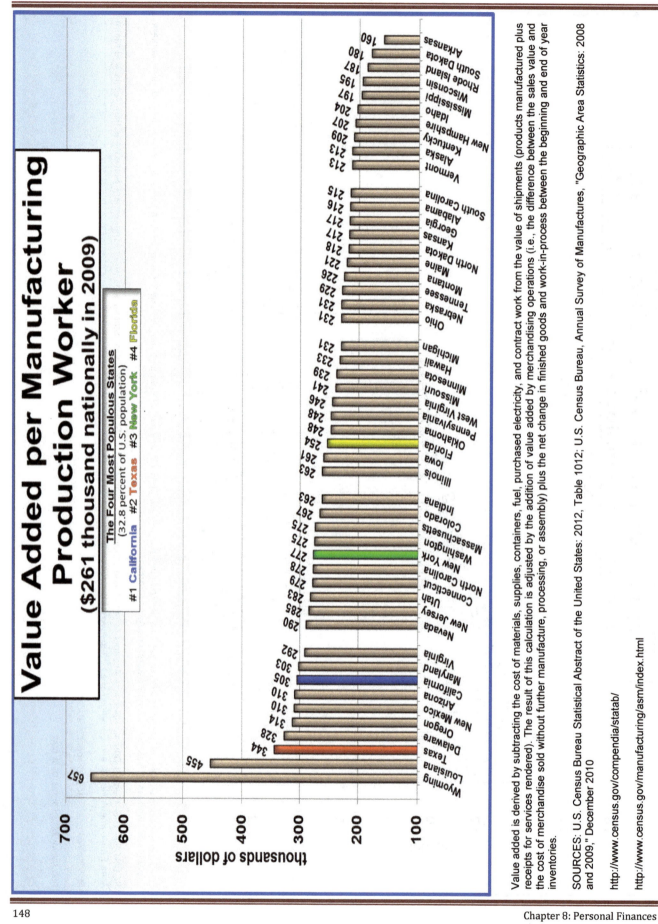

Value Added per Manufacturing Production Worker
($261 thousand nationally in 2009)

The Four Most Populous States
(32.8 percent of U.S. population)
#1 California   #2 Texas   #3 New York   #4 Florida

State	Value
Wyoming	657
Louisiana	455
Texas	344
Delaware	328
Oregon	314
New Mexico	310
Arizona	310
California	305
Maryland	303
Virginia	292
Nevada	290
New Jersey	285
Utah	283
Connecticut	279
North Carolina	278
New York	277
Washington	275
Massachusetts	275
Colorado	267
Indiana	263
Illinois	263
Iowa	261
Florida	254
Oklahoma	248
Pennsylvania	248
West Virginia	246
Missouri	241
Minnesota	239
Hawaii	233
Michigan	231
Ohio	231
Nebraska	231
Tennessee	229
Montana	226
Maine	221
North Dakota	218
Kansas	217
Georgia	217
Alabama	216
South Carolina	215
Vermont	213
Alaska	213
Kentucky	209
New Hampshire	207
Idaho	204
Mississippi	197
Wisconsin	195
Rhode Island	187
South Dakota	180
Arkansas	160

thousands of dollars

Value added is derived by subtracting the cost of materials, supplies, containers, fuel, purchased electricity, and contract work from the value of shipments (products manufactured plus receipts for services rendered). The result of this calculation is adjusted by the addition of value added by merchandising operations (i.e., the difference between the sales value and the cost of merchandise sold without further manufacture, processing, or assembly) plus the net change in finished goods and work-in-process between the beginning and end of year inventories.

SOURCES: U.S. Census Bureau Statistical Abstract of the United States: 2012, Table 1012; U.S. Census Bureau, Annual Survey of Manufactures, "Geographic Area Statistics: 2008 and 2009," December 2010

http://www.census.gov/compendia/statab/

http://www.census.gov/manufacturing/asm/index.html

Bankruptcy Filings

(5.1 per 1,000 persons nationally in 2010 [1.6 million total])

The Four Most Populous States
(32.8 percent of U.S. population)
#1 California #2 Texas #3 New York #4 Florida

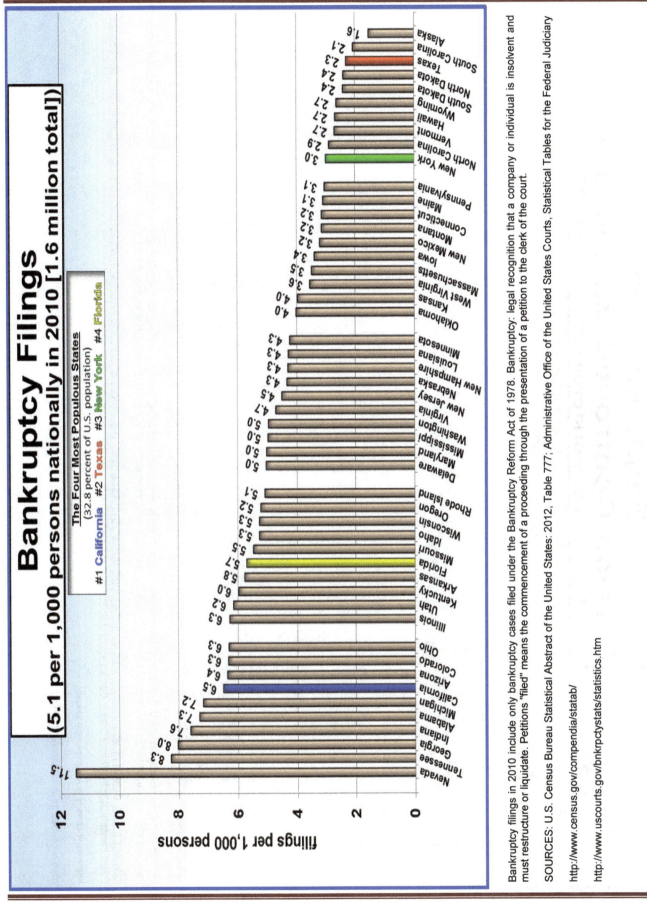

State	Filings per 1,000 persons
Nevada	11.5
Tennessee	8.3
Georgia	8.0
Indiana	7.6
Alabama	7.3
Michigan	7.2
California	6.5
Arizona	6.4
Colorado	6.3
Ohio	6.3
Illinois	6.3
Utah	6.2
Kentucky	6.0
Arkansas	5.8
Florida	5.7
Missouri	5.5
Idaho	5.3
Wisconsin	5.3
Oregon	5.2
Rhode Island	5.1
Delaware	5.0
Maryland	5.0
Mississippi	5.0
Washington	5.0
Virginia	4.7
New Jersey	4.5
Nebraska	4.3
New Hampshire	4.3
Louisiana	4.3
Minnesota	4.3
Oklahoma	4.0
Kansas	4.0
West Virginia	3.6
Massachusetts	3.5
Iowa	3.4
New Mexico	3.2
Montana	3.2
Connecticut	3.2
Maine	3.1
Pennsylvania	3.1
New York	3.0
North Carolina	2.9
Vermont	2.7
Hawaii	2.7
Wyoming	2.7
South Dakota	2.4
North Dakota	2.4
Texas	2.3
South Carolina	2.1
Alaska	1.6

filings per 1,000 persons

Bankruptcy filings in 2010 include only bankruptcy cases filed under the Bankruptcy Reform Act of 1978. Bankruptcy: legal recognition that a company or individual is insolvent and must restructure or liquidate. Petitions "filed" means the commencement of a proceeding through the presentation of a petition to the clerk of the court.

SOURCES: U.S. Census Bureau Statistical Abstract of the United States: 2012, Table 777; Administrative Office of the United States Courts, Statistical Tables for the Federal Judiciary

http://www.census.gov/compendia/statab/

http://www.uscourts.gov/bnkrpctystats/statistics.htm

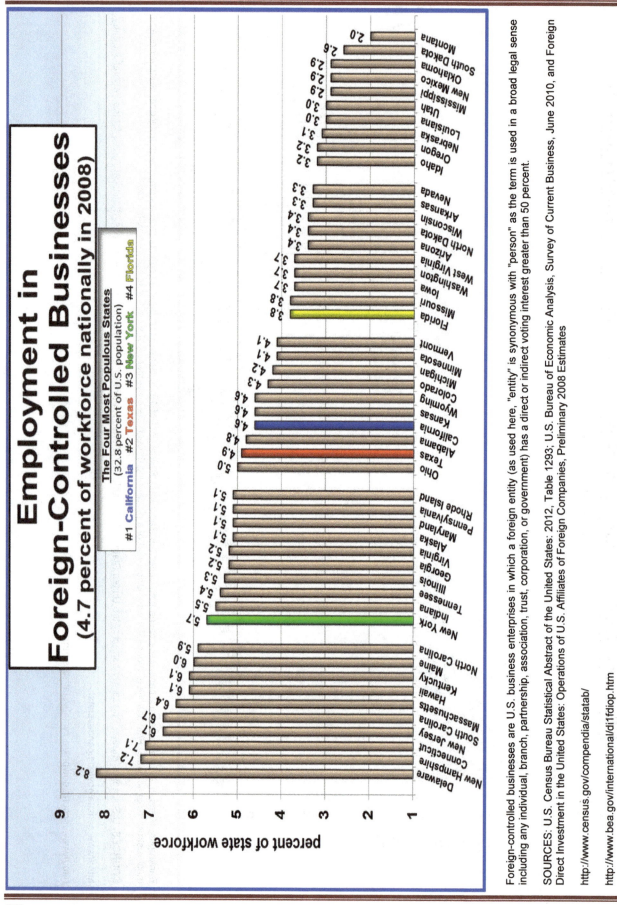

Employment in Foreign-Controlled Businesses
(4.7 percent of workforce nationally in 2008)

The Four Most Populous States
(32.8 percent of U.S. population)
#1 California   #2 Texas   #3 New York   #4 Florida

percent of state workforce

State	Percent
Delaware	8.2
New Hampshire	7.2
Connecticut	7.1
New Jersey	6.7
South Carolina	6.7
Massachusetts	6.4
Hawaii	6.1
Kentucky	6.1
Maine	6.0
North Carolina	5.9
New York	5.7
Indiana	5.5
Tennessee	5.4
Illinois	5.3
Georgia	5.2
Virginia	5.2
Alaska	5.1
Maryland	5.1
Pennsylvania	5.1
Rhode Island	5.1
Ohio	5.0
Texas	4.9
Alabama	4.8
California	4.6
Kansas	4.6
Wyoming	4.6
Colorado	4.3
Michigan	4.2
Minnesota	4.1
Vermont	4.1
Florida	3.8
Missouri	3.8
Iowa	3.7
Washington	3.7
West Virginia	3.7
Arizona	3.4
North Dakota	3.4
Wisconsin	3.4
Arkansas	3.3
Nevada	3.3
Idaho	3.2
Oregon	3.2
Nebraska	3.1
Louisiana	3.0
Utah	3.0
Mississippi	2.9
New Mexico	2.9
Oklahoma	2.9
South Dakota	2.6
Montana	2.0

Foreign-controlled businesses are U.S. business enterprises in which a foreign entity (as used here, "entity" is synonymous with "person" as the term is used in a broad legal sense including any individual, branch, partnership, association, trust, corporation, or government) has a direct or indirect voting interest greater than 50 percent.

SOURCES: U.S. Census Bureau Statistical Abstract of the United States: 2012, Table 1293; U.S. Bureau of Economic Analysis, Survey of Current Business, June 2010, and Foreign Direct Investment in the United States: Operations of U.S. Affiliates of Foreign Companies, Preliminary 2008 Estimates

http://www.census.gov/compendia/statab/

http://www.bea.gov/international/di1fdiop.htm

Chapter 9: State Economy Overview

Alaska is the only state that does not have a personal income tax or a state general sales tax. However, Alaska collected $9,770 per capita through severance tax in 2008—the most of any state. Severance taxes are taxes imposed distinctively on removal of natural products (e.g., oil) from land or water. Alaska's $9,140 state debt per capita was second behind Massachusetts' $10,980 state debt per capita which is triple the national average and sixteen times Tennessee's.

Massachusetts' investment in research and development was the highest in the nation and three times the national average.

New Hampshire has no state sales tax and had the lowest overall state tax rate per capita, at 1/6th the level of Connecticut, the highest.

Washington had the highest state gasoline tax at 37.5 cents per gallon compared with Georgia which had the lowest gasoline tax at 7.5 cents per gallon.

California's gross domestic product (GDP) in 2011 was the nation's highest at $1.96 trillion, however, on a per capita basis, it was only 72 percent of Delaware's.

One-third of the nation's total exports come from Texas, California, and New York.

Florida had the lowest number of state employees at 10 per 1,000 persons, while Hawaii had the highest at 44 per 1,000 persons.

Local taxes per capita in New York were five times higher than in Vermont. In 2010, the cost of living in Manhattan was 2.17 times the national average while the cost of living in Harlingen Texas was .83 times the national average.

The unemployment rate in the first quarter of 2012 was highest in Nevada at 12.3 percent and lowest in North Dakota at 3.4 percent.

~

State Economy Summary Table

States Legend: ▮ Highest 10% ▯ Middle 80% ▮ Lowest 10%

Metric	Page
State Personal Income Tax per Capita	153
State General Sales Tax per Capita	154
State Taxes per Capita by Source	155
Local Government Taxes per Capita by Source	156
State Gasoline Tax	157
State Debt per Capita	158
State Severance Tax on Businesses per Capita	159
Lottery Revenue	160
Unemployment Rate	161
State Employees per Resident	162
Cost of Living Composite Index for Highest City in 2010	163
Cost of Living Composite Index for Lowest City in 2010	164
Cost of Living Composite Index Range in 2010	165
Gross Domestic Product	166
Gross Domestic Product per Capita	167
Manufacturing Portion of Gross Domestic Product	168
Exports of Goods	169
Research and Development	170
State Arts Agency Appropriations	171

[1] one of seven states with no personal income tax
[2] one of five states with no sales tax
[3] one of eighteen states with no severance tax
[4] one of eight states with no lottery

State Personal Income Tax per Capita

($832 nationally in 2011)

The Four Most Populous States
(32.8 percent of U.S. population)
#1 California #2 Texas #3 New York #4 Florida

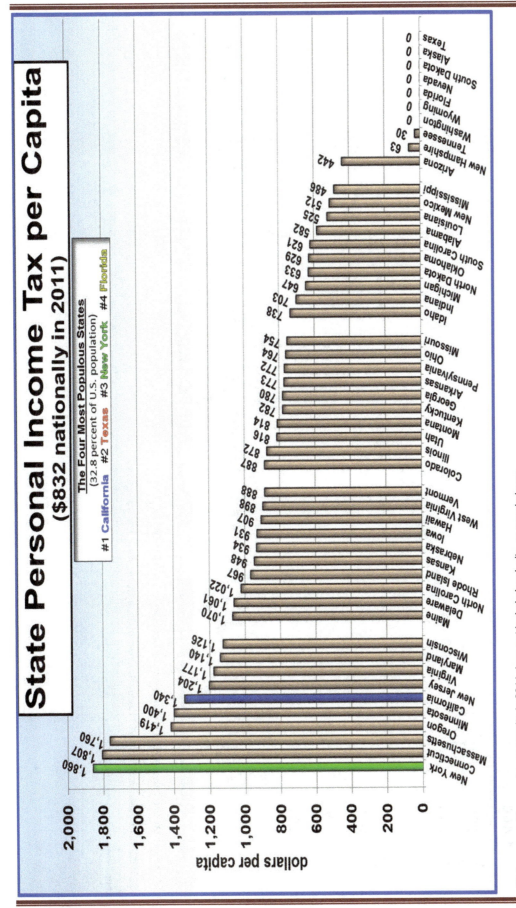

State	dollars per capita
New York	1,860
Connecticut	1,807
Massachusetts	1,760
Oregon	1,419
Minnesota	1,400
California	1,340
New Jersey	1,204
Virginia	1,177
Maryland	1,140
Wisconsin	1,126
Maine	1,070
Delaware	1,061
North Carolina	1,022
Rhode Island	967
Kansas	948
Nebraska	934
Iowa	931
Hawaii	907
West Virginia	898
Vermont	888
Colorado	887
Illinois	872
Utah	816
Montana	814
Kentucky	782
Georgia	780
Arkansas	773
Pennsylvania	772
Ohio	764
Missouri	754
Idaho	738
Indiana	703
Michigan	647
North Dakota	633
Oklahoma	629
South Carolina	621
Alabama	582
Louisiana	525
New Mexico	512
Mississippi	486
Arizona	442
New Hampshire	63
Tennessee	30
Washington	0
Wyoming	0
Florida	0
Nevada	0
South Dakota	0
Alaska	0
Texas	0

State personal income tax per capita in 2011 does not include local, city, or county taxes.

SOURCE: U.S. Census Bureau, 2011 Annual Survey of State Government Tax Collections

http://www.census.gov/govs/statetax/

State General Sales Tax per Capita
($753 nationally in 2011)

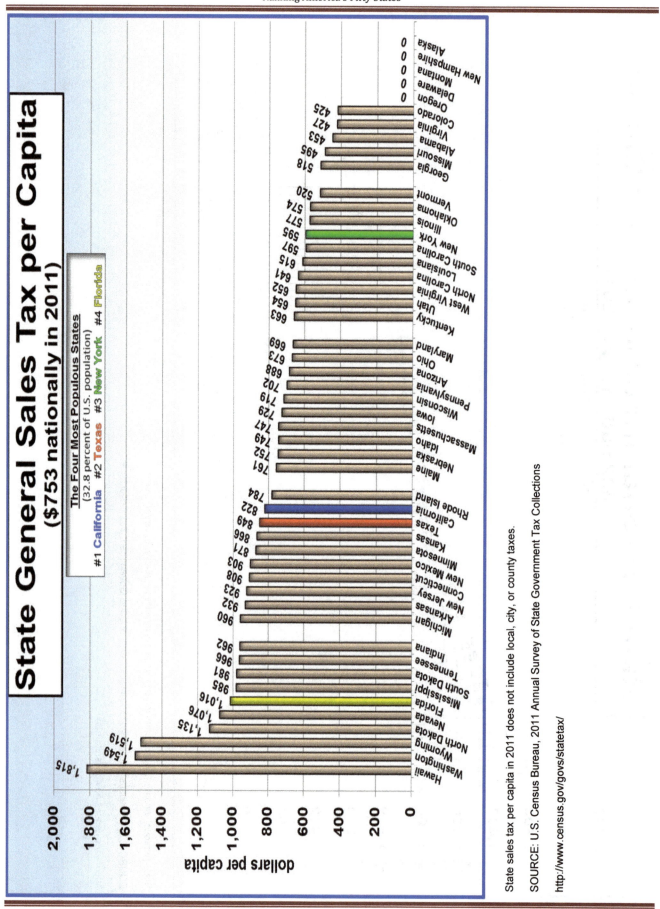

The Four Most Populous States
(32.8 percent of U.S. population)
#1 California #2 Texas #3 New York #4 Florida

State	dollars per capita
Hawaii	1,815
Washington	1,549
Wyoming	1,519
North Dakota	1,135
Nevada	1,076
Florida	1,016
Mississippi	985
South Dakota	981
Tennessee	966
Indiana	962
Michigan	960
Arkansas	932
New Jersey	923
Connecticut	908
New Mexico	903
Minnesota	871
Kansas	866
Texas	849
California	822
Rhode Island	784
Maine	761
Nebraska	752
Idaho	749
Massachusetts	747
Iowa	729
Wisconsin	719
Pennsylvania	702
Arizona	688
Ohio	673
Maryland	669
Kentucky	663
Utah	654
West Virginia	652
North Carolina	641
Louisiana	615
South Carolina	597
New York	595
Illinois	577
Oklahoma	574
Vermont	520
Georgia	518
Missouri	495
Alabama	453
Virginia	427
Colorado	425
Oregon	0
Delaware	0
Montana	0
New Hampshire	0
Alaska	0

State sales tax per capita in 2011 does not include local, city, or county taxes.

SOURCE: U.S. Census Bureau, 2011 Annual Survey of State Government Tax Collections

http://www.census.gov/govs/statetax/

State Taxes per Capita by Source
($1,713 nationally in 2011)

The Four Most Populous States
(32.8 percent of U.S. population)
#1 California #2 Texas #3 New York #4 Florida

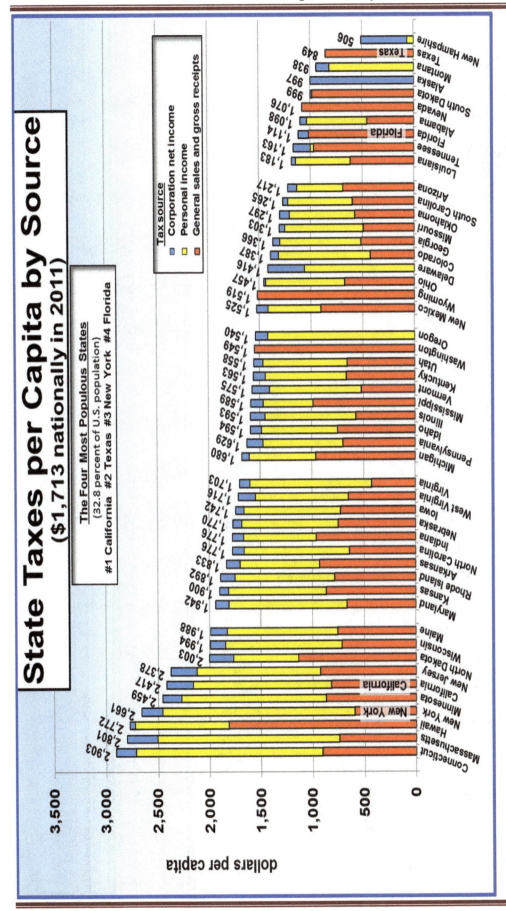

Tax source
- Corporation net income
- Personal income
- General sales and gross receipts

State taxes per capita in 2011 do not include local, city, or county taxes.

SOURCE: U.S. Census Bureau, 2011 Annual Survey of State Government Tax Collections

http://www.census.gov/govs/statetax/

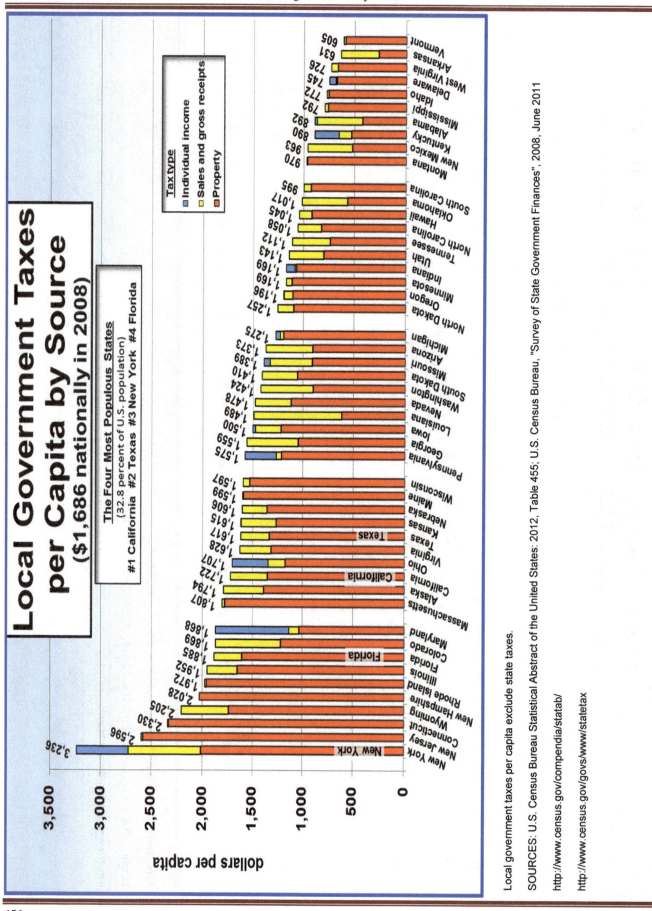

Local Government Taxes per Capita by Source
($1,686 nationally in 2008)

The Four Most Populous States
(32.8 percent of U.S. population)
#1 California #2 Texas #3 New York #4 Florida

Tax type
- Individual income
- Sales and gross receipts
- Property

New York	3,236
New Jersey	2,596
Connecticut	2,330
Wyoming	2,205
New Hampshire	2,028
Rhode Island	1,972
Illinois	1,952
Florida	1,885
Colorado	1,869
Maryland	1,868
Massachusetts	1,807
Alaska	1,794
California	1,722
Ohio	1,707
Virginia	1,628
Texas	1,617
Kansas	1,615
Nebraska	1,606
Maine	1,599
Wisconsin	1,597
Pennsylvania	1,575
Georgia	1,559
Iowa	1,500
Louisiana	1,489
Nevada	1,478
Washington	1,424
South Dakota	1,410
Missouri	1,389
Arizona	1,373
Michigan	1,275
North Dakota	1,257
Oregon	1,196
Minnesota	1,169
Indiana	1,169
Utah	1,143
Tennessee	1,112
North Carolina	1,058
Hawaii	1,045
Oklahoma	1,017
South Carolina	995
Montana	970
New Mexico	963
Kentucky	890
Alabama	892
Mississippi	792
Idaho	772
Delaware	745
West Virginia	726
Arkansas	631
Vermont	605

dollars per capita

3,500 3,000 2,500 2,000 1,500 1,000 500 0

Local government taxes per capita exclude state taxes.

SOURCES: U.S. Census Bureau Statistical Abstract of the United States: 2012, Table 455; U.S. Census Bureau, "Survey of State Government Finances", 2008, June 2011

http://www.census.gov/compendia/statab/

http://www.census.gov/govs/www/statetax

State Gasoline Tax
(21.8 cents per gallon nationally in 2009)

The Four Most Populous States
(32.8 percent of U.S. population)
#1 California   #2 Texas   #3 New York   #4 Florida

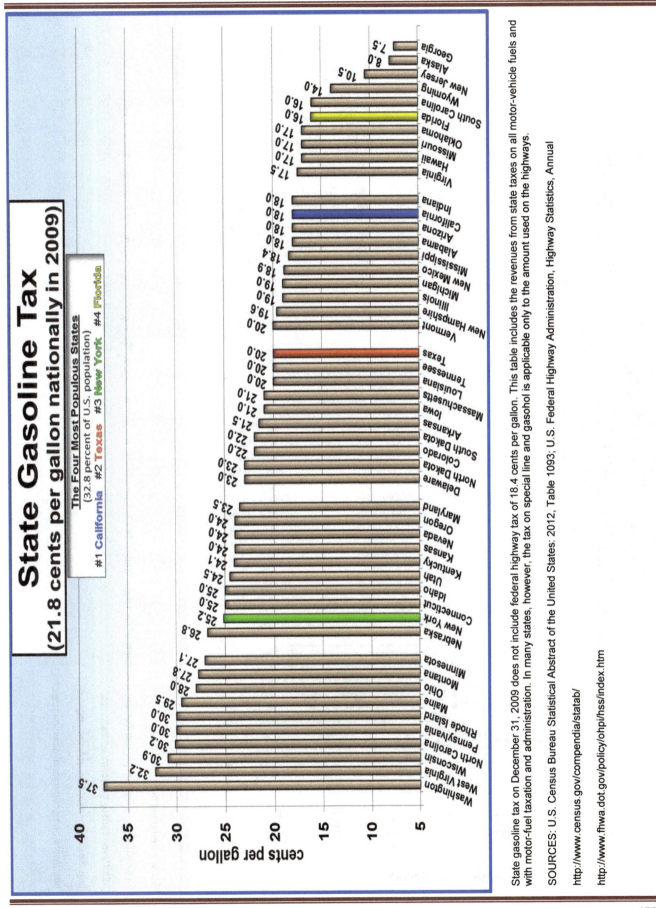

cents per gallon

State	cents per gallon
Washington	37.5
West Virginia	32.2
Wisconsin	30.9
North Carolina	30.2
Pennsylvania	30.0
Rhode Island	30.0
Maine	29.5
Ohio	28.0
Montana	27.8
Minnesota	27.1
Nebraska	26.8
New York	25.2
Connecticut	25.0
Idaho	25.0
Utah	24.5
Kentucky	24.1
Kansas	24.0
Nevada	24.0
Oregon	24.0
Maryland	23.5
Delaware	23.0
North Dakota	23.0
Colorado	22.0
South Dakota	22.0
Arkansas	21.5
Iowa	21.0
Massachusetts	21.0
Louisiana	20.0
Tennessee	20.0
Texas	20.0
Vermont	20.0
New Hampshire	19.6
Illinois	19.0
Michigan	19.0
New Mexico	18.9
Mississippi	18.4
Alabama	18.0
Arizona	18.0
California	18.0
Indiana	18.0
Virginia	17.5
Hawaii	17.0
Missouri	17.0
Oklahoma	17.0
Florida	16.0
South Carolina	16.0
Wyoming	14.0
New Jersey	10.5
Alaska	8.0
Georgia	7.5

State gasoline tax on December 31, 2009 does not include federal highway tax of 18.4 cents per gallon. This table includes the revenues from state taxes on all motor-vehicle fuels and with motor-fuel taxation and administration. In many states, however, the tax on special line and gasohol is applicable only to the amount used on the highways.

SOURCES: U.S. Census Bureau Statistical Abstract of the United States: 2012, Table 1093; U.S. Federal Highway Administration, Highway Statistics, Annual

http://www.census.gov/compendia/statab/

http://www.fhwa.dot.gov/policy/ohpi/hss/index.htm

State Debt per Capita
($3,259 nationally in 2008 [$1.0 trillion total])

The Four Most Populous States
(32.8 percent of U.S. population)
#1 California   #2 Texas   #3 New York   #4 Florida

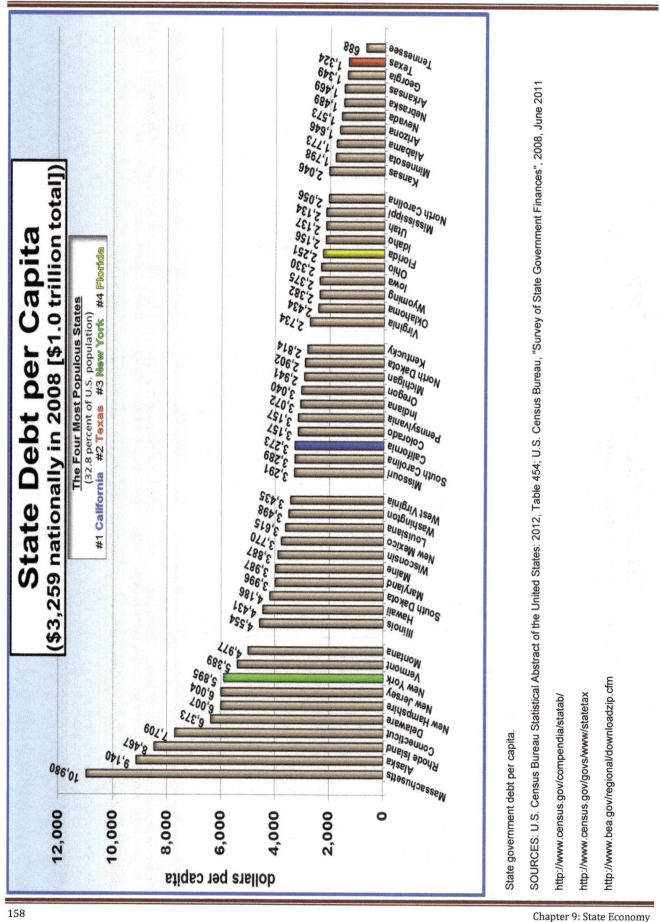

State	dollars per capita
Massachusetts	10,980
Alaska	9,140
Rhode Island	8,467
Connecticut	7,709
Delaware	6,373
New Hampshire	6,007
New Jersey	6,004
New York	5,895
Vermont	5,389
Montana	4,977
Illinois	4,554
Hawaii	4,431
South Dakota	4,186
Maryland	3,996
Maine	3,987
Wisconsin	3,887
New Mexico	3,770
Louisiana	3,615
Washington	3,498
West Virginia	3,435
Missouri	3,291
South Carolina	3,289
California	3,273
Colorado	3,157
Pennsylvania	3,157
Indiana	3,072
Oregon	3,040
Michigan	2,941
North Dakota	2,902
Kentucky	2,814
Virginia	2,734
Oklahoma	2,434
Wyoming	2,382
Iowa	2,375
Ohio	2,330
Florida	2,251
Idaho	2,156
Utah	2,137
Mississippi	2,134
North Carolina	2,056
Kansas	2,046
Minnesota	1,798
Alabama	1,773
Arizona	1,646
Nevada	1,573
Nebraska	1,489
Arkansas	1,469
Georgia	1,349
Texas	1,324
Tennessee	688

State government debt per capita.

SOURCES: U.S. Census Bureau Statistical Abstract of the United States: 2012, Table 454; U.S. Census Bureau, "Survey of State Government Finances", 2008, June 2011

http://www.census.gov/compendia/statab/

http://www.census.gov/govs/www/statetax

http://www.bea.gov/regional/downloadzip.cfm

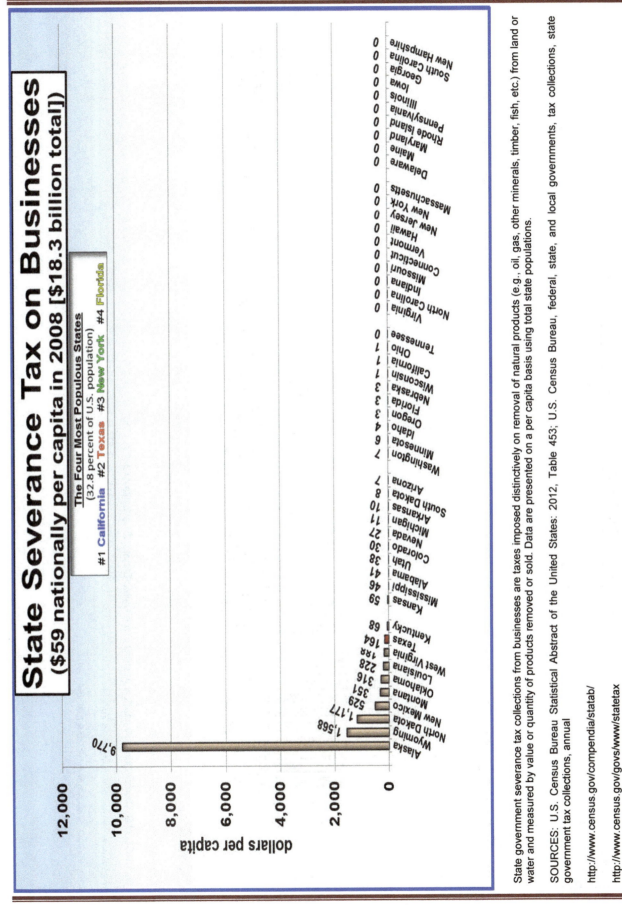

State Severance Tax on Businesses
($59 nationally per capita in 2008 [$18.3 billion total])

The Four Most Populous States
(32.8 percent of U.S. population)
#1 California   #2 Texas   #3 New York   #4 Florida

State	dollars per capita
Alaska	9,770
Wyoming	1,568
North Dakota	1,177
New Mexico	529
Montana	351
Oklahoma	316
Louisiana	228
West Virginia	188
Texas	164
Kentucky	68
Kansas	59
Mississippi	46
Alabama	41
Utah	38
Colorado	30
Nevada	27
Michigan	11
Arkansas	10
South Dakota	8
Arizona	7
Washington	7
Minnesota	6
Idaho	4
Oregon	3
Florida	3
Nebraska	1
Wisconsin	1
California	1
Ohio	1
Tennessee	0
Virginia	0
North Carolina	0
Indiana	0
Missouri	0
Connecticut	0
Vermont	0
Hawaii	0
New Jersey	0
New York	0
Massachusetts	0
Delaware	0
Maine	0
Rhode Island	0
Pennsylvania	0
Illinois	0
Iowa	0
Georgia	0
South Carolina	0
New Hampshire	0

State government severance tax collections from businesses are taxes imposed distinctively on removal of natural products (e.g., oil, gas, other minerals, timber, fish, etc.) from land or water and measured by value or quantity of products removed or sold. Data are presented on a per capita basis using total state populations.

SOURCES: U.S. Census Bureau Statistical Abstract of the United States: 2012, Table 453; U.S. Census Bureau, federal, state, and local governments, tax collections, state government tax collections, annual

http://www.census.gov/compendia/statab/

http://www.census.gov/govs/www/statetax

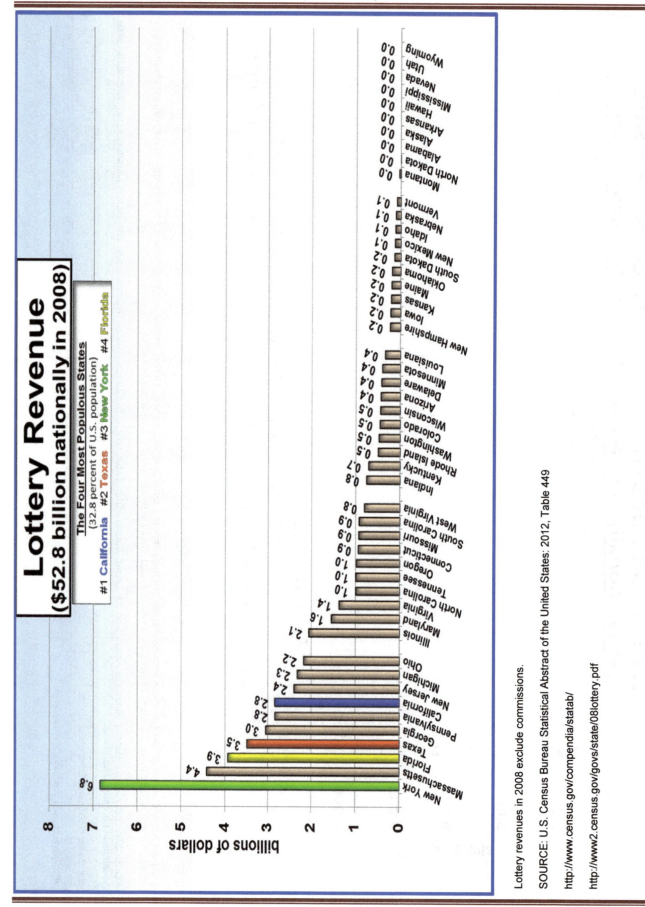

Lottery Revenue
($52.8 billion nationally in 2008)

The Four Most Populous States
(32.8 percent of U.S. population)
#1 California   #2 Texas   #3 New York   #4 Florida

State	billions of dollars
New York	6.8
Massachusetts	4.4
Florida	3.9
Texas	3.5
Georgia	3.0
Pennsylvania	2.8
California	2.8
New Jersey	2.4
Michigan	2.3
Ohio	2.2
Illinois	2.1
Maryland	1.6
Virginia	1.4
North Carolina	1.0
Tennessee	1.0
Oregon	1.0
Connecticut	0.9
Missouri	0.9
South Carolina	0.9
West Virginia	0.8
Indiana	0.8
Kentucky	0.7
Rhode Island	0.5
Washington	0.5
Colorado	0.5
Wisconsin	0.5
Arizona	0.4
Delaware	0.4
Minnesota	0.4
Louisiana	0.4
New Hampshire	0.2
Iowa	0.2
Kansas	0.2
Maine	0.2
Oklahoma	0.2
South Dakota	0.2
New Mexico	0.1
Idaho	0.1
Nebraska	0.1
Vermont	0.1
Montana	0.0
North Dakota	0.0
Alabama	0.0
Alaska	0.0
Arkansas	0.0
Hawaii	0.0
Mississippi	0.0
Nevada	0.0
Utah	0.0
Wyoming	0.0

Lottery revenues in 2008 exclude commissions.

SOURCE: U.S. Census Bureau Statistical Abstract of the United States: 2012, Table 449

http://www.census.gov/compendia/statab/

http://www2.census.gov/govs/state/08lottery.pdf

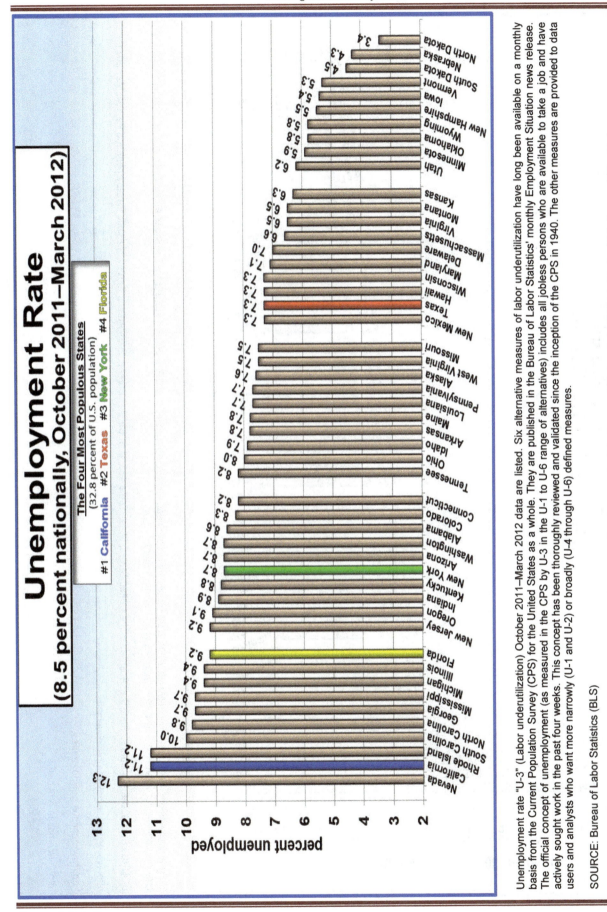

Unemployment Rate
(8.5 percent nationally, October 2011–March 2012)

The Four Most Populous States
(32.8 percent of U.S. population)
#1 California #2 Texas #3 New York #4 Florida

State	percent unemployed
Nevada	12.3
California	11.2
Rhode Island	11.2
South Carolina	10.0
North Carolina	9.8
Georgia	9.7
Mississippi	9.7
Michigan	9.4
Illinois	9.4
Florida	9.2
New Jersey	9.2
Oregon	9.1
Indiana	8.9
Kentucky	8.8
New York	8.7
Arizona	8.7
Washington	8.7
Alabama	8.6
Colorado	8.3
Connecticut	8.2
Tennessee	8.2
Ohio	8.0
Idaho	7.9
Arkansas	7.8
Maine	7.8
Louisiana	7.7
Pennsylvania	7.7
Alaska	7.6
West Virginia	7.5
Missouri	7.5
New Mexico	7.3
Texas	7.3
Hawaii	7.3
Wisconsin	7.1
Maryland	7.0
Delaware	6.6
Massachusetts	6.5
Virginia	6.5
Montana	6.3
Kansas	6.2
Utah	5.9
Minnesota	5.8
Oklahoma	5.8
Wyoming	5.5
New Hampshire	5.4
Iowa	5.3
Vermont	4.5
South Dakota	4.3
Nebraska	3.4
North Dakota	3.4

Unemployment rate "U-3" (Labor underutilization) October 2011–March 2012 data are listed. Six alternative measures of labor underutilization have long been available on a monthly basis from the Current Population Survey (CPS) for the United States as a whole. They are published in the Bureau of Labor Statistics' monthly Employment Situation news release. The official concept of unemployment (as measured in the CPS by U-3 in the U-1 to U-6 range of alternatives) includes all jobless persons who are available to take a job and have actively sought work in the past four weeks. This concept has been thoroughly reviewed and validated since the inception of the CPS in 1940. The other measures are provided to data users and analysts who want more narrowly (U-1 and U-2) or broadly (U-4 through U-6) defined measures.

SOURCE: Bureau of Labor Statistics (BLS)

http://www.bls.gov/data/

State Employees per Resident
(14.3 per one thousand residents nationally in 2009)

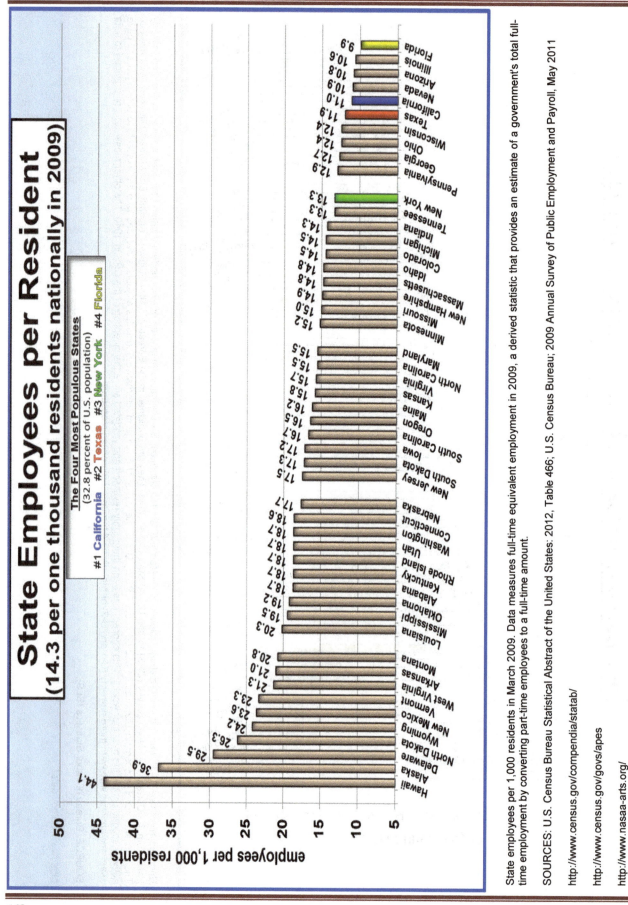

The Four Most Populous States
(32.8 percent of U.S. population)
#1 California #2 Texas #3 New York #4 Florida

Hawaii 44.1
Alaska 36.9
Delaware 29.5
North Dakota 26.3
Wyoming 24.2
New Mexico 23.6
Vermont 23.3
West Virginia 21.3
Arkansas 21.0
Montana 20.8
Louisiana 20.3
Mississippi 19.5
Oklahoma 19.2
Alabama 18.7
Kentucky 18.7
Rhode Island 18.7
Utah 18.7
Washington 18.6
Connecticut 17.7
Nebraska 17.7
New Jersey 17.5
South Dakota 17.3
Iowa 17.2
South Carolina 16.7
Oregon 16.5
Maine 16.2
Kansas 15.8
Virginia 15.7
North Carolina 15.5
Maryland 15.5
Minnesota 15.2
Missouri 15.0
New Hampshire 14.9
Massachusetts 14.8
Idaho 14.8
Colorado 14.5
Michigan 14.5
Indiana 14.3
Tennessee 13.3
New York 13.3
Pennsylvania 12.9
Georgia 12.7
Ohio 12.4
Wisconsin 12.4
Texas 11.9
California 11.0
Nevada 10.9
Arizona 10.8
Illinois 10.6
Florida 9.9

employees per 1,000 residents

State employees per 1,000 residents in March 2009. Data measures full-time equivalent employment in 2009, a derived statistic that provides an estimate of a government's total full-time employment by converting part-time employees to a full-time amount.

SOURCES: U.S. Census Bureau Statistical Abstract of the United States: 2012, Table 466; U.S. Census Bureau; 2009 Annual Survey of Public Employment and Payroll, May 2011

http://www.census.gov/compendia/statab/

http://www.census.gov/govs/apes

http://www.nasaa-arts.org/

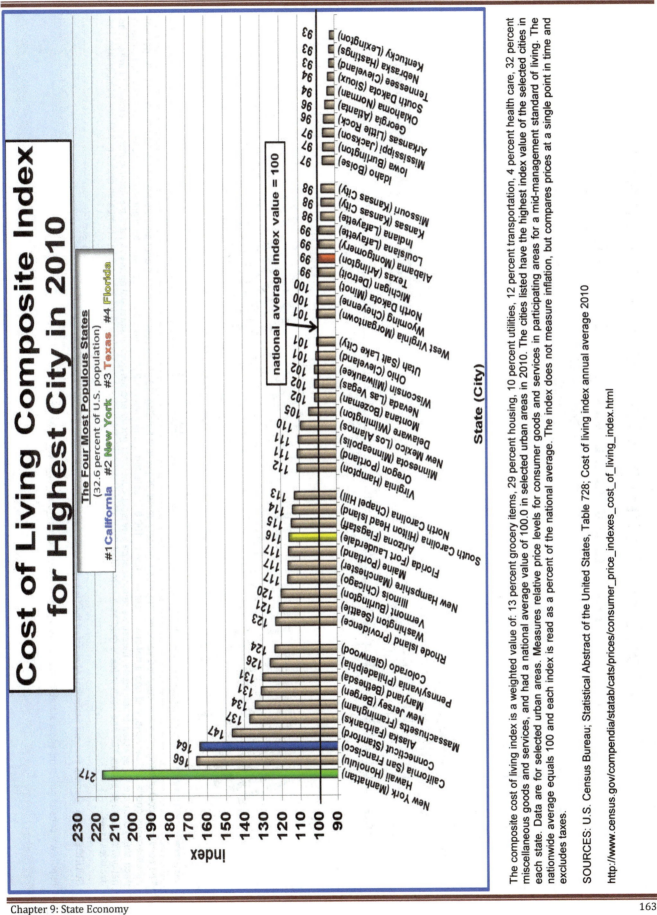

Cost of Living Composite Index for Highest City in 2010

The Four Most Populous States
(32.6 percent of U.S. population)
#1 California   #2 New York   #3 Texas   #4 Florida

national average index value = 100

State (City)	Index
New York (Manhattan)	217
Hawaii (Honolulu)	166
California (San Francisco)	164
Connecticut (Stamford)	147
Alaska (Fairbanks)	137
Massachusetts (Framingham)	134
New Jersey (Bergen)	131
Maryland (Bethesda)	131
Pennsylvania (Philadelphia)	126
Colorado (Glenwood)	124
Rhode Island (Providence)	123
Washington (Seattle)	121
Vermont (Burlington)	120
Illinois (Chicago)	117
New Hampshire (Manchester)	117
Maine (Portland)	117
Florida (Fort Lauderdale)	116
Arizona (Flagstaff)	115
South Carolina (Hilton Head Island)	114
North Carolina (Chapel Hill)	113
Virginia (Hampton)	112
Oregon (Portland)	111
Minnesota (Minneapolis)	111
New Mexico (Los Alamos)	110
Delaware (Wilmington)	105
Montana (Bozeman)	102
Nevada (Las Vegas)	102
Wisconsin (Milwaukee)	102
Ohio (Cleveland)	101
Utah (Salt Lake City)	101
West Virginia (Morgantown)	101
Wyoming (Cheyenne)	100
North Dakota (Minot)	100
Michigan (Detroit)	99
Texas (Arlington)	99
Alabama (Montgomery)	99
Louisiana (Lafayette)	99
Indiana (Lafayette)	98
Kansas (Kansas City)	98
Missouri (Kansas City)	98
Idaho (Boise)	97
Iowa (Burlington)	97
Mississippi (Jackson)	97
Arkansas (Little Rock)	96
Georgia (Atlanta)	96
Oklahoma (Norman)	94
South Dakota (Sioux)	94
Tennessee (Cleveland)	93
Nebraska (Hastings)	93
Kentucky (Lexington)	93

The composite cost of living index is a weighted value of: 13 percent grocery items, 29 percent housing, 10 percent utilities, 12 percent transportation, 4 percent health care, 32 percent miscellaneous goods and services, and had a national average value of 100.0 in selected urban areas in 2010. The cities listed have the highest index value of the selected cities in each state. Data are for selected urban areas. Measures relative price levels for consumer goods and services in participating areas for a mid-management standard of living. The nationwide average equals 100 and each index is read as a percent of the national average. The index does not measure inflation, but compares prices at a single point in time and excludes taxes.

SOURCES: U.S. Census Bureau; Statistical Abstract of the United States, Table 728; Cost of living index annual average 2010

http://www.census.gov/compendia/statab/cats/prices/consumer_price_indexes_cost_of_living_index.html

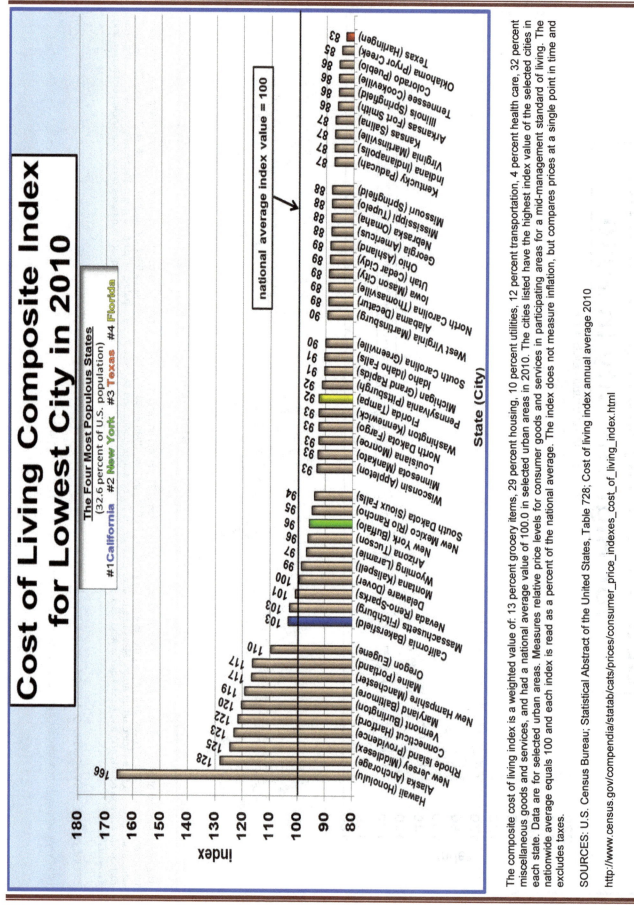

Cost of Living Composite Index for Lowest City in 2010

The Four Most Populous States
(32.6 percent of U.S. population)

#1 California   #2 New York   #3 Texas   #4 Florida

national average index value = 100

State (City)	Index
Hawaii (Honolulu)	166
Alaska (Anchorage)	128
New Jersey (Middlesex)	125
Rhode Island (Providence)	123
Connecticut (Hartford)	122
Vermont (Burlington)	120
Maryland (Baltimore)	119
New Hampshire (Manchester)	117
Maine (Portland)	117
Oregon (Eugene)	110
California (Bakersfield)	103
Massachusetts (Fitchburg)	103
Nevada (Reno-Sparks)	101
Delaware (Dover)	100
Montana (Kalispell)	99
Wyoming (Laramie)	97
Arizona (Tucson)	96
New York (Buffalo)	96
New Mexico (Rio Rancho)	95
South Dakota (Sioux Falls)	94
Wisconsin (Appleton)	93
Minnesota (Mankato)	93
Louisiana (Monroe)	93
North Dakota (Fargo)	93
Washington (Kennewick)	93
Florida (Tampa)	92
Pennsylvania (Pittsburgh)	92
Michigan (Grand Rapids)	91
Idaho (Idaho Falls)	91
South Carolina (Greenville)	90
West Virginia (Martinsburg)	90
Alabama (Decatur)	90
North Carolina (Thomasville)	89
Iowa (Mason City)	89
Utah (Cedar City)	89
Ohio (Ashland)	89
Georgia (Americus)	88
Nebraska (Omaha)	88
Mississippi (Tupelo)	88
Missouri (Springfield)	88
Kentucky (Paducah)	87
Indiana (Indianapolis)	87
Virginia (Martinsville)	87
Kansas (Salina)	87
Arkansas (Fort Smith)	86
Illinois (Springfield)	86
Tennessee (Cookeville)	86
Colorado (Pueblo)	86
Oklahoma (Pryor Creek)	85
Texas (Harlingen)	83

The composite cost of living index is a weighted value of: 13 percent grocery items, 29 percent housing, 10 percent utilities, 12 percent transportation, 4 percent health care, 32 percent miscellaneous goods and services, and had a national average value of 100.0 in selected urban areas in 2010. The cities listed have the highest index value of the selected cities in each state. Data are for selected urban areas. Measures relative price levels for consumer goods and services in participating areas for a mid-management standard of living. The nationwide average equals 100 and each index is read as a percent of the national average. The index does not measure inflation, but compares prices at a single point in time and excludes taxes.

SOURCES: U.S. Census Bureau; Statistical Abstract of the United States, Table 728; Cost of living index annual average 2010

http://www.census.gov/compendia/statab/cats/prices/consumer_price_indexes_cost_of_living_index.html

Chapter 9: State Economy

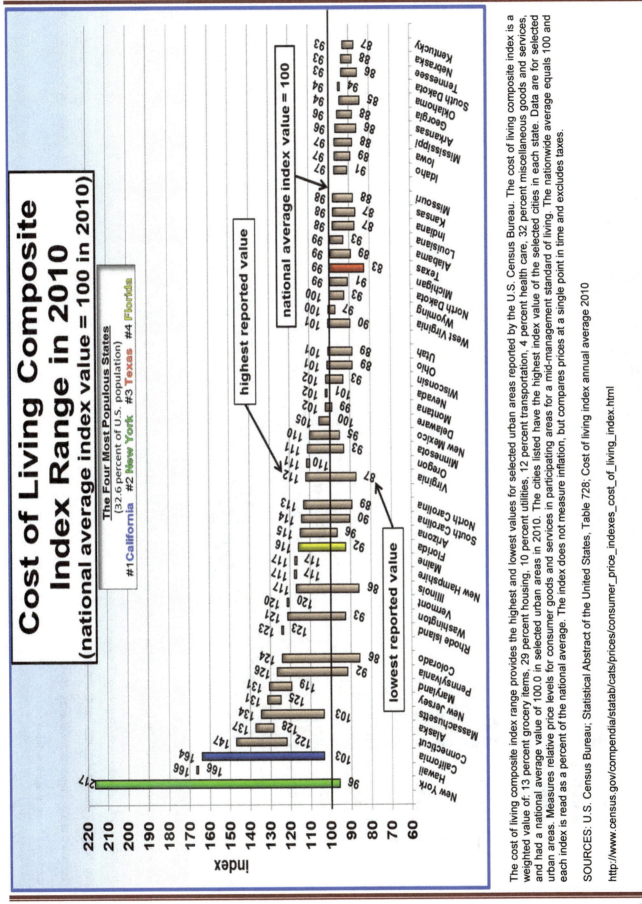

Cost of Living Composite Index Range in 2010

(national average index value = 100 in 2010)

The Four Most Populous States
(32.6 percent of U.S. population)

#1 California   #2 New York   #3 Texas   #4 Florida

highest reported value

national average index value = 100

lowest reported value

The cost of living composite index range provides the highest and lowest values for selected urban areas reported by the U.S. Census Bureau. The cost of living composite index is a weighted value of: 13 percent grocery items, 29 percent housing, 10 percent utilities, 12 percent transportation, 4 percent health care, 32 percent miscellaneous goods and services, and had a national average value of 100.0 in selected urban areas in 2010. The cities listed have the highest index value of the selected cities in each state. Data are for selected urban areas. Measures relative price levels for consumer goods and services in participating areas for a mid-management standard of living. The nationwide average equals 100 and each index is read as a percent of the national average. The index does not measure inflation, but compares prices at a single point in time and excludes taxes.

SOURCES: U.S. Census Bureau; Statistical Abstract of the United States, Table 728; Cost of living index annual average 2010

http://www.census.gov/compendia/statab/cats/prices/consumer_price_indexes_cost_of_living_index.html

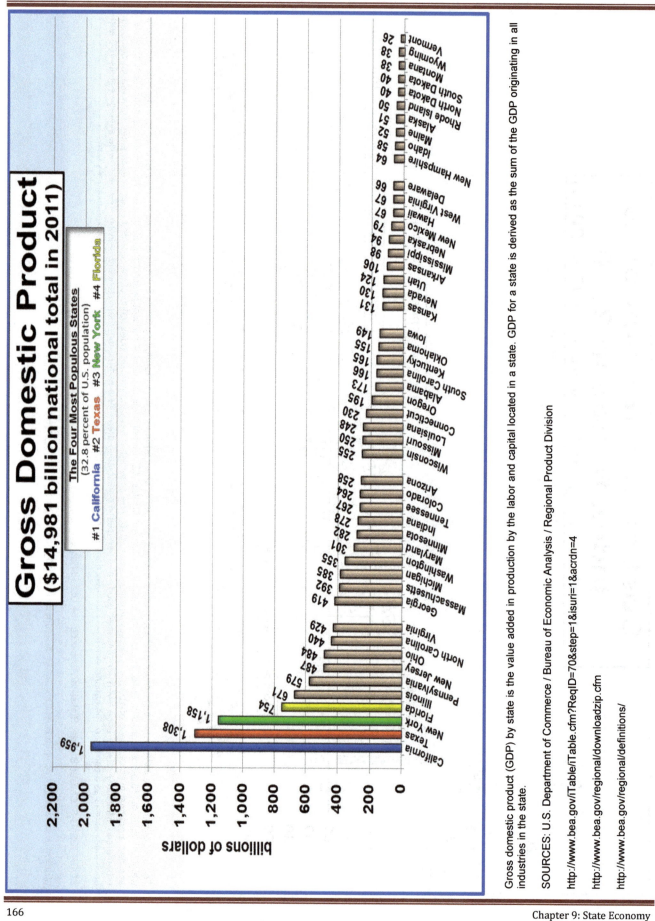

Gross Domestic Product
($14,981 billion national total in 2011)

The Four Most Populous States
(32.8 percent of U.S. population)
#1 California   #2 Texas   #3 New York   #4 Florida

billions of dollars

California	1,959
Texas	1,308
New York	1,158
Florida	754
Illinois	671
Pennsylvania	579
New Jersey	487
Ohio	484
North Carolina	440
Virginia	429
Georgia	419
Massachusetts	392
Michigan	385
Washington	355
Maryland	301
Minnesota	282
Indiana	278
Tennessee	267
Colorado	264
Arizona	258
Wisconsin	255
Missouri	250
Louisiana	248
Connecticut	230
Oregon	195
Alabama	173
South Carolina	166
Kentucky	165
Oklahoma	155
Iowa	149
Kansas	131
Nevada	130
Utah	124
Arkansas	106
Mississippi	98
Nebraska	94
New Mexico	79
Hawaii	67
West Virginia	67
Delaware	66
New Hampshire	64
Idaho	58
Maine	52
Alaska	51
Rhode Island	50
North Dakota	40
South Dakota	40
Montana	38
Wyoming	38
Vermont	26

Gross domestic product (GDP) by state is the value added in production by the labor and capital located in a state. GDP for a state is derived as the sum of the GDP originating in all industries in the state.

SOURCES: U.S. Department of Commerce / Bureau of Economic Analysis / Regional Product Division

http://www.bea.gov/iTable/iTable.cfm?ReqID=70&step=1&isuri=1&acrdn=4

http://www.bea.gov/regional/downloadzip.cfm

http://www.bea.gov/regional/definitions/

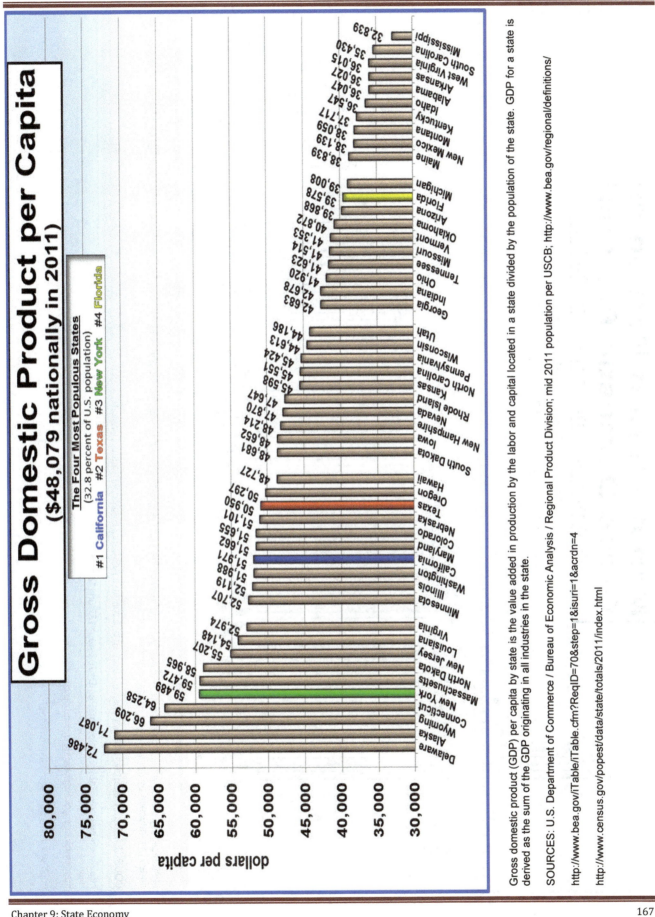

Gross Domestic Product per Capita
($48,079 nationally in 2011)

The Four Most Populous States
(32.8 percent of U.S. population)
#1 California #2 Texas #3 New York #4 Florida

Gross domestic product (GDP) per capita by state is the value added in production by the labor and capital located in a state divided by the population of the state. GDP for a state is derived as the sum of the GDP originating in all industries in the state.

SOURCES: U.S. Department of Commerce / Bureau of Economic Analysis / Regional Product Division; mid 2011 population per USCB; http://www.bea.gov/regional/definitions/

http://www.bea.gov/iTable/iTable.cfm?ReqID=70&step=1&isuri=1&acrdn=4

http://www.census.gov/popest/data/state/totals/2011/index.html

State	GDP per capita
Delaware	72,486
Alaska	71,087
Wyoming	66,209
Connecticut	64,258
New York	59,489
Massachusetts	59,472
North Dakota	58,965
New Jersey	55,207
Louisiana	54,148
Virginia	52,974
Minnesota	52,707
Illinois	52,119
Washington	51,988
California	51,971
Maryland	51,662
Colorado	51,655
Nebraska	51,101
Texas	50,950
Oregon	50,297
Hawaii	48,727
South Dakota	48,681
Iowa	48,652
New Hampshire	48,214
Nevada	47,870
Rhode Island	47,647
Kansas	45,598
North Carolina	45,551
Pennsylvania	45,424
Wisconsin	44,613
Utah	44,186
Georgia	42,683
Indiana	42,678
Ohio	41,920
Tennessee	41,623
Missouri	41,514
Vermont	41,353
Oklahoma	40,872
Arizona	39,868
Florida	39,578
Michigan	39,008
Maine	38,839
New Mexico	38,139
Montana	38,059
Kentucky	37,717
Idaho	36,547
Alabama	36,047
Arkansas	36,027
West Virginia	36,015
South Carolina	35,430
Mississippi	32,839

Manufacturing Portion of Gross Domestic Product
(12.3 percent nationally in 2011)

The Four Most Populous States
(32.8 percent of U.S. population)
#1 California   #2 Texas   #3 New York   #4 Florida

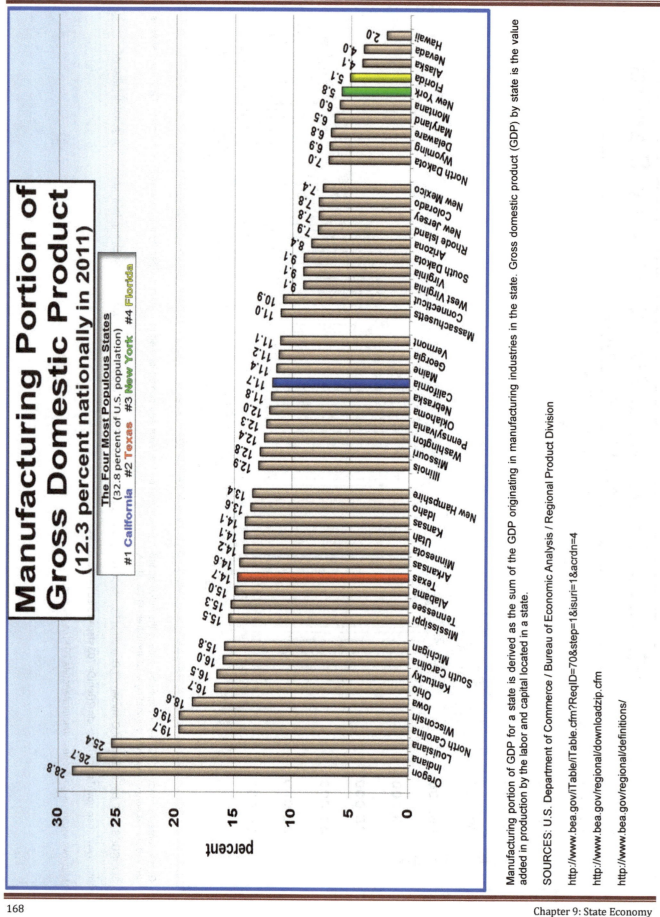

State	Percent
Oregon	28.8
Indiana	26.7
Louisiana	25.4
North Carolina	19.7
Wisconsin	19.6
Iowa	18.6
Ohio	16.7
Kentucky	16.5
South Carolina	16.0
Michigan	15.8
Mississippi	15.5
Tennessee	15.3
Alabama	15.0
Texas	14.7
Arkansas	14.6
Minnesota	14.2
Utah	14.1
Kansas	14.1
Idaho	13.6
New Hampshire	13.4
Illinois	12.9
Missouri	12.8
Washington	12.4
Pennsylvania	12.3
Oklahoma	12.0
Nebraska	11.8
California	11.7
Maine	11.4
Georgia	11.2
Vermont	11.1
Massachusetts	11.0
Connecticut	10.9
West Virginia	9.1
Virginia	9.1
South Dakota	9.1
Arizona	8.4
Rhode Island	7.9
New Jersey	7.8
Colorado	7.8
New Mexico	7.4
North Dakota	7.0
Wyoming	6.9
Delaware	6.8
Maryland	6.5
Montana	6.0
New York	5.8
Florida	5.1
Alaska	4.1
Nevada	4.0
Hawaii	2.0

percent

Manufacturing portion of GDP for a state is derived as the sum of the GDP originating in manufacturing industries in the state. Gross domestic product (GDP) by state is the value added in production by the labor and capital located in a state.

SOURCES: U.S. Department of Commerce / Bureau of Economic Analysis / Regional Product Division

http://www.bea.gov/iTable/iTable.cfm?ReqID=70&step=1&isuri=1&acrdn=4

http://www.bea.gov/regional/downloadzip.cfm

http://www.bea.gov/regional/definitions/

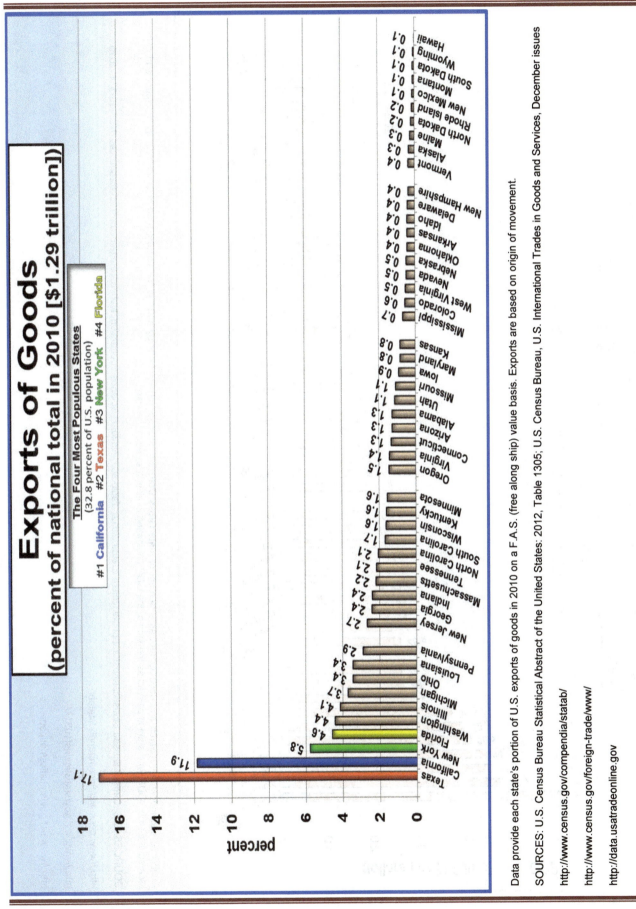

Exports of Goods
(percent of national total in 2010 [$1.29 trillion])

The Four Most Populous States
(32.8 percent of U.S. population)
#1 California   #2 Texas   #3 New York   #4 Florida

State	Percent
Texas	17.1
California	11.9
New York	5.8
Florida	4.6
Washington	4.4
Illinois	4.1
Michigan	3.7
Ohio	3.4
Louisiana	3.4
Pennsylvania	2.9
New Jersey	2.7
Georgia	2.4
Indiana	2.4
Massachusetts	2.2
Tennessee	2.1
North Carolina	2.1
South Carolina	1.7
Wisconsin	1.6
Kentucky	1.6
Minnesota	1.6
Oregon	1.5
Virginia	1.4
Connecticut	1.3
Arizona	1.3
Alabama	1.3
Utah	1.1
Missouri	1.1
Iowa	0.9
Maryland	0.8
Kansas	0.8
Mississippi	0.7
Colorado	0.6
West Virginia	0.5
Nevada	0.5
Nebraska	0.5
Oklahoma	0.4
Arkansas	0.4
Idaho	0.4
Delaware	0.4
New Hampshire	0.4
Vermont	0.4
Alaska	0.3
Maine	0.3
North Dakota	0.2
Rhode Island	0.2
New Mexico	0.1
Montana	0.1
South Dakota	0.1
Wyoming	0.1
Hawaii	0.1

percent

Data provide each state's portion of U.S. exports of goods in 2010 on a F.A.S. (free along ship) value basis. Exports are based on origin of movement.

SOURCES: U.S. Census Bureau Statistical Abstract of the United States: 2012, Table 1305; U.S. Census Bureau, U.S. International Trades in Goods and Services, December issues

http://www.census.gov/compendia/statab/

http://www.census.gov/foreign-trade/www/

http://data.usatradeonline.gov

Research and Development

($23.1 per $1,000 of GDP nationally in 2007)

The Four Most Populous States
(32.8 percent of U.S. population)
#1 California #2 Texas #3 New York #4 Florida

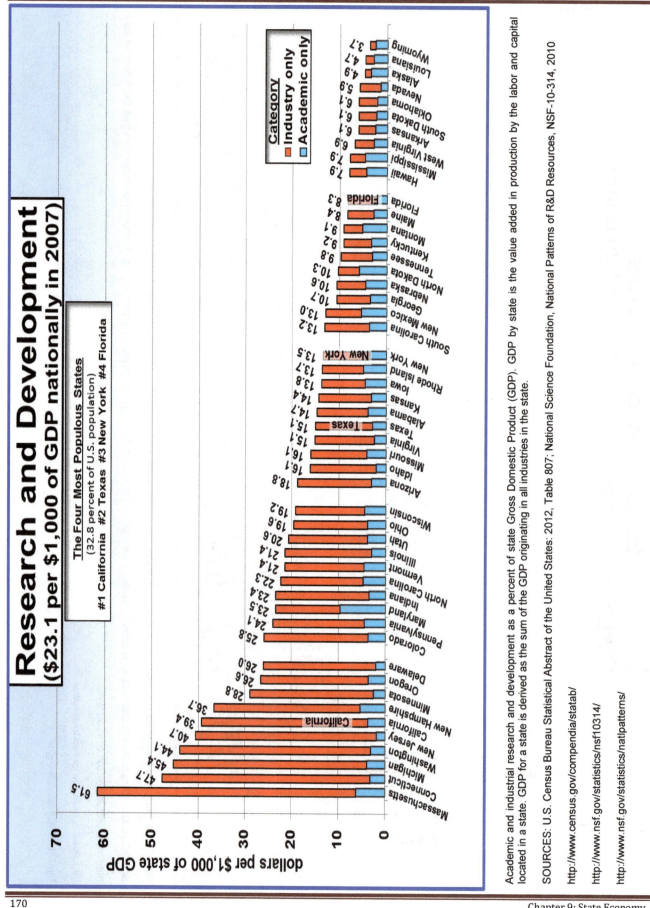

Category
- Industry only
- Academic only

dollars per $1,000 of state GDP

Massachusetts	61.5
Connecticut	47.7
Michigan	45.4
Washington	44.1
New Jersey	40.7
California	39.4
New Hampshire	36.7
Minnesota	28.8
Oregon	26.6
Delaware	26.0
Colorado	25.8
Pennsylvania	24.1
Maryland	23.5
Indiana	23.4
North Carolina	22.3
Vermont	21.4
Illinois	21.4
Utah	20.6
Ohio	19.6
Wisconsin	19.2
Arizona	18.8
Idaho	16.1
Missouri	16.1
Virginia	15.1
Texas	15.1
Alabama	14.7
Kansas	14.4
Iowa	13.8
Rhode Island	13.7
New York	13.5
South Carolina	13.2
New Mexico	13.0
Georgia	10.7
Nebraska	10.6
North Dakota	10.3
Tennessee	9.8
Kentucky	9.2
Montana	9.1
Maine	8.4
Florida	8.3
Hawaii	7.9
Mississippi	7.9
West Virginia	6.9
Arkansas	6.1
South Dakota	6.1
Oklahoma	6.1
Nevada	5.9
Alaska	4.9
Louisiana	4.7
Wyoming	3.7

Academic and industrial research and development as a percent of state Gross Domestic Product (GDP). GDP by state is the value added in production by the labor and capital located in a state. GDP for a state is derived as the sum of the GDP originating in all industries in the state.

SOURCES: U.S. Census Bureau Statistical Abstract of the United States: 2012, Table 807; National Science Foundation, National Patterns of R&D Resources, NSF-10-314, 2010

http://www.census.gov/compendia/statab/

http://www.nsf.gov/statistics/nsf10314/

http://www.nsf.gov/statistics/natlpatterns/

State Arts Agency Appropriations
($.88 per capita nationally in 2011 [$272 million total])

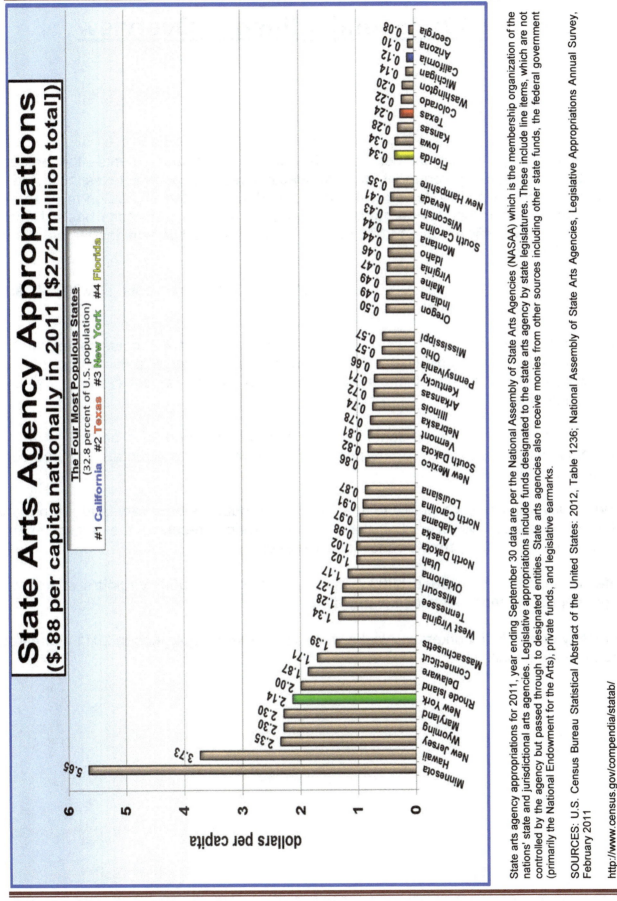

The Four Most Populous States
(32.8 percent of U.S. population)
#1 California   #2 Texas   #3 New York   #4 Florida

State	dollars per capita
Minnesota	5.65
Hawaii	3.73
New Jersey	2.35
Wyoming	2.30
Maryland	2.30
New York	2.14
Rhode Island	2.00
Delaware	1.87
Connecticut	1.71
Massachusetts	1.39
West Virginia	1.34
Tennessee	1.28
Missouri	1.27
Oklahoma	1.17
Utah	1.02
North Dakota	1.02
Alaska	0.98
Alabama	0.97
North Carolina	0.91
Louisiana	0.87
New Mexico	0.86
South Dakota	0.82
Vermont	0.81
Nebraska	0.78
Illinois	0.74
Arkansas	0.72
Kentucky	0.71
Pennsylvania	0.66
Ohio	0.57
Mississippi	0.57
Oregon	0.50
Indiana	0.49
Maine	0.49
Virginia	0.47
Idaho	0.46
Montana	0.44
South Carolina	0.44
Wisconsin	0.43
Nevada	0.41
New Hampshire	0.35
Florida	0.34
Iowa	0.34
Kansas	0.28
Texas	0.24
Colorado	0.22
Washington	0.20
Michigan	0.14
California	0.12
Arizona	0.10
Georgia	0.08

State arts agency appropriations for 2011, year ending September 30 data are per the National Assembly of State Arts Agencies (NASAA) which is the membership organization of the nations' state and jurisdictional arts agencies. Legislative appropriations include funds designated to the state arts agency by state legislatures. These include line items, which are not controlled by the agency but passed through to designated entities. State arts agencies also receive monies from other sources including other state funds, the federal government (primarily the National Endowment for the Arts), private funds, and legislative earmarks.

SOURCES: U.S. Census Bureau Statistical Abstract of the United States: 2012, Table 1236; National Assembly of State Arts Agencies, Legislative Appropriations Annual Survey, February 2011

http://www.census.gov/compendia/statab/

Chapter 10: Federal Influence Overview

In 2009, Virginia was the largest net beneficiary of federal disbursements—the amount disbursed by the federal government after subtracting federal income taxes collected—receiving $97 billion while New Jersey was the largest donor, paying $23 billion more to the federal government than the federal government disbursed. On a per capita basis, Hawaii was the largest net beneficiary at $14,076 per capita, while Delaware was the largest donor per capita at $6,064.

Alaska was the largest beneficiary per capita of federal disbursements at $20,400 and approximately double the national average.

Federal tax collections per capita were highest in Delaware and 4.7 times more than in Mississippi. Residents of Connecticut paid the highest effective federal personal income tax rate at 10.5 percent and had the highest federal personal income tax per capita. It was 3.8 times more than Mississippi's.

In Mississippi, 19.4 percent of residents received food stamps and 31.4 percent were on Medicaid. Nationally, 13.0 percent of the population received food stamps and 20.0 percent were recipients of Medicaid.

The federal government contributes to the funding of public elementary and secondary education in all states, however, Louisiana and Mississippi received the largest share, measured as a percent each state's educational expenditures.

The defense department awarded $303 billion in contracts in 2009. Virginia's share was $4,800 per capita, the most per capita of any state.

Approximately one-in-four workers in Alaska were government employees in 2011 compared with one-in-seven nationally.

~

Federal Influence Summary Table

States Legend: ■ Highest 10% □ Middle 80% ■ Lowest 10%

Page	Metric
174	Federal Personal Income Taxes Paid per Capita
175	Federal Personal Income Tax Rate Paid
176	Federal Tax Revenues per Capita
177	U.S. Federal Expenditure Distribution*
178	Federal Disbursements per Capita
179	Federal Disbursements in Excess of Taxes Collected
180	Federal Disbursements in Excess of Taxes per Capita
181	Federal Aid to State and Local Government per Capita
182	Food Stamp Recipients
183	Medicaid Payments
184	Medicaid Recipients
185	Supplemental Security Income per Capita
186	Federal Financing of Public K-12 Education
187	Federal Highway Subsidies per Capita
188	Federal Subsidies for Agriculture
189	Homeland Security Grants per Capita
190	Defense Department Payroll per Capita
191	Defense Department Personnel
192	Defense Department Contract Awards
193	Government Employment

States (columns, left to right): Alabama, Alaska, Arizona, Arkansas, California, Colorado, Connecticut, Delaware, Florida, Georgia, Hawaii, Idaho, Illinois, Indiana, Iowa, Kansas, Kentucky, Louisiana, Maine, Maryland, Massachusetts, Michigan, Minnesota, Mississippi, Missouri, Montana, Nebraska, Nevada, New Hampshire, New Jersey, New Mexico, New York, North Carolina, North Dakota, Ohio, Oklahoma, Oregon, Pennsylvania, Rhode Island, South Carolina, South Dakota, Tennessee, Texas, Utah, Vermont, Virginia, Washington, West Virginia, Wisconsin, Wyoming

* data for U.S. Federal Expenditure Distribution are national and not state specific

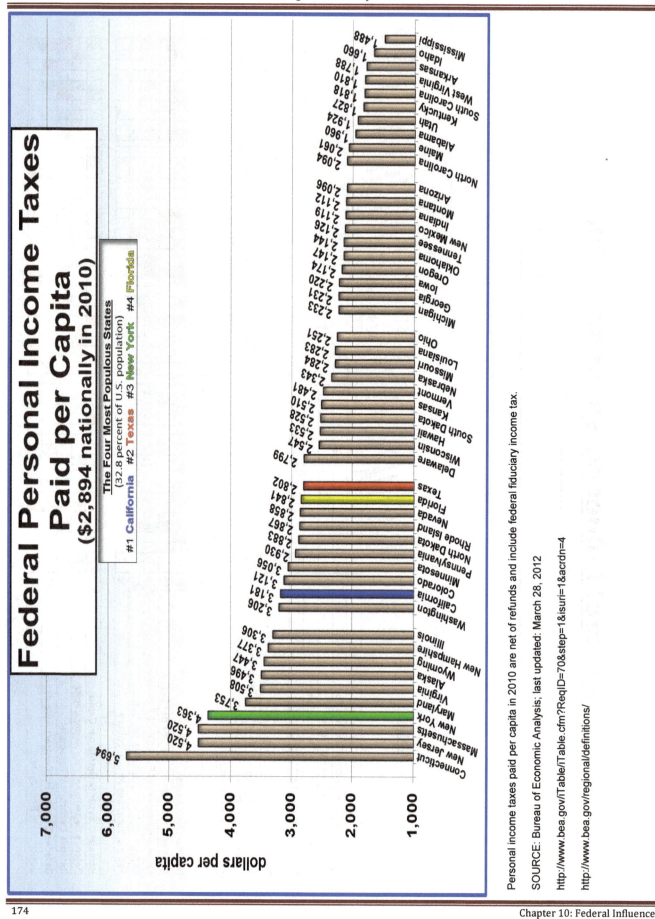

Federal Personal Income Taxes Paid per Capita

($2,894 nationally in 2010)

The Four Most Populous States
(32.8 percent of U.S. population)
#1 California #2 Texas #3 New York #4 Florida

State	dollars per capita
Connecticut	5,694
New Jersey	4,520
Massachusetts	4,520
New York	4,363
Maryland	3,753
Virginia	3,508
Alaska	3,496
Wyoming	3,447
New Hampshire	3,377
Illinois	3,306
Washington	3,206
California	3,181
Colorado	3,121
Minnesota	3,056
Pennsylvania	2,930
North Dakota	2,883
Rhode Island	2,867
Nevada	2,858
Florida	2,841
Texas	2,802
Delaware	2,799
Wisconsin	2,547
Hawaii	2,533
South Dakota	2,528
Kansas	2,510
Vermont	2,481
Nebraska	2,343
Missouri	2,284
Louisiana	2,283
Ohio	2,251
Michigan	2,233
Georgia	2,231
Iowa	2,220
Oregon	2,174
Oklahoma	2,147
Tennessee	2,144
New Mexico	2,126
Indiana	2,119
Montana	2,112
Arizona	2,096
North Carolina	2,094
Maine	2,061
Alabama	1,960
Utah	1,924
Kentucky	1,827
South Carolina	1,818
West Virginia	1,810
Arkansas	1,788
Idaho	1,660
Mississippi	1,488

Personal income taxes paid per capita in 2010 are net of refunds and include federal fiduciary income tax.

SOURCE: Bureau of Economic Analysis; last updated: March 28, 2012

http://www.bea.gov/iTable/iTable.cfm?ReqID=70&step=1&isuri=1&acrdn=4

http://www.bea.gov/regional/definitions/

Federal Personal Income Tax Rate Paid
(7.2 percent nationally in 2010)

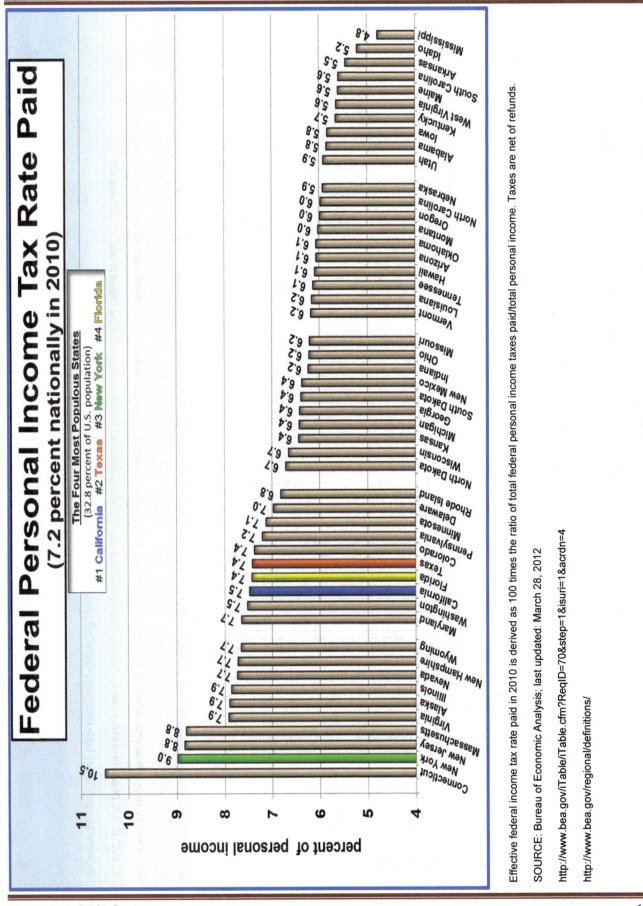

The Four Most Populous States
(32.8 percent of U.S. population)
#1 California   #2 Texas   #3 New York   #4 Florida

State	percent of personal income
Connecticut	10.5
New York	9.0
New Jersey	8.8
Massachusetts	8.8
Virginia	7.9
Alaska	7.9
Illinois	7.9
Nevada	7.7
New Hampshire	7.7
Wyoming	7.7
Maryland	7.7
Washington	7.5
California	7.5
Florida	7.4
Texas	7.4
Colorado	7.4
Pennsylvania	7.2
Minnesota	7.1
Delaware	7.0
Rhode Island	6.8
North Dakota	6.7
Wisconsin	6.7
Kansas	6.4
Michigan	6.4
Georgia	6.4
South Dakota	6.4
New Mexico	6.4
Indiana	6.2
Ohio	6.2
Missouri	6.2
Vermont	6.2
Louisiana	6.2
Tennessee	6.1
Hawaii	6.1
Arizona	6.1
Oklahoma	6.1
Montana	6.0
Oregon	6.0
North Carolina	6.0
Nebraska	5.9
Utah	5.9
Alabama	5.8
Iowa	5.8
Kentucky	5.7
West Virginia	5.6
Maine	5.6
South Carolina	5.6
Arkansas	5.5
Idaho	5.2
Mississippi	4.8

Effective federal income tax rate paid in 2010 is derived as 100 times the ratio of total federal personal income taxes paid/total personal income. Taxes are net of refunds.

SOURCE: Bureau of Economic Analysis; last updated: March 28, 2012

http://www.bea.gov/iTable/iTable.cfm?ReqID=70&step=1&isuri=1&acrdn=4

http://www.bea.gov/regional/definitions/

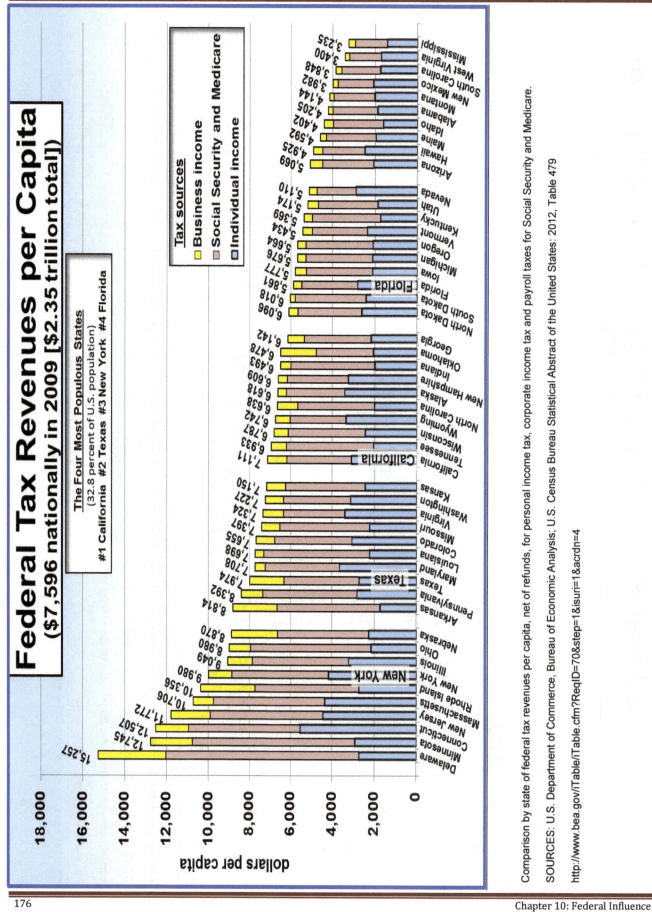

Federal Tax Revenues per Capita
($7,596 nationally in 2009 [$2.35 trillion total])

The Four Most Populous States
(32.8 percent of U.S. population)
#1 California #2 Texas #3 New York #4 Florida

Tax sources
- Business income
- Social Security and Medicare
- Individual income

dollars per capita

Delaware	15,257
Minnesota	12,745
Connecticut	12,507
New Jersey	11,772
Massachusetts	10,706
Rhode Island	10,356
New York	9,980
Illinois	9,049
Ohio	8,980
Nebraska	8,870
Arkansas	8,814
Pennsylvania	8,392
Texas	7,974
Maryland	7,708
Louisiana	7,698
Colorado	7,655
Missouri	7,397
Virginia	7,324
Washington	7,227
Kansas	7,150
California	7,111
Tennessee	6,933
Wisconsin	6,787
Wyoming	6,742
North Carolina	6,638
Alaska	6,618
New Hampshire	6,609
Indiana	6,493
Oklahoma	6,478
Georgia	6,142
North Dakota	6,960
South Dakota	6,018
Florida	5,861
Iowa	5,777
Michigan	5,676
Oregon	5,664
Vermont	5,434
Kentucky	5,369
Utah	5,174
Nevada	5,110
Arizona	5,069
Hawaii	4,925
Maine	4,592
Idaho	4,402
Alabama	4,205
Montana	4,144
New Mexico	3,982
South Carolina	3,848
West Virginia	3,400
Mississippi	3,235

Comparison by state of federal tax revenues per capita, net of refunds, for personal income tax, corporate income tax and payroll taxes for Social Security and Medicare.

SOURCES: U.S. Department of Commerce, Bureau of Economic Analysis; U.S. Census Bureau Statistical Abstract of the United States: 2012, Table 479

http://www.bea.gov/iTable/iTable.cfm?ReqID=70&step=1&isuri=1&acrdn=4

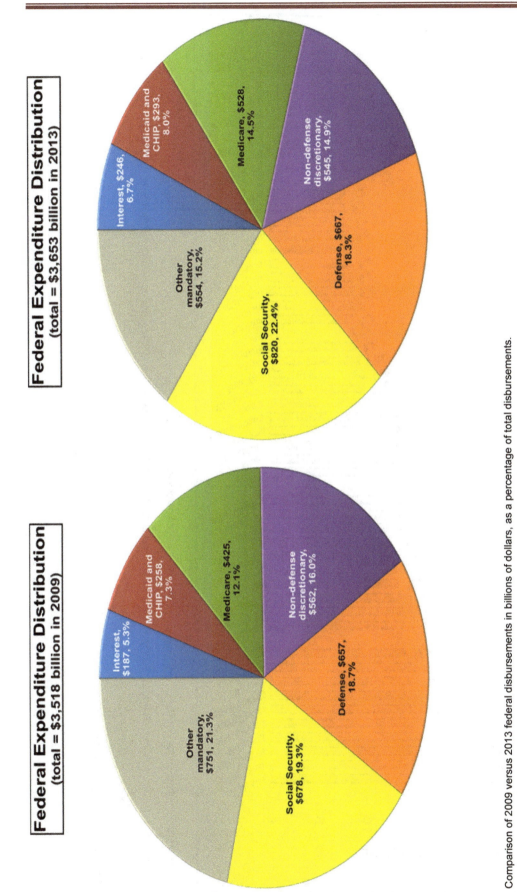

Federal Expenditure Distribution
(total = $3,653 billion in 2013)

Interest, $246, 6.7%

Medicaid and CHIP, $293, 8.0%

Medicare, $528, 14.5%

Non-defense discretionary, $545, 14.9%

Other mandatory, $554, 15.2%

Social Security, $820, 22.4%

Defense, $667, 18.3%

Federal Expenditure Distribution
(total = $3,518 billion in 2009)

Interest, $187, 5.3%

Medicaid and CHIP, $258, 7.3%

Medicare, $425, 12.1%

Non-defense discretionary, $562, 16.0%

Other mandatory, $751, 21.3%

Social Security, $678, 19.3%

Defense, $657, 18.7%

Comparison of 2009 versus 2013 federal disbursements in billions of dollars, as a percentage of total disbursements.

SOURCE: White House Office of Management and Budget (OMB)

http://www.whitehouse.gov/sites/default/files/omb/budget/fy2013/assets/technical_analyses.pdf

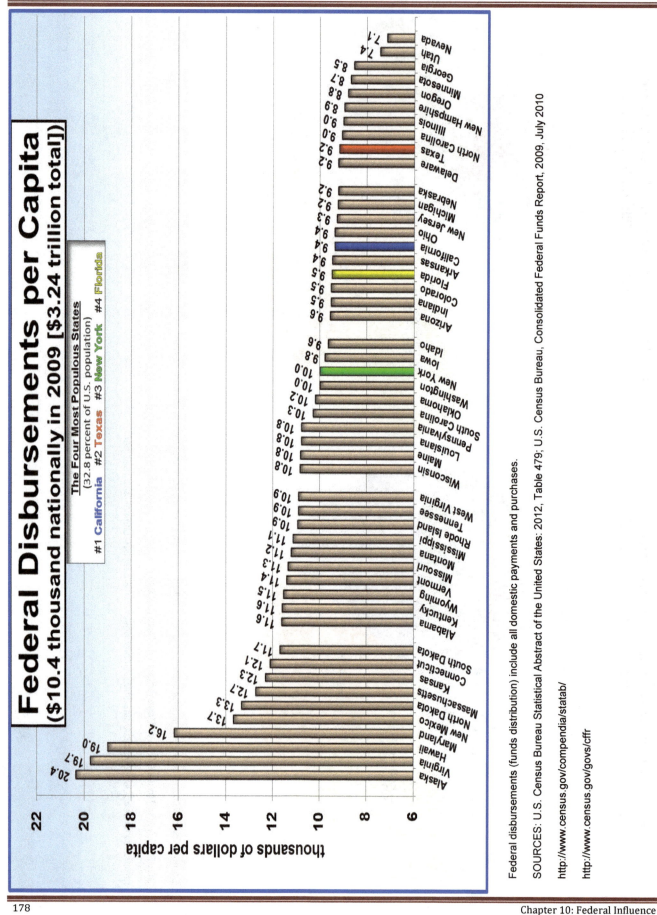

Federal Disbursements per Capita
($10.4 thousand nationally in 2009 [$3.24 trillion total])

The Four Most Populous States
(32.8 percent of U.S. population)
#1 California   #2 Texas   #3 New York   #4 Florida

thousands of dollars per capita

Alaska	20.4
Virginia	19.7
Hawaii	19.0
Maryland	16.2
New Mexico	13.7
North Dakota	13.3
Massachusetts	12.7
Kansas	12.3
Connecticut	12.1
South Dakota	11.7
Alabama	11.6
Kentucky	11.6
Wyoming	11.5
Vermont	11.4
Missouri	11.3
Montana	11.2
Mississippi	11.1
Rhode Island	10.9
Tennessee	10.9
West Virginia	10.9
Wisconsin	10.8
Maine	10.8
Louisiana	10.8
Pennsylvania	10.8
South Carolina	10.3
Oklahoma	10.2
Washington	10.0
New York	10.0
Iowa	9.8
Idaho	9.6
Arizona	9.6
Indiana	9.5
Colorado	9.5
Florida	9.5
Arkansas	9.4
California	9.4
Ohio	9.4
New Jersey	9.3
Michigan	9.2
Nebraska	9.2
Delaware	9.2
Texas	9.2
North Carolina	9.0
Illinois	9.0
New Hampshire	8.9
Oregon	8.8
Minnesota	8.7
Georgia	8.5
Utah	7.4
Nevada	7.1

Federal disbursements (funds distribution) include all domestic payments and purchases.

SOURCES: U.S. Census Bureau Statistical Abstract of the United States: 2012, Table 479; U.S. Census Bureau, Consolidated Federal Funds Report, 2009, July 2010

http://www.census.gov/compendia/statab/

http://www.census.gov/govs/cffr

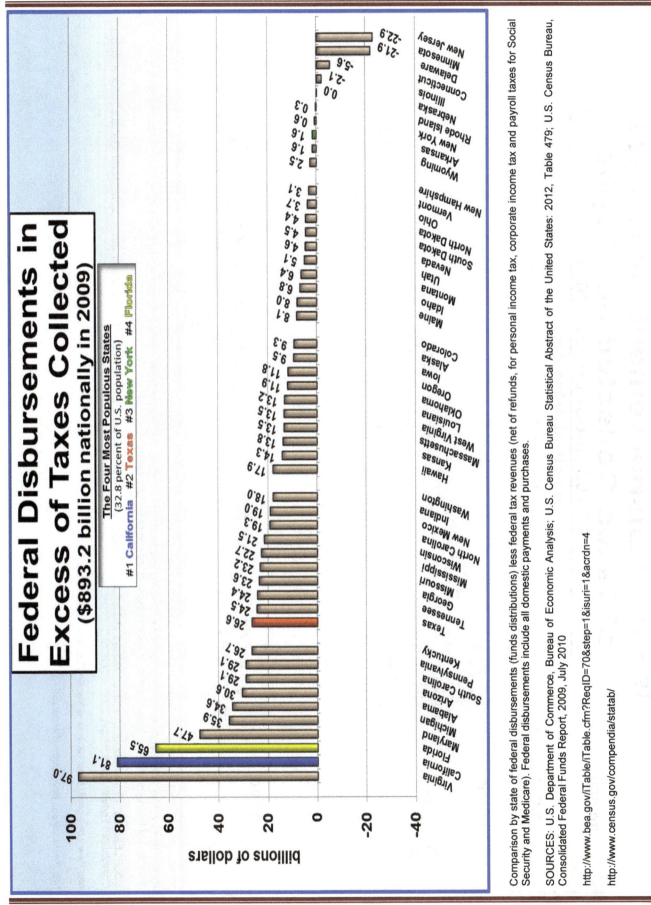

Federal Disbursements in Excess of Taxes Collected
($893.2 billion nationally in 2009)

The Four Most Populous States
(32.8 percent of U.S. population)
#1 California #2 Texas #3 New York #4 Florida

billions of dollars

Virginia	97.0
California	81.1
Florida	65.5
Maryland	47.7
Michigan	35.9
Alabama	34.6
Arizona	30.6
South Carolina	29.1
Pennsylvania	29.1
Kentucky	26.7
Texas	26.6
Tennessee	24.5
Georgia	24.4
Missouri	23.6
Mississippi	23.2
Wisconsin	22.7
North Carolina	21.5
New Mexico	19.3
Indiana	19.0
Washington	18.0
Hawaii	17.9
Kansas	14.3
Massachusetts	13.8
West Virginia	13.5
Louisiana	13.2
Oklahoma	11.9
Oregon	11.8
Iowa	9.5
Alaska	9.3
Colorado	8.1
Maine	8.0
Idaho	6.8
Montana	6.4
Utah	5.1
Nevada	4.6
South Dakota	4.5
North Dakota	4.4
Ohio	3.7
Vermont	3.1
New Hampshire	2.5
Wyoming	1.6
Arkansas	1.6
New York	0.6
Rhode Island	0.3
Nebraska	0.0
Illinois	-2.1
Connecticut	-5.6
Delaware	-21.9
Minnesota	-22.9
New Jersey	-22.9

Comparison by state of federal disbursements (funds distributions) less federal tax revenues (net of refunds, for personal income tax, corporate income tax and payroll taxes for Social Security and Medicare). Federal disbursements include all domestic payments and purchases.

SOURCES: U.S. Department of Commerce, Bureau of Economic Analysis; U.S. Census Bureau Statistical Abstract of the United States: 2012, Table 479; U.S. Census Bureau, Consolidated Federal Funds Report, 2009, July 2010

http://www.bea.gov/iTable/iTable.cfm?ReqID=70&step=1&isuri=1&acrdn=4

http://www.census.gov/compendia/statab/

Federal Disbursements in Excess of Taxes Collected per Capita
($2,799 nationally in 2009)

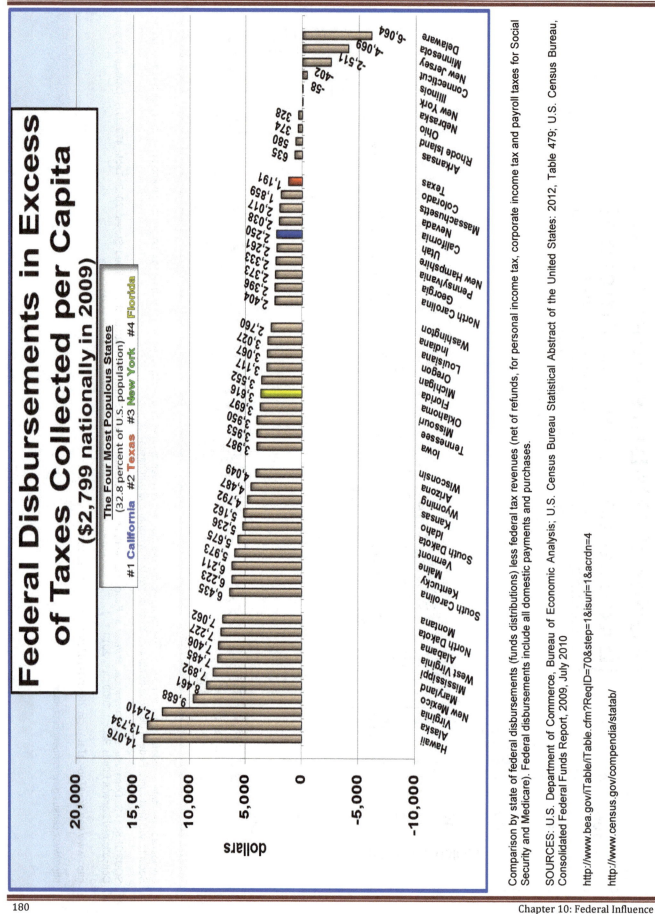

The Four Most Populous States
(32.8 percent of U.S. population)
#1 California   #2 Texas   #3 New York   #4 Florida

Hawaii	14,076
Alaska	13,734
Virginia	12,410
New Mexico	9,688
Maryland	8,461
Mississippi	7,892
West Virginia	7,485
Alabama	7,406
North Dakota	7,227
Montana	7,062
South Carolina	6,435
Kentucky	6,223
Maine	6,211
Vermont	5,973
South Dakota	5,675
Idaho	5,236
Kansas	5,162
Wyoming	4,792
Arizona	4,487
Wisconsin	4,049
Tennessee	3,987
Missouri	3,953
Oklahoma	3,950
Florida	3,697
Michigan	3,616
Oregon	3,552
Louisiana	3,117
Indiana	3,067
Washington	3,027
North Carolina	2,760
Georgia	2,404
Pennsylvania	2,396
New Hampshire	2,373
Utah	2,333
California	2,261
Nevada	2,250
Massachusetts	2,038
Colorado	2,017
Texas	1,859
Arkansas	1,191
Rhode Island	635
Ohio	580
Nebraska	374
New York	328
Illinois	-58
Connecticut	402
New Jersey	-2,511
Minnesota	-4,069
Delaware	-6,064

dollars

20,000   15,000   10,000   5,000   0   -5,000   -10,000

Comparison by state of federal disbursements (funds distributions) less federal tax revenues (net of refunds, for personal income tax, corporate income tax and payroll taxes for Social Security and Medicare). Federal disbursements include all domestic payments and purchases.

SOURCES: U.S. Department of Commerce, Bureau of Economic Analysis; U.S. Census Bureau Statistical Abstract of the United States: 2012, Table 479; U.S. Census Bureau, Consolidated Federal Funds Report, 2009, July 2010

http://www.bea.gov/iTable/iTable.cfm?ReqID=70&step=1&isuri=1&acrdn=4

http://www.census.gov/compendia/statab/

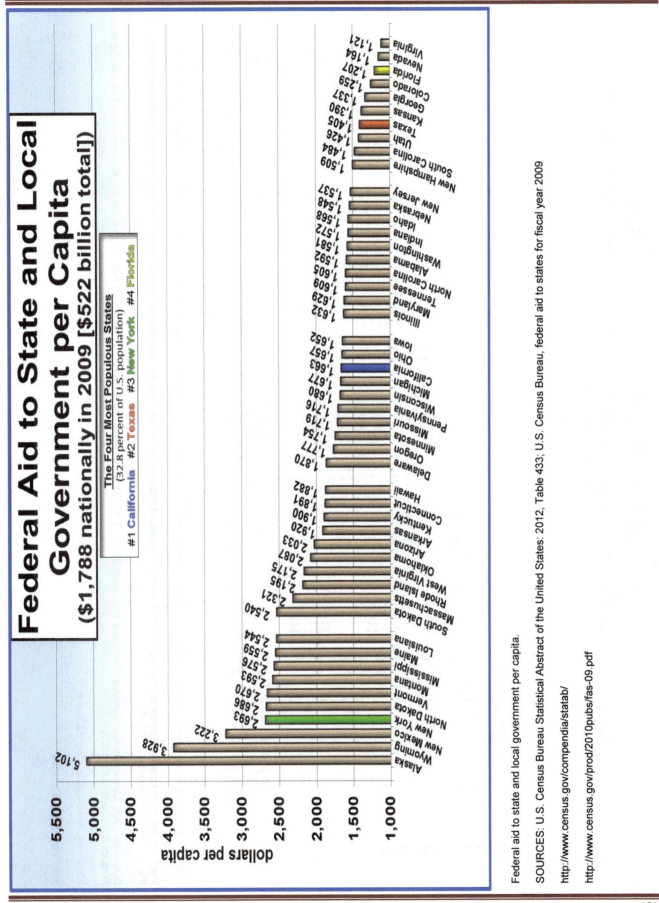

Federal Aid to State and Local Government per Capita
($1,788 nationally in 2009 [$522 billion total])

The Four Most Populous States
(32.8 percent of U.S. population)
#1 California   #2 Texas   #3 New York   #4 Florida

State	dollars per capita
Alaska	5,102
Wyoming	3,928
New Mexico	3,222
New York	2,693
North Dakota	2,686
Vermont	2,670
Montana	2,593
Mississippi	2,576
Maine	2,559
Louisiana	2,544
South Dakota	2,540
Massachusetts	2,321
Rhode Island	2,195
West Virginia	2,175
Oklahoma	2,087
Arizona	2,033
Arkansas	1,920
Kentucky	1,900
Connecticut	1,891
Hawaii	1,882
Delaware	1,870
Oregon	1,777
Minnesota	1,754
Missouri	1,719
Pennsylvania	1,716
Wisconsin	1,680
Michigan	1,677
California	1,663
Ohio	1,657
Iowa	1,652
Illinois	1,632
Maryland	1,629
Tennessee	1,609
North Carolina	1,605
Alabama	1,592
Washington	1,581
Indiana	1,572
Idaho	1,568
Nebraska	1,548
New Jersey	1,537
New Hampshire	1,509
South Carolina	1,484
Utah	1,426
Texas	1,405
Kansas	1,390
Georgia	1,337
Colorado	1,259
Florida	1,207
Nevada	1,164
Virginia	1,121

Federal aid to state and local government per capita.

SOURCES: U.S. Census Bureau Statistical Abstract of the United States: 2012, Table 433; U.S. Census Bureau, federal aid to states for fiscal year 2009

http://www.census.gov/compendia/statab/

http://www.census.gov/prod/2010pubs/fas-09.pdf

Food Stamp Recipients

(13.0 percent of persons nationally in 2010 [$64.7 billion total])

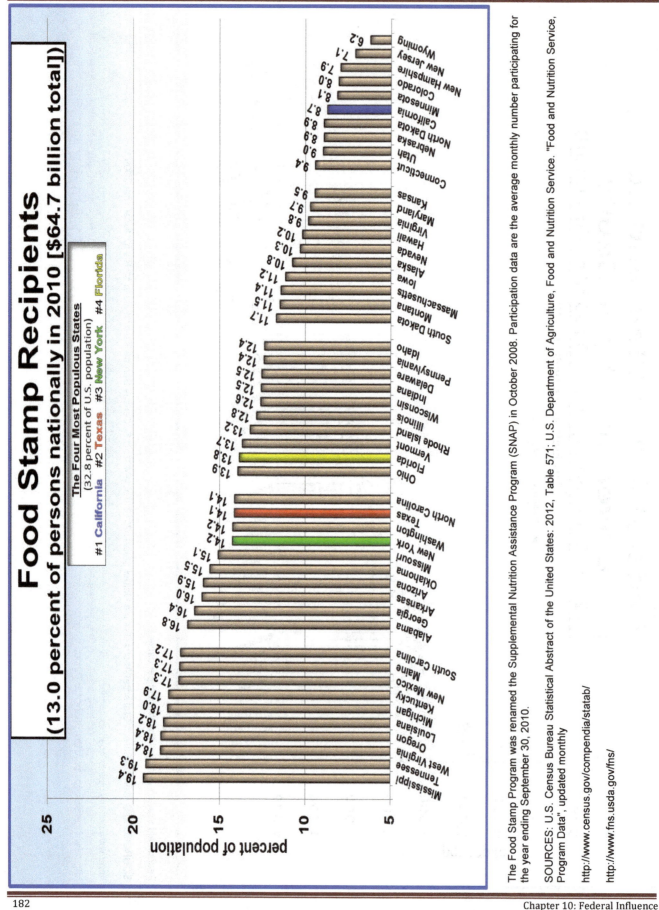

The Four Most Populous States
(32.8 percent of U.S. population)
#1 California #2 Texas #3 New York #4 Florida

State	percent of population
Mississippi	19.4
Tennessee	19.3
West Virginia	18.4
Oregon	18.4
Louisiana	18.2
Michigan	18.0
Kentucky	17.9
New Mexico	17.3
Maine	17.3
South Carolina	17.2
Alabama	16.8
Georgia	16.4
Arkansas	16.0
Arizona	15.9
Oklahoma	15.5
Missouri	15.1
New York	14.2
Washington	14.2
Texas	14.1
North Carolina	14.1
Ohio	13.9
Florida	13.8
Vermont	13.7
Rhode Island	13.2
Illinois	12.8
Wisconsin	12.6
Indiana	12.5
Delaware	12.5
Pennsylvania	12.4
Idaho	12.4
South Dakota	11.7
Montana	11.5
Massachusetts	11.4
Iowa	11.2
Alaska	10.8
Nevada	10.3
Hawaii	10.2
Virginia	9.8
Maryland	9.7
Kansas	9.5
Connecticut	9.4
Utah	9.0
Nebraska	8.9
North Dakota	8.9
California	8.7
Minnesota	8.1
Colorado	8.0
New Hampshire	7.9
New Jersey	7.1
Wyoming	6.2

The Food Stamp Program was renamed the Supplemental Nutrition Assistance Program (SNAP) in October 2008. Participation data are the average monthly number participating for the year ending September 30, 2010.

SOURCES: U.S. Census Bureau Statistical Abstract of the United States: 2012, Table 571; U.S. Department of Agriculture, Food and Nutrition Service. "Food and Nutrition Service, Program Data", updated monthly

http://www.census.gov/compendia/statab/

http://www.fns.usda.gov/fns/

Medicaid Payments
($317.99 billion nationally in 2009)

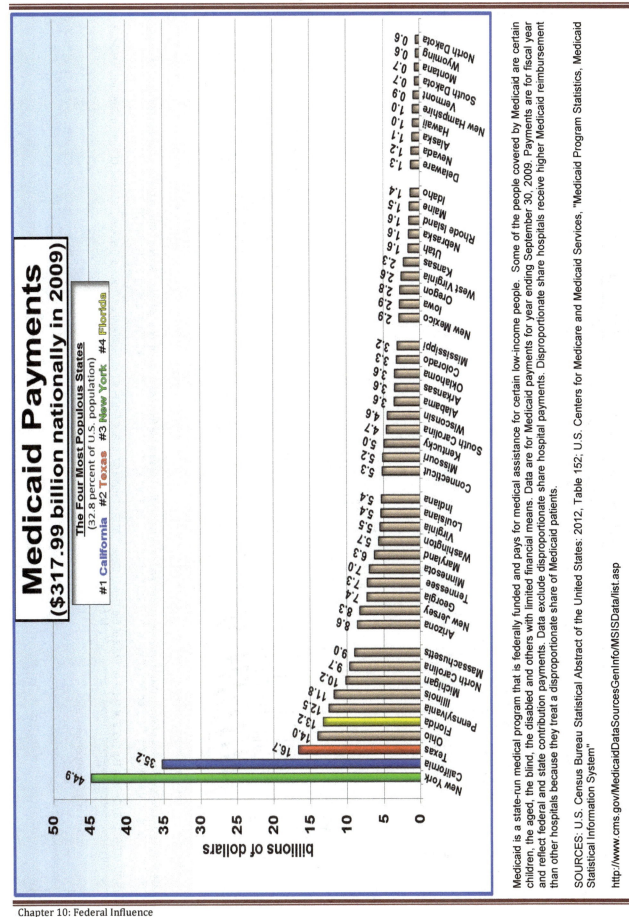

The Four Most Populous States
(32.8 percent of U.S. population)
#1 California   #2 Texas   #3 New York   #4 Florida

billions of dollars

New York	44.9
California	35.2
Texas	16.7
Ohio	14.0
Florida	13.2
Pennsylvania	12.5
Illinois	11.8
Michigan	10.2
North Carolina	9.7
Massachusetts	9.0
Arizona	8.6
New Jersey	8.3
Georgia	7.4
Tennessee	7.3
Minnesota	7.0
Maryland	6.3
Washington	5.7
Virginia	5.5
Louisiana	5.4
Indiana	5.4
Connecticut	5.3
Missouri	5.2
Kentucky	5.0
South Carolina	4.7
Wisconsin	4.6
Alabama	3.6
Arkansas	3.6
Oklahoma	3.6
Colorado	3.3
Mississippi	3.2
New Mexico	2.9
Iowa	2.9
Oregon	2.8
West Virginia	2.6
Kansas	2.3
Utah	1.6
Nebraska	1.6
Rhode Island	1.6
Maine	1.5
Idaho	1.4
Delaware	1.3
Nevada	1.2
Alaska	1.1
Hawaii	1.0
New Hampshire	1.0
Vermont	0.9
South Dakota	0.7
Montana	0.7
Wyoming	0.6
North Dakota	0.6

Medicaid is a state-run medical program that is federally funded and pays for medical assistance for certain low-income people. Some of the people covered by Medicaid are certain children, the aged, the blind, the disabled and others with limited financial means. Data are for Medicaid payments for year ending September 30, 2009. Payments are for fiscal year and reflect federal and state contribution payments. Data exclude disproportionate share hospital payments. Disproportionate share hospitals receive higher Medicaid reimbursement than other hospitals because they treat a disproportionate share of Medicaid patients.

SOURCES: U.S. Census Bureau Statistical Abstract of the United States: 2012, Table 152; U.S. Centers for Medicare and Medicaid Services, "Medicaid Program Statistics, Medicaid Statistical Information System"

http://www.cms.gov/MedicaidDataSourcesGenInfo/MSISData/list.asp

http://www.census.gov/compendia/statab/

Medicaid Recipients
(20.0 percent of population nationally in 2009)

The Four Most Populous States
(32.8 percent of U.S. population)
#1 California #2 Texas #3 New York #4 Florida

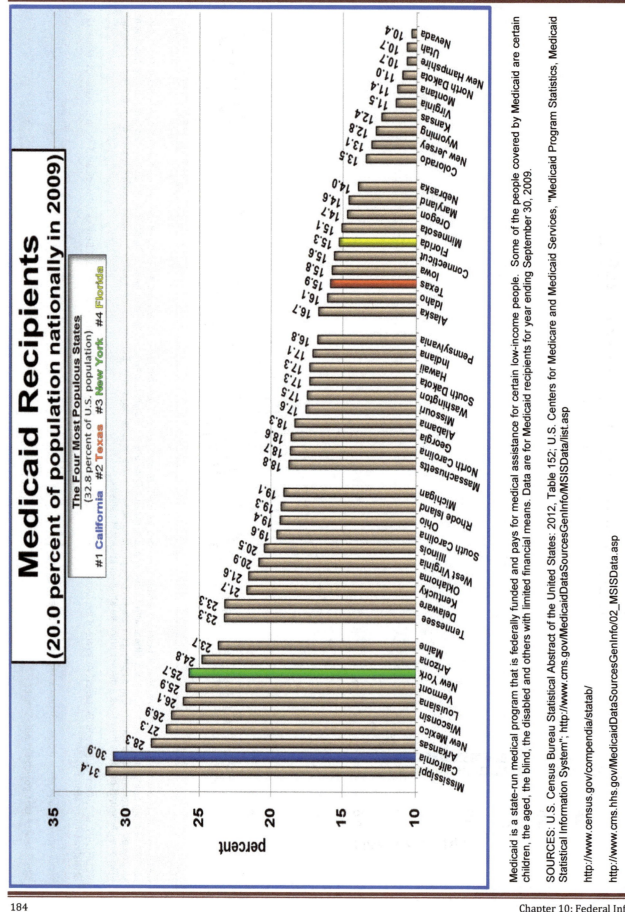

State	Percent
Mississippi	31.4
California	30.9
Arkansas	28.3
New Mexico	27.3
Wisconsin	26.9
Louisiana	26.1
Vermont	25.9
New York	25.7
Arizona	24.8
Maine	23.7
Tennessee	23.3
Delaware	23.3
Kentucky	21.7
Oklahoma	21.6
West Virginia	20.9
Illinois	20.5
South Carolina	19.6
Ohio	19.4
Rhode Island	19.3
Michigan	19.1
Massachusetts	18.8
North Carolina	18.7
Georgia	18.6
Alabama	18.3
Missouri	17.6
Washington	17.5
South Dakota	17.3
Hawaii	17.3
Indiana	17.1
Pennsylvania	16.8
Alaska	16.7
Idaho	16.1
Texas	15.9
Iowa	15.8
Connecticut	15.6
Florida	15.3
Minnesota	15.1
Oregon	14.7
Maryland	14.6
Nebraska	14.0
Colorado	13.5
New Jersey	13.1
Wyoming	12.8
Kansas	12.4
Virginia	11.5
Montana	11.4
North Dakota	11.0
New Hampshire	10.7
Utah	10.7
Nevada	10.4

Medicaid is a state-run medical program that is federally funded and pays for medical assistance for certain low-income people. Some of the people covered by Medicaid are certain children, the aged, the blind, the disabled and others with limited financial means. Data are for Medicaid recipients for year ending September 30, 2009.

SOURCES: U.S. Census Bureau Statistical Abstract of the United States: 2012, Table 152; U.S. Centers for Medicare and Medicaid Services, "Medicaid Program Statistics, Medicaid Statistical Information System"; http://www.cms.gov/MedicaidDataSourcesGenInfo/MSISData/list.asp

http://www.census.gov/compendia/statab/

http://www.cms.hhs.gov/MedicaidDataSourcesGenInfo/02_MSISData.asp

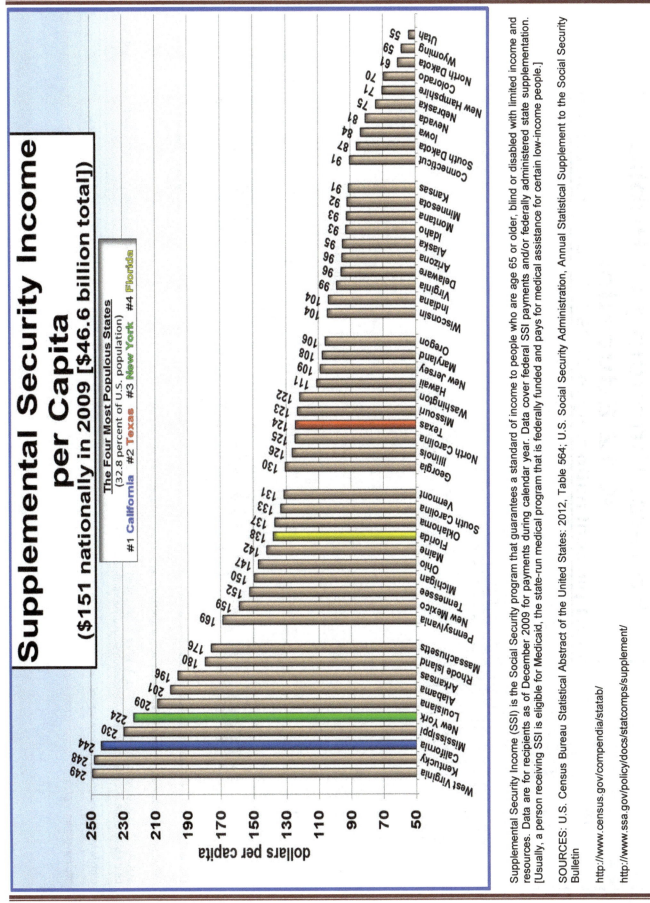

Supplemental Security Income per Capita

($151 nationally in 2009 [$46.6 billion total])

The Four Most Populous States
(32.8 percent of U.S. population)
#1 California   #2 Texas   #3 New York   #4 Florida

State	dollars per capita
West Virginia	249
Kentucky	248
California	244
Mississippi	230
New York	224
Louisiana	209
Alabama	201
Arkansas	196
Rhode Island	180
Massachusetts	176
Pennsylvania	169
New Mexico	159
Tennessee	152
Michigan	150
Ohio	147
Maine	142
Florida	138
Oklahoma	137
South Carolina	133
Vermont	131
Georgia	130
Illinois	126
North Carolina	125
Texas	124
Missouri	123
Washington	122
Hawaii	111
New Jersey	109
Maryland	108
Oregon	106
Wisconsin	104
Indiana	104
Virginia	99
Delaware	96
Arizona	96
Alaska	95
Idaho	93
Montana	93
Minnesota	92
Kansas	91
Connecticut	91
South Dakota	87
Iowa	84
Nevada	81
Nebraska	75
New Hampshire	71
Colorado	70
North Dakota	61
Wyoming	59
Utah	55

Supplemental Security Income (SSI) is the Social Security program that guarantees a standard of income to people who are age 65 or older, blind or disabled with limited income and resources. Data are for recipients as of December 2009 for payments during calendar year. Data cover federal SSI payments and/or federally administered state supplementation. [Usually, a person receiving SSI is eligible for Medicaid, the state-run medical program that is federally funded and pays for medical assistance for certain low-income people.]

SOURCES: U.S. Census Bureau Statistical Abstract of the United States: 2012, Table 564; U.S. Social Security Administration, Annual Statistical Supplement to the Social Security Bulletin

http://www.census.gov/compendia/statab/

http://www.ssa.gov/policy/docs/statcomps/supplement/

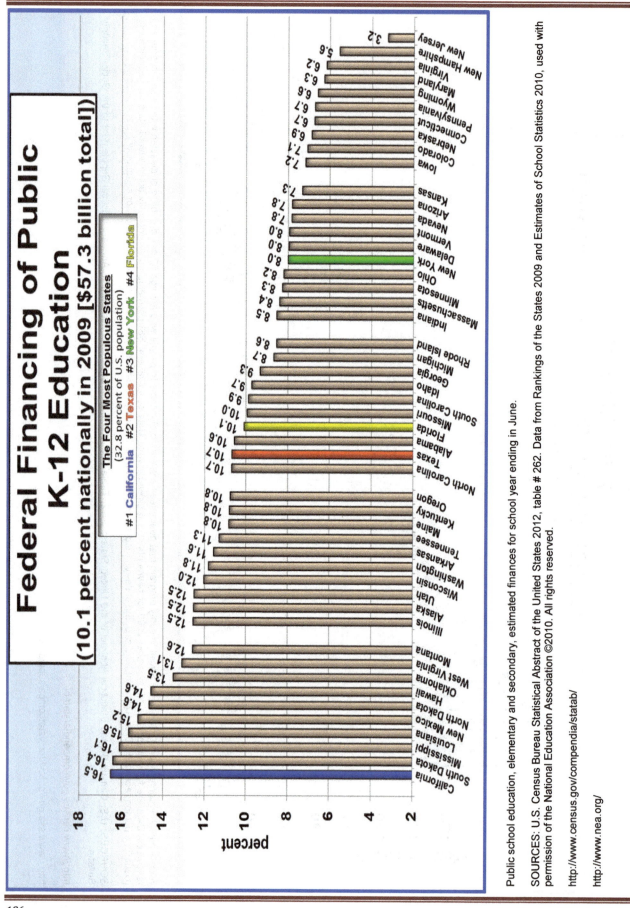

Federal Financing of Public K-12 Education
(10.1 percent nationally in 2009 [$57.3 billion total])

The Four Most Populous States
(32.8 percent of U.S. population)
#1 California   #2 Texas   #3 New York   #4 Florida

State	percent
California	16.5
South Dakota	16.4
Mississippi	16.1
Louisiana	15.6
New Mexico	15.2
North Dakota	14.6
Hawaii	14.6
Oklahoma	13.5
West Virginia	13.1
Montana	12.6
Illinois	12.5
Alaska	12.5
Utah	12.5
Wisconsin	12.0
Washington	11.8
Arkansas	11.6
Tennessee	11.3
Maine	10.8
Kentucky	10.8
Oregon	10.8
North Carolina	10.7
Texas	10.7
Alabama	10.6
Florida	10.1
Missouri	10.0
South Carolina	9.9
Idaho	9.7
Georgia	9.3
Michigan	8.7
Rhode Island	8.6
Indiana	8.5
Massachusetts	8.4
Minnesota	8.3
Ohio	8.2
New York	8.0
Delaware	8.0
Vermont	8.0
Nevada	7.8
Arizona	7.8
Kansas	7.3
Iowa	7.2
Colorado	7.1
Nebraska	6.9
Connecticut	6.7
Pennsylvania	6.7
Wyoming	6.6
Maryland	6.3
Virginia	6.2
New Hampshire	5.6
New Jersey	3.2

Public school education, elementary and secondary, estimated finances for school year ending in June.

SOURCES: U.S. Census Bureau Statistical Abstract of the United States 2012, table # 262. Data from Rankings of the States 2009 and Estimates of School Statistics 2010, used with permission of the National Education Association ©2010. All rights reserved.

http://www.census.gov/compendia/statab/

http://www.nea.org/

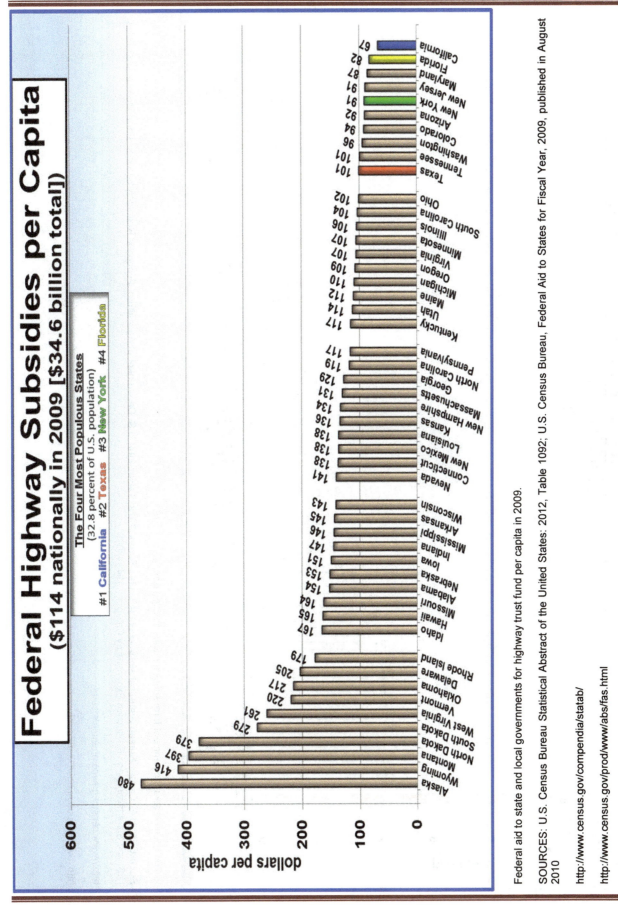

Federal Highway Subsidies per Capita
($114 nationally in 2009 [$34.6 billion total])

The Four Most Populous States
(32.8 percent of U.S. population)
#1 California #2 Texas #3 New York #4 Florida

State	dollars per capita
California	67
Florida	82
Maryland	87
New Jersey	91
New York	91
Arizona	92
Colorado	94
Washington	96
Tennessee	101
Texas	101
Ohio	102
South Carolina	104
Illinois	106
Minnesota	107
Virginia	107
Oregon	109
Michigan	110
Maine	112
Utah	114
Kentucky	117
Pennsylvania	117
North Carolina	119
Georgia	129
Massachusetts	131
New Hampshire	134
Kansas	136
Louisiana	138
New Mexico	138
Connecticut	138
Nevada	141
Wisconsin	143
Arkansas	145
Mississippi	146
Indiana	147
Iowa	151
Nebraska	153
Alabama	154
Missouri	164
Hawaii	165
Idaho	167
Rhode Island	179
Delaware	205
Oklahoma	217
Vermont	220
West Virginia	261
South Dakota	279
North Dakota	379
Montana	397
Wyoming	416
Alaska	480

Federal aid to state and local governments for highway trust fund per capita in 2009.

SOURCES: U.S. Census Bureau Statistical Abstract of the United States: 2012, Table 1092; U.S. Census Bureau, Federal Aid to States for Fiscal Year, 2009, published in August 2010

http://www.census.gov/compendia/statab/

http://www.census.gov/prod/www/abs/fas.html

Federal Subsidies for Agriculture
(percent of nation's $12.3 billion in 2009)

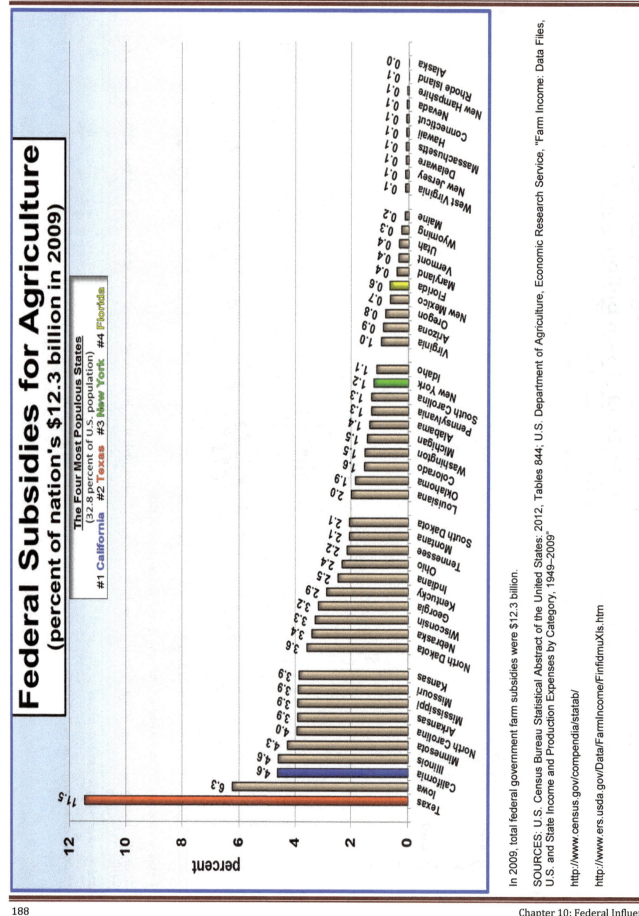

The Four Most Populous States
(32.8 percent of U.S. population)
#1 California #2 Texas #3 New York #4 Florida

State	Percent
Texas	11.5
Iowa	6.3
California	4.6
Illinois	4.6
Minnesota	4.3
North Carolina	4.0
Arkansas	3.9
Mississippi	3.9
Missouri	3.9
Kansas	3.9
North Dakota	3.6
Nebraska	3.4
Wisconsin	3.3
Georgia	3.2
Kentucky	2.9
Indiana	2.5
Ohio	2.4
Tennessee	2.2
Montana	2.1
South Dakota	2.1
Louisiana	2.0
Oklahoma	1.9
Colorado	1.6
Washington	1.5
Michigan	1.5
Alabama	1.4
Pennsylvania	1.3
South Carolina	1.3
New York	1.2
Idaho	1.1
Virginia	1.0
Arizona	0.9
Oregon	0.8
New Mexico	0.7
Florida	0.6
Maryland	0.4
Vermont	0.4
Utah	0.4
Wyoming	0.3
Maine	0.2
West Virginia	0.1
New Jersey	0.1
Delaware	0.1
Massachusetts	0.1
Hawaii	0.1
Connecticut	0.1
Nevada	0.1
New Hampshire	0.1
Rhode Island	0.1
Alaska	0.0

In 2009, total federal government farm subsidies were $12.3 billion.

SOURCES: U.S. Census Bureau Statistical Abstract of the United States: 2012, Tables 844; U.S. Department of Agriculture, Economic Research Service, "Farm Income: Data Files, U.S. and State Income and Production Expenses by Category, 1949–2009"

http://www.census.gov/compendia/statab/

http://www.ers.usda.gov/Data/FarmIncome/FinfidmuXls.htm

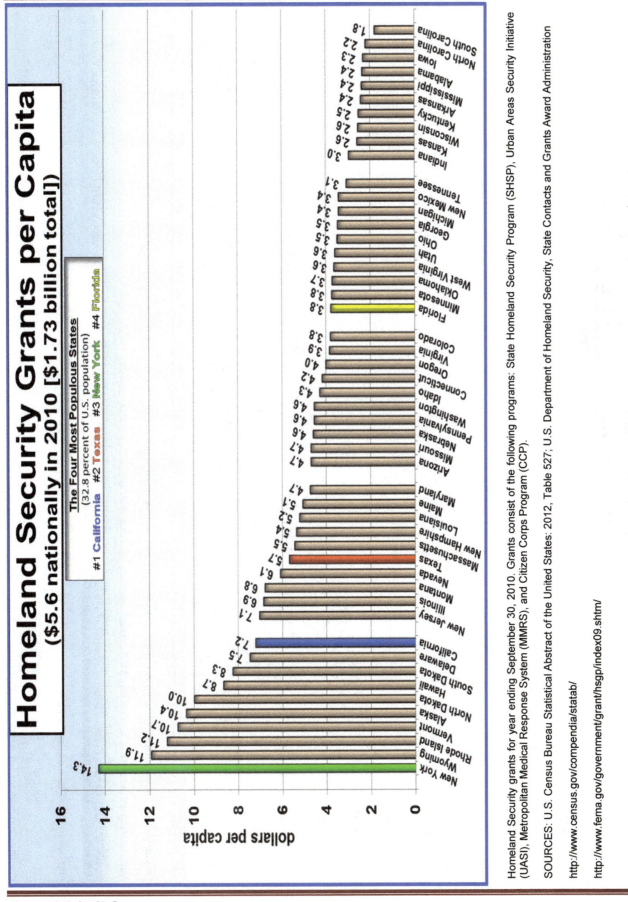

Homeland Security Grants per Capita
($5.6 nationally in 2010 [$1.73 billion total])

The Four Most Populous States
(32.8 percent of U.S. population)
#1 California   #2 Texas   #3 New York   #4 Florida

State	dollars per capita
New York	14.3
Wyoming	11.9
Rhode Island	11.2
Vermont	10.7
Alaska	10.4
North Dakota	10.0
Hawaii	8.7
South Dakota	8.3
Delaware	7.5
California	7.2
New Jersey	7.1
Illinois	6.9
Montana	6.8
Nevada	6.1
Texas	5.7
Massachusetts	5.5
New Hampshire	5.4
Louisiana	5.2
Maine	5.1
Maryland	4.7
Arizona	4.7
Missouri	4.7
Nebraska	4.6
Pennsylvania	4.6
Washington	4.6
Idaho	4.3
Connecticut	4.2
Oregon	4.0
Virginia	3.9
Colorado	3.8
Florida	3.8
Minnesota	3.8
Oklahoma	3.7
West Virginia	3.6
Utah	3.6
Ohio	3.5
Georgia	3.5
Michigan	3.4
New Mexico	3.4
Tennessee	3.1
Indiana	3.0
Kansas	2.6
Wisconsin	2.6
Kentucky	2.5
Arkansas	2.4
Mississippi	2.4
Alabama	2.4
Iowa	2.3
North Carolina	2.2
South Carolina	1.8

Homeland Security grants for year ending September 30, 2010. Grants consist of the following programs: State Homeland Security Program (SHSP), Urban Areas Security Initiative (UASI), Metropolitan Medical Response System (MMRS), and Citizen Corps Program (CCP).

SOURCES: U.S. Census Bureau Statistical Abstract of the United States: 2012, Table 527; U.S. Department of Homeland Security, State Contacts and Grants Award Administration

http://www.census.gov/compendia/statab/

http://www.fema.gov/government/grant/hsgp/index09.shtm/

Defense Department Payroll per Capita
($633 nationally in 2009 [$195.2 billion total])

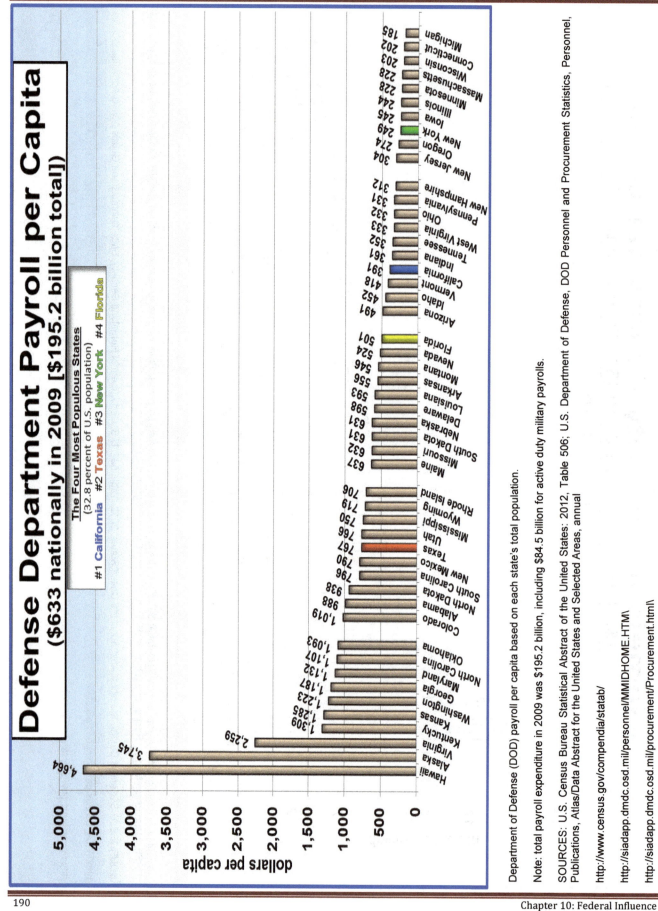

The Four Most Populous States
(32.8 percent of U.S. population)
#1 California   #2 Texas   #3 New York   #4 Florida

State	dollars per capita
Hawaii	4,664
Alaska	3,745
Virginia	2,259
Kentucky	1,309
Kansas	1,285
Washington	1,223
Georgia	1,187
Maryland	1,132
North Carolina	1,107
Oklahoma	1,093
Colorado	1,019
Alabama	988
North Dakota	938
South Carolina	796
New Mexico	790
Texas	767
Utah	766
Mississippi	750
Wyoming	719
Rhode Island	706
Maine	637
Missouri	632
South Dakota	631
Nebraska	631
Delaware	598
Louisiana	593
Arkansas	556
Montana	546
Nevada	524
Florida	501
Arizona	491
Idaho	452
Vermont	418
California	391
Indiana	361
Tennessee	352
West Virginia	333
Ohio	332
Pennsylvania	331
New Hampshire	312
New Jersey	304
Oregon	274
New York	249
Iowa	245
Illinois	244
Minnesota	228
Massachusetts	228
Wisconsin	203
Connecticut	202
Michigan	185

Department of Defense (DOD) payroll per capita based on each state's total population.

Note: total payroll expenditure in 2009 was $195.2 billion, including $84.5 billion for active duty military payrolls.

SOURCES: U.S. Census Bureau Statistical Abstract of the United States: 2012, Table 506; U.S. Department of Defense, DOD Personnel and Procurement Statistics, Personnel, Publications, Atlas/Data Abstract for the United States and Selected Areas, annual

http://www.census.gov/compendia/statab/

http://siadapp.dmdc.osd.mil/personnel/MMIDHOME.HTM\

http://siadapp.dmdc.osd.mil/procurement/Procurement.html\

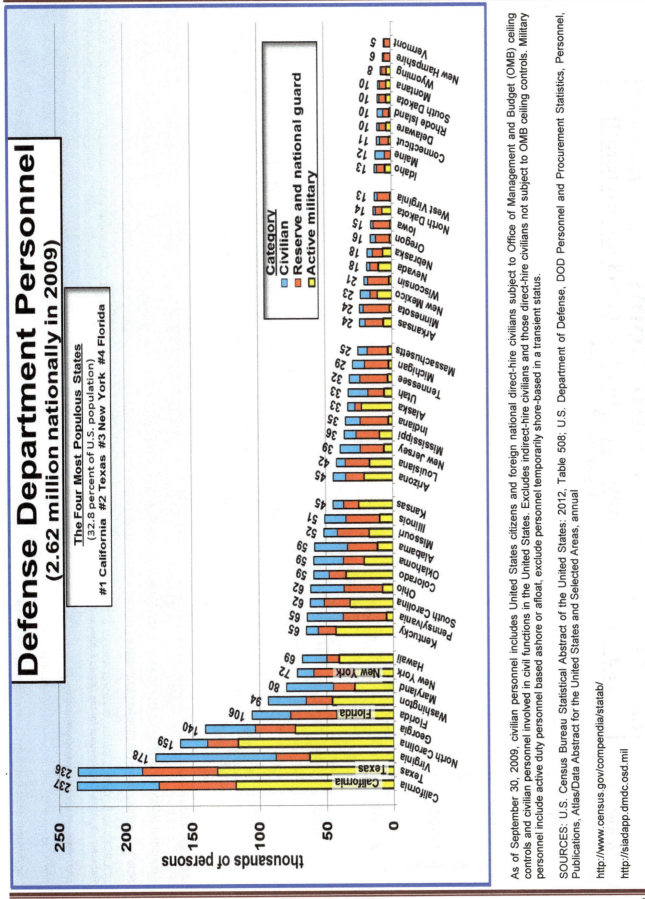

Defense Department Personnel
(2.62 million nationally in 2009)

The Four Most Populous States
(32.8 percent of U.S. population)
#1 California #2 Texas #3 New York #4 Florida

Category
- Civilian
- Reserve and national guard
- Active military

thousands of persons

California	237
Texas	236
Virginia	178
North Carolina	159
Georgia	140
Florida	106
Washington	94
Maryland	80
New York	72
Hawaii	69
Kentucky	65
Pennsylvania	65
South Carolina	62
Ohio	62
Colorado	59
Oklahoma	59
Alabama	59
Missouri	52
Illinois	51
Kansas	45
Arizona	45
Louisiana	42
New Jersey	39
Mississippi	36
Indiana	35
Alaska	33
Utah	33
Tennessee	32
Michigan	29
Massachusetts	25
Arkansas	24
Minnesota	24
New Mexico	23
Wisconsin	21
Nevada	18
Nebraska	18
Oregon	16
Iowa	15
North Dakota	14
West Virginia	13
Idaho	13
Maine	12
Connecticut	11
Delaware	10
Rhode Island	10
South Dakota	10
Montana	10
Wyoming	8
New Hampshire	6
Vermont	5

As of September 30, 2009, civilian personnel includes United States citizens and foreign national direct-hire civilians subject to Office of Management and Budget (OMB) ceiling controls and civilian personnel involved in civil functions in the United States. Excludes indirect-hire civilians and those direct-hire civilians not subject to OMB ceiling controls. Military personnel include active duty personnel based ashore or afloat, exclude personnel temporarily shore-based in a transient status.

SOURCES: U.S. Census Bureau Statistical Abstract of the United States: 2012, Table 508; U.S. Department of Defense, DOD Personnel and Procurement Statistics, Personnel, Publications, Atlas/Data Abstract for the United States and Selected Areas, annual

http://www.census.gov/compendia/statab/

http://siadapp.dmdc.osd.mil

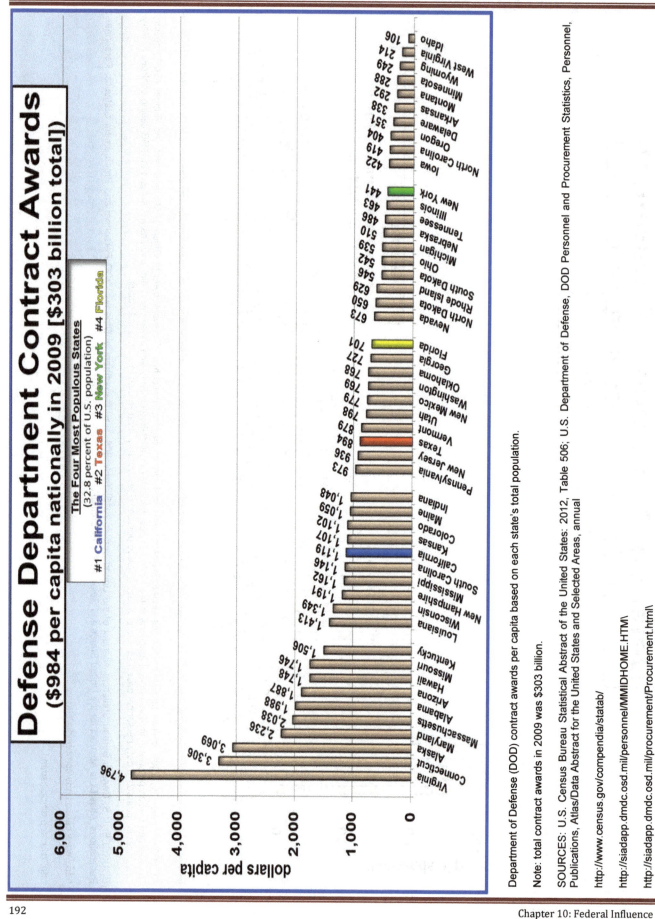

Defense Department Contract Awards
($984 per capita nationally in 2009 [$303 billion total])

The Four Most Populous States
(32.8 percent of U.S. population)
#1 California #2 Texas #3 New York #4 Florida

dollars per capita

Virginia	4,796
Connecticut	3,306
Alaska	3,069
Maryland	2,236
Massachusetts	2,038
Alabama	1,988
Arizona	1,887
Hawaii	1,748
Missouri	1,746
Kentucky	1,506
Louisiana	1,413
Wisconsin	1,349
New Hampshire	1,191
Mississippi	1,162
South Carolina	1,146
California	1,119
Kansas	1,107
Colorado	1,102
Maine	1,059
Indiana	1,048
Pennsylvania	973
New Jersey	936
Texas	894
Vermont	879
Utah	798
New Mexico	779
Washington	769
Oklahoma	768
Georgia	727
Florida	701
Nevada	673
North Dakota	650
Rhode Island	629
South Dakota	546
Ohio	542
Michigan	539
Nebraska	510
Tennessee	486
Illinois	463
New York	441
Iowa	422
North Carolina	419
Oregon	404
Delaware	351
Arkansas	338
Montana	292
Minnesota	288
Wyoming	249
West Virginia	214
Idaho	106

Department of Defense (DOD) contract awards per capita based on each state's total population.

Note: total contract awards in 2009 was $303 billion.

SOURCES: U.S. Census Bureau Statistical Abstract of the United States: 2012, Table 506; U.S. Department of Defense, DOD Personnel and Procurement Statistics, Personnel, Publications, Atlas/Data Abstract for the United States and Selected Areas, annual

http://www.census.gov/compendia/statab/

http://siadapp.dmdc.osd.mil/personnel/MMIDHOME.HTM\

http://siadapp.dmdc.osd.mil/procurement/Procurement.html\

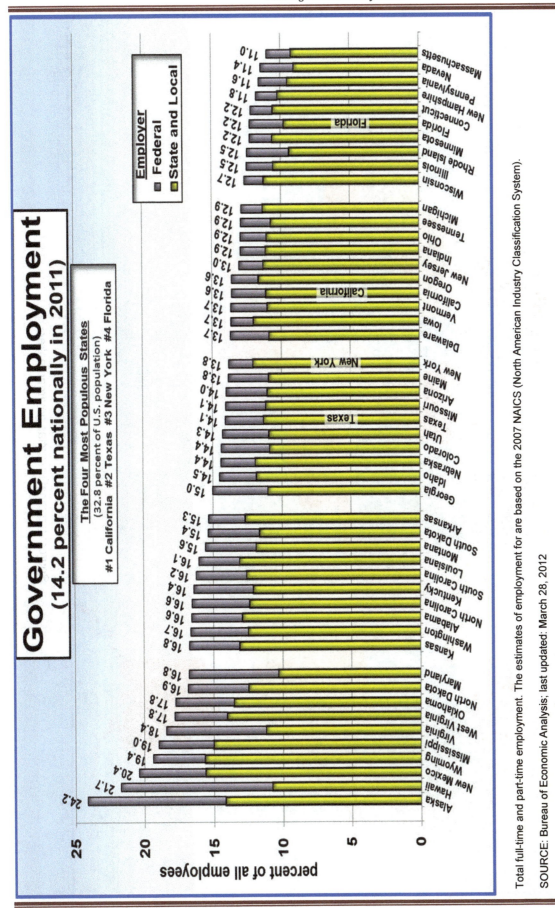

Government Employment
(14.2 percent nationally in 2011)

The Four Most Populous States
(32.8 percent of U.S. population)
#1 California #2 Texas #3 New York #4 Florida

Total full-time and part-time employment. The estimates of employment for are based on the 2007 NAICS (North American Industry Classification System).

SOURCE: Bureau of Economic Analysis; last updated: March 28, 2012

http://www.bea.gov/iTable/iTable.cfm?ReqID=70&step=1&isuri=1&acrdn=4

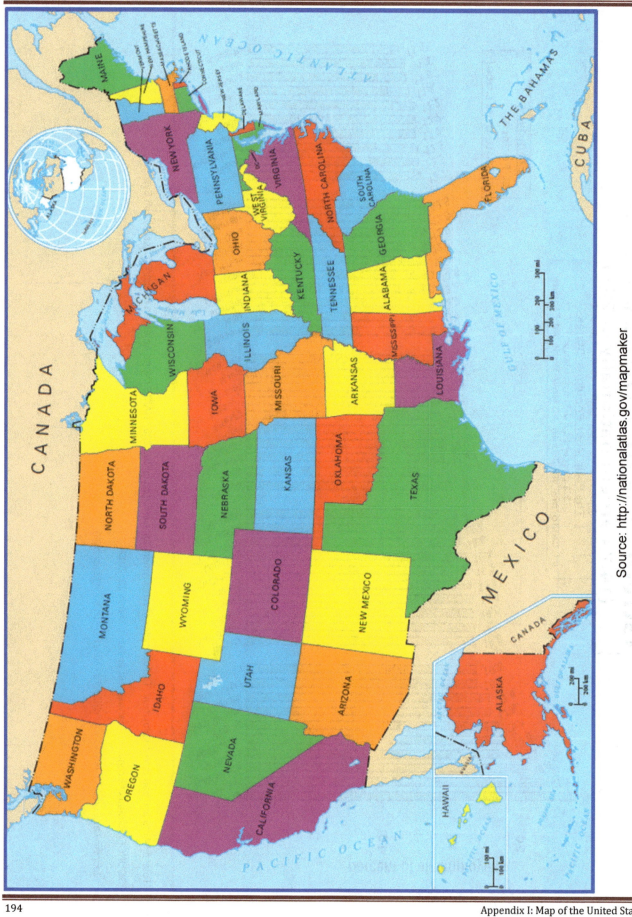

Source: http://nationalatlas.gov/mapmaker

~ <u>Top and Bottom Ranked States</u> ~
In alphabetical order

Alabama

Not highest or lowest for any metric

Ranking	Alaska	Page
Highest	Suicide Rate (per 100,000 residents in 2007)	29
Highest	Criminal Justice Expenditures (dollars per capita in 2007)	90
Highest	Lowest Air Temperature on Record (degrees Fahrenheit, 1885–2010)	99
Highest	Relative Humidity (annual, average afternoon for selected cities, 1986–2009)	107
Highest	Cloudy Days (average, annual percentage for selected cities, 1986–2009)	108
Highest	Snow, Hail, Ice Pellets, and Sleet (average, annual for selected cities, 1960–2008)	110
Highest	Air Quality "Good" Days for Best County (percent of days rated "good" best county	112
Highest	Toxic Chemical Releases (pounds in 2009)	114
Highest	Land Area (square miles)	117
Highest	State Severance Tax on Businesses (dollars per capita in 2008)	159
Highest	Federal Tax Revenues per Capita (dollars in 2009)	178
Highest	Federal Aid to State and Local Government per Capita (dollars in 2009)	181
Highest	Federal Highway Subsidies per Capita (dollars in 2009)	187
Highest	Government Employment (percent in 2011)	193
1 of 5 states with 0	State General Sales Tax (dollars per capita in 2011)	154
1 of 7 states with 0	Storm Major Disaster Declarations (1953–2012)	97
1 of 8 states with 0	State Personal Income Tax (dollars per capita in 2011)	153
Lowest	Population Over Age 64 (percent in 2010)	16
Lowest	Old Age Dependency Ratio (persons over age 64 per 100 persons ages 18–64)	17
Lowest	Population Density (persons per square mile in 2011)	18
Lowest	Patents Issued to Residents (per 100,000 residents in 2010)	58
Lowest	College Freshmen Migrated from Other States (persons in 2008)	77
Lowest	Summer Air Temperature (degrees Fahrenheit, 1971–2000)	102
Lowest	Cooling Degree Days (annual, average for selected cities, 1986–2009)	106
Lowest	Exports of Agricultural Products (percent of national total in 2009)	120
Lowest	Farm Crops Market (percent of nation's total in 2009)	121
Lowest	Farm Livestock Market (percent of nation's total in 2009)	122
Lowest	Households with Annual Income Below $15,000 (percent in 2009)	136
Lowest	Bankruptcy Filings (per 1,000 persons in 2010)	149
Lowest	Federal Subsidies for Agriculture (percent of nation's total in 2009)	188

Ranking	Arizona	Page
1 of 4 states with 0 in selected cities	Snow, Hail, Ice Pellets, and Sleet (average, annual for selected cities, 1960–2008)	110
Lowest	Expenditures per Capita for Public K–12 Education (dollars in 2009)	66
Lowest	Relative Humidity (annual, average afternoon for selected cities, 1986–2009)	107
Lowest	Cloudy Days (average, annual percentage for selected cities, 1986–2009)	108
Lowest	Air Quality "Good" Days for Average County (percent of days rated "good" across all counties	111

Ranking	Arkansas	Page
Highest	Households Without Internet Usage (percent in 2010)	55
Lowest	Manufacturing Employee Annual Payroll (dollars in 2009)	146
Lowest	Value Added per Manufacturing Production Worker (dollars in 2009)	148

Ranking	California	Page
Highest	Population (persons in 2012)	3
Highest	Residents Born Outside the United States (percent in 2009)	7
Highest	Births to Foreign-Born Women (percent in 2009)	9
Highest	Births by Race and Hispanic Origin (in 2009)	10
Highest	Foreign Language Spoken at Home (percent of households in 2009)	14
Highest	Population Living in Urban Areas (percent in 2000)	19
Highest	Same-Sex Couple Households (thousands in 2010)	45
Highest	U.S. Congressional Seats Held by Political Party (seats in 2013 for 113th Congress)	54
Highest	State Park Recreation Visitors (persons in 2010)	60
Highest	National Park Recreation Visitors (persons in 2010)	61
Highest	Pupil-to-Teacher Ratio (in 2011)	65
Highest	Higher Education Degrees Conferred (in 2007)	75
Highest	Motor Vehicle Theft Rate (per 100,000 persons in 2010)	86
Highest	Earthquake and Flood Major Disaster Declarations (1953–2012)	96
Highest	Highest Air Temperature on Record (degrees Fahrenheit, 1885–2010)	100
Highest	Forest Lands (acres in 2010)	118
Highest	Exports of Agricultural Products (percent of national total in 2009)	120
Highest	Farm Crops Market (percent of nation's total in 2009)	121
Highest	Gross Domestic Product (dollars in 2011)	166
Highest	Federal Financing of Public K–12 Education (percent in 2009)	186
Highest	Defense Department Personnel (persons in 2009)	191
1 of 4 states with 0 in selected cities	Snow, Hail, Ice Pellets, and Sleet (average, annual for selected cities, 1960–2008)	110
Lowest	Total Degree Days (annual average for selected cities, 1986–2009)	104
Lowest	Federal Highway Subsidies per Capita (dollars in 2009)	187

Ranking	Colorado	Page
Lowest	Adult Obesity Rate (percent in 2011)	26

Ranking	Connecticut	Page
Highest	Personal Income per Capita (dollars in 2010)	134
Highest	Households with Annual Income Over $200,000 (percent in 2009)	137
Highest	Employee Annual Wages (dollars in 2009)	145
Highest	State Taxes by Source (dollars per capita in 2011)	155
Highest	Federal Personal Income Taxes Paid per Capita (dollars in 2010)	174
Highest	Federal Personal Income Tax Rate Paid (percent in 2010)	175
Lowest	National Park Recreation Visitors (persons in 2010)	61

Ranking	Delaware	Page
Highest	Abortion Rate (1 per 1,000 women in 2008)	42
Highest	Incoming State Criminal Court Cases (per 100,000 persons in 2009)	91
Highest	Employment in Foreign–Controlled Businesses (percent of workforce in 2008)	150
Highest	Gross Domestic Product per Capita (dollars in 2011)	167
Highest	Federal Tax Revenues per Capita (dollars in 2009)	176
1 of 5 states with 0	State General Sales Tax (dollars per capita in 2011)	154
Lowest	Air Quality "Good" Days for Best County (percent of days rated "good" best county)	112
Lowest	Mineral Production (dollars in 2010)	131
Lowest	Federal Disbursements per Capita (dollars in 2009)	178
Lowest	Federal Disbursements in Excess of Taxes per Capita (dollars in 2009)	180

Ranking	Florida	Page
Highest	Net Immigration (persons, 2000–2009)	5
Highest	Population Over Age 64 (percent in 2010)	16
Highest	Old Age Dependency Ratio (persons over age 64 per 100 persons ages 18–64)	17
Highest	Identity Theft Victims (per 100,000 persons in 2010)	87
1 of 4 states with 0 in selected cities	Snow, Hail, Ice Pellets, and Sleet (average, annual for selected cities, 1960–2008)	110
1 of 8 states with 0	State Personal Income Tax (dollars per capita in 2011)	153
Lowest	Volunteer Rate (percent of persons in 2010)	49
Lowest	State Employees per Resident (in 2009)	162

Ranking	Georgia	Page
Lowest	State Gasoline Tax (cents per gallon in 2009)	157
Lowest	State Arts Agency Appropriations (dollars per capita in 2011)	171

Ranking	Hawaii	Page
Highest	Residents by Race–Other than White (percent in 2010)	11
Highest	Minority Students Grades K–12 (percent in 2011)	13
Highest	Life Expectancy (years in 2000)	22
Highest	Voter Selection for President in 2012 (Obama's percent margin)	51
Highest	Voter Selection for President in 2008 (Obama's percent margin)	52
Highest	Winter Air Temperature (degrees Fahrenheit, 1971–2000)	101
Highest	Cooling Degree Days (annual, average for selected cities, 1986–2009)	106
Highest	Annual Precipitation (average, annual inches,1971–2000)	109
Highest	Owner Occupied Housing Values (median home value in 2009)	141
Highest	Rental Housing Cost (average rental cost per month in 2009)	143
Highest	State General Sales Tax (dollars per capita in 2011)	154
Highest	State Employees per Resident (in 2009)	162
Highest	Cost of Living Composite Index for Lowest City in 2010	164
Highest	Federal Disbursements in Excess of Taxes per Capita (dollars in 2009)	180
Highest	Defense Department Payroll per Capita (dollars in 2009)	190
1 of 4 states with 0 in selected cities	Snow, Hail, Ice Pellets, and Sleet (average, annual for selected cities, 1960–2008)	110
Lowest	Eligible Voters who Voted for President (percent in 2012)	50
Lowest	Lowest Air Temperature on Record (degrees Fahrenheit, 1885–2010)	99
Lowest	Highest Air Temperature on Record (degrees Fahrenheit, 1885–2010)	100
Lowest	Air Temperature Range (degrees Fahrenheit, 1971–2000)	103
Lowest	Heating Degree Days (annual, average for selected cities, 1986–2009)	105
Lowest	Employees in Manufacturing (percent of all employees in 2010)	147
Lowest	Manufacturing Portion of Gross Domestic Product (percent in 2011)	168
Lowest	Exports of Goods (percent of national total in 2010)	169

Ranking	Idaho	Page
1 of 7 states with 0	Storm Major Disaster Declarations (1953–2012)	97
Lowest	Physicians per 100,000 Residents (in 2009)	36
Lowest	Defense Department Contract Awards (dollars per capita in 2009)	192

Illinois	
Not highest or lowest for any metric	

Ranking	Indiana	Page
Highest	Employees in Manufacturing (percent of all employees in 2010)	147
Lowest	Divorce Rate (per 1,000 residents in 2009)	44

Ranking	Iowa	Page
Lowest	Infant Mortality Rate (deaths per 1,000 live births in 2009)	23
Lowest	Illicit Drug Use—Other than Marijuana (percent in 2007–2008)	30
Lowest	Marijuana Use (percent in 2007–2008)	31

Kansas

Not highest or lowest for any metric

Ranking	Kentucky	Page
Highest	Cigarette Smoking by Adults (percent in 2009)	28
Lowest	Cost of Living Composite Index for Highest City in 2010	163
Lowest	Cost of Living Composite Index Range in 2010	165

Ranking	Louisiana	Page
Highest	Murder Rate (per 100,000 persons in 2009)	83
Highest	Prisoners (per 100,000 persons in 2009)	88
Lowest	Life Expectancy (years in 2000)	22
Lowest	Grade 4 Reading Proficiency Levels (in 2009)	67

Ranking	Maine	Page
Highest	Median Age (years old in 2010)	15
Highest	Residents who Voted for Congress (percent of voting age persons in 2010)	53
Lowest	Violent Crime Rate (per 100,000 persons in 2010)	82
Lowest	Prisoners (per 100,000 persons in 2009)	88
Lowest	Criminal Justice Expenditures (dollars per capita in 2007)	90

Ranking	Maryland	Page
Highest	Median Household Income (dollars in 2009)	135
Lowest	Daily Newspaper Circulation (per 100 persons in 2009)	56

Ranking	Massachusetts	Page
Highest	Physicians per 100,000 Residents (in 2009)	36
Highest	Grade 4 Reading Proficiency Levels (in 2009)	67
Highest	Grade 4 Math Proficiency Levels (in 2009)	68
Highest	Grade 8 Reading Proficiency Levels (score in 2009)	70
Highest	Grade 8 Math Proficiency Levels (score in 2009)	71
Highest	Tertiary Education Attainment (percent in 2009)	74
Highest	Child Abuse and Neglect Victims (per 100,000 children in 2009)	84
Highest	State Debt (dollars per capita in 2008)	158
Highest	Research and Development (dollars per $1,000 of GDP in 2007)	170

Ranking	Massachusetts - continued	Page
Lowest of 49 states	Incoming State Criminal Court Cases (per 100,000 persons in 2009)	91
Lowest	Traffic Fatality Rate (deaths per 10,000 persons in 2010)	34
Lowest	Persons Without Health Insurance (percent in 2009)	35
Lowest	Government Employment (percent in 2011)	193

Ranking	Michigan	Page
Lowest	Population Growth (percent, 2000–to–2010)	4
Lowest	Defense Department Payroll per Capita (dollars in 2009)	190

Ranking	Minnesota	Page
Highest	Eligible Voters who Voted for President (percent in 2012)	50
Highest	Total Degree Days (annual average for selected cities, 1986–2009)	104
Highest	Heating Degree Days (annual, average for selected cities, 1986–2009)	105
Highest	State Arts Agency Appropriations (dollars per capita in 2011)	171

Ranking	Mississippi	Page
Highest	Infant Mortality Rate (deaths per 1,000 live births in 2009)	23
Highest	Pre-Term Births (percent in 2010)	24
Highest	Low Birth Weight Babies (percent in 2009)	25
Highest	Adult Obesity Rate (percent in 2011)	26
Highest	Births to Unmarried Women (percent in 2009)	39
Highest	Births to Teenage Mothers (percent in 2009)	40
Highest	Births to Women Below Poverty Level (percent in 2009)	41
Highest	Households with Annual Income Below $15,000 (percent in 2009)	136
Highest	Individuals Below Poverty Level (percent in 2009)	138
Highest	Food Stamp Recipients (percent of persons)	182
Highest	Medicaid Recipients (percent of population in 2009)	184
Lowest of 44 states	Grade 4 Science Proficiency Levels (score in 2009)	69
Lowest of 44 states	Grade 8 Science Proficiency Levels (score in 2009)	72
Lowest	Marriage Rate (per 1,000 residents in 2009)	43
Lowest	Library Visits per Capita (in 2008)	57
Lowest	Grade 4 Math Proficiency Levels (in 2009)	68
Lowest	Grade 8 Reading Proficiency Levels (score in 2009)	70
Lowest	Grade 8 Math Proficiency Levels (score in 2009)	71
Lowest	Personal Income per Capita (dollars in 2010)	134
Lowest	Median Household Income (dollars in 2009)	135
Lowest	Households with Annual Income Over $200,000 (percent in 2009)	137
Lowest	Gross Domestic Product per Capita (dollars in 2011)	167
Lowest	Federal Personal Income Taxes Paid per Capita (dollars in 2010)	174
Lowest	Federal Personal Income Tax Rate Paid (percent in 2010)	175

Ranking	Mississippi-continued	Page
Lowest	Federal Tax Revenues per Capita (dollars in 2009)	176

Missouri

Not highest or lowest for any metric

Ranking	Montana	Page
Highest	Air Quality "Good" Days for Average County (percent of days rated "good" across all counties	111
Highest	Demonstrated Coal Reserves (percent of nation's total in 2009)	128
Highest	Single-Family Housing Price Index (in 2010)	142
1 of 5 states with 0	State General Sales Tax (dollars per capita in 2011)	154
1 of 7 states with 0	Storm Major Disaster Declarations (1953–2012)	97
Lowest	Births to Foreign-Born Women (percent in 2009)	9
Lowest	Employment in Foreign-Controlled Businesses (percent of workforce in 2008)	150

Nebraska

Not highest or lowest for any metric

Ranking	Nevada	Page
Highest	Population Growth (percent, 2000–to–2010)	4
Highest	Residents Born in a Different State (percent in 2009)	6
Highest	Marriages Rate (per 1,000 residents in 2009)	43
Highest	Divorce Rate (per 1,000 residents in 2009)	44
Highest	Violent Crime Rate (per 100,000 persons in 2010)	82
Highest	Mineral Production (dollars in 2010)	131
Highest	Bankruptcy Filings (per 1,000 persons in 2010)	149
Highest	Unemployment Rate (percent, October 2011–March 2012)	161
1 of 7 states with 0	Storm Major Disaster Declarations (1953–2012)	97
1 of 8 states with 0	State Personal Income Tax (dollars per capita in 2011)	153
Lowest	Annual Precipitation (average, annual inches,1971–2000)	109
Lowest	Single-Family Housing Price Index (in 2010)	142
Lowest	Medicaid Recipients (percent of population in 2009)	184

Ranking	New Hampshire	Page
1 of 5 states with 0	State General Sales Tax (dollars per capita in 2011)	154
Lowest	Births to Teenage Mothers (percent in 2009)	40
Lowest	Murder Rate (per 100,000 persons in 2009)	83
Lowest	Individuals Below Poverty Level (percent in 2009)	138
Lowest	State Taxes by Source (dollars per capita in 2011)	155

Ranking	New Jersey	Page
Lowest of 49 states	Firearms Background Checks Rate (checks per 1,000 persons in 2010)	62
Lowest	Suicide Rate (per 100,000 residents in 2007)	29
Lowest	College Freshmen Enrolled in their Home State (percent in 2008)	76
Lowest	College Freshmen Interstate Migration Ratio (entering/leaving in 2008)	78
Lowest	Net Interstate Migration of College Freshmen (persons in 2009)	79
Lowest	Federal Disbursements in Excess of Taxes Collected (dollars in 2009)	179
Lowest	Federal Financing of Public K–12 Education (percent in 2009)	186
Highest	Population Density (persons per square mile in 2011)	18
Highest	Incoming State Trial Court Cases (per 100,000 persons in 2008)	92

Ranking	New Mexico	Page
Highest	Residents of Hispanic or Latino Origin (percent in 2010)	12
1 of 7 states with 0	Storm Major Disaster Declarations (1953–2012)	97

Ranking	New York	Page
Highest of 42 states with lottery	Lottery Revenue (dollars in 2008)	160
Highest	Jewish Population (percent of population in 2010)	47
Highest	Foreign Visitors (persons in 2010)	59
Highest	Labor Union Membership (percent of workers in 2010)	144
Highest	State Personal Income Tax (dollars per capita in 2011)	153
Highest	Local Government Taxes by Source (dollars per capita in 2008)	156
Highest	Cost of Living Composite Index for Highest City in 2010	163
Highest	Cost of Living Composite Index Range in 2010	165
Highest	Medicaid Payments (dollars in 2009)	183
Highest	Homeland Security Grants per Capita (dollars in 2010)	189
1 of 8 states with 0	State Personal Income Tax (dollars per capita in 2011)	153
Lowest	Net Immigration (persons, 2000–2009)	5
Lowest	Residents Born in a Different State (percent in 2009)	6
Lowest	Energy Consumption per Capita (BTUs per capita in 2008)	123
Lowest	Home Ownership Rate (percent of households in 2010)	140

Ranking	North Carolina	Page
Lowest	Labor Union Membership (percent of workers in 2010)	144

Ranking	North Dakota	Page
Highest	Binge Alcohol Drinkers (percent in 2007–2008)	32
Highest	Alcohol–Impaired Traffic Fatalities (percent of traffic fatalities in 2010)	33
Highest	Grade 8 Science Proficiency Levels (score in 2009)	72

Ranking	North Dakota - continued	Page
Highest	Air Temperature Range (degrees Fahrenheit, 1971–2000)	103
Lowest	Same–Sex Couple Households (thousands in 2010)	45
Lowest	Pupil–to–Teacher Ratio (in 2011)	65
Lowest	Winter Air Temperature (degrees Fahrenheit, 1971–2000)	101
Lowest	Unemployment Rate (percent, October 2011–March 2012)	161
Lowest	Medicaid Payments (dollars in 2009)	183

Ranking	Ohio	Page
Highest	Library Visits per Capita (in 2008)	57

Oklahoma
Not highest or lowest for any metric

Ranking	Ohio	Page
Highest	Manufacturing Portion of Gross Domestic Product (percent in 2011)	168
1 of 5 states with 0	State General Sales Tax (dollars per capita in 2011)	154
1 of 7 states with 0	Storm Major Disaster Declarations (1953–2012)	97
Lowest	Christian Church Adherents (percent of population in 2009)	46

Ranking	Pennsylvania	Page
Highest	College Freshmen Migrated from Other States (persons in 2008)	77
Highest	Net Interstate Migration of College Freshmen (persons in 2009)	79
Lowest	Child Abuse and Neglect Victims (per 100,000 children in 2009)	84

Ranking	Rhode Island	Page
Highest	Illicit Drug Use—Other than Marijuana (percent in 2007–2008)	30
Highest	Marijuana Use (percent in 2007–2008)	31
Lowest	Major Disaster/Fire Management Assistance Declarations (1953–2012)	95
Lowest	Land Area (square miles)	117
Lowest	Forest Lands (acres in 2010)	118
Lowest	Farm Land (percent of nation's total in 2010)	119
Lowest	Renewable energy production (percent of nation's total in 2010)	130

Ranking	South Carolina	Page
Lowest	Earthquake and Flood Major Disaster Declarations (1953–2012)	96
Lowest	Homeland Security Grants per Capita (dollars in 2010)	189

Ranking	South Dakota	Page
1 of 8 states with 0	State Personal Income Tax (dollars per capita in 2011)	153
Lowest	Low Birth Weight Babies (percent in 2009)	25

Ranking	South Dakota - continued	Page
Lowest	Jewish Population (percent of population in 2010)	47
Lowest	Property Crime Rate (per 100,000 persons in 2009)	85
Lowest	Identity Theft Victims (per 100,000 persons in 2010)	87
Lowest	Employee Annual Wages (dollars in 2009)	145

Ranking	Tennessee	Page
Lowest of 49 states	Incoming State Trial Court Cases (per 100,000 persons in 2008)	92
Lowest	State Debt (dollars per capita in 2008)	158

Ranking	Texas	Page
Highest	Persons Without Health Insurance (percent in 2009)	35
Highest	Property Crime Rate (per 100,000 persons in 2009)	85
Highest	Prisoner Executions (1977–2010)	89
Highest	Major Disaster/Fire Management Assistance Declarations (1953–2012)	95
Highest	Storm Major Disaster Declarations (1953–2012)	97
Highest	Wildfire Management Assistance Declarations (1953–2012)	98
Highest	Summer Air Temperature (degrees Fahrenheit, 1971–2000)	102
Highest	Carbon Dioxide Emissions (percent of nation's total in 2010)	113
Highest	Farm Land (percent of nation's total in 2010)	119
Highest	Farm Livestock Market (percent of nation's total in 2009)	122
Highest	Crude Oil Proved Reserves (percent of nation's total in 2009)	124
Highest	Crude Petroleum Production (percent nation's total in 2010)	125
Highest	Natural Gas Proved Reserves (percent of nation's total in 2009)	126
Highest	Natural Gas Marketed Production (percent of nation's total in 2009)	127
Highest	Exports of Goods (percent of national total in 2010)	169
Highest	Federal Subsidies for Agriculture (percent of nation's total in 2009)	188
1 of 8 states with 0	State Personal Income Tax (dollars per capita in 2011)	153
Lowest	Residents who Voted for Congress (percent of voting age persons in 2010)	53
Lowest	High School Graduation Rate (percent in 2009)	73
Lowest	Cost of Living Composite Index for Lowest City in 2010	164

Ranking	Utah	Page
Highest of 49 states	Firearms Background Checks Rate (checks per 1,000 persons in 2010)	62
Highest	Birth Rate (births per 1,000 women in 2009)	8
Highest	Christian Church Adherents (percent of population in 2009)	46
Highest	Charitable Contributions per Capita (dollars in 2008)	48
Highest	Volunteer Rate (percent of persons in 2010)	49
Highest	College Freshmen Enrolled in their Home State (percent in 2008)	76
Highest	College Freshmen Interstate Migration Ratio (entering/leaving in 2008)	78
Lowest	Median Age (years old in 2010)	15
Lowest	Age-Adjusted Cancer Death Rates (deaths per 100,000 persons in 2009)	27

Ranking	Utah - continued	Page
Lowest	Cigarette Smoking by Adults (percent in 2009)	28
Lowest	Binge Alcohol Drinkers (percent in 2007–2008)	32
Lowest	Alcohol-Impaired Traffic Fatalities (percent of traffic fatalities in 2010)	33
Lowest	Births to Unmarried Women (percent in 2009)	39
Lowest	Births to Women Below Poverty Level (percent in 2009)	41
Lowest	Voter Selection for President in 2012 (Obama's percent margin)	51
Lowest	Households Without Internet Usage (percent in 2010)	55
Lowest	Supplemental Security Income per Capita (dollars in 2009)	185

Ranking	Vermont	Page
Highest	Patents Issued to Residents (per 100,000 residents in 2010)	58
Highest	Nuclear Power Generation of Electricity (percent of state's electricity generation in 2009)	129
Lowest	Birth Rate (births per 1,000 women in 2009)	8
Lowest	Births by Race and Hispanic Origin (in 2009)	10
Lowest	Residents by Race–other than White (percent in 2010)	11
Lowest	Minority Students Grades K–12 (percent in 2011)	13
Lowest	Population Living in Urban Areas (percent in 2000)	19
Lowest	Pre-Term Births (percent in 2010)	24
Lowest	State Park Recreation Visitors (persons in 2010)	60
Lowest	Motor Vehicle Theft Rate (per 100,000 persons in 2010)	86
Lowest	Carbon Dioxide Emissions (percent of nation's total in 2010)	113
Lowest	Toxic Chemical Releases (pounds in 2009)	114
Lowest	Local Government Taxes by Source (dollars per capita in 2008)	156
Lowest	Gross Domestic Product (dollars in 2011)	166
Lowest	Defense Department Personnel (persons in 2009)	191

Ranking	Virginia	Page
Highest	Daily Newspaper Circulation (per 100 persons in 2009)	56
Highest	Grade 4 Science Proficiency Levels (score in 2009)	69
Highest	Federal Disbursements in Excess of Taxes Collected (dollars in 2009)	179
Highest	Defense Department Contract Awards (dollars per capita in 2009)	192
Lowest	Federal Aid to State and Local Government per Capita (dollars in 2009)	181

Ranking	Washington	Page
Highest	Renewable energy production (percent of nation's total in 2010)	130
Highest	State Gasoline Tax (cents per gallon in 2009)	157
1 of 7 states with 0	Storm Major Disaster Declarations (1953–2012)	97
1 of 8 states with 0	State Personal Income Tax (dollars per capita in 2011)	153

Ranking	West Virginia	Page
Highest	Age-Adjusted Cancer Death Rates (deaths per 100,000 persons in 2009)	27
Highest	Home Ownership Rate (percent of households in 2010)	140
Highest	Supplemental Security Income per Capita (dollars in 2009)	185
Lowest	Residents Born Outside the United States (percent in 2009)	7
Lowest	Residents of Hispanic or Latino Origin (percent in 2010)	12
Lowest	Foreign Language Spoken at Home (percent of households in 2009)	14
Lowest	Charitable Contributions per Capita (dollars in 2008)	48
Lowest	Tertiary Education Attainment (percent in 2009)	74
Lowest	Individuals with Net Worth Over $2.0 million (dollars in 2007)	139
Lowest	Owner Occupied Housing Values (median home value in 2009)	141
Lowest	Rental Housing Cost (average rental cost per month in 2009)	143

Wisconsin

Not highest or lowest for any metric

Ranking	Wyoming	Page
Highest	Traffic Fatality Rate (deaths per 10,000 persons in 2010)	34
Highest	Expenditures per Capita for Public K–12 Education (dollars in 2009)	66
Highest	High School Graduation Rate (percent in 2009)	73
Highest	Energy Consumption per Capita (BTUs per capita in 2008)	123
Highest	Individuals with Net Worth Over $2.0 million (dollars in 2007)	139
Highest	Manufacturing Employee Annual Payroll (dollars in 2009)	146
Highest	Value Added per Manufacturing Production Worker (dollars in 2009)	148
1 of 8 states with 0	State Personal Income Tax (dollars per capita in 2011)	153
Lowest	Population (persons in 2012)	3
Lowest	Abortion Rate (1 per 1,000 women in 2008)	42
Lowest	Voter Selection for President in 2008 (Obama's percent margin)	52
Lowest	U.S. Congressional Seats Held by Political Party (seats in 2013 for 113th Congress)	54
Lowest	Higher Education Degrees Conferred (in 2007)	75
Lowest	Research and Development (dollars per $1,000 of GDP in 2007)	170
Lowest	Food Stamp Recipients (percent of persons)	182

~ Resources ~

The following sources were selected for data mining used to create the charts in this book. The author judges these sources to be unbiased and apolitical, however all data should be viewed with some skepticism. Updates to these databases occur at varying intervals ranging from weekly to multiple years, depending on the source and the parameter. Generally, demographic-type databases tend to be updated in one-to-five year intervals, whereas other data, especially related to economics, may be updated daily.

Database Resources	Website Portals
Corporation for National and Community Service	http://www.volunteeringinamerica.gov/export.cfm
Federal Bureau of Investigation	http://www.fbi.gov/
Federal Emergency Management Agency	http://www.fema.gov/disasters/grid/state
National Center for Educational Statistics	http://nces.ed.gov/datatools/
National Highway Traffic Safety Administration	http://www-nrd.nhtsa.dot.gov/Cats/index.aspx
National Oceanic and Atmospheric Administration	http://www.ncdc.noaa.gov/
U.S. Bureau of Economic Analysis	http://www.bea.gov/
U.S. Bureau of Labor Statistics	http://www.bls.gov/
U.S. Census Bureau	http://www.census.gov/compendia/statab/
U.S. Center for Disease Control	http://www.cdc.gov/nchs/pressroom/stats_states.htm
U.S. Energy Information Administration	http://www.eia.gov/
U.S. Environmental Protection Agency	http://www.epa.gov/airdata/
United States Election Project	http://elections.gmu.edu/Turnout_2012G.html
White House	http://www.whitehouse.gov/sites/default/files/omb/budget/fy2013/assets/technical_analyses.pdf

~ <u>Index</u> ~

<u>Page</u>

C

D

E

L

M

T

U

V

W, X, Y, Z

~